IF YOU CAN'T BEAT 'EM, EAT 'EM

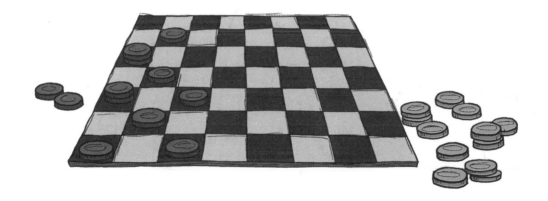

OTHER BOOKS BY JIM TOOMEY

Sherman's Lagoon: Ate That, What's Next?

Poodle: The Other White Meat

An Illustrated Guide to Shark Etiquette

Another Day in Paradise

Greetings from Sherman's Lagoon

Surf's Up!

The Shark Diaries

Catch of the Day

A Day at the Beach

Surfer Safari

Planet of the Hairless Beach Apes

Yarns and Shanties (and Other Nautical Baloney)

Sharks Just Wanna Have Fun

Confessions of a Swinging Single Sea Turtle

Discover Your Inner Hermit Crab

Never Bite Anything That Bites Back

Think Like a Shark

Here We Go Again

Lunch Wore a Speedo

Tales From the Deep: That Are Completely Fabricated

Happy as a Clam

Onward and Downward

The Adventures of Superfish and His Superfishal Friends

TREASURIES

Sherman's Lagoon 1991 to 2001: Greatest Hits and Near Misses

In Shark Years I'm Dead: Sherman's Lagoon Turns Fifteen

IF YOU CAN'T BEAT 'EM, EAT 'EM

The Twenty-Fourth Sherman's Lagoon Collection

JIM TOOMEY

Andrews McMeel
PUBLISHING®

To Anne Thomas, who helped me see humor in everything.

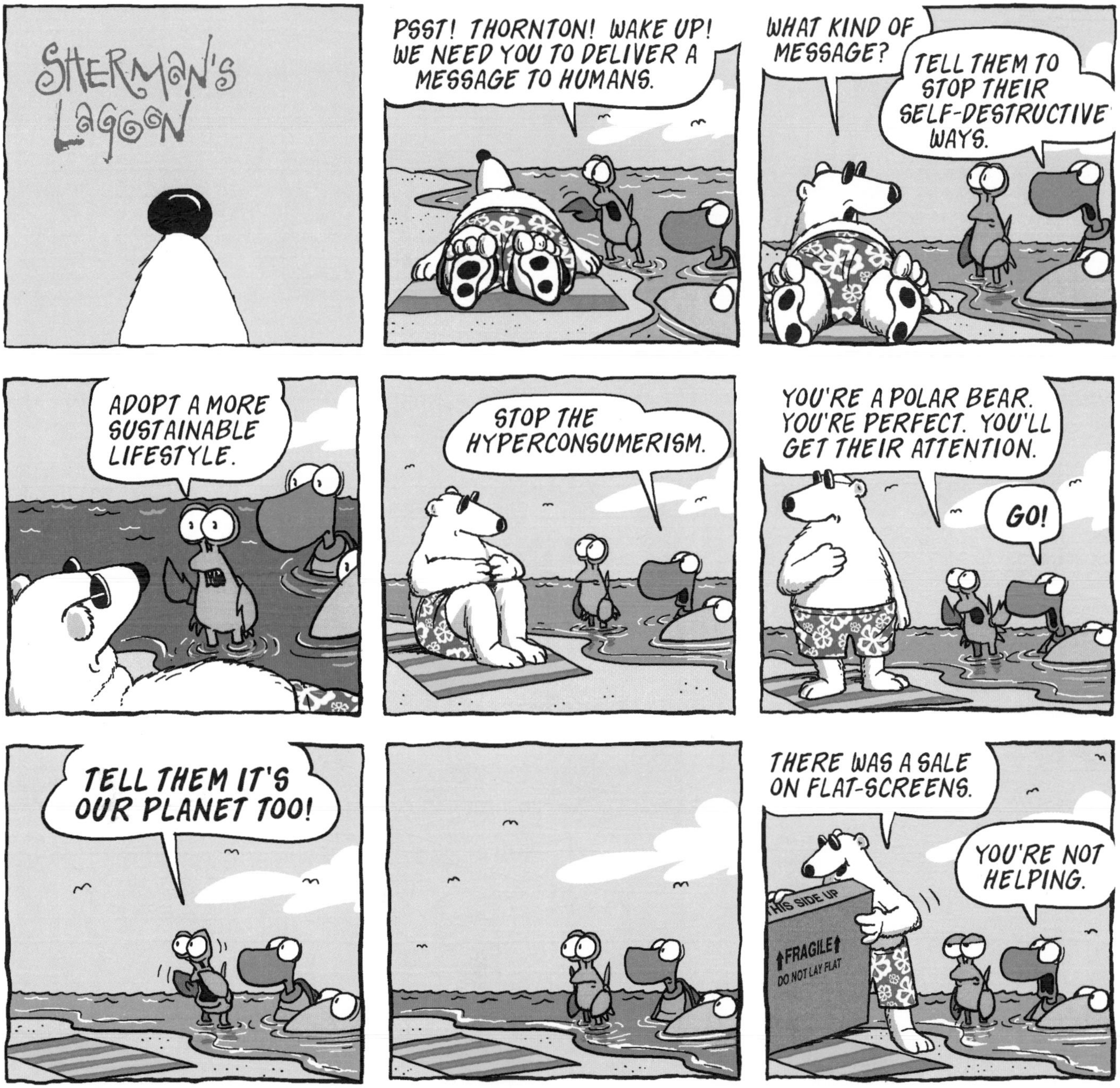
SHERMAN'S LAGOON
PSST! THORNTON! WAKE UP! WE NEED YOU TO DELIVER A MESSAGE TO HUMANS.
WHAT KIND OF MESSAGE?
TELL THEM TO STOP THEIR SELF-DESTRUCTIVE WAYS.
ADOPT A MORE SUSTAINABLE LIFESTYLE.
STOP THE HYPERCONSUMERISM.
YOU'RE A POLAR BEAR. YOU'RE PERFECT. YOU'LL GET THEIR ATTENTION.
GO!
TELL THEM IT'S OUR PLANET TOO!
THERE WAS A SALE ON FLAT-SCREENS.
THIS SIDE UP
FRAGILE
DO NOT LAY FLAT
YOU'RE NOT HELPING.

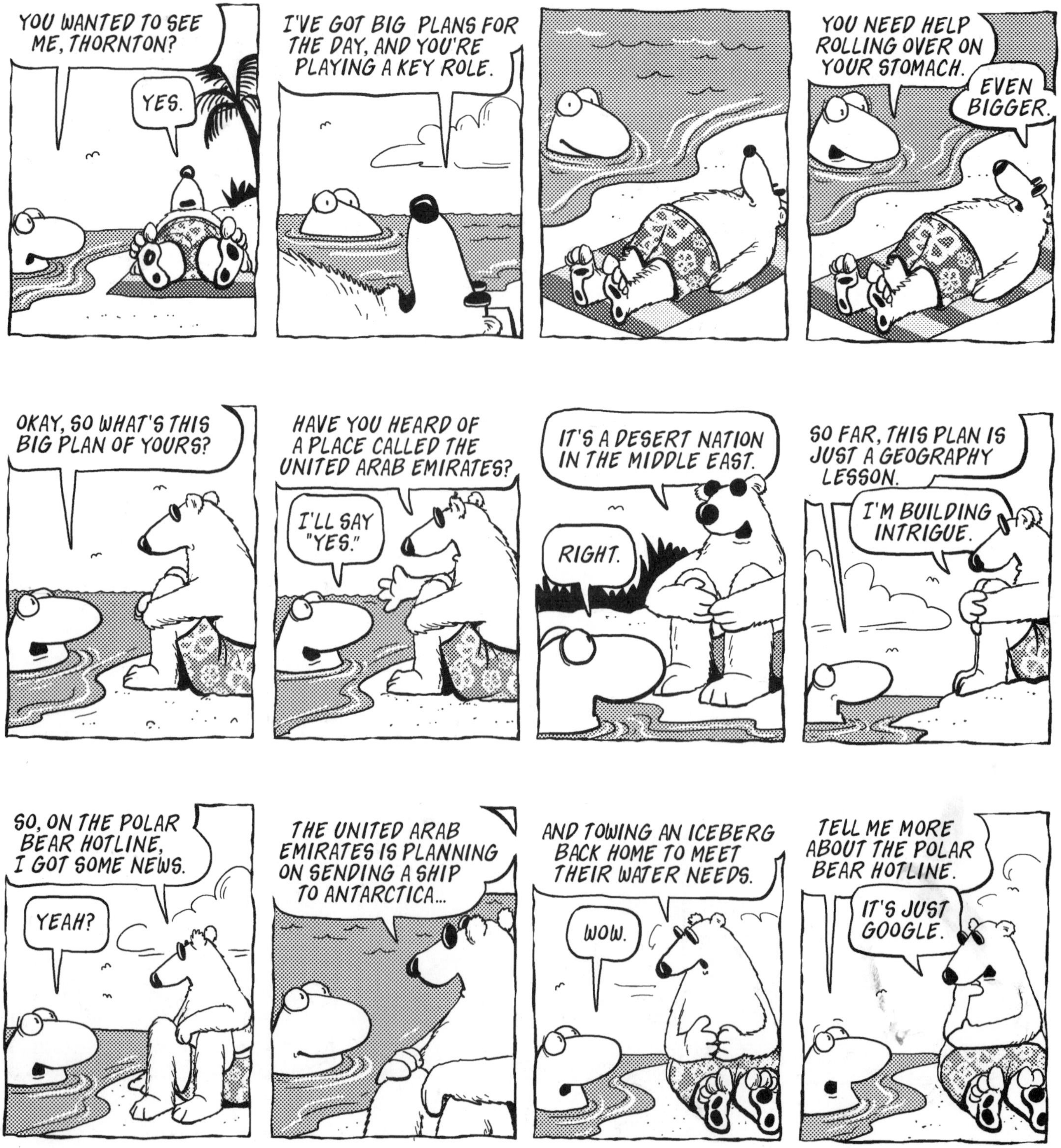
YOU WANTED TO SEE ME, THORNTON?
YES.
I'VE GOT BIG PLANS FOR THE DAY, AND YOU'RE PLAYING A KEY ROLE.
YOU NEED HELP ROLLING OVER ON YOUR STOMACH.
EVEN BIGGER.
OKAY, SO WHAT'S THIS BIG PLAN OF YOURS?
HAVE YOU HEARD OF A PLACE CALLED THE UNITED ARAB EMIRATES?
I'LL SAY "YES."
IT'S A DESERT NATION IN THE MIDDLE EAST.
RIGHT.
SO FAR, THIS PLAN IS JUST A GEOGRAPHY LESSON.
I'M BUILDING INTRIGUE.
SO, ON THE POLAR BEAR HOTLINE, I GOT SOME NEWS.
YEAH?
THE UNITED ARAB EMIRATES IS PLANNING ON SENDING A SHIP TO ANTARCTICA...
AND TOWING AN ICEBERG BACK HOME TO MEET THEIR WATER NEEDS.
WOW.
TELL ME MORE ABOUT THE POLAR BEAR HOTLINE.
IT'S JUST GOOGLE.

SO, THIS ICEBERG THAT THE UNITED ARAB EMIRATES IS AFTER...
UH-HUH.
I THINK WE SHOULD HIJACK IT EN ROUTE AND BRING IT HERE.
WE COULD SUPPLY THE LAGOON WITH SMOOTHIES FOR YEARS.
YOU'RE THE ONLY ONE THAT DRINKS SMOOTHIES.
THEN DECADES!
SO, WHAT DO YOU SAY, SHERMAN? YOU UP FOR A LITTLE ADVENTURE?
I DON'T KNOW.
ISN'T HIJACKING AN ICEBERG WRONG?
ONLY IF YOU LOOK AT IT FROM THE ASPECT THAT TAKING SOMETHING THAT'S NOT YOURS IS WRONG.
WHAT OTHER ASPECT IS THERE?
CONVINCING YOU WAS SUPPOSED TO BE THE EASY PART OF THIS.
MEGAN, I'LL BE AWAY FOR A FEW DAYS.
IS THIS ANOTHER ONE OF YOUR BIZARRE QUESTS THAT I ALWAYS FIND DIFFICULT TO COMPREHEND?
NOT AT ALL.
I'M GOING TO HELP THORNTON HIJACK AN ICEBERG BOUND FOR THE UNITED ARAB EMIRATES.
WEAR MITTENS.
GOOD IDEA.

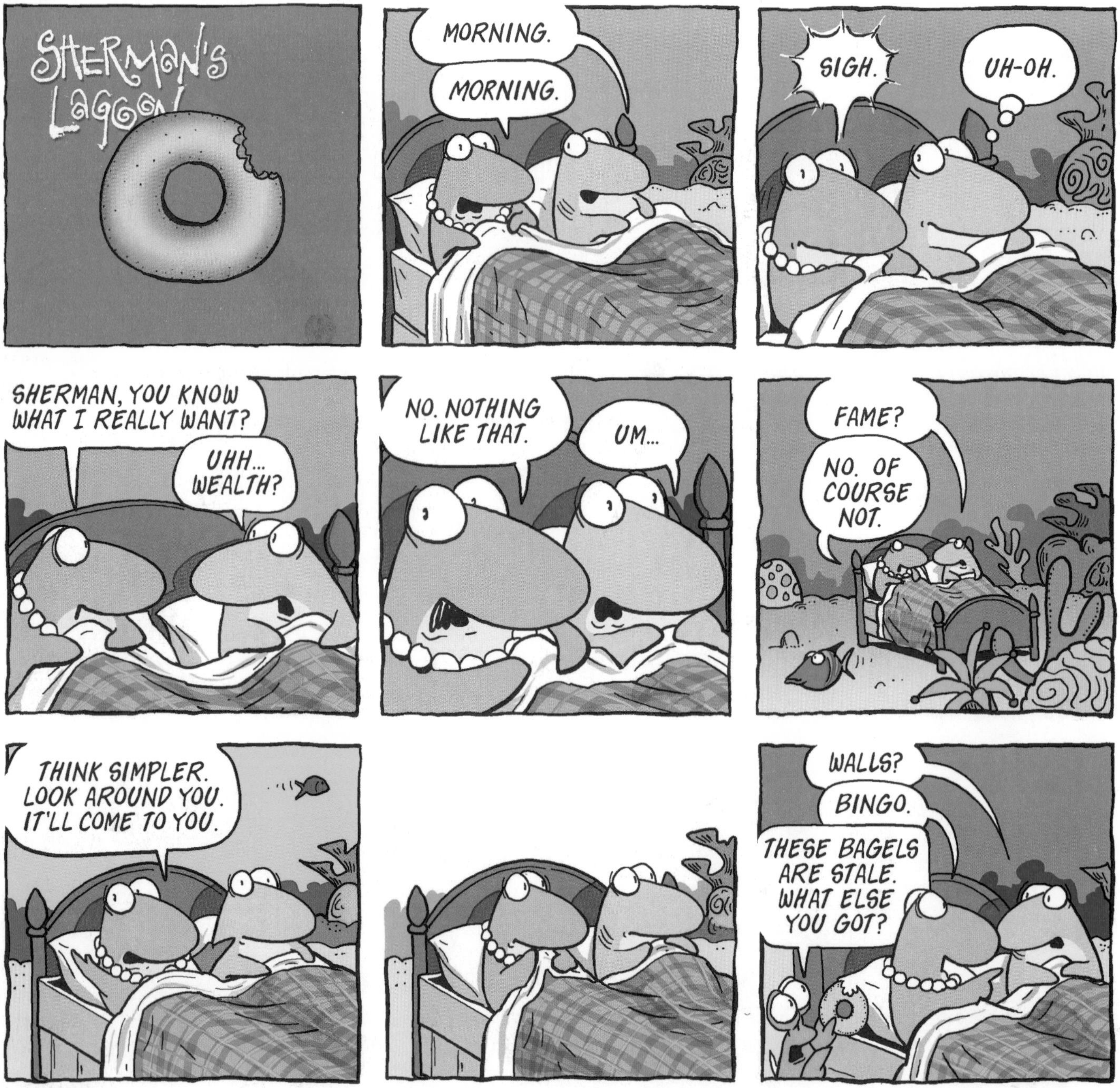
SHERMAN'S LAGOON
MORNING.
MORNING.
SIGH.
UH-OH.
SHERMAN, YOU KNOW WHAT I REALLY WANT?
UHH... WEALTH?
NO. NOTHING LIKE THAT.
UM...
FAME?
NO. OF COURSE NOT.
THINK SIMPLER. LOOK AROUND YOU. IT'LL COME TO YOU.
WALLS?
BINGO.
THESE BAGELS ARE STALE. WHAT ELSE YOU GOT?

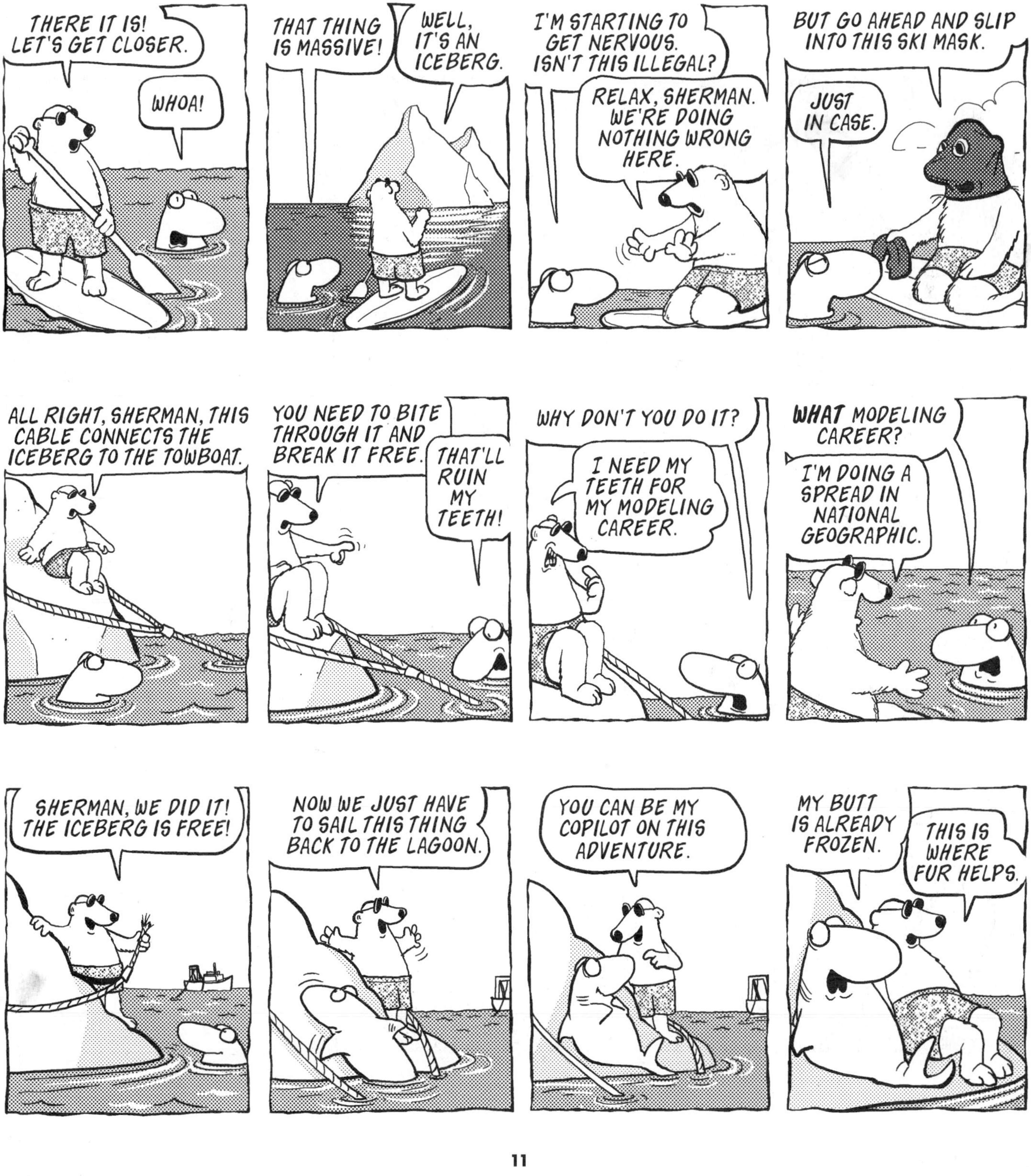
THERE IT IS! LET'S GET CLOSER.
WHOA!
THAT THING IS MASSIVE!
WELL, IT'S AN ICEBERG.
I'M STARTING TO GET NERVOUS. ISN'T THIS ILLEGAL?
RELAX, SHERMAN. WE'RE DOING NOTHING WRONG HERE.
BUT GO AHEAD AND SLIP INTO THIS SKI MASK.
JUST IN CASE.
ALL RIGHT, SHERMAN, THIS CABLE CONNECTS THE ICEBERG TO THE TOWBOAT.
YOU NEED TO BITE THROUGH IT AND BREAK IT FREE.
THAT'LL RUIN MY TEETH!
WHY DON'T YOU DO IT?
I NEED MY TEETH FOR MY MODELING CAREER.
WHAT MODELING CAREER?
I'M DOING A SPREAD IN NATIONAL GEOGRAPHIC.
SHERMAN, WE DID IT! THE ICEBERG IS FREE!
NOW WE JUST HAVE TO SAIL THIS THING BACK TO THE LAGOON.
YOU CAN BE MY COPILOT ON THIS ADVENTURE.
MY BUTT IS ALREADY FROZEN.
THIS IS WHERE FUR HELPS.

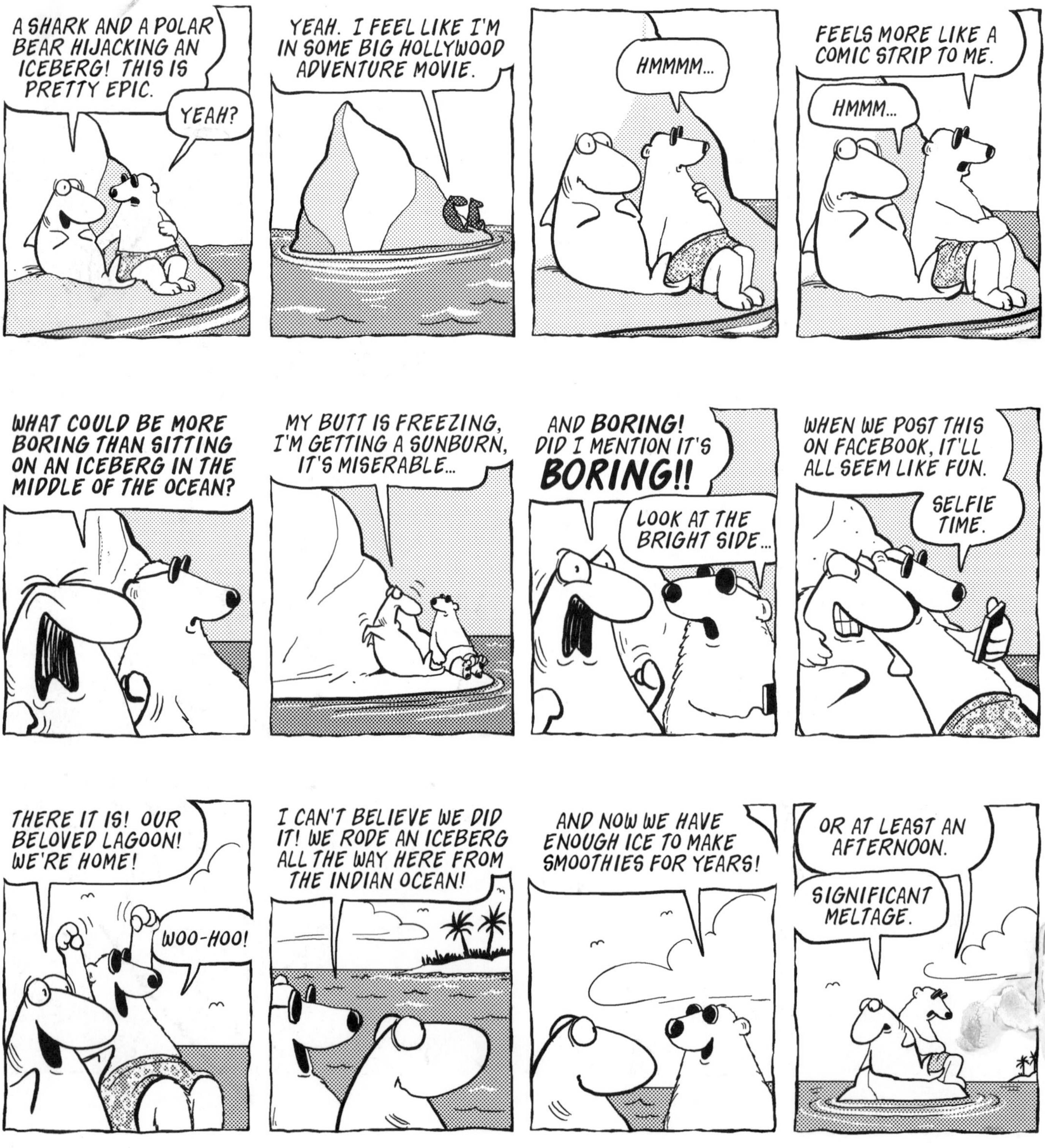
A SHARK AND A POLAR BEAR HIJACKING AN ICEBERG! THIS IS PRETTY EPIC.
YEAH?
YEAH. I FEEL LIKE I'M IN SOME BIG HOLLYWOOD ADVENTURE MOVIE.
HMMMM...
FEELS MORE LIKE A COMIC STRIP TO ME.
HMMM...
WHAT COULD BE MORE BORING THAN SITTING ON AN ICEBERG IN THE MIDDLE OF THE OCEAN?
MY BUTT IS FREEZING, I'M GETTING A SUNBURN, IT'S MISERABLE...
AND BORING! DID I MENTION IT'S BORING!!
LOOK AT THE BRIGHT SIDE...
WHEN WE POST THIS ON FACEBOOK, IT'LL ALL SEEM LIKE FUN.
SELFIE TIME.
THERE IT IS! OUR BELOVED LAGOON! WE'RE HOME!
WOO-HOO!
I CAN'T BELIEVE WE DID IT! WE RODE AN ICEBERG ALL THE WAY HERE FROM THE INDIAN OCEAN!
AND NOW WE HAVE ENOUGH ICE TO MAKE SMOOTHIES FOR YEARS!
OR AT LEAST AN AFTERNOON.
SIGNIFICANT MELTAGE.

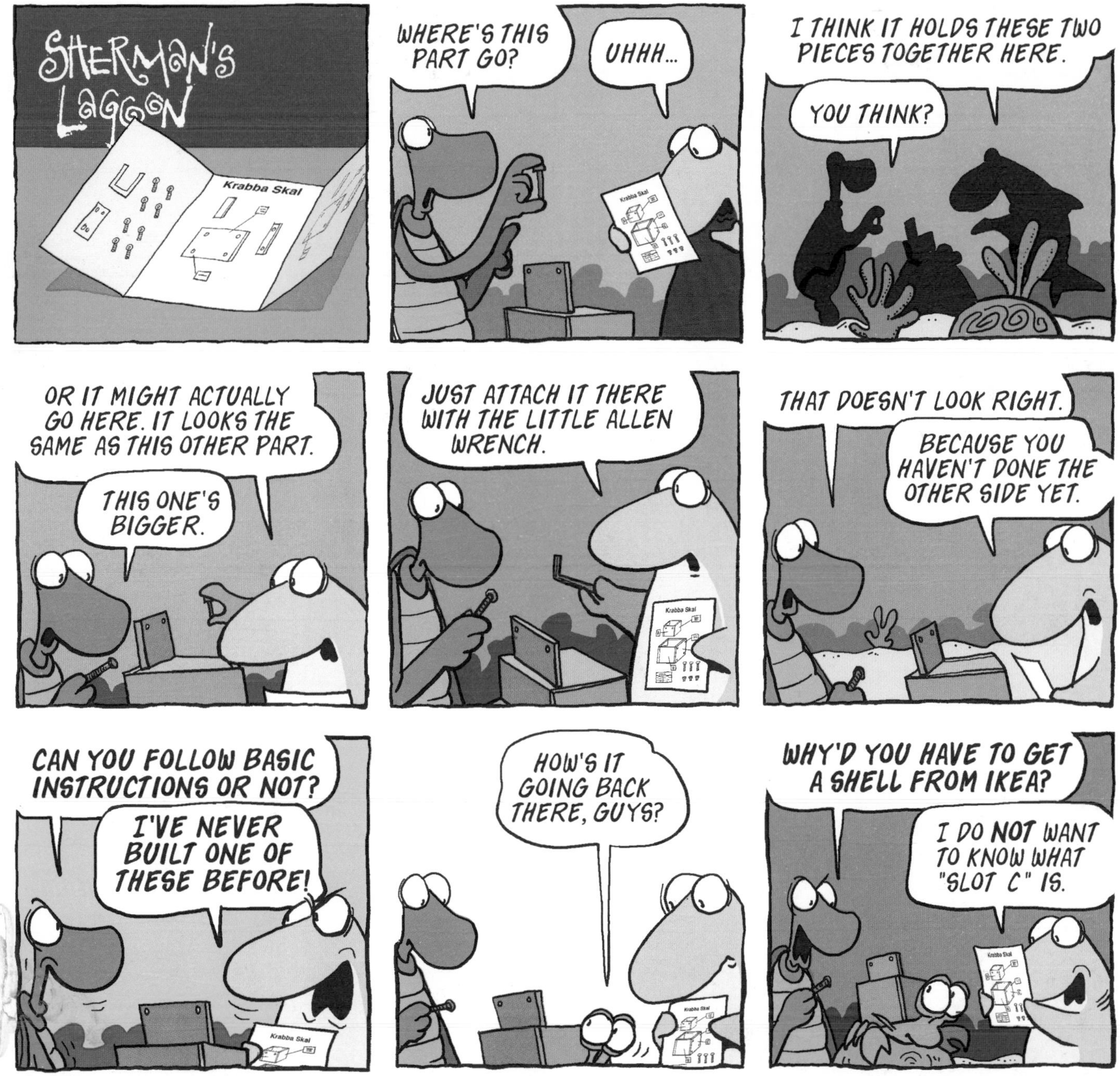
SHERMAN'S LAGOON
Krabba Skal
WHERE'S THIS PART GO?
UHHH...
I THINK IT HOLDS THESE TWO PIECES TOGETHER HERE.
YOU THINK?
OR IT MIGHT ACTUALLY GO HERE. IT LOOKS THE SAME AS THIS OTHER PART.
THIS ONE'S BIGGER.
JUST ATTACH IT THERE WITH THE LITTLE ALLEN WRENCH.
THAT DOESN'T LOOK RIGHT.
BECAUSE YOU HAVEN'T DONE THE OTHER SIDE YET.
CAN YOU FOLLOW BASIC INSTRUCTIONS OR NOT?
I'VE NEVER BUILT ONE OF THESE BEFORE!
HOW'S IT GOING BACK THERE, GUYS?
WHY'D YOU HAVE TO GET A SHELL FROM IKEA?
I DO **NOT** WANT TO KNOW WHAT "SLOT C" IS.

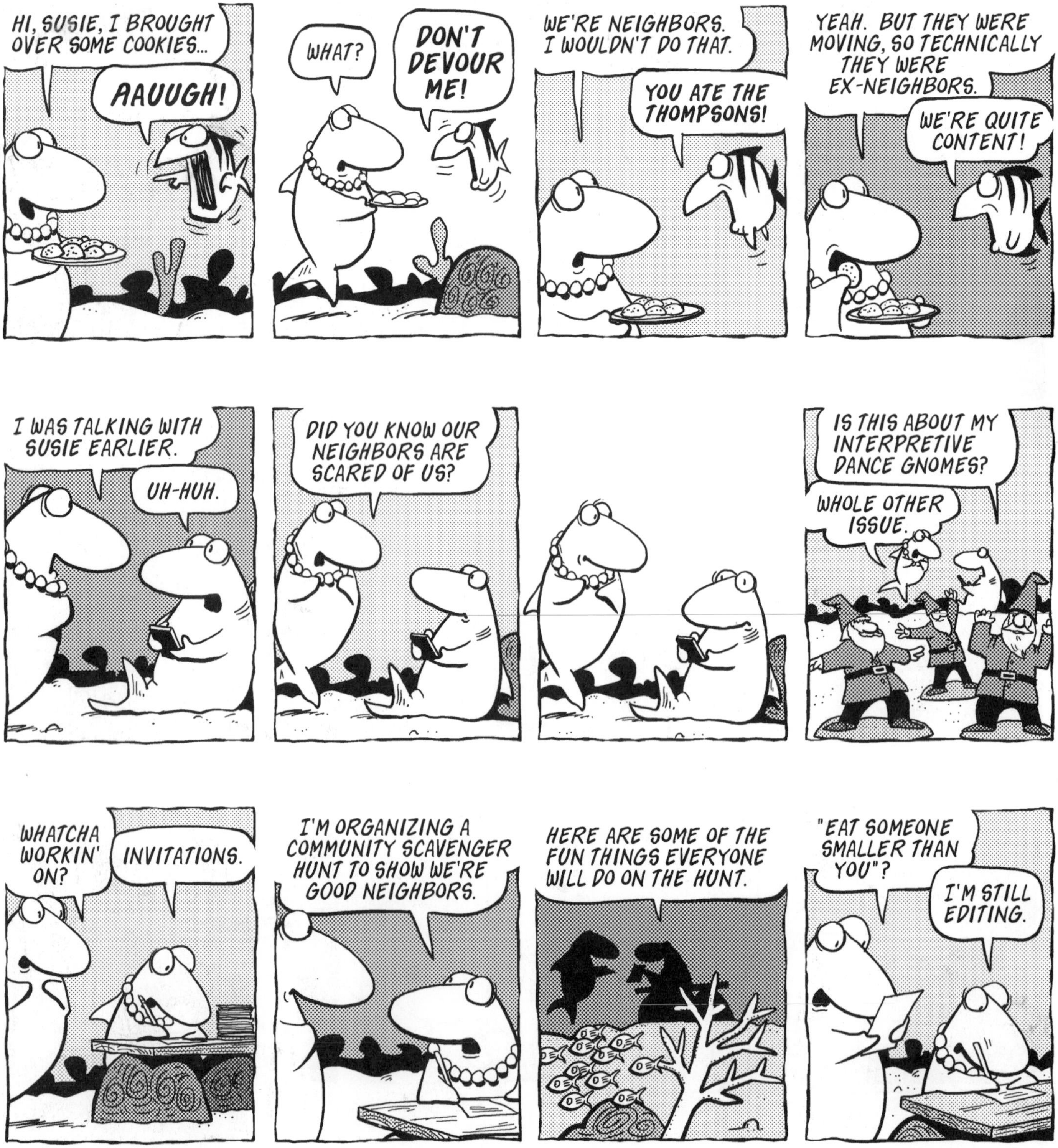

HI, SUSIE, I BROUGHT OVER SOME COOKIES...
AAUUGH!
WHAT?
DON'T DEVOUR ME!
WE'RE NEIGHBORS. I WOULDN'T DO THAT.
YOU ATE THE THOMPSONS!
YEAH. BUT THEY WERE MOVING, SO TECHNICALLY THEY WERE EX-NEIGHBORS.
WE'RE QUITE CONTENT!
I WAS TALKING WITH SUSIE EARLIER.
UH-HUH.
DID YOU KNOW OUR NEIGHBORS ARE SCARED OF US?
IS THIS ABOUT MY INTERPRETIVE DANCE GNOMES?
WHOLE OTHER ISSUE.
WHATCHA WORKIN' ON?
INVITATIONS.
I'M ORGANIZING A COMMUNITY SCAVENGER HUNT TO SHOW WE'RE GOOD NEIGHBORS.
HERE ARE SOME OF THE FUN THINGS EVERYONE WILL DO ON THE HUNT.
"EAT SOMEONE SMALLER THAN YOU"?
I'M STILL EDITING.

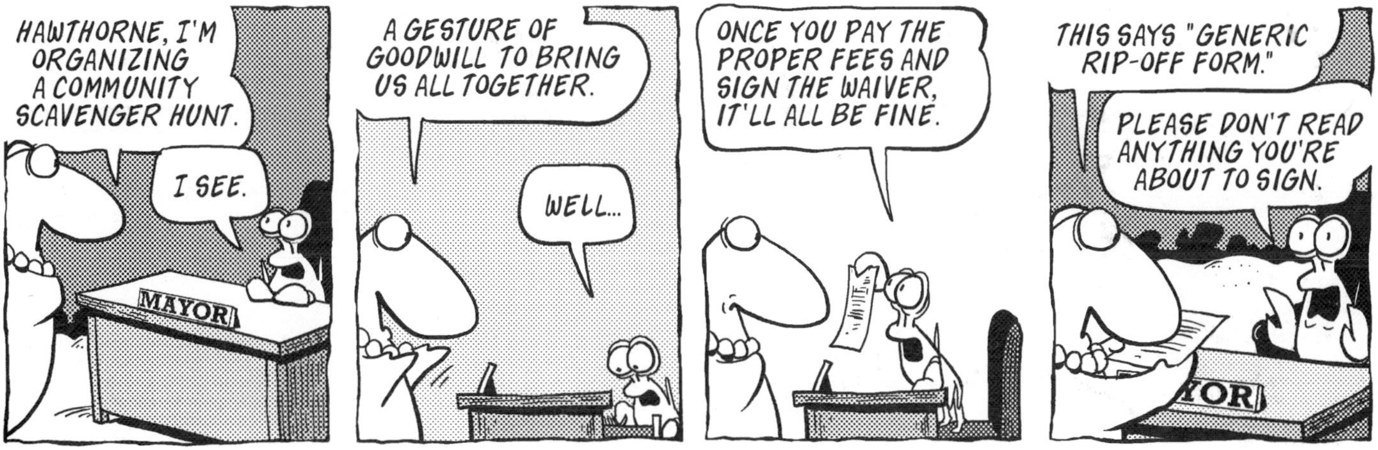
HAWTHORNE, I'M ORGANIZING A COMMUNITY SCAVENGER HUNT.
I SEE.
MAYOR
A GESTURE OF GOODWILL TO BRING US ALL TOGETHER.
WELL...
ONCE YOU PAY THE PROPER FEES AND SIGN THE WAIVER, IT'LL ALL BE FINE.
THIS SAYS "GENERIC RIP-OFF FORM."
PLEASE DON'T READ ANYTHING YOU'RE ABOUT TO SIGN.
YOR

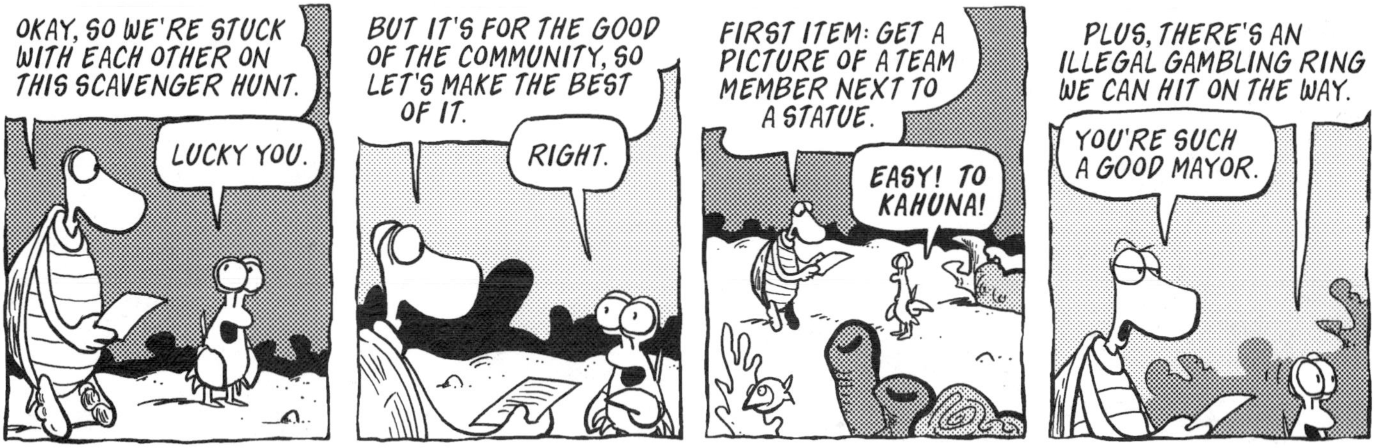
OKAY, SO WE'RE STUCK WITH EACH OTHER ON THIS SCAVENGER HUNT.
LUCKY YOU.
BUT IT'S FOR THE GOOD OF THE COMMUNITY, SO LET'S MAKE THE BEST OF IT.
RIGHT.
FIRST ITEM: GET A PICTURE OF A TEAM MEMBER NEXT TO A STATUE.
EASY! TO KAHUNA!
PLUS, THERE'S AN ILLEGAL GAMBLING RING WE CAN HIT ON THE WAY.
YOU'RE SUCH A GOOD MAYOR.

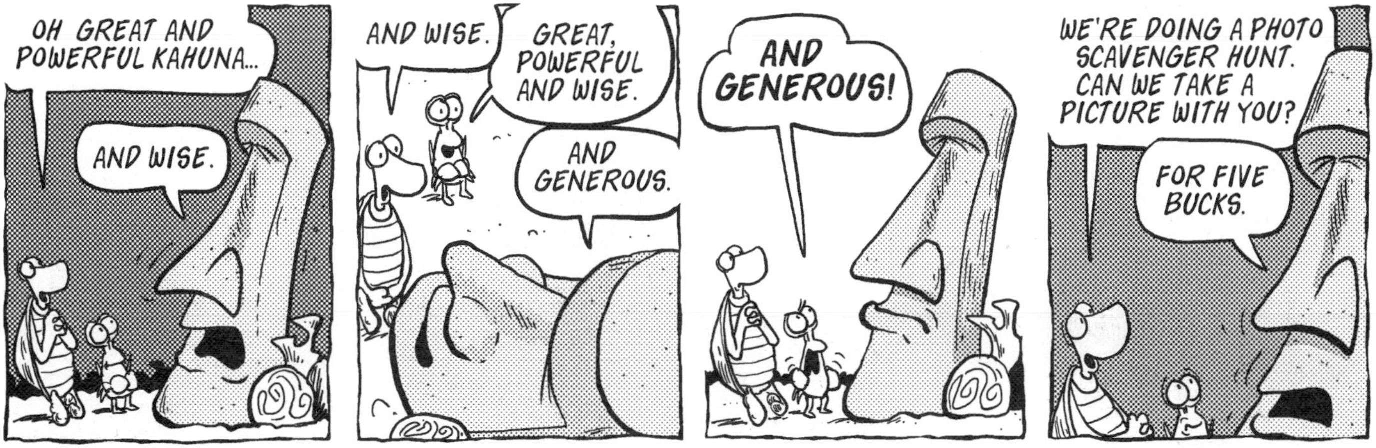
OH GREAT AND POWERFUL KAHUNA...
AND WISE.
AND WISE.
GREAT, POWERFUL AND WISE.
AND GENEROUS.
AND GENEROUS!
WE'RE DOING A PHOTO SCAVENGER HUNT. CAN WE TAKE A PICTURE WITH YOU?
FOR FIVE BUCKS.

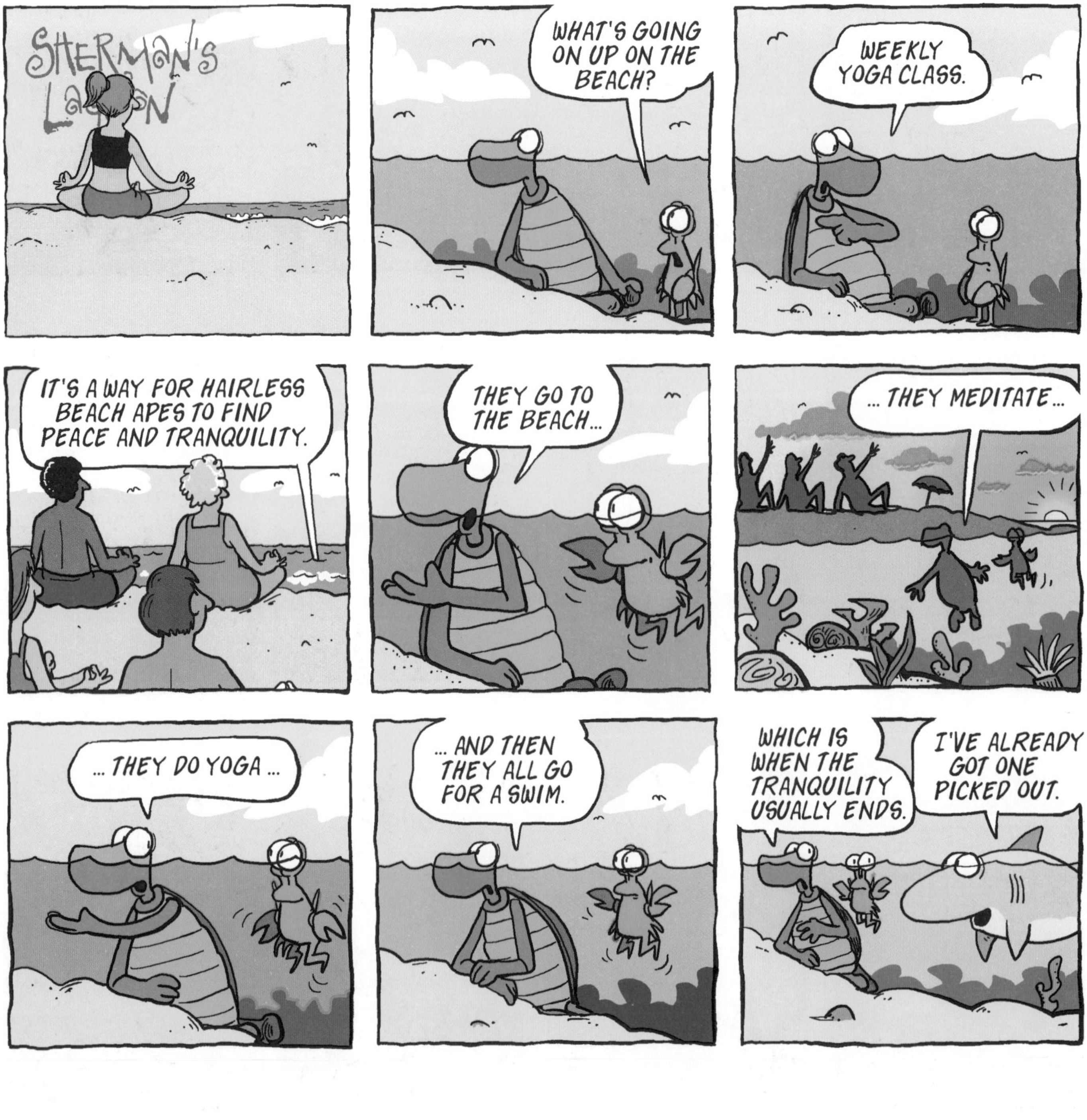
SHERMAN'S LAGOON
WHAT'S GOING ON UP ON THE BEACH?
WEEKLY YOGA CLASS.
IT'S A WAY FOR HAIRLESS BEACH APES TO FIND PEACE AND TRANQUILITY.
THEY GO TO THE BEACH...
... THEY MEDITATE ...
... THEY DO YOGA ...
... AND THEN THEY ALL GO FOR A SWIM.
WHICH IS WHEN THE TRANQUILITY USUALLY ENDS.
I'VE ALREADY GOT ONE PICKED OUT.

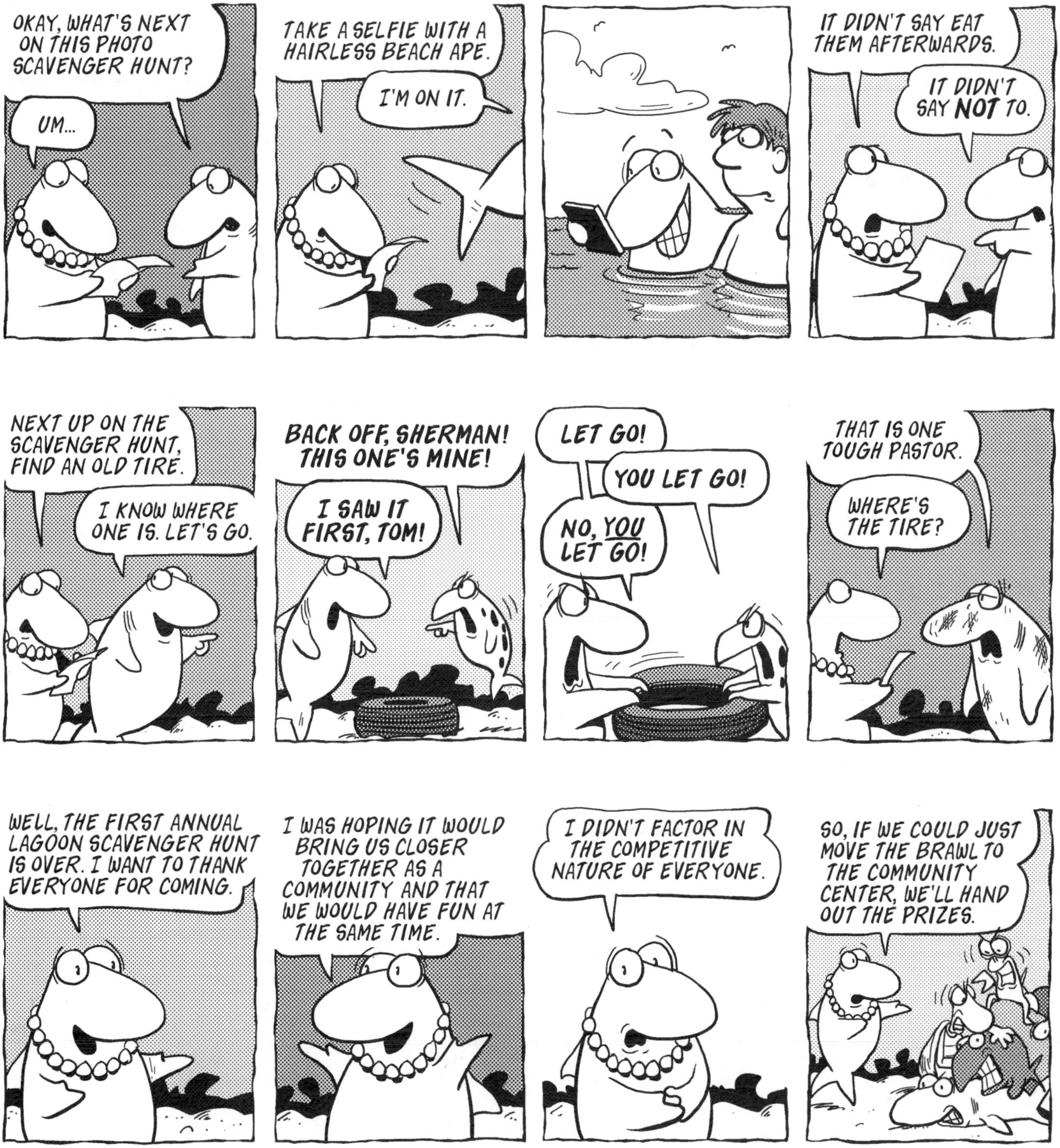
OKAY, WHAT'S NEXT ON THIS PHOTO SCAVENGER HUNT?
UM...
TAKE A SELFIE WITH A HAIRLESS BEACH APE.
I'M ON IT.
IT DIDN'T SAY EAT THEM AFTERWARDS.
IT DIDN'T SAY NOT TO.
NEXT UP ON THE SCAVENGER HUNT, FIND AN OLD TIRE.
I KNOW WHERE ONE IS. LET'S GO.
BACK OFF, SHERMAN! THIS ONE'S MINE!
I SAW IT FIRST, TOM!
LET GO!
YOU LET GO!
NO, YOU LET GO!
THAT IS ONE TOUGH PASTOR.
WHERE'S THE TIRE?
WELL, THE FIRST ANNUAL LAGOON SCAVENGER HUNT IS OVER. I WANT TO THANK EVERYONE FOR COMING.
I WAS HOPING IT WOULD BRING US CLOSER TOGETHER AS A COMMUNITY AND THAT WE WOULD HAVE FUN AT THE SAME TIME.
I DIDN'T FACTOR IN THE COMPETITIVE NATURE OF EVERYONE.
SO, IF WE COULD JUST MOVE THE BRAWL TO THE COMMUNITY CENTER, WE'LL HAND OUT THE PRIZES.

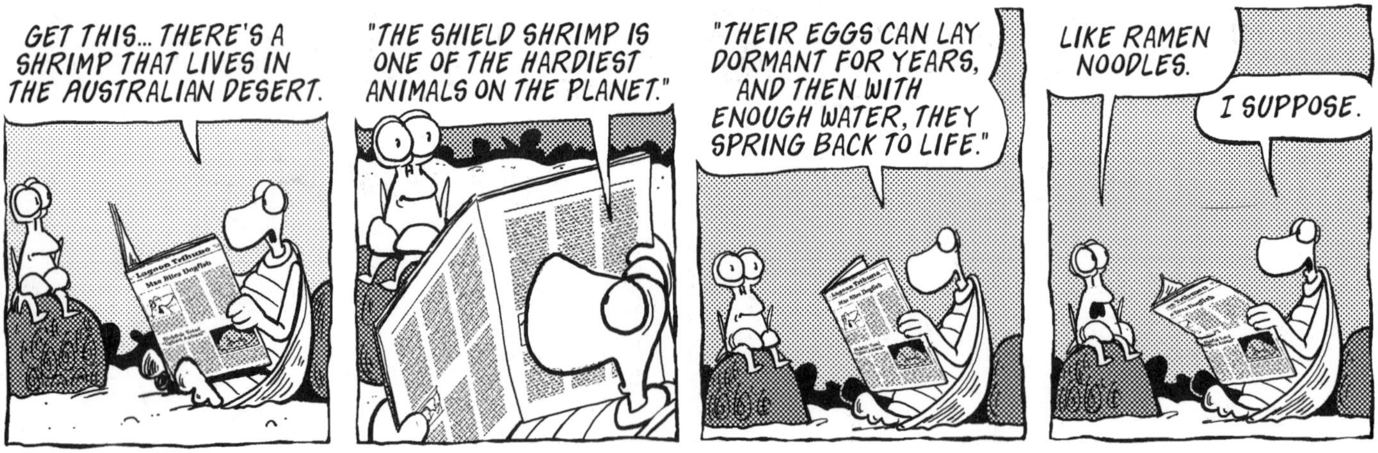
GET THIS... THERE'S A SHRIMP THAT LIVES IN THE AUSTRALIAN DESERT.
"THE SHIELD SHRIMP IS ONE OF THE HARDIEST ANIMALS ON THE PLANET."
"THEIR EGGS CAN LAY DORMANT FOR YEARS, AND THEN WITH ENOUGH WATER, THEY SPRING BACK TO LIFE."
LIKE RAMEN NOODLES.
I SUPPOSE.

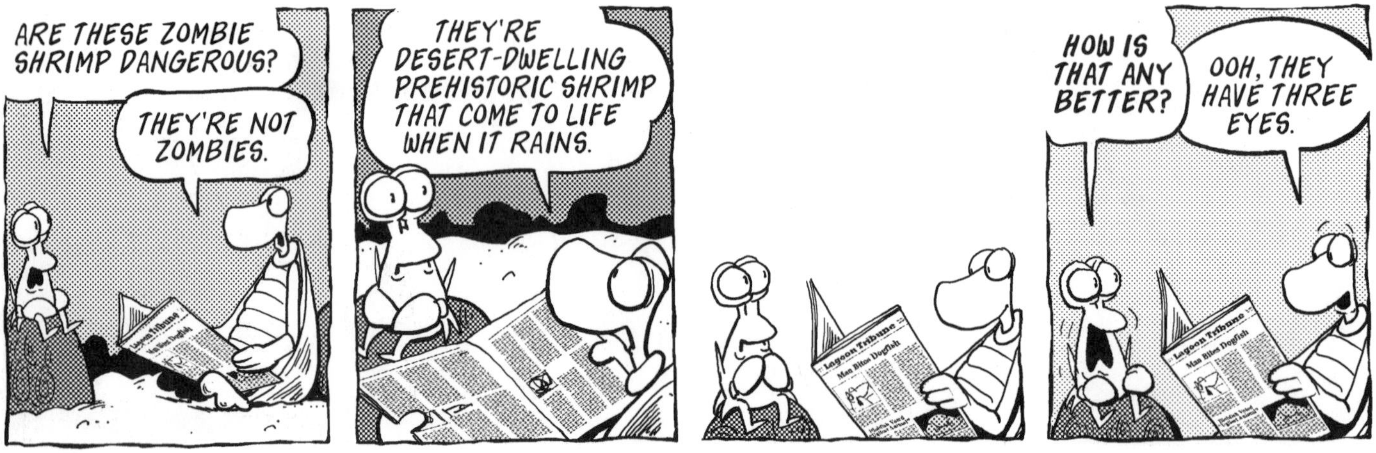
ARE THESE ZOMBIE SHRIMP DANGEROUS?
THEY'RE NOT ZOMBIES.
THEY'RE DESERT-DWELLING PREHISTORIC SHRIMP THAT COME TO LIFE WHEN IT RAINS.
HOW IS THAT ANY BETTER?
OOH, THEY HAVE THREE EYES.

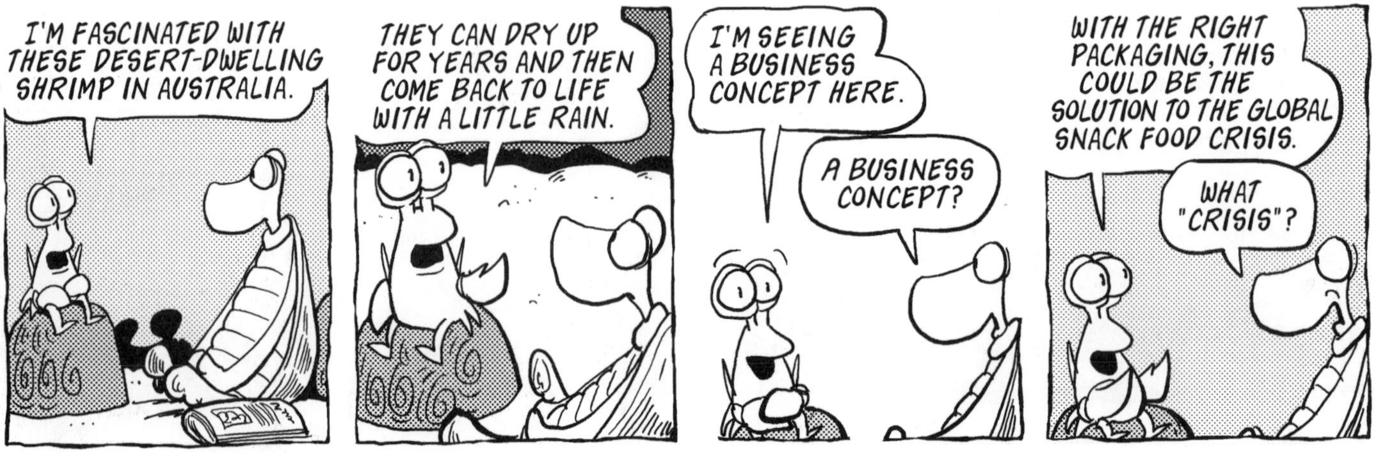
I'M FASCINATED WITH THESE DESERT-DWELLING SHRIMP IN AUSTRALIA.
THEY CAN DRY UP FOR YEARS AND THEN COME BACK TO LIFE WITH A LITTLE RAIN.
I'M SEEING A BUSINESS CONCEPT HERE.
A BUSINESS CONCEPT?
WITH THE RIGHT PACKAGING, THIS COULD BE THE SOLUTION TO THE GLOBAL SNACK FOOD CRISIS.
WHAT "CRISIS"?

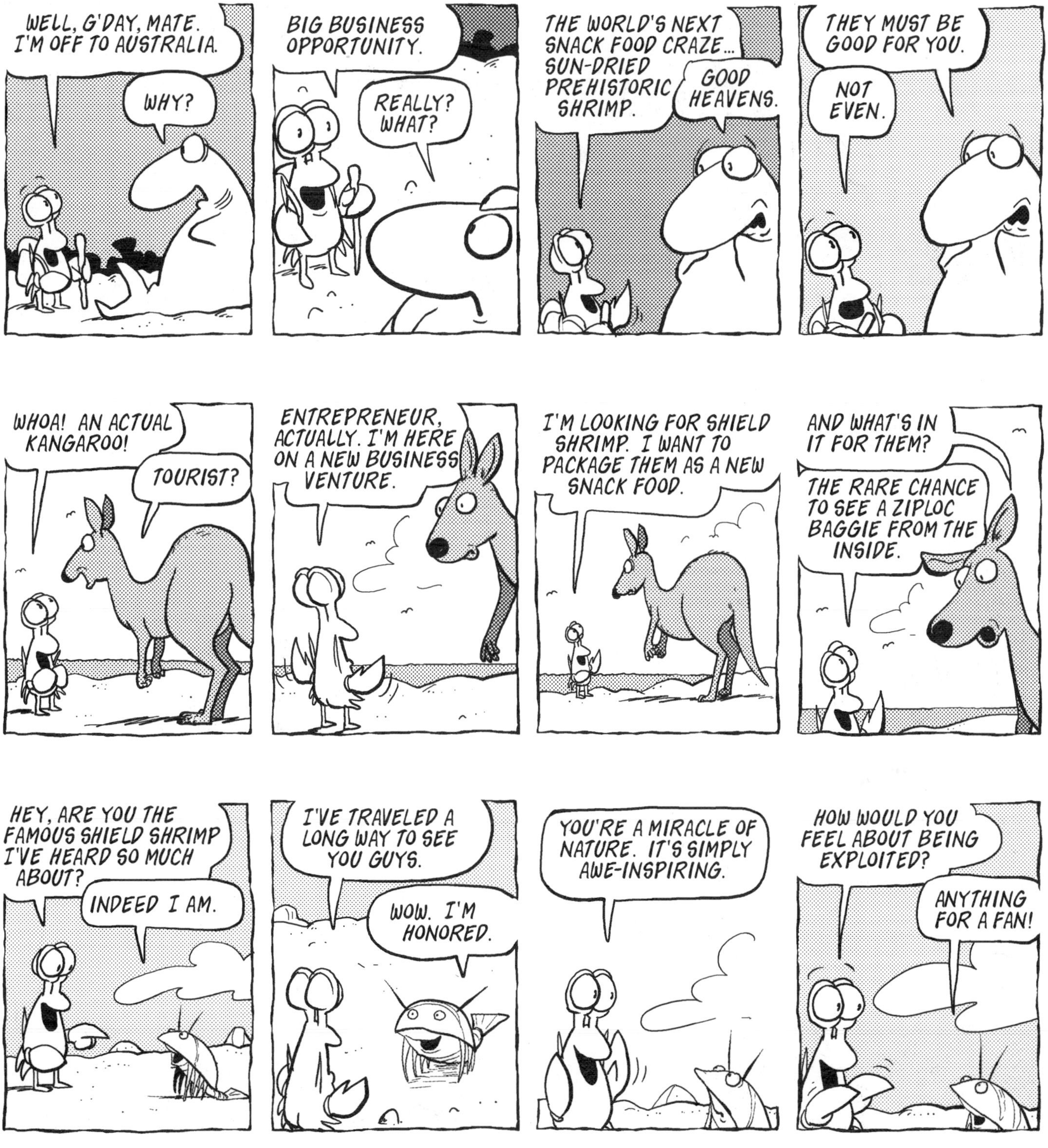
WELL, G'DAY, MATE. I'M OFF TO AUSTRALIA.
WHY?
BIG BUSINESS OPPORTUNITY.
REALLY? WHAT?
THE WORLD'S NEXT SNACK FOOD CRAZE... SUN-DRIED PREHISTORIC SHRIMP.
GOOD HEAVENS.
THEY MUST BE GOOD FOR YOU.
NOT EVEN.
WHOA! AN ACTUAL KANGAROO!
TOURIST?
ENTREPRENEUR, ACTUALLY. I'M HERE ON A NEW BUSINESS VENTURE.
I'M LOOKING FOR SHIELD SHRIMP. I WANT TO PACKAGE THEM AS A NEW SNACK FOOD.
AND WHAT'S IN IT FOR THEM?
THE RARE CHANCE TO SEE A ZIPLOC BAGGIE FROM THE INSIDE.
HEY, ARE YOU THE FAMOUS SHIELD SHRIMP I'VE HEARD SO MUCH ABOUT?
INDEED I AM.
I'VE TRAVELED A LONG WAY TO SEE YOU GUYS.
WOW. I'M HONORED.
YOU'RE A MIRACLE OF NATURE. IT'S SIMPLY AWE-INSPIRING.
HOW WOULD YOU FEEL ABOUT BEING EXPLOITED?
ANYTHING FOR A FAN!

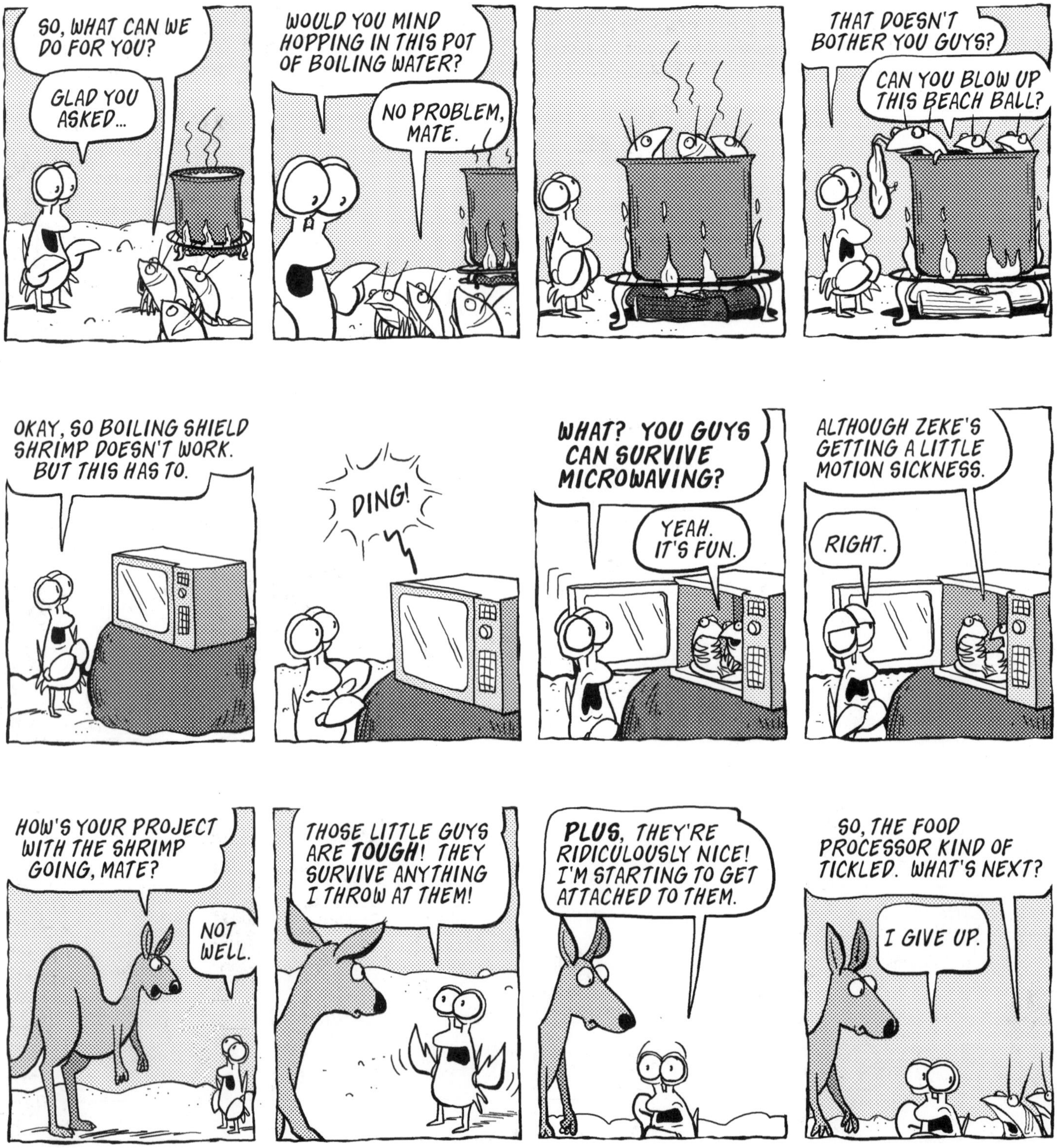
SO, WHAT CAN WE DO FOR YOU?
GLAD YOU ASKED...
WOULD YOU MIND HOPPING IN THIS POT OF BOILING WATER?
NO PROBLEM, MATE.
THAT DOESN'T BOTHER YOU GUYS?
CAN YOU BLOW UP THIS BEACH BALL?
OKAY, SO BOILING SHIELD SHRIMP DOESN'T WORK. BUT THIS HAS TO.
DING!
WHAT? YOU GUYS CAN SURVIVE MICROWAVING?
YEAH. IT'S FUN.
ALTHOUGH ZEKE'S GETTING A LITTLE MOTION SICKNESS.
RIGHT.
HOW'S YOUR PROJECT WITH THE SHRIMP GOING, MATE?
NOT WELL.
THOSE LITTLE GUYS ARE TOUGH! THEY SURVIVE ANYTHING I THROW AT THEM!
PLUS, THEY'RE RIDICULOUSLY NICE! I'M STARTING TO GET ATTACHED TO THEM.
SO, THE FOOD PROCESSOR KIND OF TICKLED. WHAT'S NEXT?
I GIVE UP.

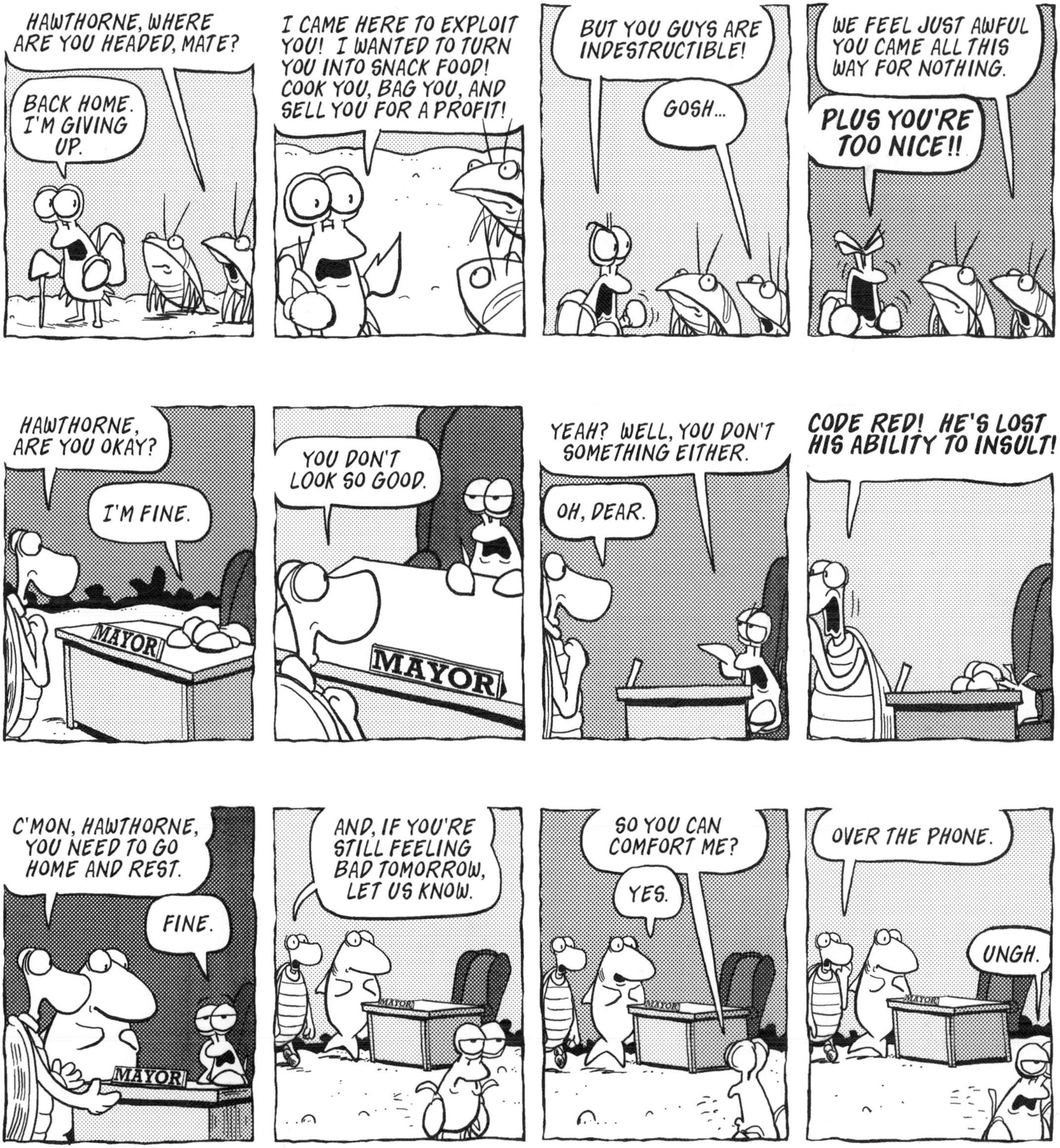
HAWTHORNE, WHERE ARE YOU HEADED, MATE?
BACK HOME. I'M GIVING UP.
I CAME HERE TO EXPLOIT YOU! I WANTED TO TURN YOU INTO SNACK FOOD! COOK YOU, BAG YOU, AND SELL YOU FOR A PROFIT!
BUT YOU GUYS ARE INDESTRUCTIBLE!
GOSH...
WE FEEL JUST AWFUL YOU CAME ALL THIS WAY FOR NOTHING.
PLUS YOU'RE TOO NICE!!
HAWTHORNE, ARE YOU OKAY?
I'M FINE.
YOU DON'T LOOK SO GOOD.
MAYOR
YEAH? WELL, YOU DON'T SOMETHING EITHER.
OH, DEAR.
CODE RED! HE'S LOST HIS ABILITY TO INSULT!
C'MON, HAWTHORNE, YOU NEED TO GO HOME AND REST.
FINE.
AND, IF YOU'RE STILL FEELING BAD TOMORROW, LET US KNOW.
SO YOU CAN COMFORT ME?
YES.
OVER THE PHONE.
UNGH.

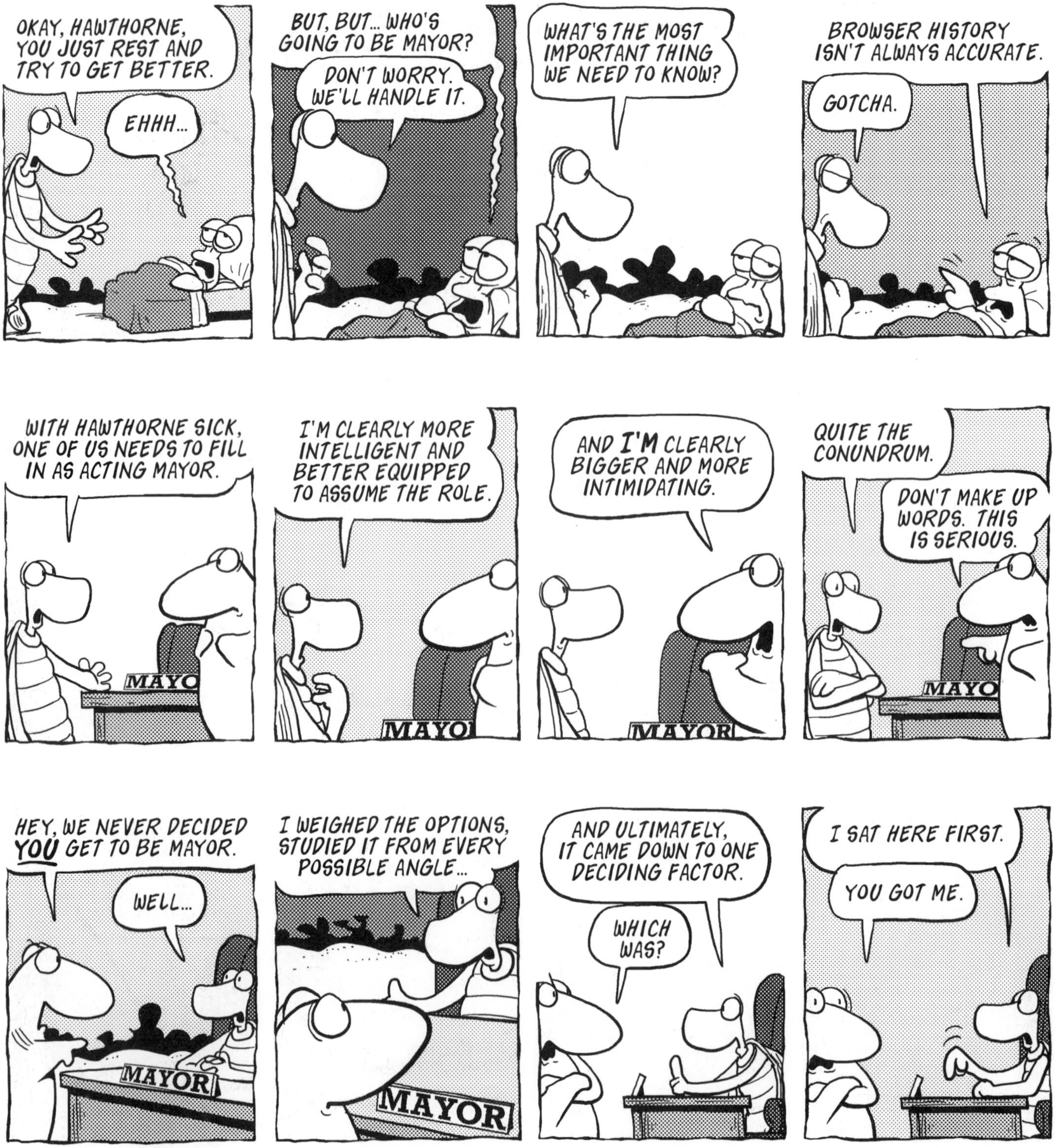
OKAY, HAWTHORNE, YOU JUST REST AND TRY TO GET BETTER.
EHHH...
BUT, BUT... WHO'S GOING TO BE MAYOR?
DON'T WORRY. WE'LL HANDLE IT.
WHAT'S THE MOST IMPORTANT THING WE NEED TO KNOW?
BROWSER HISTORY ISN'T ALWAYS ACCURATE.
GOTCHA.
WITH HAWTHORNE SICK, ONE OF US NEEDS TO FILL IN AS ACTING MAYOR.
MAYOR
I'M CLEARLY MORE INTELLIGENT AND BETTER EQUIPPED TO ASSUME THE ROLE.
AND I'M CLEARLY BIGGER AND MORE INTIMIDATING.
QUITE THE CONUNDRUM.
DON'T MAKE UP WORDS. THIS IS SERIOUS.
HEY, WE NEVER DECIDED YOU GET TO BE MAYOR.
WELL...
MAYOR
I WEIGHED THE OPTIONS, STUDIED IT FROM EVERY POSSIBLE ANGLE...
MAYOR
AND ULTIMATELY, IT CAME DOWN TO ONE DECIDING FACTOR.
WHICH WAS?
I SAT HERE FIRST.
YOU GOT ME.

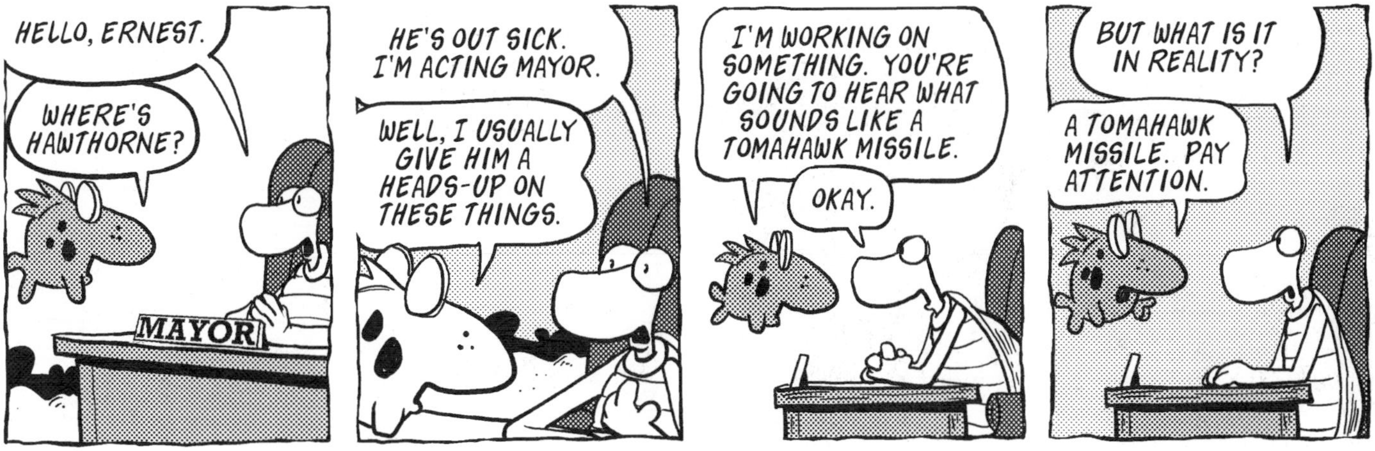
HELLO, ERNEST.
WHERE'S HAWTHORNE?
MAYOR
HE'S OUT SICK. I'M ACTING MAYOR.
WELL, I USUALLY GIVE HIM A HEADS-UP ON THESE THINGS.
I'M WORKING ON SOMETHING. YOU'RE GOING TO HEAR WHAT SOUNDS LIKE A TOMAHAWK MISSILE.
OKAY.
BUT WHAT IS IT IN REALITY?
A TOMAHAWK MISSILE. PAY ATTENTION.

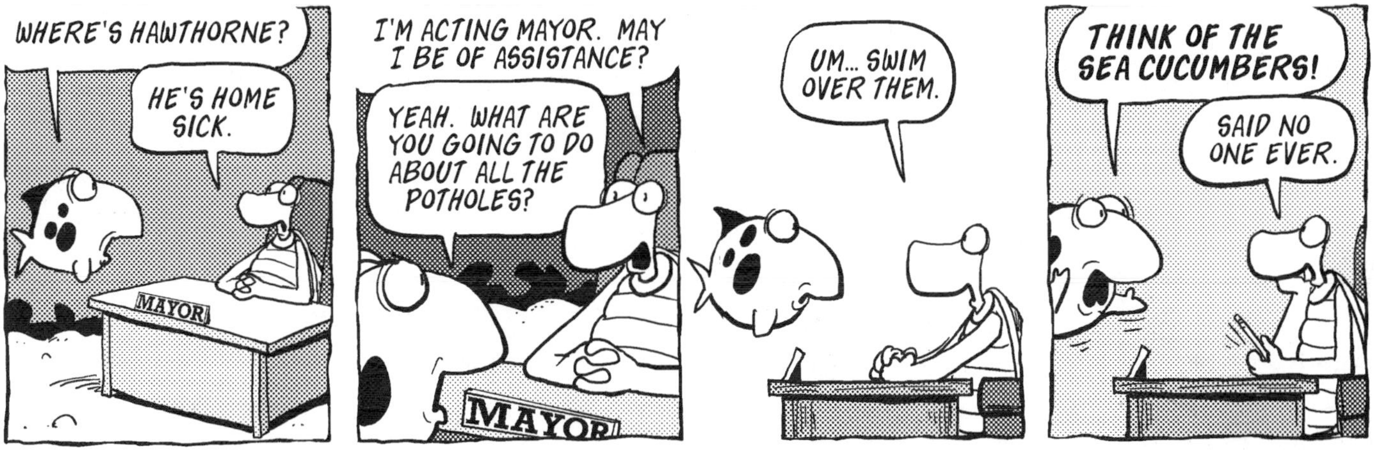
WHERE'S HAWTHORNE?
HE'S HOME SICK.
MAYOR
I'M ACTING MAYOR. MAY I BE OF ASSISTANCE?
YEAH. WHAT ARE YOU GOING TO DO ABOUT ALL THE POTHOLES?
MAYOR
UM... SWIM OVER THEM.
THINK OF THE SEA CUCUMBERS!
SAID NO ONE EVER.

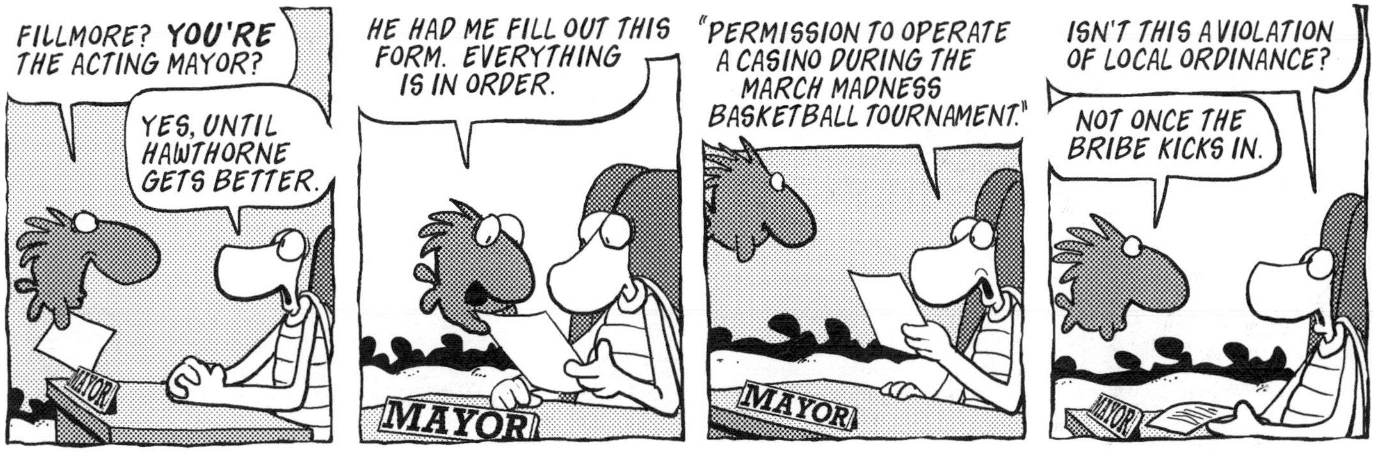
FILLMORE? YOU'RE THE ACTING MAYOR?
YES, UNTIL HAWTHORNE GETS BETTER.
MAYOR
HE HAD ME FILL OUT THIS FORM. EVERYTHING IS IN ORDER.
MAYOR
"PERMISSION TO OPERATE A CASINO DURING THE MARCH MADNESS BASKETBALL TOURNAMENT."
MAYOR
ISN'T THIS A VIOLATION OF LOCAL ORDINANCE?
NOT ONCE THE BRIBE KICKS IN.
MAYOR

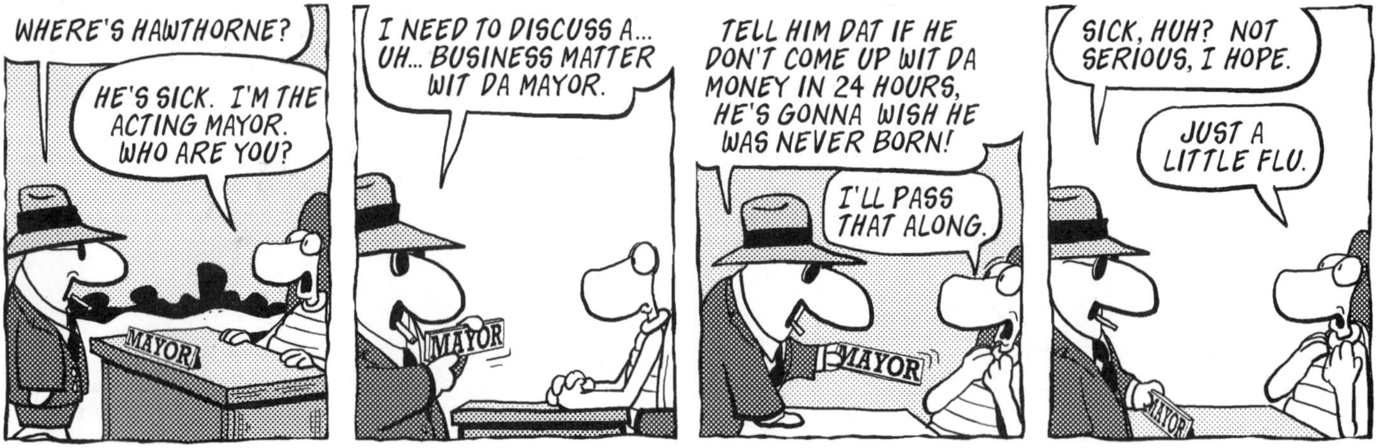
WHERE'S HAWTHORNE?
HE'S SICK. I'M THE ACTING MAYOR. WHO ARE YOU?
MAYOR
I NEED TO DISCUSS A... UH... BUSINESS MATTER WIT DA MAYOR.
MAYOR
TELL HIM DAT IF HE DON'T COME UP WIT DA MONEY IN 24 HOURS, HE'S GONNA WISH HE WAS NEVER BORN!
I'LL PASS THAT ALONG.
MAYOR
SICK, HUH? NOT SERIOUS, I HOPE.
JUST A LITTLE FLU.
MAYOR

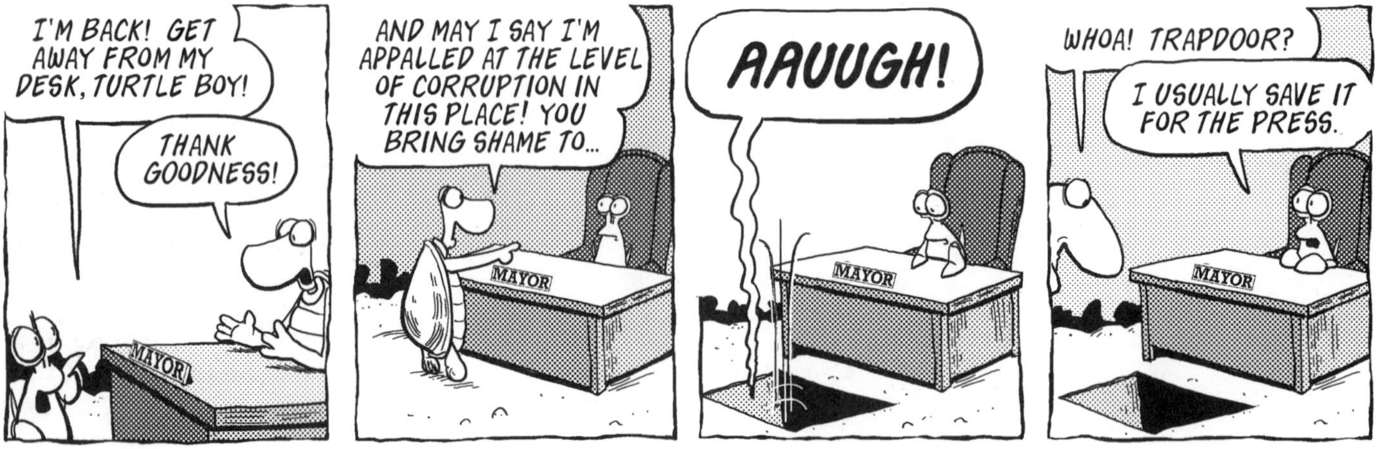
I'M BACK! GET AWAY FROM MY DESK, TURTLE BOY!
THANK GOODNESS!
MAYOR
AND MAY I SAY I'M APPALLED AT THE LEVEL OF CORRUPTION IN THIS PLACE! YOU BRING SHAME TO...
MAYOR
AAUUGH!
MAYOR
WHOA! TRAPDOOR?
I USUALLY SAVE IT FOR THE PRESS.
MAYOR

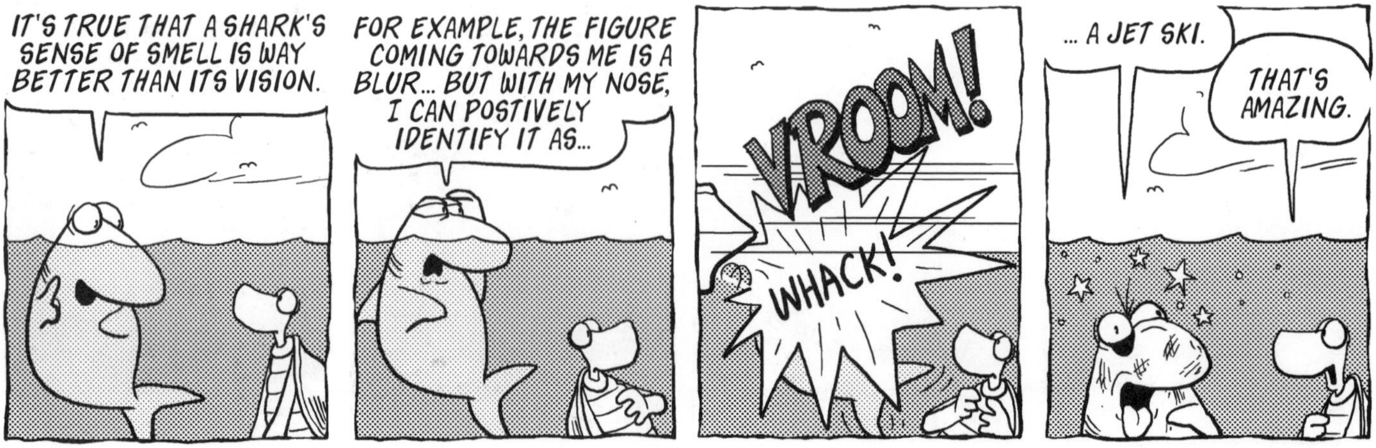
IT'S TRUE THAT A SHARK'S SENSE OF SMELL IS WAY BETTER THAN ITS VISION.
FOR EXAMPLE, THE FIGURE COMING TOWARDS ME IS A BLUR... BUT WITH MY NOSE, I CAN POSTIVELY IDENTIFY IT AS...
VROOM!
WHACK!
... A JET SKI.
THAT'S AMAZING.

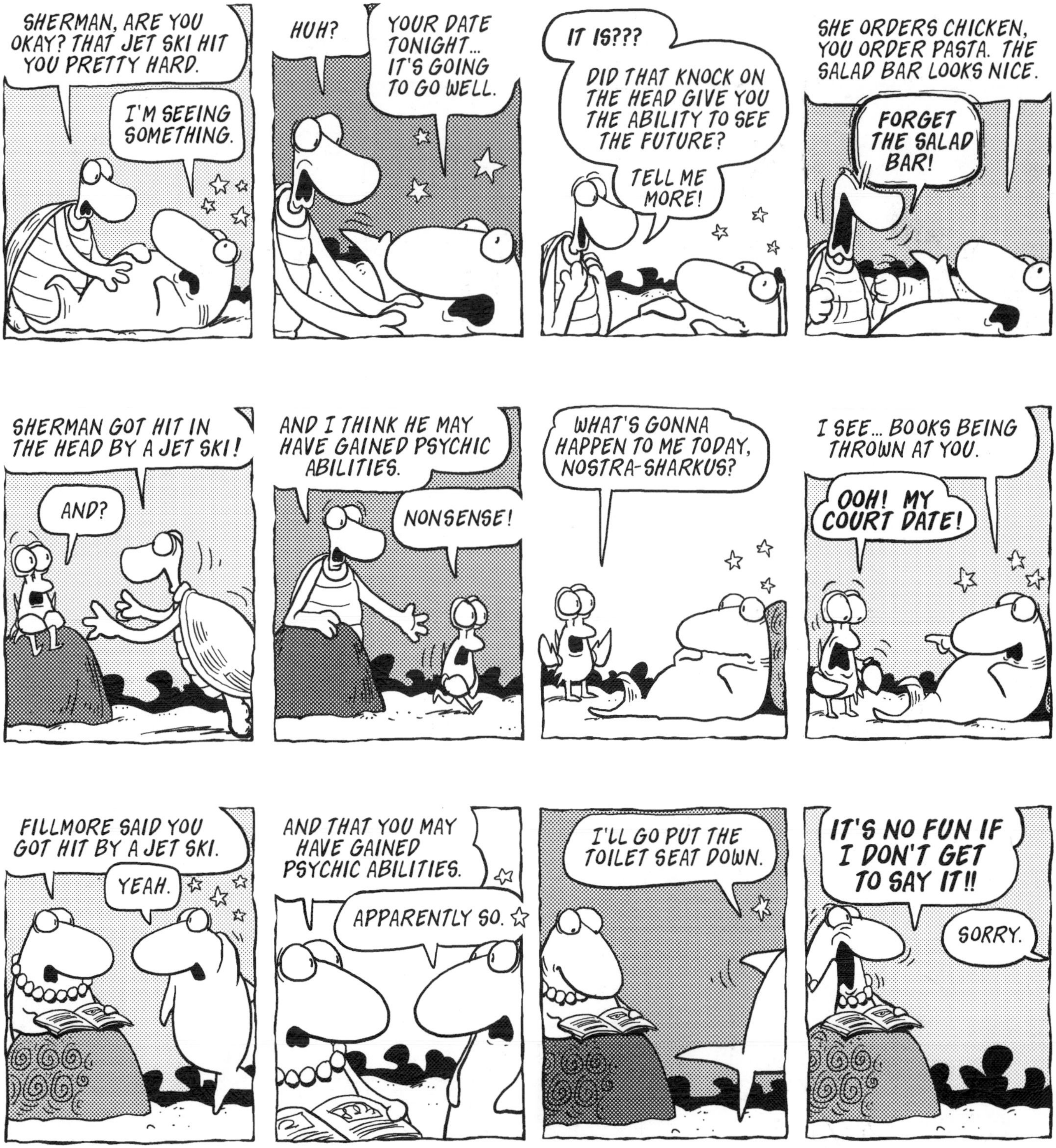
SHERMAN, ARE YOU OKAY? THAT JET SKI HIT YOU PRETTY HARD.
I'M SEEING SOMETHING.
HUH?
YOUR DATE TONIGHT... IT'S GOING TO GO WELL.
IT IS???
DID THAT KNOCK ON THE HEAD GIVE YOU THE ABILITY TO SEE THE FUTURE?
TELL ME MORE!
SHE ORDERS CHICKEN, YOU ORDER PASTA. THE SALAD BAR LOOKS NICE.
FORGET THE SALAD BAR!
SHERMAN GOT HIT IN THE HEAD BY A JET SKI!
AND?
AND I THINK HE MAY HAVE GAINED PSYCHIC ABILITIES.
NONSENSE!
WHAT'S GONNA HAPPEN TO ME TODAY, NOSTRA-SHARKUS?
I SEE... BOOKS BEING THROWN AT YOU.
OOH! MY COURT DATE!
FILLMORE SAID YOU GOT HIT BY A JET SKI.
YEAH.
AND THAT YOU MAY HAVE GAINED PSYCHIC ABILITIES.
APPARENTLY SO.
I'LL GO PUT THE TOILET SEAT DOWN.
IT'S NO FUN IF I DON'T GET TO SAY IT!!
SORRY.

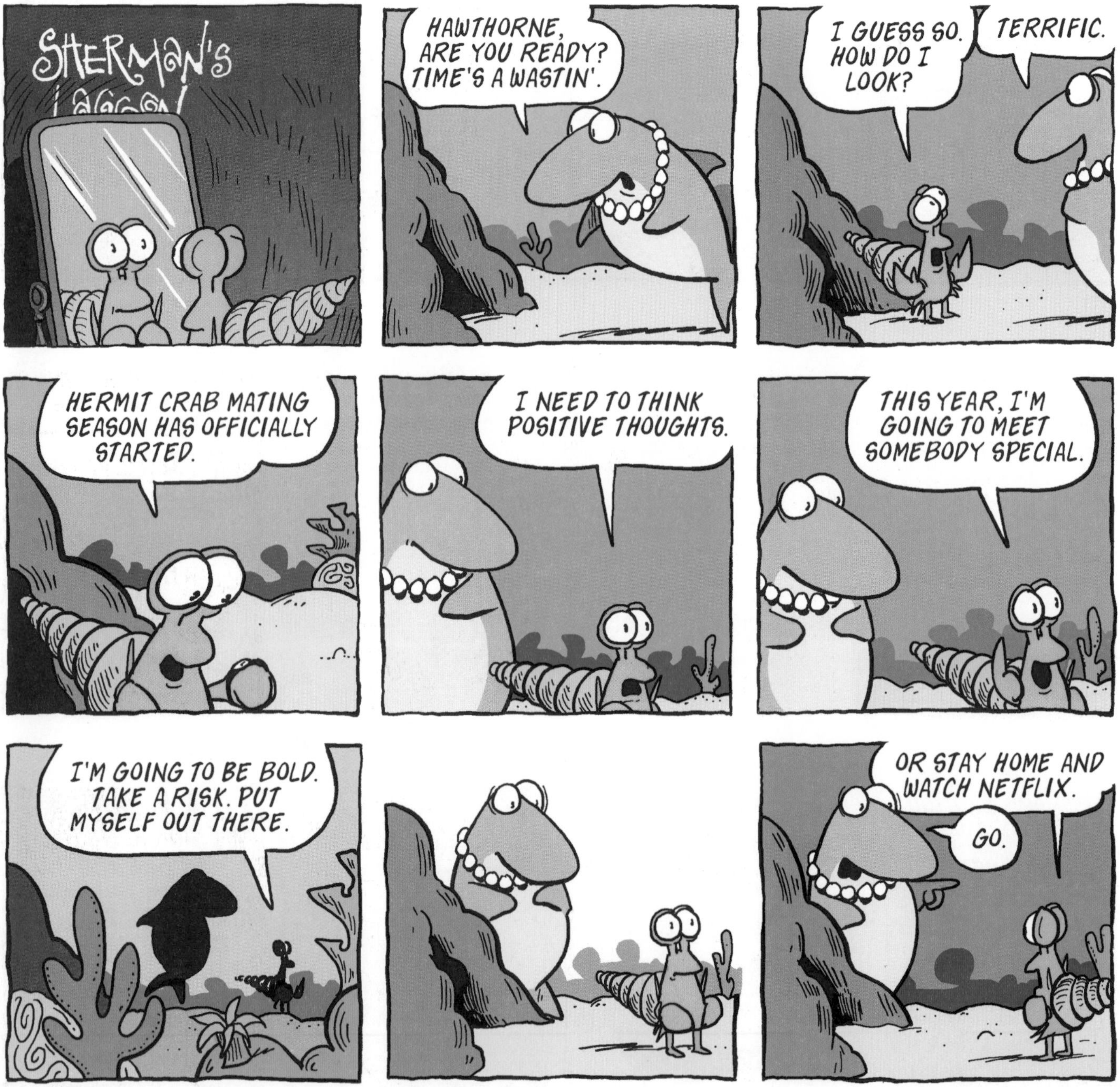
SHERMAN'S LAGOON
HAWTHORNE, ARE YOU READY? TIME'S A WASTIN'.
I GUESS SO. HOW DO I LOOK?
TERRIFIC.
HERMIT CRAB MATING SEASON HAS OFFICIALLY STARTED.
I NEED TO THINK POSITIVE THOUGHTS.
THIS YEAR, I'M GOING TO MEET SOMEBODY SPECIAL.
I'M GOING TO BE BOLD. TAKE A RISK. PUT MYSELF OUT THERE.
OR STAY HOME AND WATCH NETFLIX.
GO.

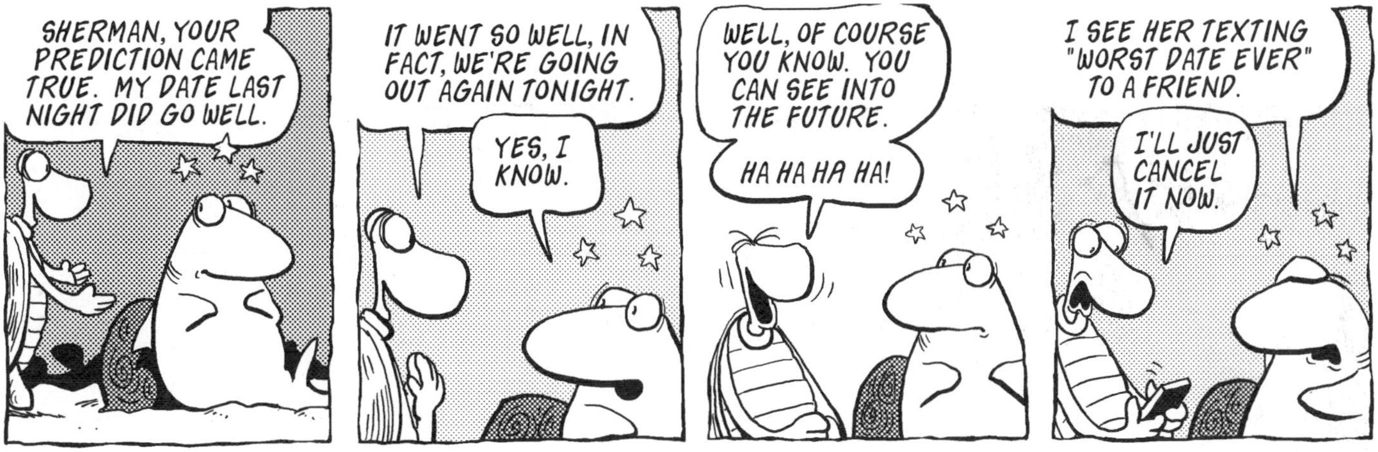
SHERMAN, YOUR PREDICTION CAME TRUE. MY DATE LAST NIGHT DID GO WELL.
IT WENT SO WELL, IN FACT, WE'RE GOING OUT AGAIN TONIGHT.
YES, I KNOW.
WELL, OF COURSE YOU KNOW. YOU CAN SEE INTO THE FUTURE.
HA HA HA HA!
I SEE HER TEXTING "WORST DATE EVER" TO A FRIEND.
I'LL JUST CANCEL IT NOW.

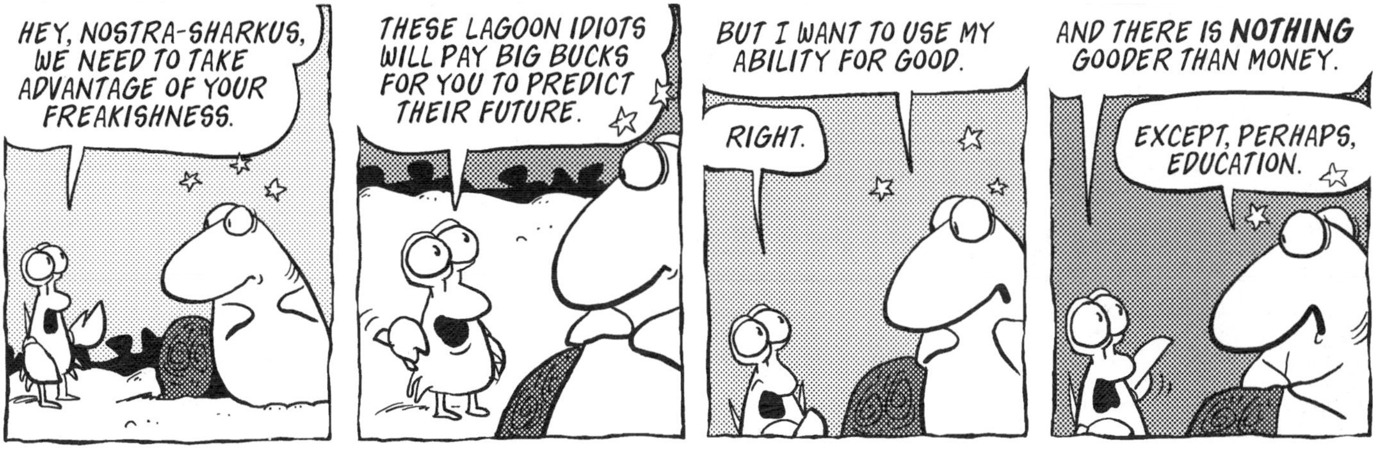
HEY, NOSTRA-SHARKUS, WE NEED TO TAKE ADVANTAGE OF YOUR FREAKISHNESS.
THESE LAGOON IDIOTS WILL PAY BIG BUCKS FOR YOU TO PREDICT THEIR FUTURE.
BUT I WANT TO USE MY ABILITY FOR GOOD.
RIGHT.
AND THERE IS **NOTHING** GOODER THAN MONEY.
EXCEPT, PERHAPS, EDUCATION.

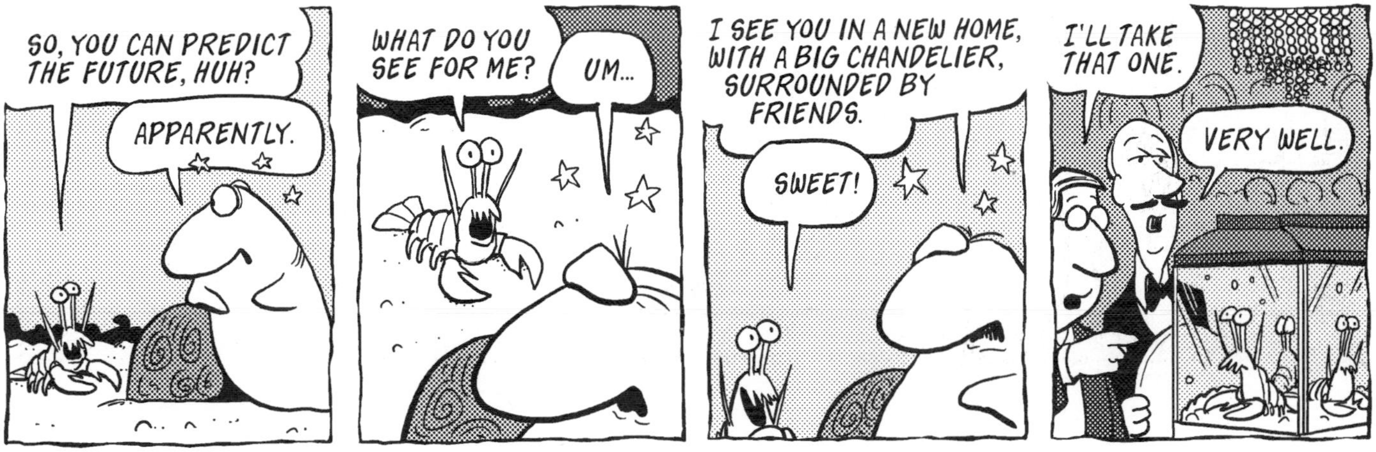
SO, YOU CAN PREDICT THE FUTURE, HUH?
APPARENTLY.
WHAT DO YOU SEE FOR ME?
UM...
I SEE YOU IN A NEW HOME, WITH A BIG CHANDELIER, SURROUNDED BY FRIENDS.
SWEET!
I'LL TAKE THAT ONE.
VERY WELL.

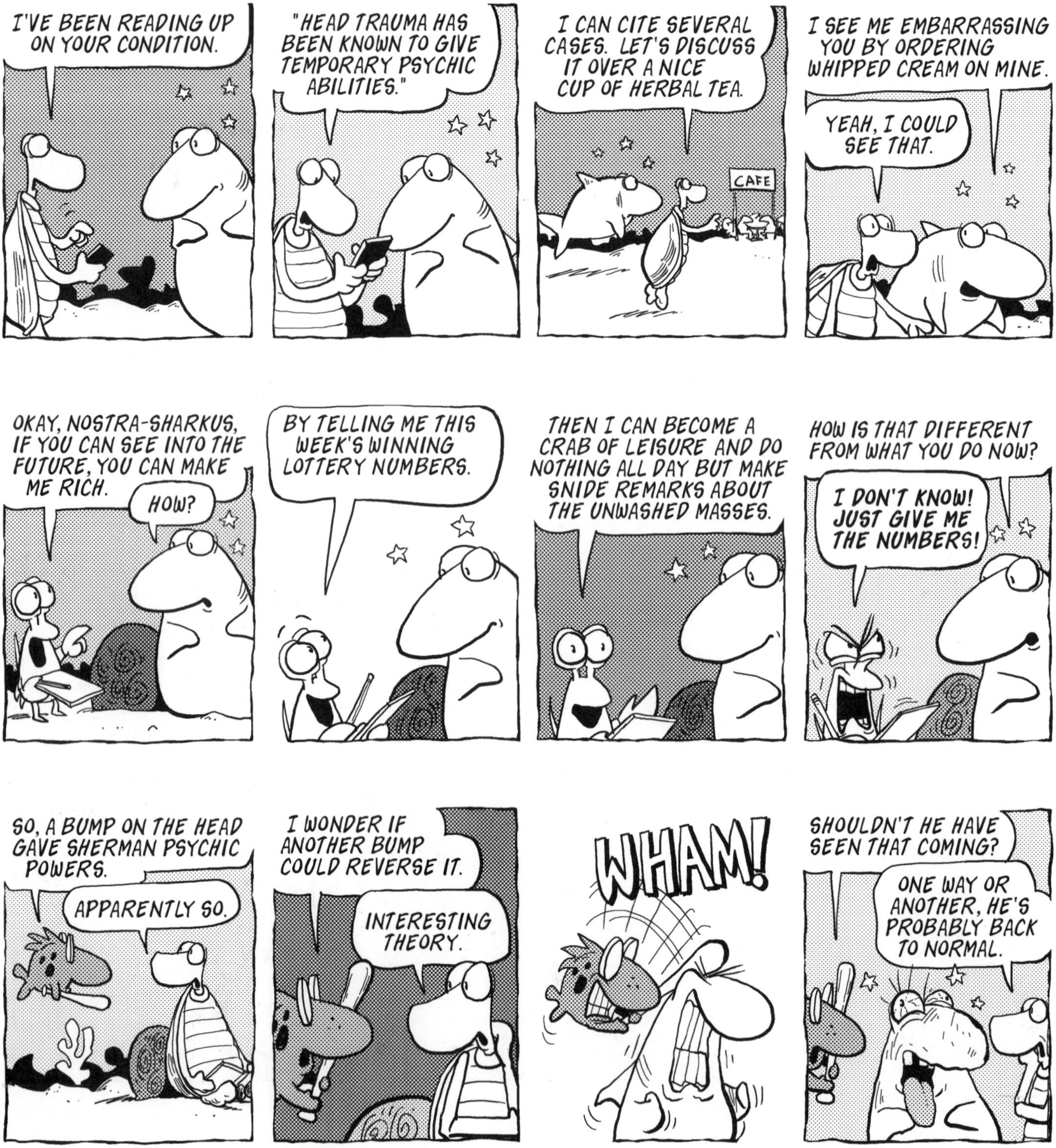
I'VE BEEN READING UP ON YOUR CONDITION.
"HEAD TRAUMA HAS BEEN KNOWN TO GIVE TEMPORARY PSYCHIC ABILITIES."
I CAN CITE SEVERAL CASES. LET'S DISCUSS IT OVER A NICE CUP OF HERBAL TEA.
CAFE
I SEE ME EMBARRASSING YOU BY ORDERING WHIPPED CREAM ON MINE.
YEAH, I COULD SEE THAT.
OKAY, NOSTRA-SHARKUS, IF YOU CAN SEE INTO THE FUTURE, YOU CAN MAKE ME RICH.
HOW?
BY TELLING ME THIS WEEK'S WINNING LOTTERY NUMBERS.
THEN I CAN BECOME A CRAB OF LEISURE AND DO NOTHING ALL DAY BUT MAKE SNIDE REMARKS ABOUT THE UNWASHED MASSES.
HOW IS THAT DIFFERENT FROM WHAT YOU DO NOW?
I DON'T KNOW! JUST GIVE ME THE NUMBERS!
SO, A BUMP ON THE HEAD GAVE SHERMAN PSYCHIC POWERS.
APPARENTLY SO.
I WONDER IF ANOTHER BUMP COULD REVERSE IT.
INTERESTING THEORY.
WHAM!
SHOULDN'T HE HAVE SEEN THAT COMING?
ONE WAY OR ANOTHER, HE'S PROBABLY BACK TO NORMAL.

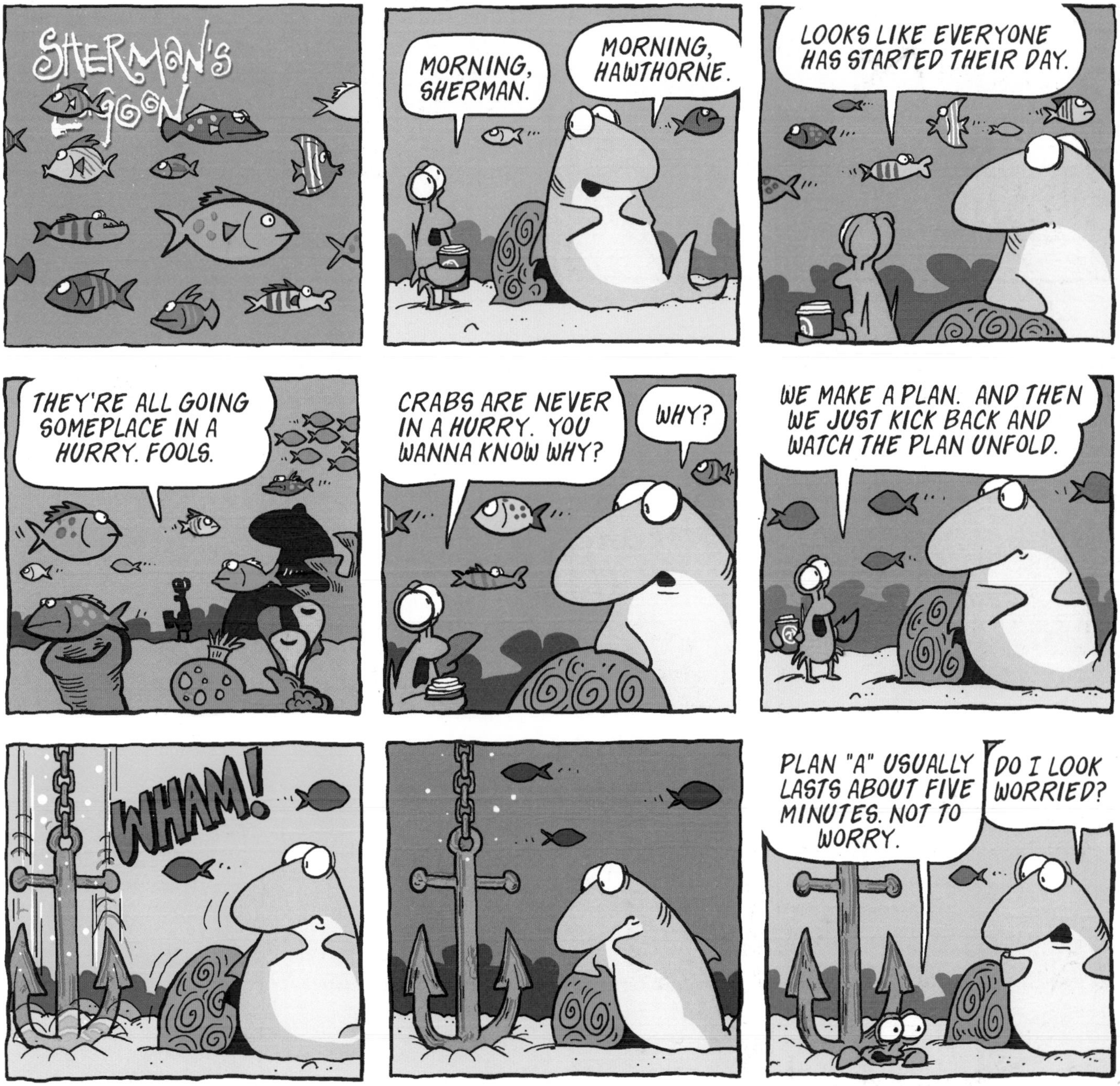
SHERMAN'S LAGOON
MORNING, SHERMAN.
MORNING, HAWTHORNE.
LOOKS LIKE EVERYONE HAS STARTED THEIR DAY.
THEY'RE ALL GOING SOMEPLACE IN A HURRY. FOOLS.
CRABS ARE NEVER IN A HURRY. YOU WANNA KNOW WHY?
WHY?
WE MAKE A PLAN. AND THEN WE JUST KICK BACK AND WATCH THE PLAN UNFOLD.
WHAM!
PLAN "A" USUALLY LASTS ABOUT FIVE MINUTES. NOT TO WORRY.
DO I LOOK WORRIED?

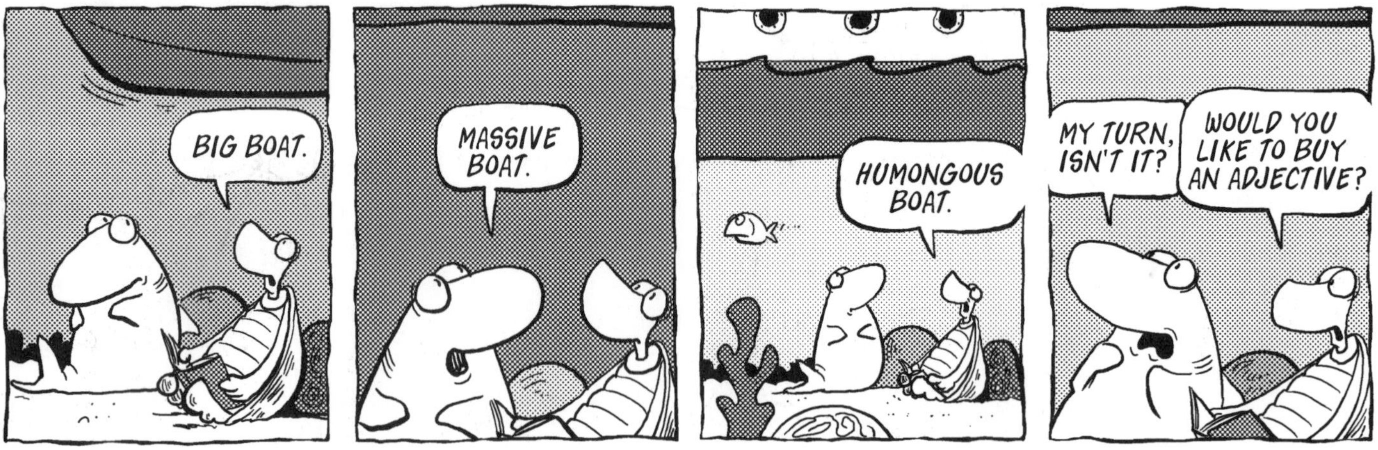
BIG BOAT.
MASSIVE BOAT.
HUMONGOUS BOAT.
MY TURN, ISN'T IT?
WOULD YOU LIKE TO BUY AN ADJECTIVE?

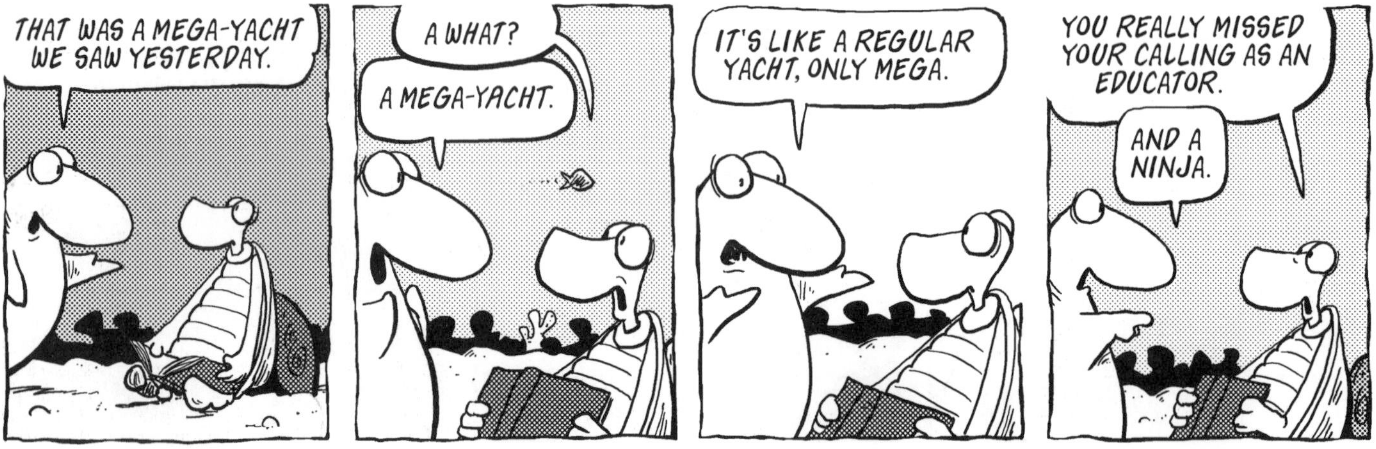
THAT WAS A MEGA-YACHT WE SAW YESTERDAY.
A WHAT?
A MEGA-YACHT.
IT'S LIKE A REGULAR YACHT, ONLY MEGA.
YOU REALLY MISSED YOUR CALLING AS AN EDUCATOR.
AND A NINJA.

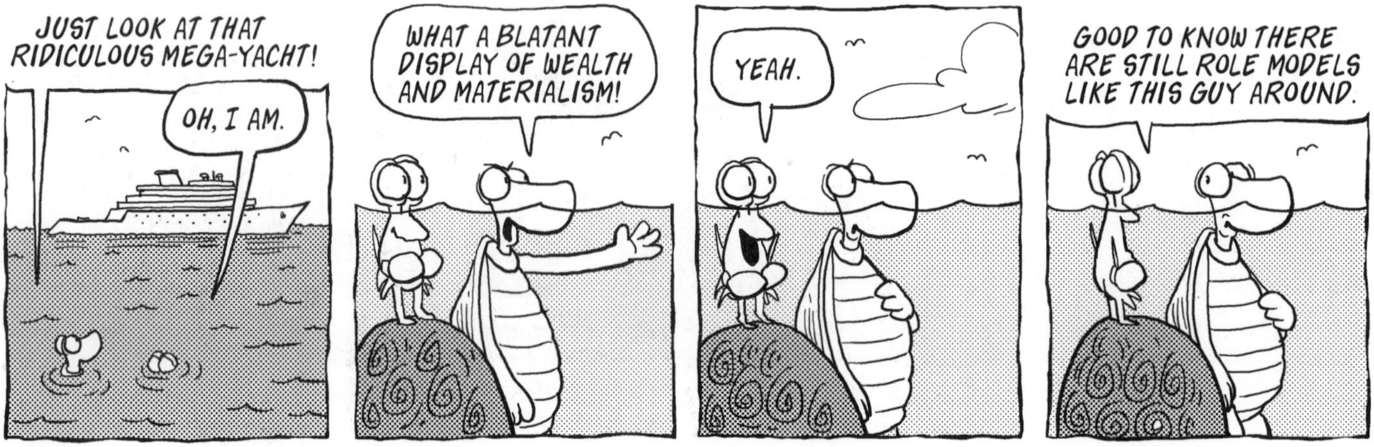
JUST LOOK AT THAT RIDICULOUS MEGA-YACHT!
OH, I AM.
WHAT A BLATANT DISPLAY OF WEALTH AND MATERIALISM!
YEAH.
GOOD TO KNOW THERE ARE STILL ROLE MODELS LIKE THIS GUY AROUND.

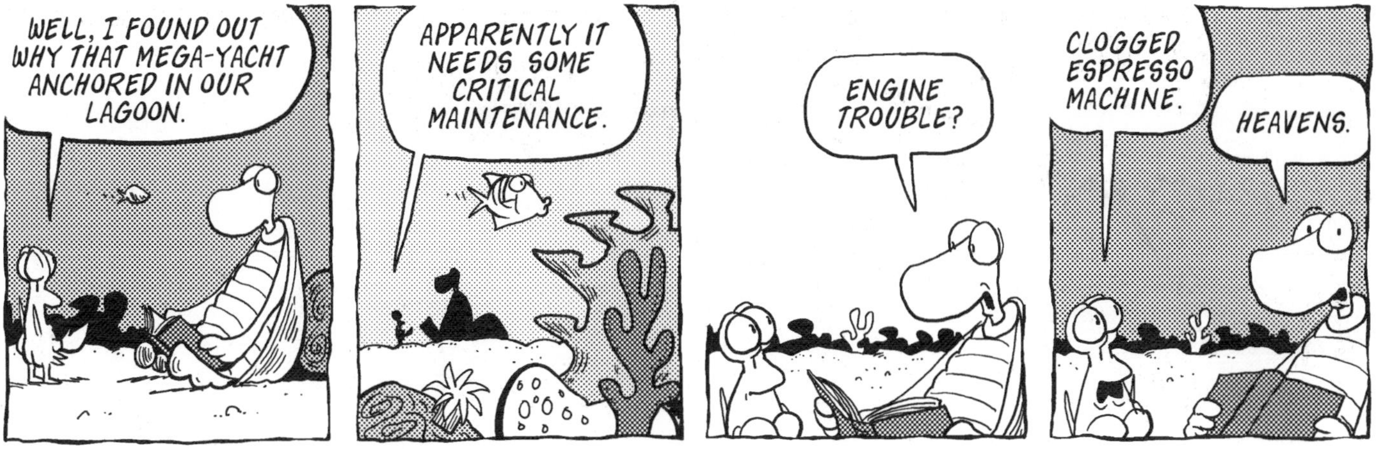
WELL, I FOUND OUT WHY THAT MEGA-YACHT ANCHORED IN OUR LAGOON.
APPARENTLY IT NEEDS SOME CRITICAL MAINTENANCE.
ENGINE TROUBLE?
CLOGGED ESPRESSO MACHINE.
HEAVENS.

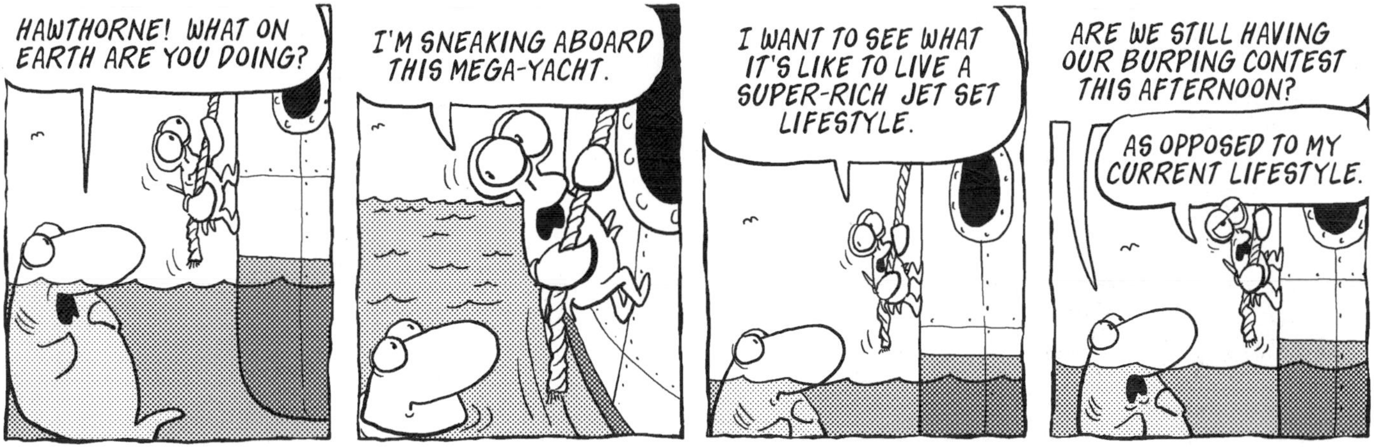
HAWTHORNE! WHAT ON EARTH ARE YOU DOING?
I'M SNEAKING ABOARD THIS MEGA-YACHT.
I WANT TO SEE WHAT IT'S LIKE TO LIVE A SUPER-RICH JET SET LIFESTYLE.
ARE WE STILL HAVING OUR BURPING CONTEST THIS AFTERNOON?
AS OPPOSED TO MY CURRENT LIFESTYLE.

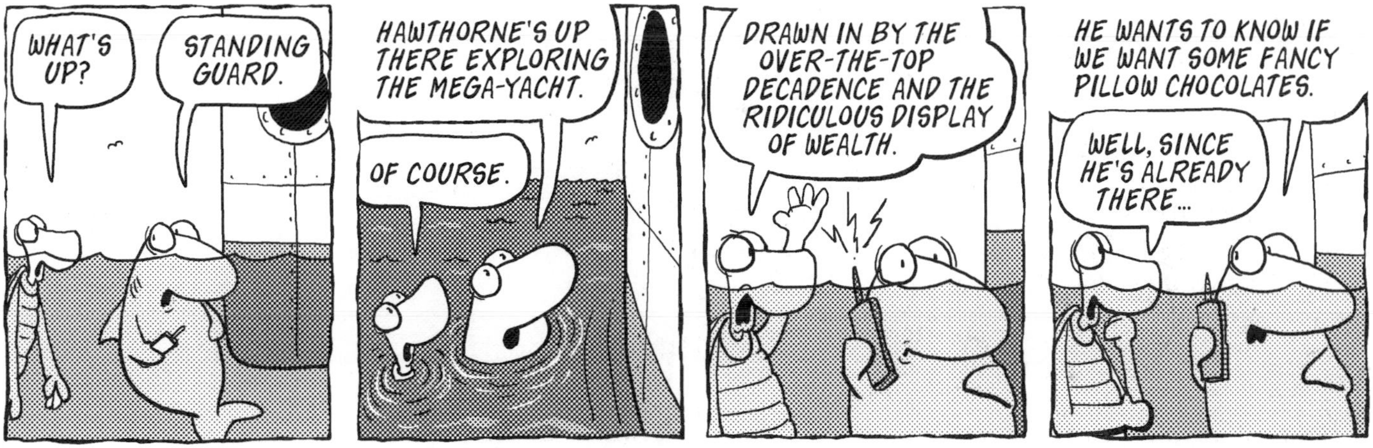
WHAT'S UP?
STANDING GUARD.
HAWTHORNE'S UP THERE EXPLORING THE MEGA-YACHT.
OF COURSE.
DRAWN IN BY THE OVER-THE-TOP DECADENCE AND THE RIDICULOUS DISPLAY OF WEALTH.
HE WANTS TO KNOW IF WE WANT SOME FANCY PILLOW CHOCOLATES.
WELL, SINCE HE'S ALREADY THERE...

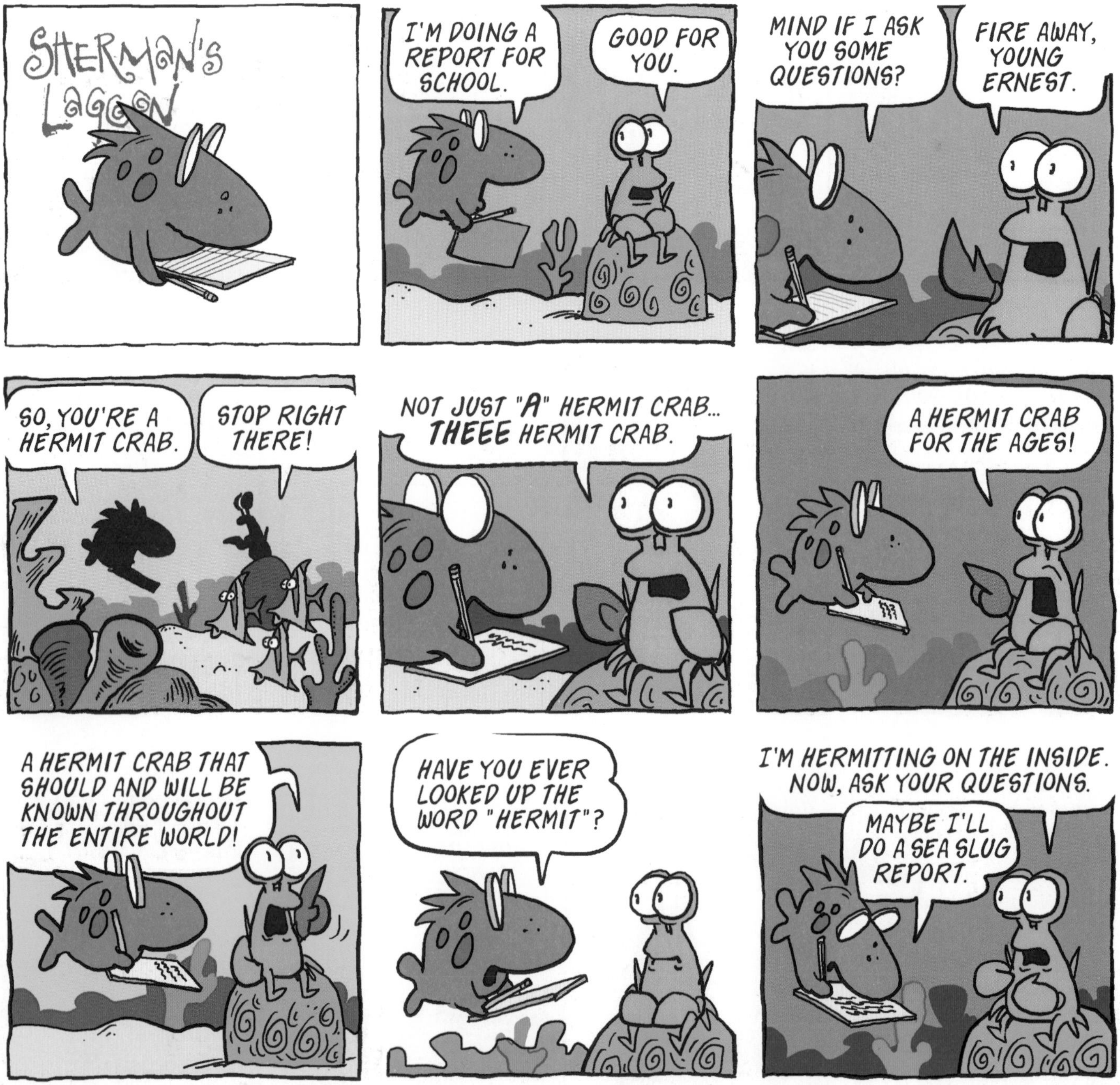
SHERMAN'S LAGOON
I'M DOING A REPORT FOR SCHOOL.
GOOD FOR YOU.
MIND IF I ASK YOU SOME QUESTIONS?
FIRE AWAY, YOUNG ERNEST.
SO, YOU'RE A HERMIT CRAB.
STOP RIGHT THERE!
NOT JUST "A" HERMIT CRAB... THEEE HERMIT CRAB.
A HERMIT CRAB FOR THE AGES!
A HERMIT CRAB THAT SHOULD AND WILL BE KNOWN THROUGHOUT THE ENTIRE WORLD!
HAVE YOU EVER LOOKED UP THE WORD "HERMIT"?
I'M HERMITTING ON THE INSIDE. NOW, ASK YOUR QUESTIONS.
MAYBE I'LL DO A SEA SLUG REPORT.

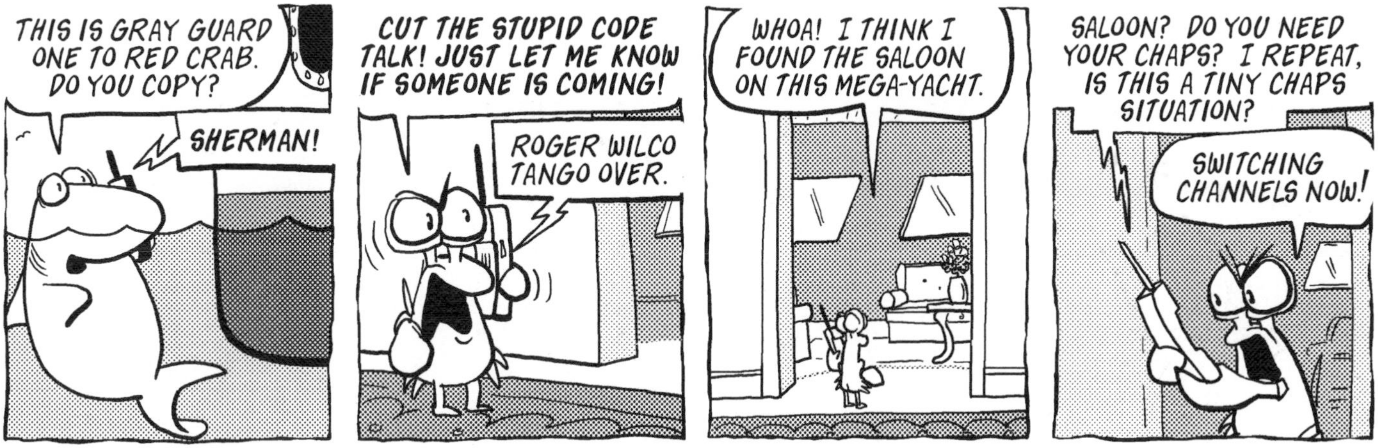
THIS IS GRAY GUARD ONE TO RED CRAB. DO YOU COPY?
SHERMAN!
CUT THE STUPID CODE TALK! JUST LET ME KNOW IF SOMEONE IS COMING!
ROGER WILCO TANGO OVER.
WHOA! I THINK I FOUND THE SALOON ON THIS MEGA-YACHT.
SALOON? DO YOU NEED YOUR CHAPS? I REPEAT, IS THIS A TINY CHAPS SITUATION?
SWITCHING CHANNELS NOW!

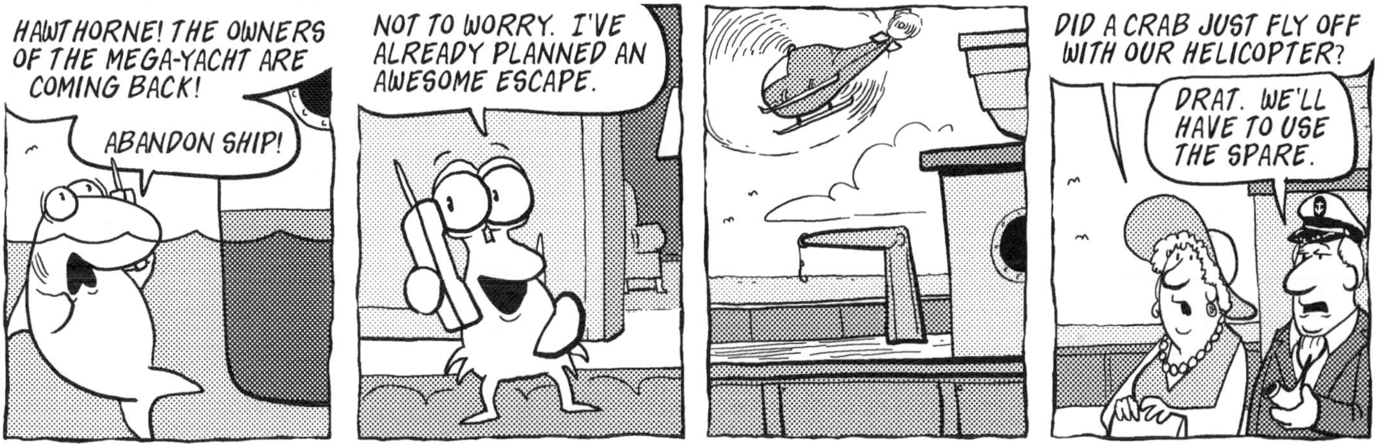
HAWTHORNE! THE OWNERS OF THE MEGA-YACHT ARE COMING BACK!
ABANDON SHIP!
NOT TO WORRY. I'VE ALREADY PLANNED AN AWESOME ESCAPE.
DID A CRAB JUST FLY OFF WITH OUR HELICOPTER?
DRAT. WE'LL HAVE TO USE THE SPARE.

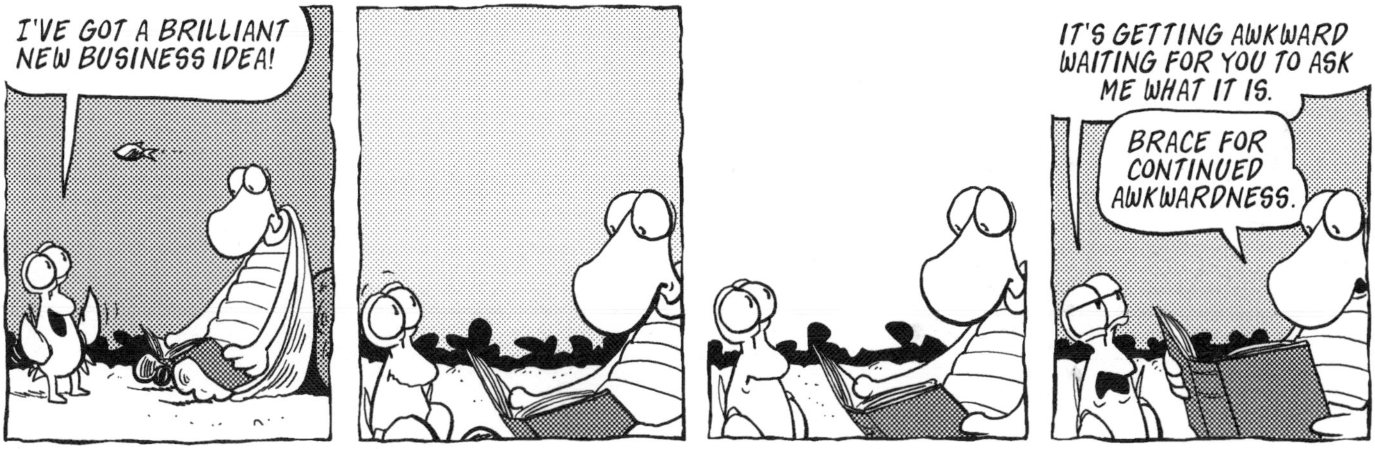
I'VE GOT A BRILLIANT NEW BUSINESS IDEA!
IT'S GETTING AWKWARD WAITING FOR YOU TO ASK ME WHAT IT IS.
BRACE FOR CONTINUED AWKWARDNESS.

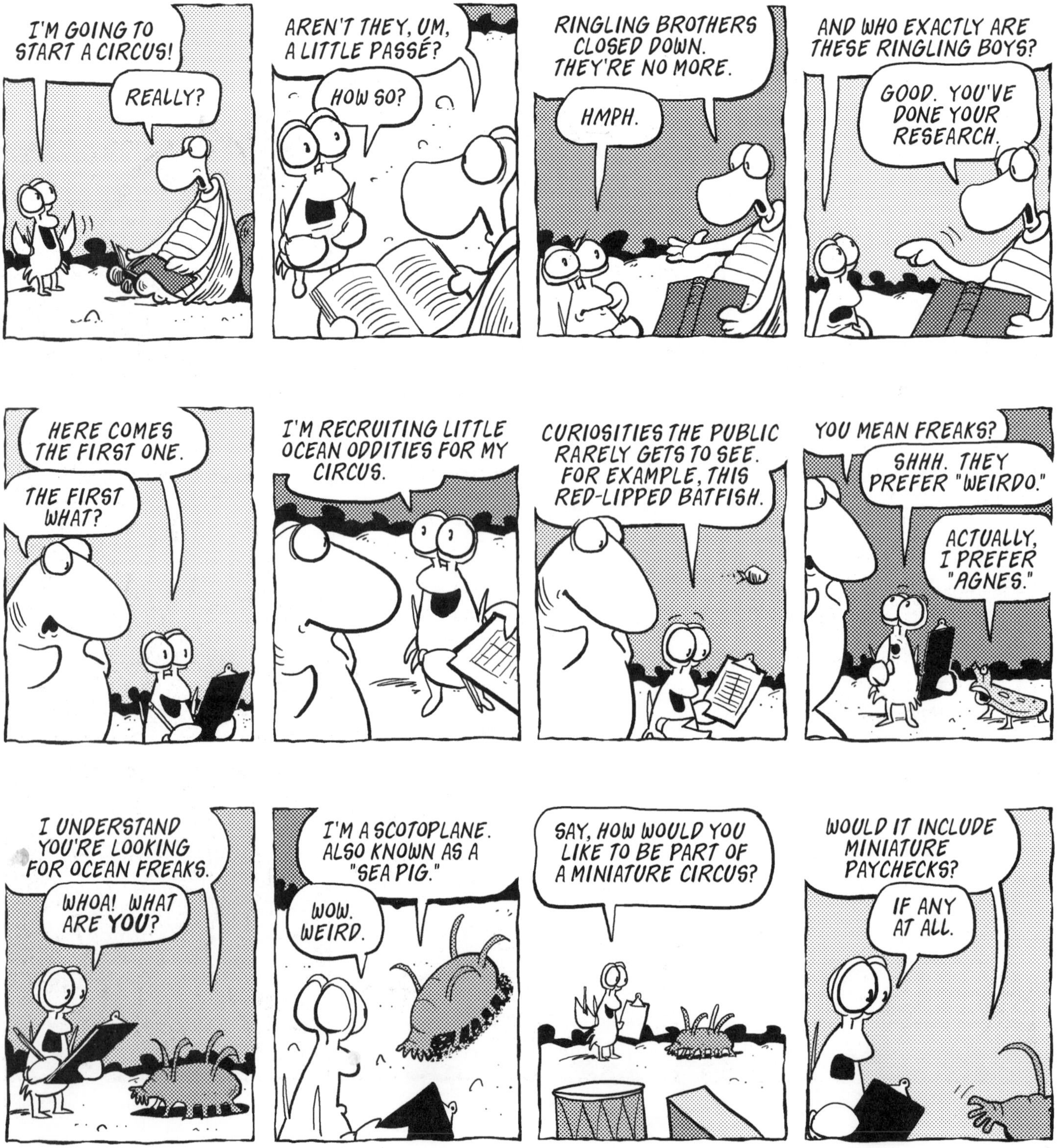
I'M GOING TO START A CIRCUS!
REALLY?
AREN'T THEY, UM, A LITTLE PASSÉ?
HOW SO?
RINGLING BROTHERS CLOSED DOWN. THEY'RE NO MORE.
HMPH.
AND WHO EXACTLY ARE THESE RINGLING BOYS?
GOOD. YOU'VE DONE YOUR RESEARCH.
HERE COMES THE FIRST ONE.
THE FIRST WHAT?
I'M RECRUITING LITTLE OCEAN ODDITIES FOR MY CIRCUS.
CURIOSITIES THE PUBLIC RARELY GETS TO SEE. FOR EXAMPLE, THIS RED-LIPPED BATFISH.
YOU MEAN FREAKS?
SHHH. THEY PREFER "WEIRDO."
ACTUALLY, I PREFER "AGNES."
I UNDERSTAND YOU'RE LOOKING FOR OCEAN FREAKS.
WHOA! WHAT ARE YOU?
I'M A SCOTOPLANE. ALSO KNOWN AS A "SEA PIG."
WOW. WEIRD.
SAY, HOW WOULD YOU LIKE TO BE PART OF A MINIATURE CIRCUS?
WOULD IT INCLUDE MINIATURE PAYCHECKS?
IF ANY AT ALL.

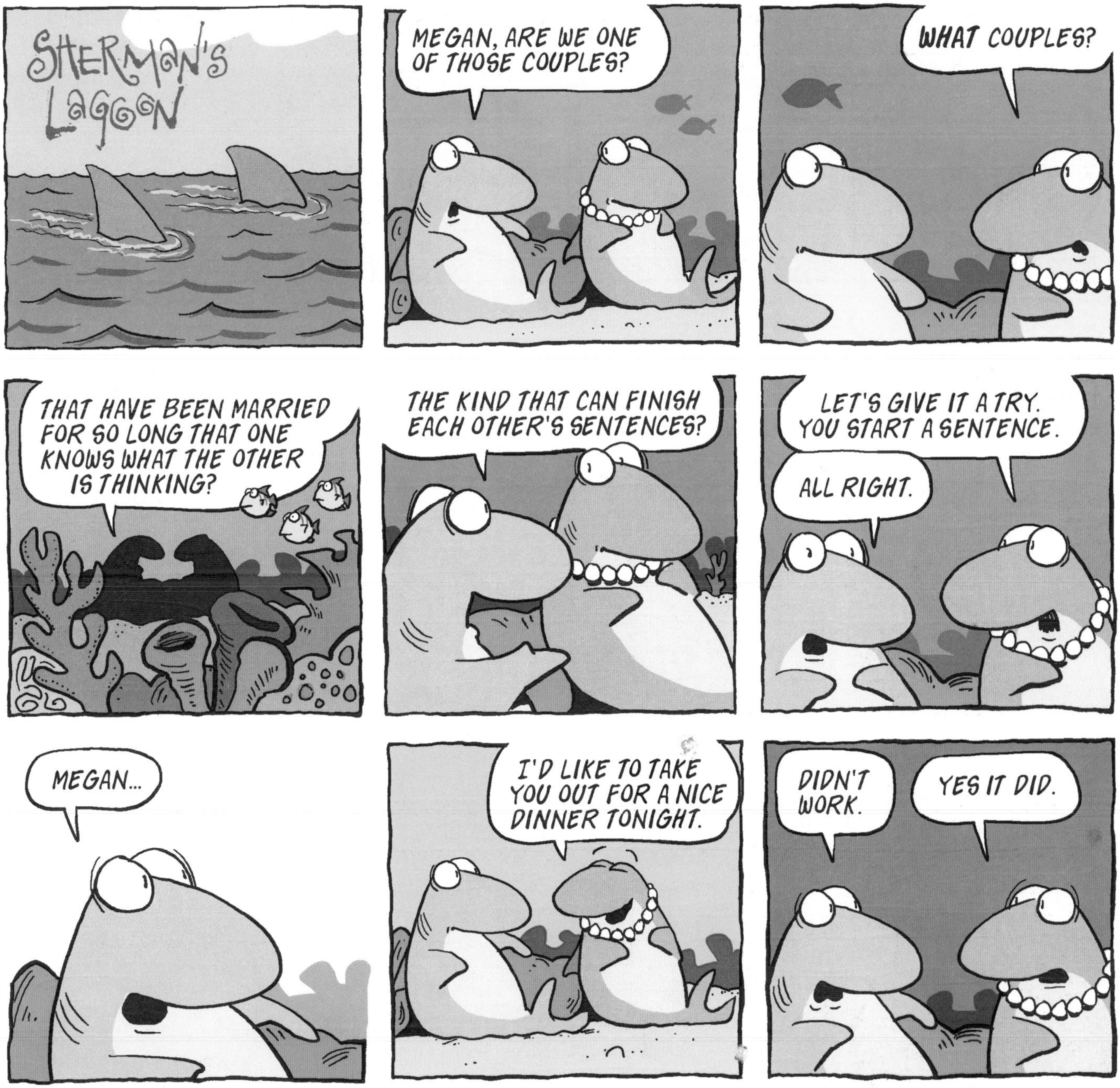
SHERMAN'S LAGOON
MEGAN, ARE WE ONE OF THOSE COUPLES?
WHAT COUPLES?
THAT HAVE BEEN MARRIED FOR SO LONG THAT ONE KNOWS WHAT THE OTHER IS THINKING?
THE KIND THAT CAN FINISH EACH OTHER'S SENTENCES?
LET'S GIVE IT A TRY. YOU START A SENTENCE.
ALL RIGHT.
MEGAN...
I'D LIKE TO TAKE YOU OUT FOR A NICE DINNER TONIGHT.
DIDN'T WORK.
YES IT DID.

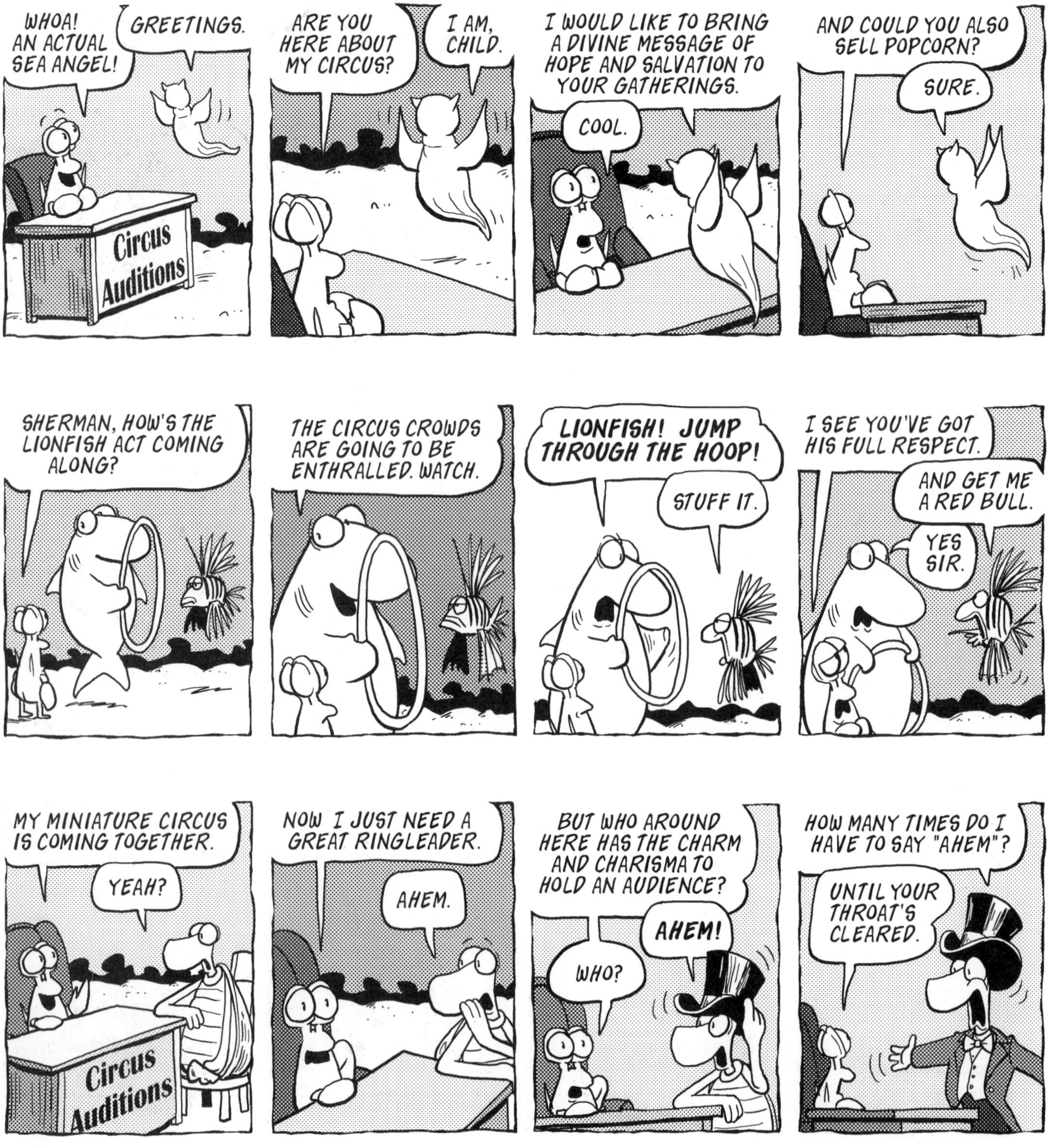
WHOA! AN ACTUAL SEA ANGEL!
GREETINGS.
Circus Auditions
ARE YOU HERE ABOUT MY CIRCUS?
I AM, CHILD.
I WOULD LIKE TO BRING A DIVINE MESSAGE OF HOPE AND SALVATION TO YOUR GATHERINGS.
COOL.
AND COULD YOU ALSO SELL POPCORN?
SURE.
SHERMAN, HOW'S THE LIONFISH ACT COMING ALONG?
THE CIRCUS CROWDS ARE GOING TO BE ENTHRALLED. WATCH.
LIONFISH! JUMP THROUGH THE HOOP!
STUFF IT.
I SEE YOU'VE GOT HIS FULL RESPECT.
AND GET ME A RED BULL.
YES SIR.
MY MINIATURE CIRCUS IS COMING TOGETHER.
YEAH?
Circus Auditions
NOW I JUST NEED A GREAT RINGLEADER.
AHEM.
BUT WHO AROUND HERE HAS THE CHARM AND CHARISMA TO HOLD AN AUDIENCE?
AHEM!
WHO?
HOW MANY TIMES DO I HAVE TO SAY "AHEM"?
UNTIL YOUR THROAT'S CLEARED.

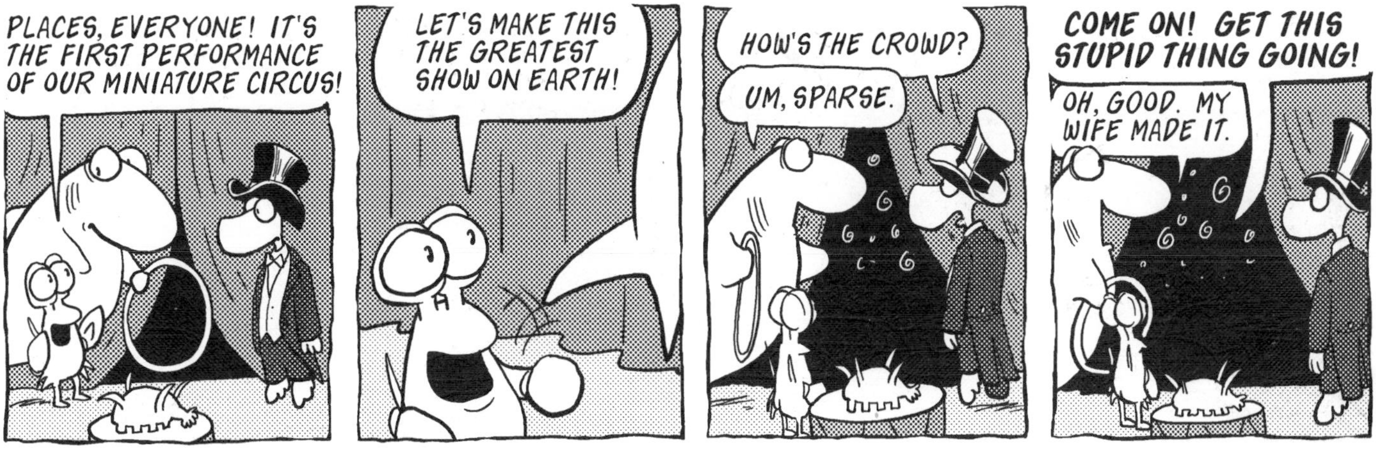
PLACES, EVERYONE! IT'S THE FIRST PERFORMANCE OF OUR MINIATURE CIRCUS!
LET'S MAKE THIS THE GREATEST SHOW ON EARTH!
HOW'S THE CROWD?
UM, SPARSE.
COME ON! GET THIS STUPID THING GOING!
OH, GOOD. MY WIFE MADE IT.

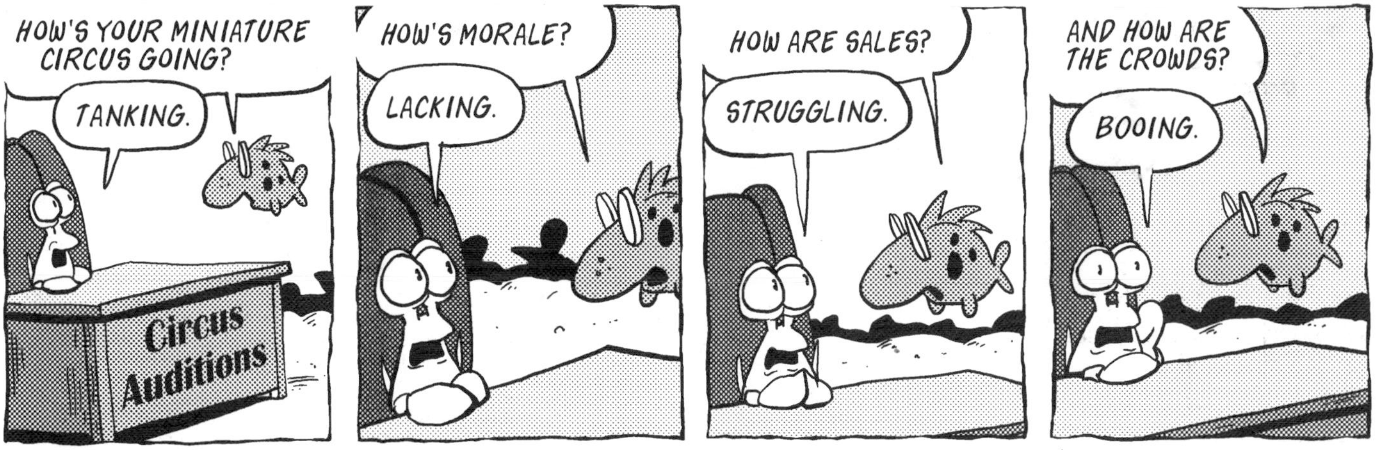
HOW'S YOUR MINIATURE CIRCUS GOING?
TANKING.
Circus Auditions
HOW'S MORALE?
LACKING.
HOW ARE SALES?
STRUGGLING.
AND HOW ARE THE CROWDS?
BOOING.

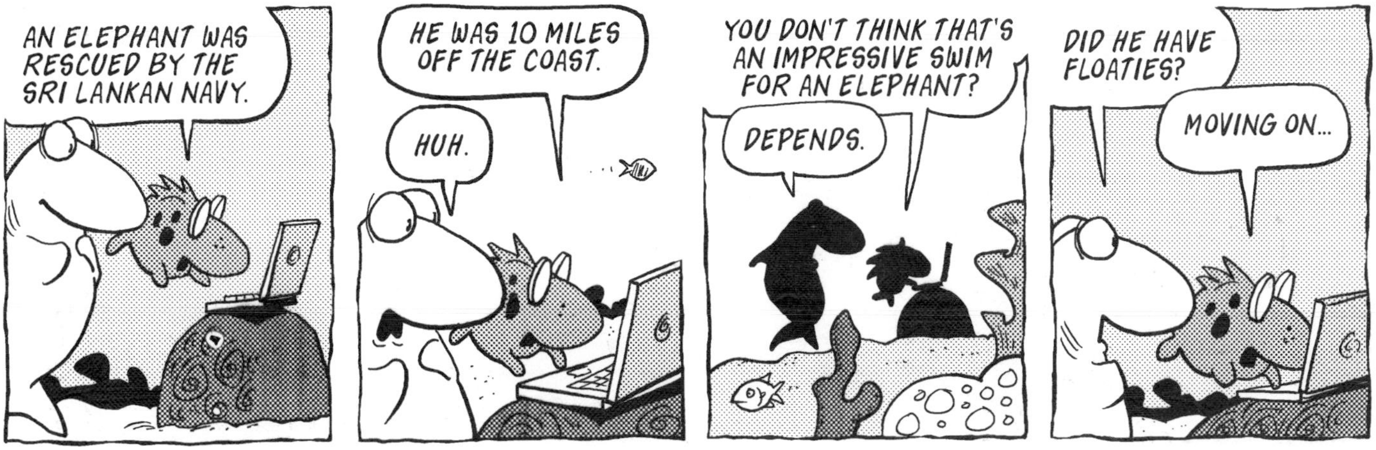
AN ELEPHANT WAS RESCUED BY THE SRI LANKAN NAVY.
HE WAS 10 MILES OFF THE COAST.
HUH.
YOU DON'T THINK THAT'S AN IMPRESSIVE SWIM FOR AN ELEPHANT?
DEPENDS.
DID HE HAVE FLOATIES?
MOVING ON...

I'M GOING TO SRI LANKA. I WANT TO MEET THAT FAMOUS SWIMMING ELEPHANT.

AND I WANT YOU TO COME WITH ME.

ME?

IT'S ALWAYS PRUDENT TO BRING SOMEONE OF YOUR HEFT AND FORTITUDE ON LONG JOURNEYS SUCH AS THIS.

AS COMPANION AND BODYGUARD?

SHADE PROVIDER.

I'M GOING TO SRI LANKA WITH ERNEST.

WHY?

TO MEET A SWIMMING ELEPHANT.

ANOTHER BUCKET-LIST ITEM?

THESE ALWAYS SOUND BETTER IN REHEARSAL.

WELL, THIS IS SRI LANKA.

BEAUTIFUL.

OOH! THAT MIGHT BE THE ELEPHANT WE'RE LOOKING FOR.

LET'S FIND OUT.

EXCUSE ME. ARE YOU THE ELEPHANT THAT WAS RESCUED BY THE NAVY?

I WASN'T RESCUED! I WAS KIDNAPPED!

OOH, PLOT TWIST.

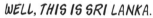

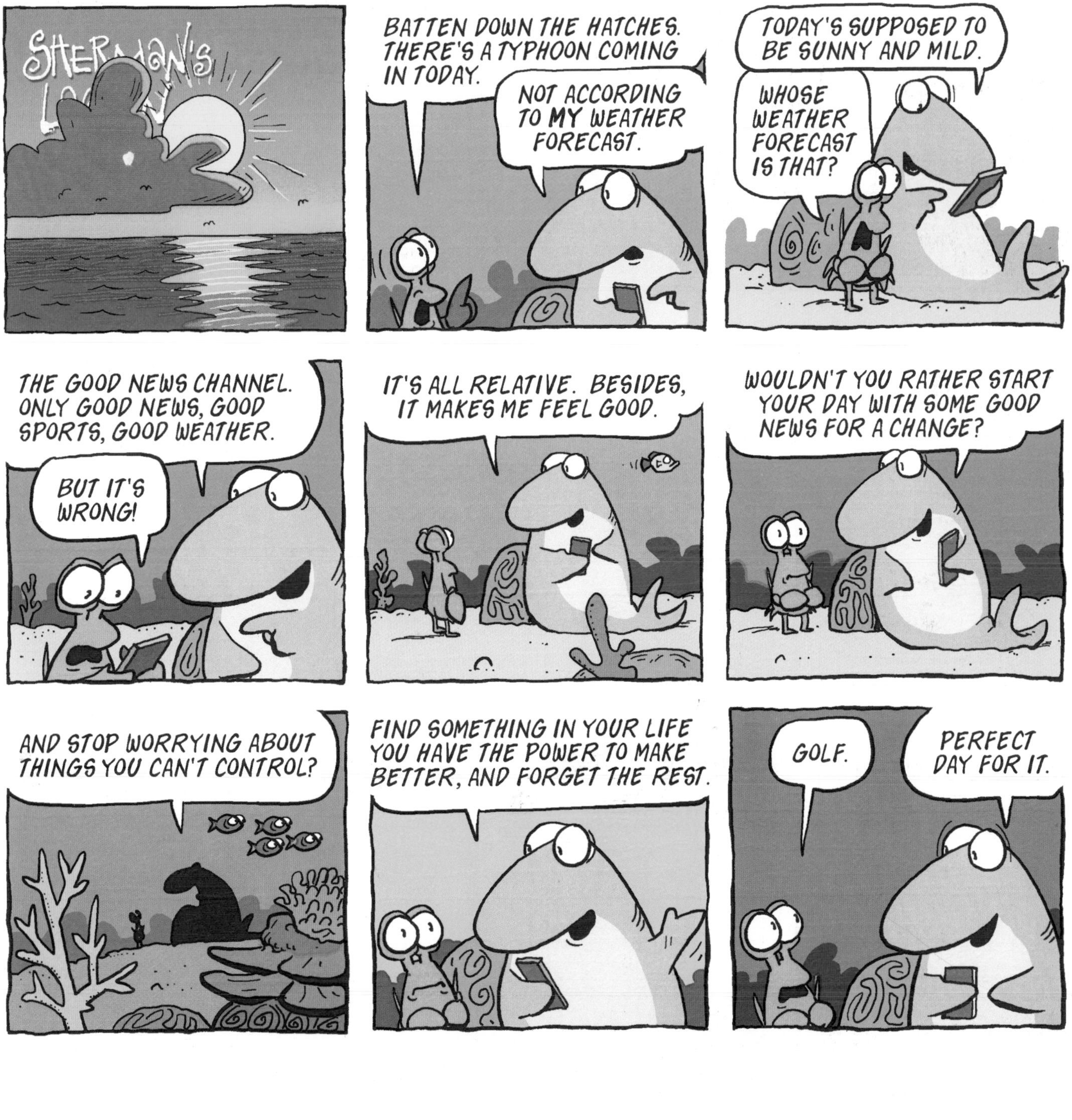
SHERMAN'S LAGOON
BATTEN DOWN THE HATCHES. THERE'S A TYPHOON COMING IN TODAY.
NOT ACCORDING TO MY WEATHER FORECAST.
TODAY'S SUPPOSED TO BE SUNNY AND MILD.
WHOSE WEATHER FORECAST IS THAT?
THE GOOD NEWS CHANNEL. ONLY GOOD NEWS, GOOD SPORTS, GOOD WEATHER.
BUT IT'S WRONG!
IT'S ALL RELATIVE. BESIDES, IT MAKES ME FEEL GOOD.
WOULDN'T YOU RATHER START YOUR DAY WITH SOME GOOD NEWS FOR A CHANGE?
AND STOP WORRYING ABOUT THINGS YOU CAN'T CONTROL?
FIND SOMETHING IN YOUR LIFE YOU HAVE THE POWER TO MAKE BETTER, AND FORGET THE REST.
GOLF.
PERFECT DAY FOR IT.

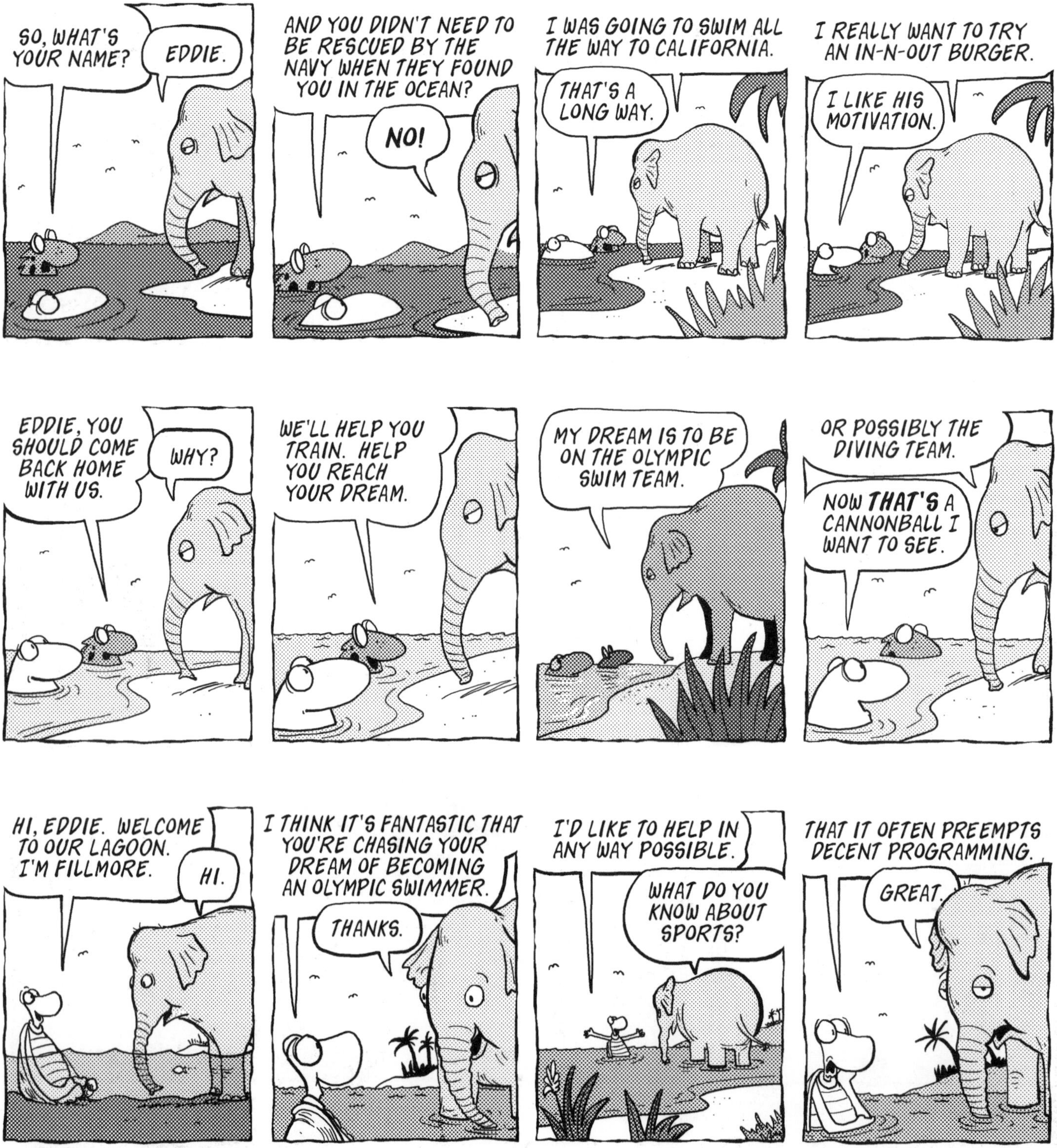
SO, WHAT'S YOUR NAME?
EDDIE.
AND YOU DIDN'T NEED TO BE RESCUED BY THE NAVY WHEN THEY FOUND YOU IN THE OCEAN?
NO!
I WAS GOING TO SWIM ALL THE WAY TO CALIFORNIA.
THAT'S A LONG WAY.
I REALLY WANT TO TRY AN IN-N-OUT BURGER.
I LIKE HIS MOTIVATION.
EDDIE, YOU SHOULD COME BACK HOME WITH US.
WHY?
WE'LL HELP YOU TRAIN. HELP YOU REACH YOUR DREAM.
MY DREAM IS TO BE ON THE OLYMPIC SWIM TEAM.
OR POSSIBLY THE DIVING TEAM.
NOW THAT'S A CANNONBALL I WANT TO SEE.
HI, EDDIE. WELCOME TO OUR LAGOON. I'M FILLMORE.
HI.
I THINK IT'S FANTASTIC THAT YOU'RE CHASING YOUR DREAM OF BECOMING AN OLYMPIC SWIMMER.
THANKS.
I'D LIKE TO HELP IN ANY WAY POSSIBLE.
WHAT DO YOU KNOW ABOUT SPORTS?
THAT IT OFTEN PREEMPTS DECENT PROGRAMMING.
GREAT.

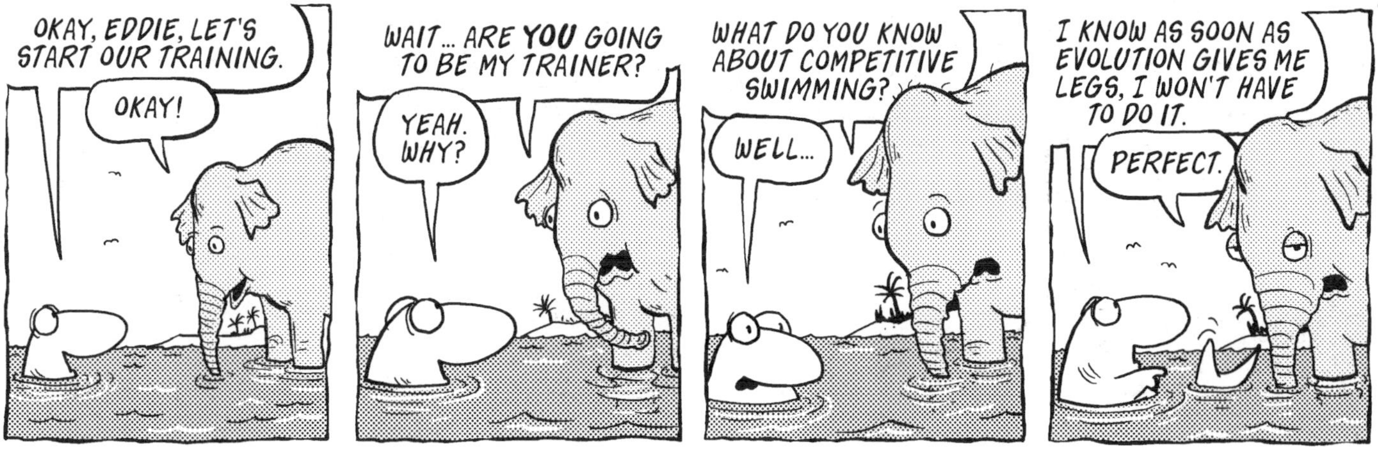
OKAY, EDDIE, LET'S START OUR TRAINING.
OKAY!
WAIT... ARE **YOU** GOING TO BE MY TRAINER?
YEAH. WHY?
WHAT DO YOU KNOW ABOUT COMPETITIVE SWIMMING?
WELL...
I KNOW AS SOON AS EVOLUTION GIVES ME LEGS, I WON'T HAVE TO DO IT.
PERFECT.

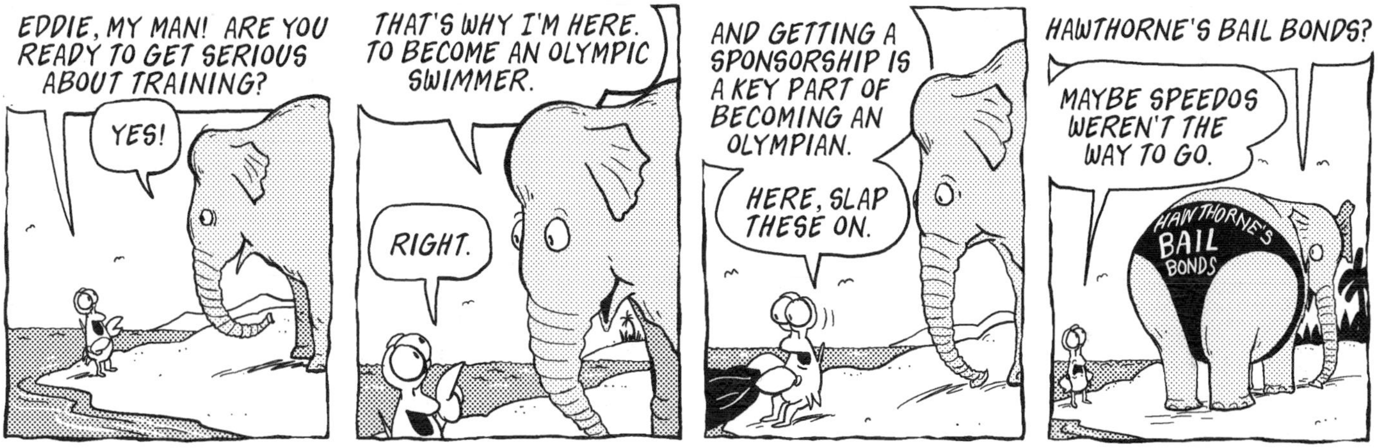
EDDIE, MY MAN! ARE YOU READY TO GET SERIOUS ABOUT TRAINING?
YES!
THAT'S WHY I'M HERE. TO BECOME AN OLYMPIC SWIMMER.
RIGHT.
AND GETTING A SPONSORSHIP IS A KEY PART OF BECOMING AN OLYMPIAN.
HERE, SLAP THESE ON.
HAWTHORNE'S BAIL BONDS?
MAYBE SPEEDOS WEREN'T THE WAY TO GO.
HAWTHORNE'S BAIL BONDS

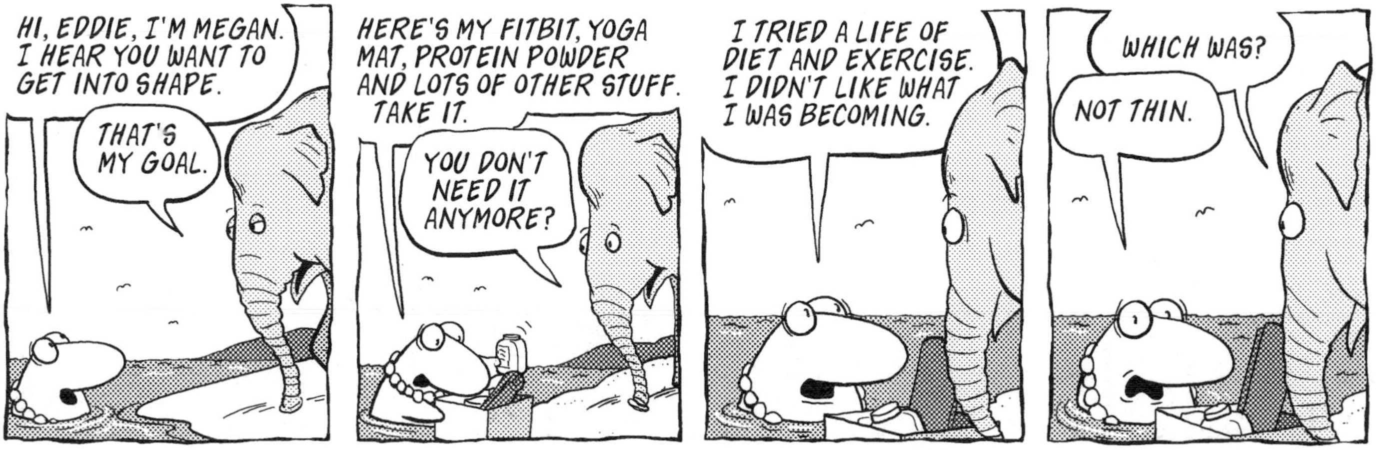
HI, EDDIE, I'M MEGAN. I HEAR YOU WANT TO GET INTO SHAPE.
THAT'S MY GOAL.
HERE'S MY FITBIT, YOGA MAT, PROTEIN POWDER AND LOTS OF OTHER STUFF. TAKE IT.
YOU DON'T NEED IT ANYMORE?
I TRIED A LIFE OF DIET AND EXERCISE. I DIDN'T LIKE WHAT I WAS BECOMING.
WHICH WAS?
NOT THIN.

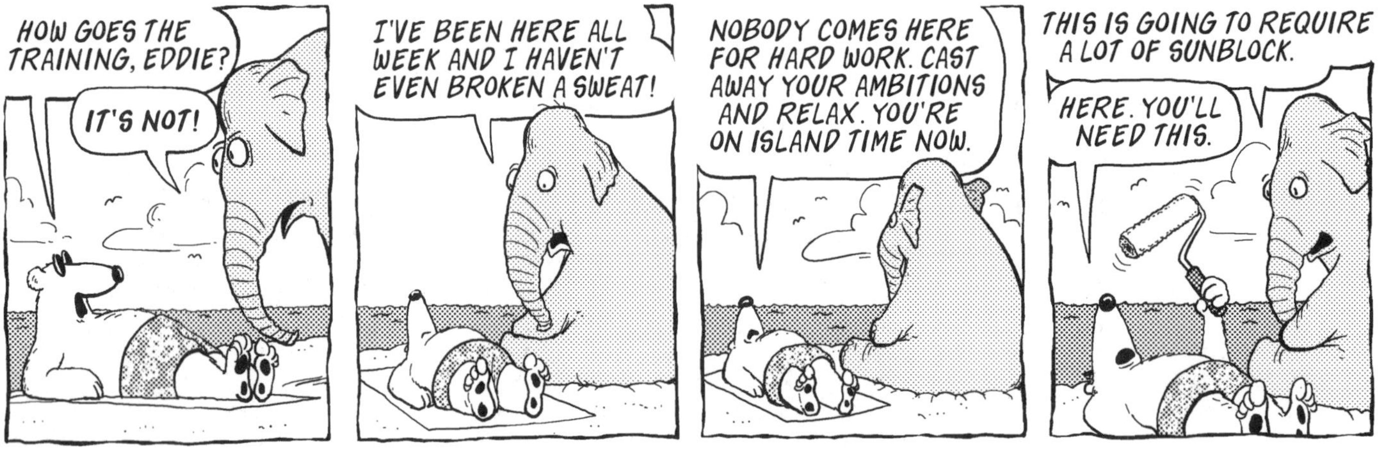
HOW GOES THE TRAINING, EDDIE?
IT'S NOT!
I'VE BEEN HERE ALL WEEK AND I HAVEN'T EVEN BROKEN A SWEAT!
NOBODY COMES HERE FOR HARD WORK. CAST AWAY YOUR AMBITIONS AND RELAX. YOU'RE ON ISLAND TIME NOW.
THIS IS GOING TO REQUIRE A LOT OF SUNBLOCK.
HERE. YOU'LL NEED THIS.

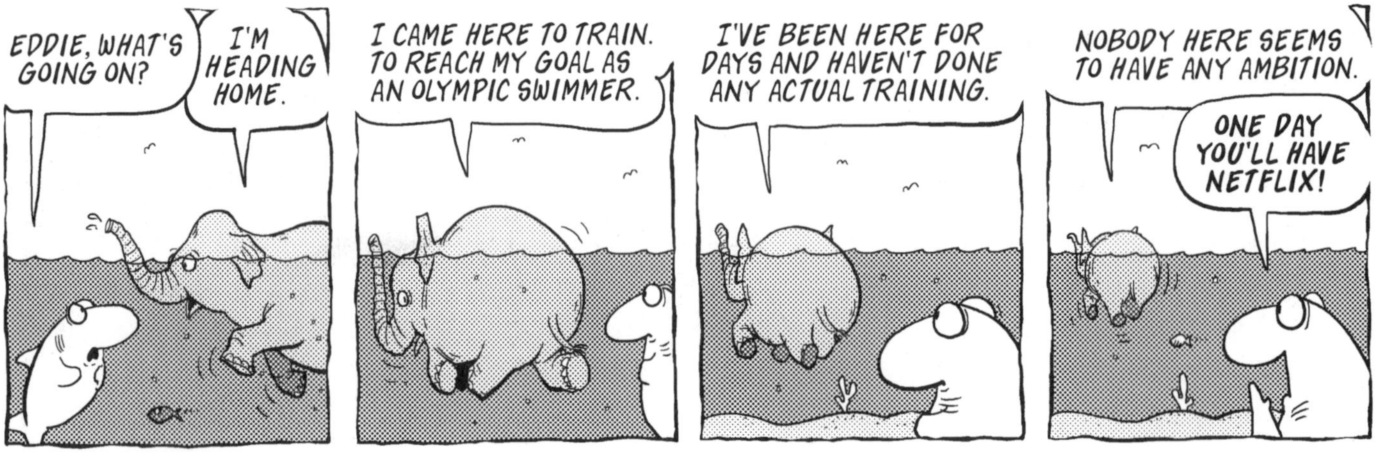
EDDIE, WHAT'S GOING ON?
I'M HEADING HOME.
I CAME HERE TO TRAIN. TO REACH MY GOAL AS AN OLYMPIC SWIMMER.
I'VE BEEN HERE FOR DAYS AND HAVEN'T DONE ANY ACTUAL TRAINING.
NOBODY HERE SEEMS TO HAVE ANY AMBITION.
ONE DAY YOU'LL HAVE NETFLIX!

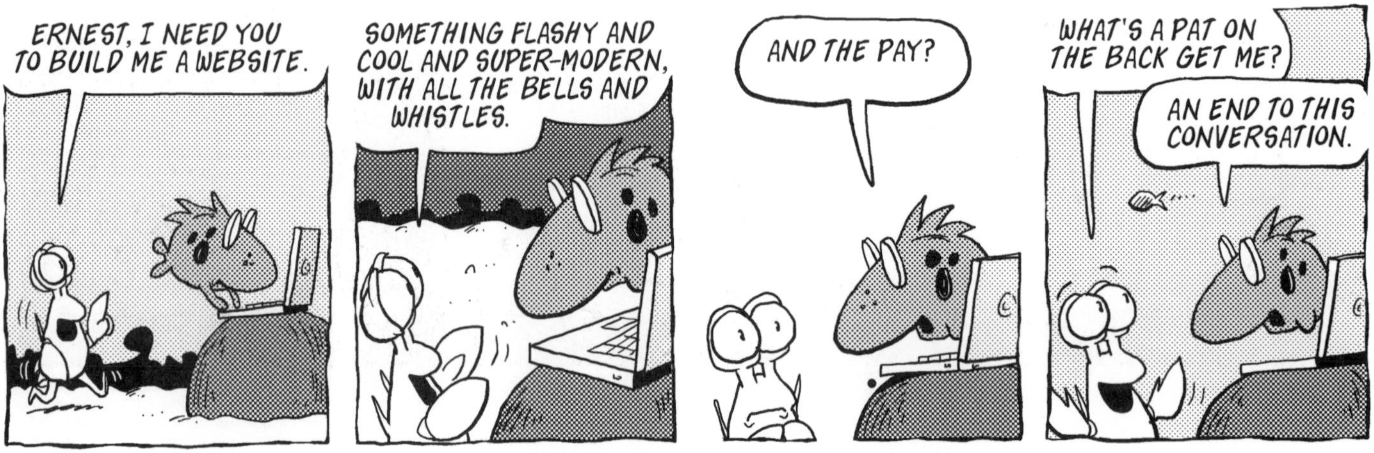
ERNEST, I NEED YOU TO BUILD ME A WEBSITE.
SOMETHING FLASHY AND COOL AND SUPER-MODERN, WITH ALL THE BELLS AND WHISTLES.
AND THE PAY?
WHAT'S A PAT ON THE BACK GET ME?
AN END TO THIS CONVERSATION.

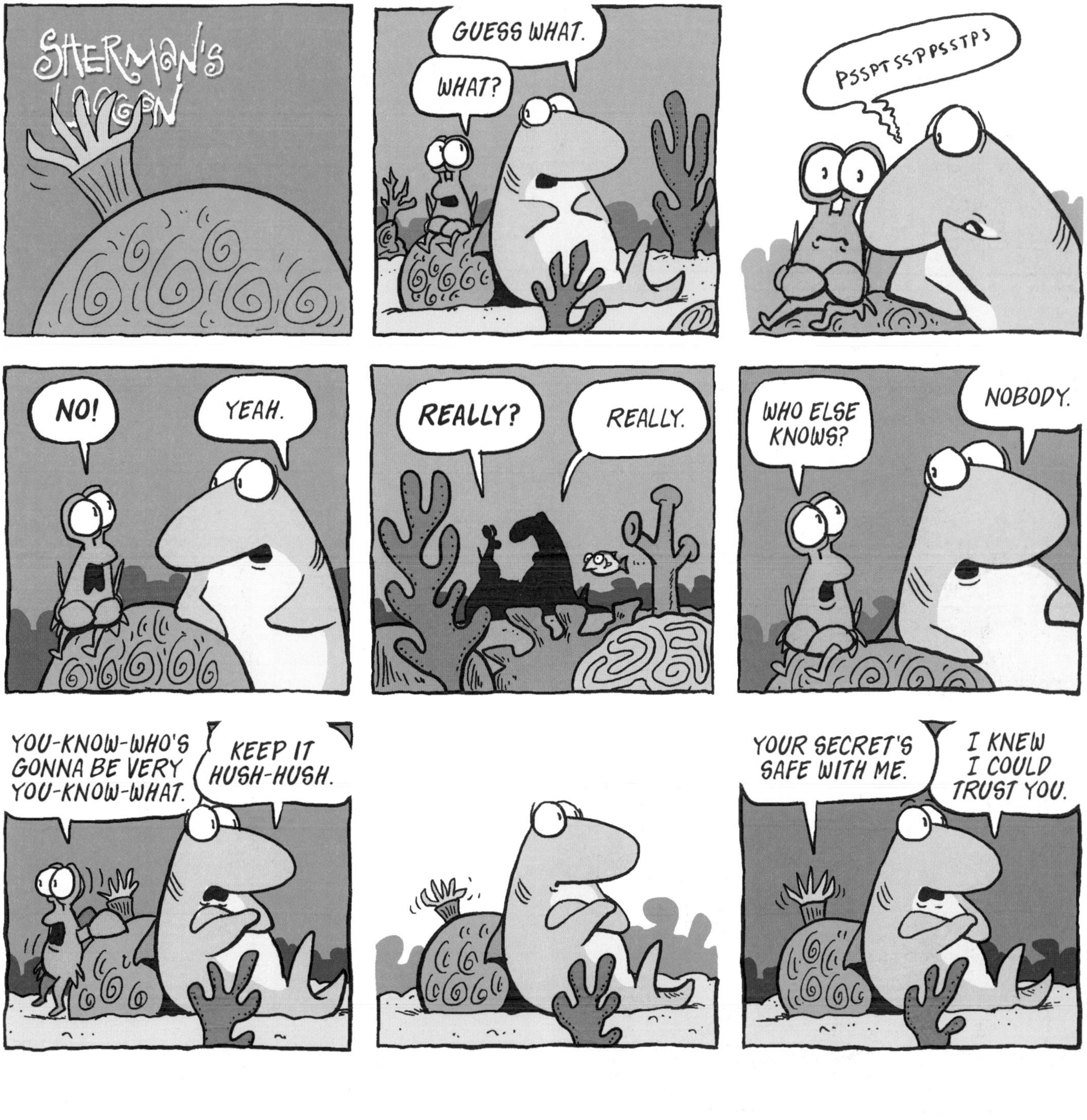
SHERMAN'S LAGOON
GUESS WHAT.
WHAT?
PSSPTSSPPSSTPS
NO!
YEAH.
REALLY?
REALLY.
WHO ELSE KNOWS?
NOBODY.
YOU-KNOW-WHO'S GONNA BE VERY YOU-KNOW-WHAT.
KEEP IT HUSH-HUSH.
YOUR SECRET'S SAFE WITH ME.
I KNEW I COULD TRUST YOU.

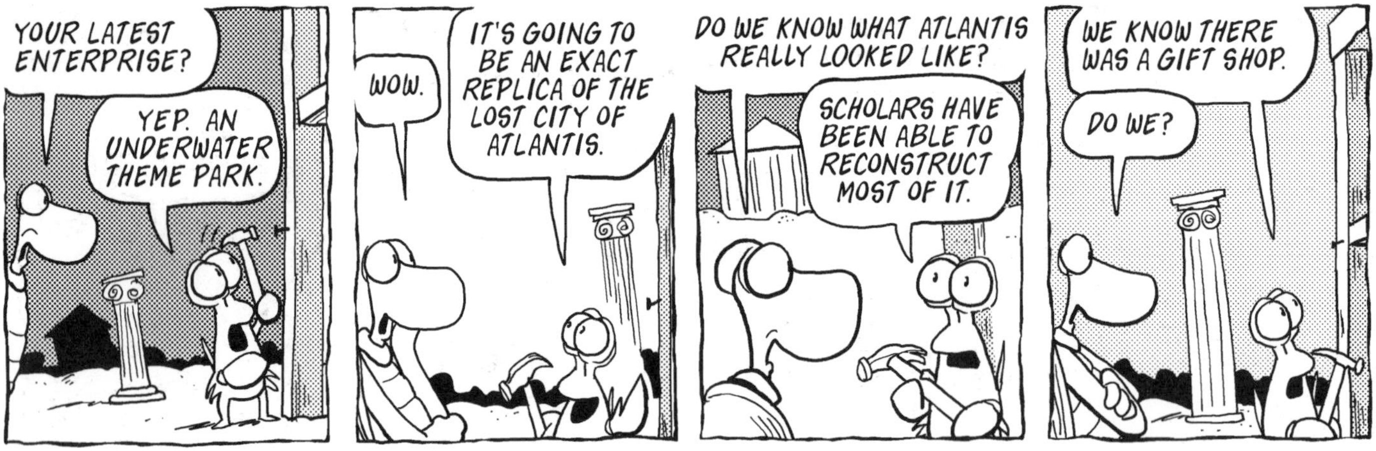
YOUR LATEST ENTERPRISE?
YEP. AN UNDERWATER THEME PARK.
WOW.
IT'S GOING TO BE AN EXACT REPLICA OF THE LOST CITY OF ATLANTIS.
DO WE KNOW WHAT ATLANTIS REALLY LOOKED LIKE?
SCHOLARS HAVE BEEN ABLE TO RECONSTRUCT MOST OF IT.
WE KNOW THERE WAS A GIFT SHOP.
DO WE?

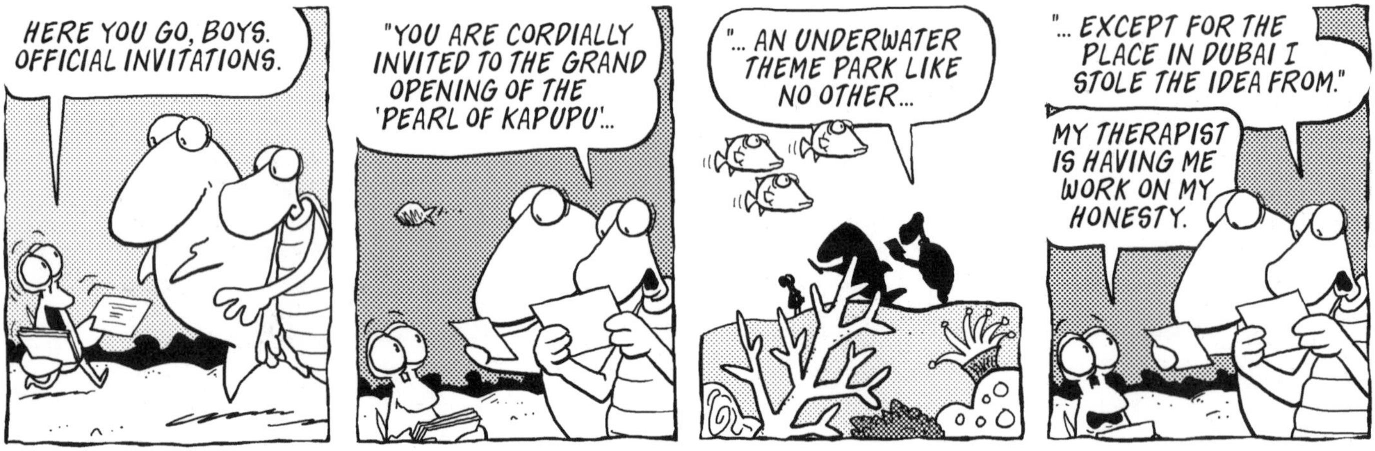
HERE YOU GO, BOYS. OFFICIAL INVITATIONS.
"YOU ARE CORDIALLY INVITED TO THE GRAND OPENING OF THE 'PEARL OF KAPUPU'...
"... AN UNDERWATER THEME PARK LIKE NO OTHER...
"... EXCEPT FOR THE PLACE IN DUBAI I STOLE THE IDEA FROM."
MY THERAPIST IS HAVING ME WORK ON MY HONESTY.

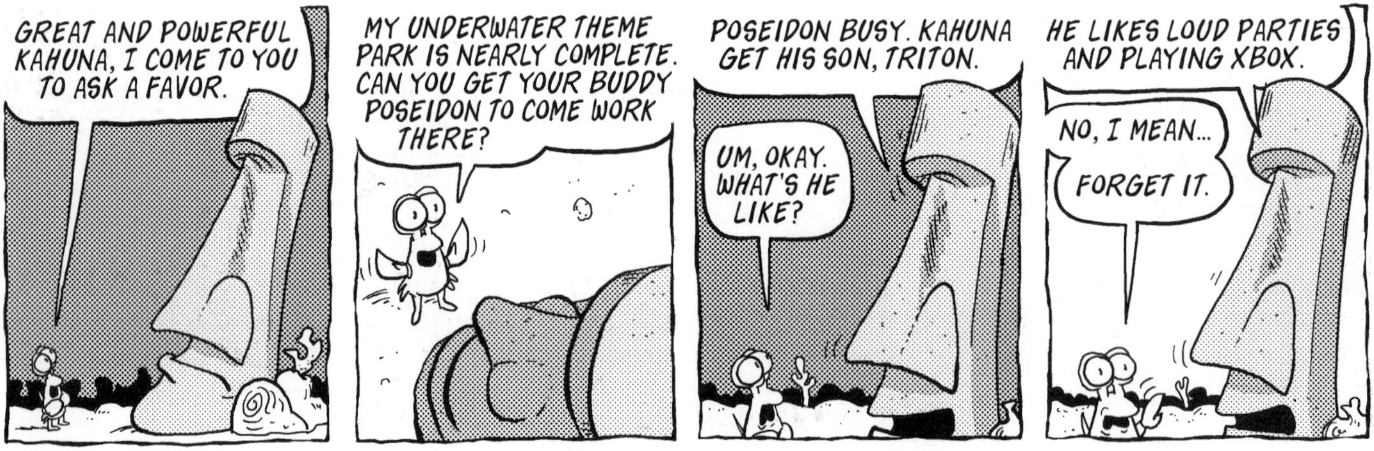
GREAT AND POWERFUL KAHUNA, I COME TO YOU TO ASK A FAVOR.
MY UNDERWATER THEME PARK IS NEARLY COMPLETE. CAN YOU GET YOUR BUDDY POSEIDON TO COME WORK THERE?
POSEIDON BUSY. KAHUNA GET HIS SON, TRITON.
UM, OKAY. WHAT'S HE LIKE?
HE LIKES LOUD PARTIES AND PLAYING XBOX.
NO, I MEAN...
FORGET IT.

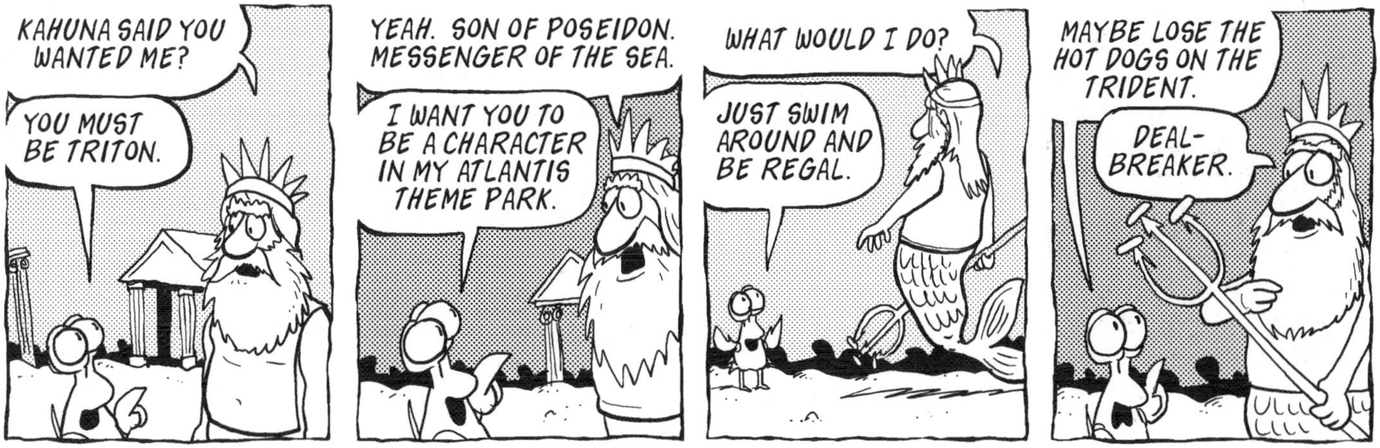
KAHUNA SAID YOU WANTED ME?
YOU MUST BE TRITON.
YEAH. SON OF POSEIDON. MESSENGER OF THE SEA.
I WANT YOU TO BE A CHARACTER IN MY ATLANTIS THEME PARK.
WHAT WOULD I DO?
JUST SWIM AROUND AND BE REGAL.
MAYBE LOSE THE HOT DOGS ON THE TRIDENT.
DEAL-BREAKER.

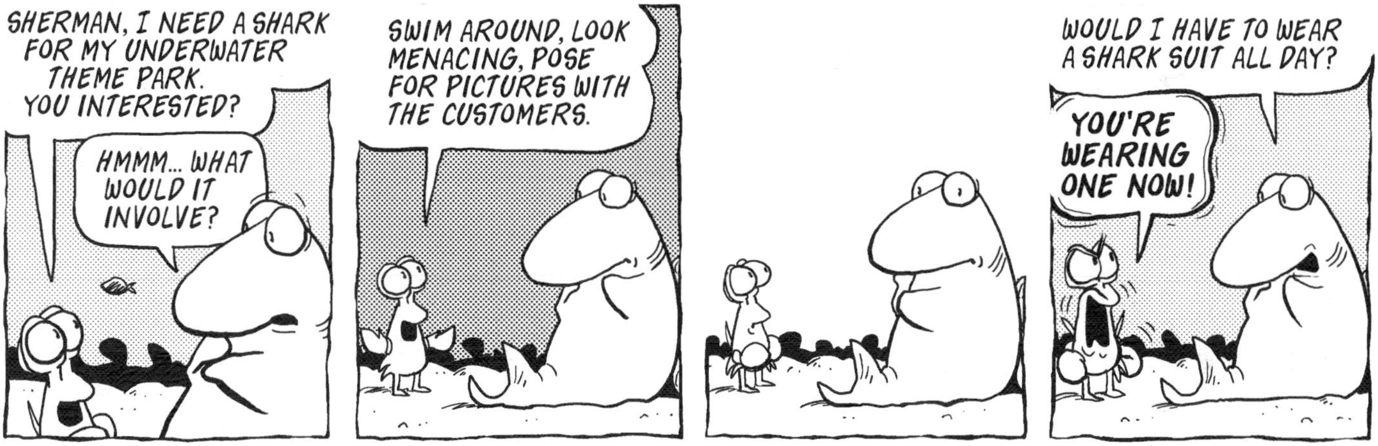
SHERMAN, I NEED A SHARK FOR MY UNDERWATER THEME PARK. YOU INTERESTED?
HMMM... WHAT WOULD IT INVOLVE?
SWIM AROUND, LOOK MENACING, POSE FOR PICTURES WITH THE CUSTOMERS.
WOULD I HAVE TO WEAR A SHARK SUIT ALL DAY?
YOU'RE WEARING ONE NOW!

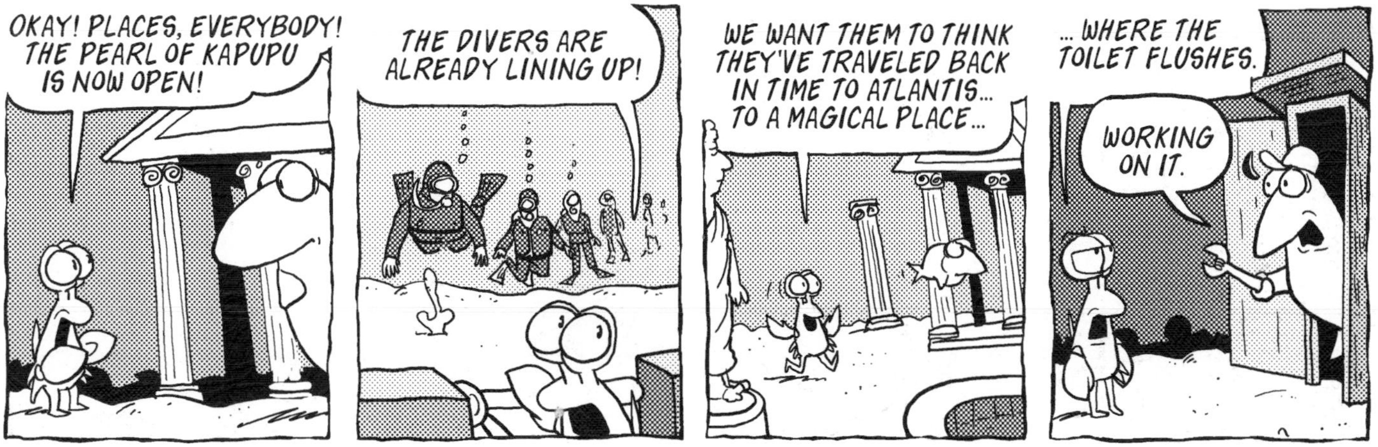
OKAY! PLACES, EVERYBODY! THE PEARL OF KAPUPU IS NOW OPEN!
THE DIVERS ARE ALREADY LINING UP!
WE WANT THEM TO THINK THEY'VE TRAVELED BACK IN TIME TO ATLANTIS... TO A MAGICAL PLACE...
... WHERE THE TOILET FLUSHES.
WORKING ON IT.

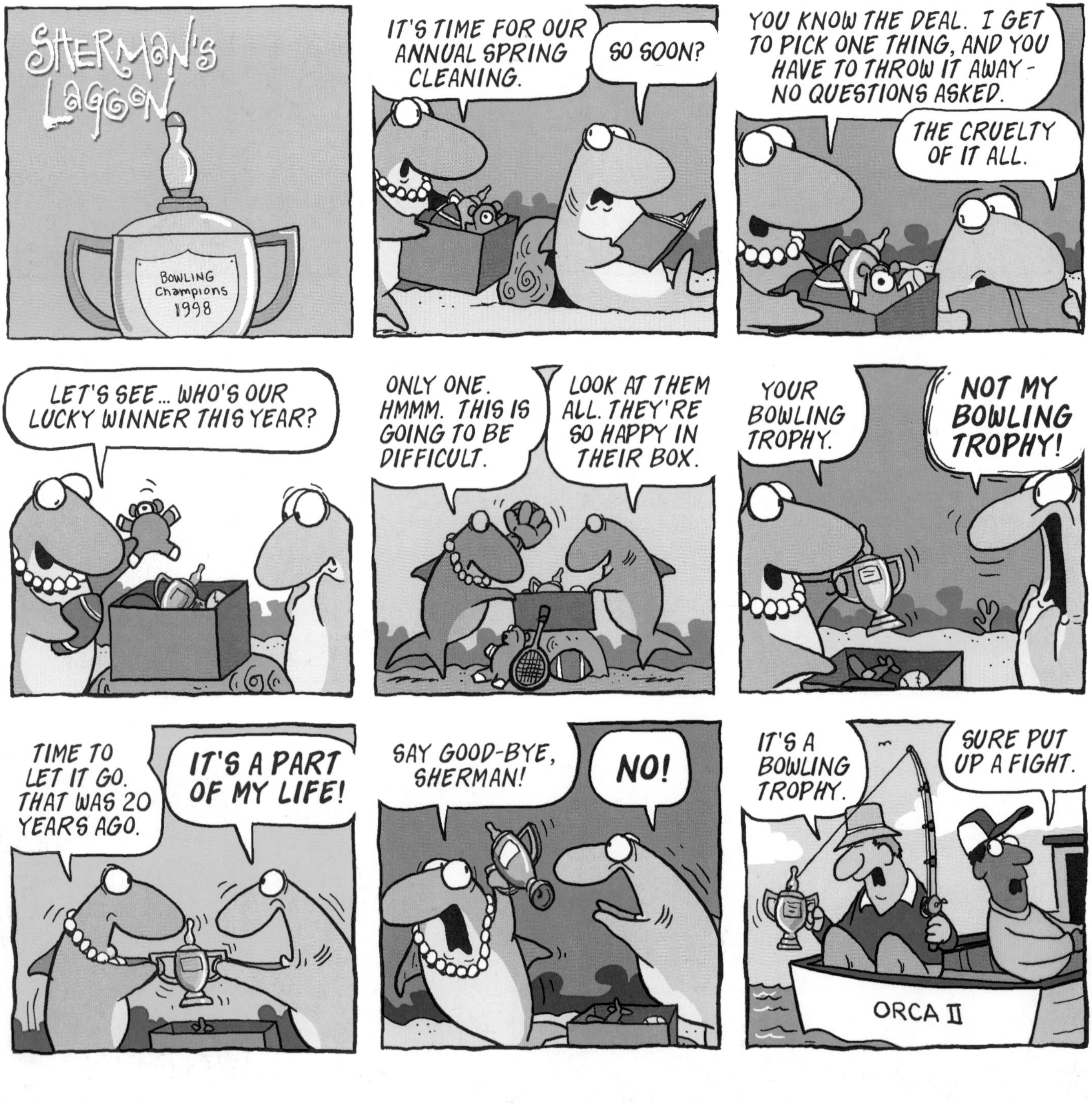

SHERMAN'S LAGOON
BOWLING Champions 1998
IT'S TIME FOR OUR ANNUAL SPRING CLEANING.
SO SOON?
YOU KNOW THE DEAL. I GET TO PICK ONE THING, AND YOU HAVE TO THROW IT AWAY - NO QUESTIONS ASKED.
THE CRUELTY OF IT ALL.
LET'S SEE... WHO'S OUR LUCKY WINNER THIS YEAR?
ONLY ONE. HMMM. THIS IS GOING TO BE DIFFICULT.
LOOK AT THEM ALL. THEY'RE SO HAPPY IN THEIR BOX.
YOUR BOWLING TROPHY.
NOT MY BOWLING TROPHY!
TIME TO LET IT GO. THAT WAS 20 YEARS AGO.
IT'S A PART OF MY LIFE!
SAY GOOD-BYE, SHERMAN!
NO!
IT'S A BOWLING TROPHY.
SURE PUT UP A FIGHT.
ORCA II

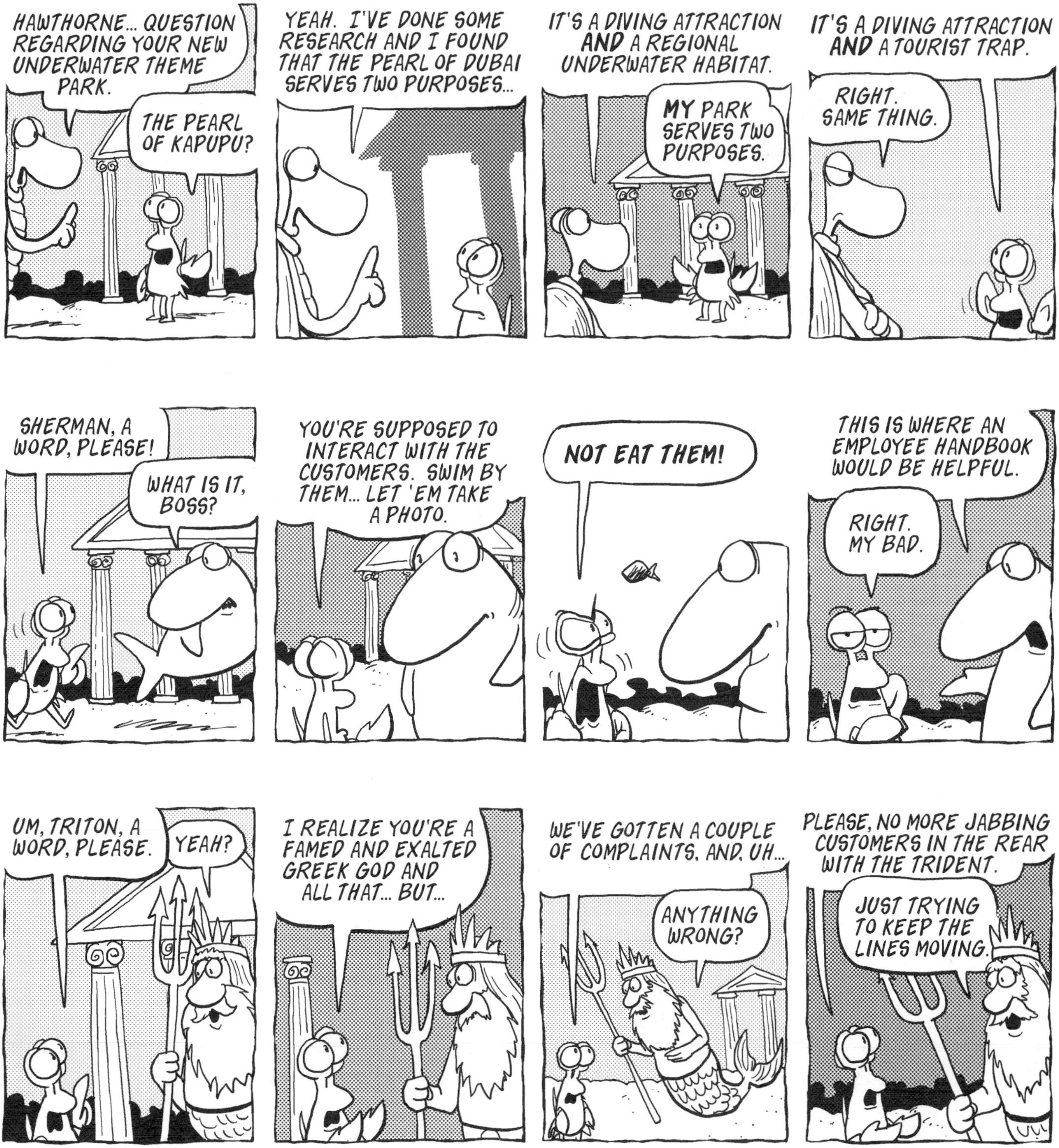
HAWTHORNE... QUESTION REGARDING YOUR NEW UNDERWATER THEME PARK.
THE PEARL OF KAPUPU?
YEAH. I'VE DONE SOME RESEARCH AND I FOUND THAT THE PEARL OF DUBAI SERVES TWO PURPOSES...
IT'S A DIVING ATTRACTION AND A REGIONAL UNDERWATER HABITAT.
MY PARK SERVES TWO PURPOSES.
IT'S A DIVING ATTRACTION AND A TOURIST TRAP.
RIGHT. SAME THING.
SHERMAN, A WORD, PLEASE!
WHAT IS IT, BOSS?
YOU'RE SUPPOSED TO INTERACT WITH THE CUSTOMERS. SWIM BY THEM... LET 'EM TAKE A PHOTO.
NOT EAT THEM!
THIS IS WHERE AN EMPLOYEE HANDBOOK WOULD BE HELPFUL.
RIGHT. MY BAD.
UM, TRITON, A WORD, PLEASE.
YEAH?
I REALIZE YOU'RE A FAMED AND EXALTED GREEK GOD AND ALL THAT... BUT...
WE'VE GOTTEN A COUPLE OF COMPLAINTS, AND, UH...
ANYTHING WRONG?
PLEASE, NO MORE JABBING CUSTOMERS IN THE REAR WITH THE TRIDENT.
JUST TRYING TO KEEP THE LINES MOVING.

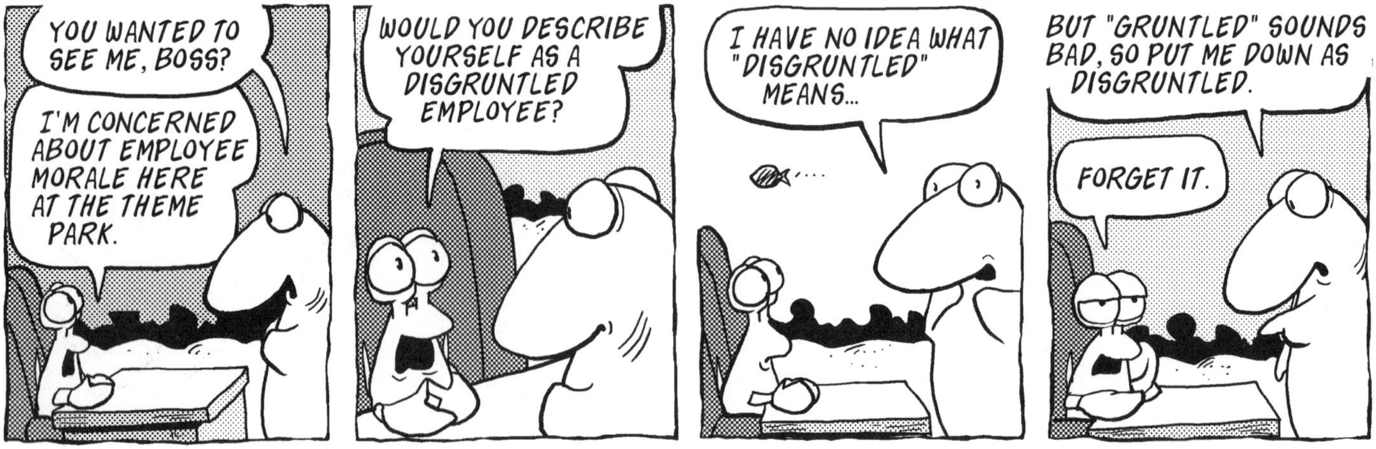
YOU WANTED TO SEE ME, BOSS?
I'M CONCERNED ABOUT EMPLOYEE MORALE HERE AT THE THEME PARK.
WOULD YOU DESCRIBE YOURSELF AS A DISGRUNTLED EMPLOYEE?
I HAVE NO IDEA WHAT "DISGRUNTLED" MEANS...
BUT "GRUNTLED" SOUNDS BAD, SO PUT ME DOWN AS DISGRUNTLED.
FORGET IT.

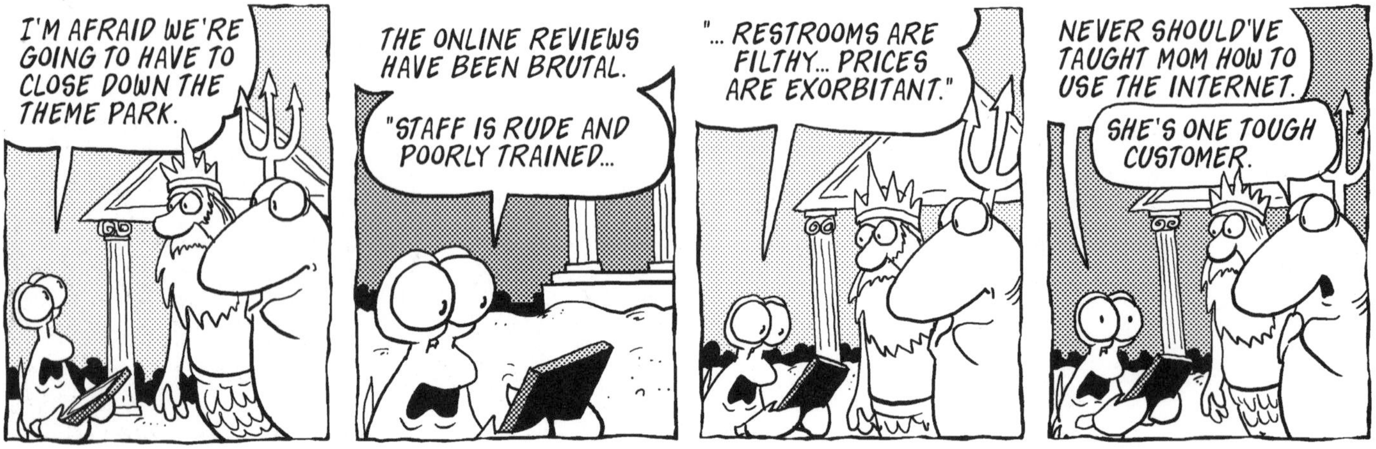
I'M AFRAID WE'RE GOING TO HAVE TO CLOSE DOWN THE THEME PARK.
THE ONLINE REVIEWS HAVE BEEN BRUTAL.
"STAFF IS RUDE AND POORLY TRAINED...
"... RESTROOMS ARE FILTHY... PRICES ARE EXORBITANT."
NEVER SHOULD'VE TAUGHT MOM HOW TO USE THE INTERNET.
SHE'S ONE TOUGH CUSTOMER.

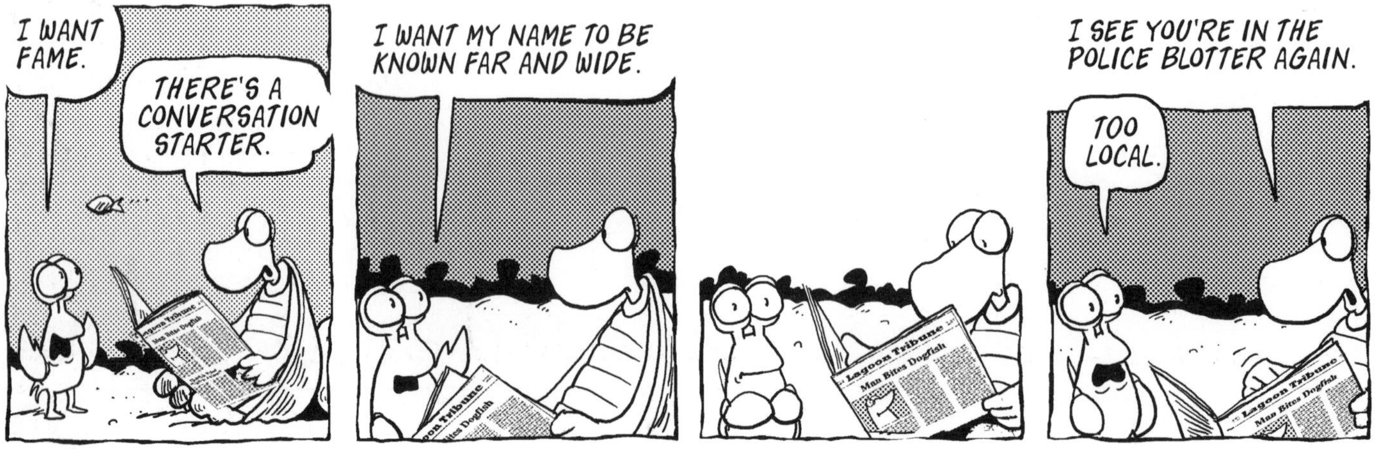
I WANT FAME.
THERE'S A CONVERSATION STARTER.
I WANT MY NAME TO BE KNOWN FAR AND WIDE.
Lagoon Tribune
Man Bites Dogfish
I SEE YOU'RE IN THE POLICE BLOTTER AGAIN.
TOO LOCAL.

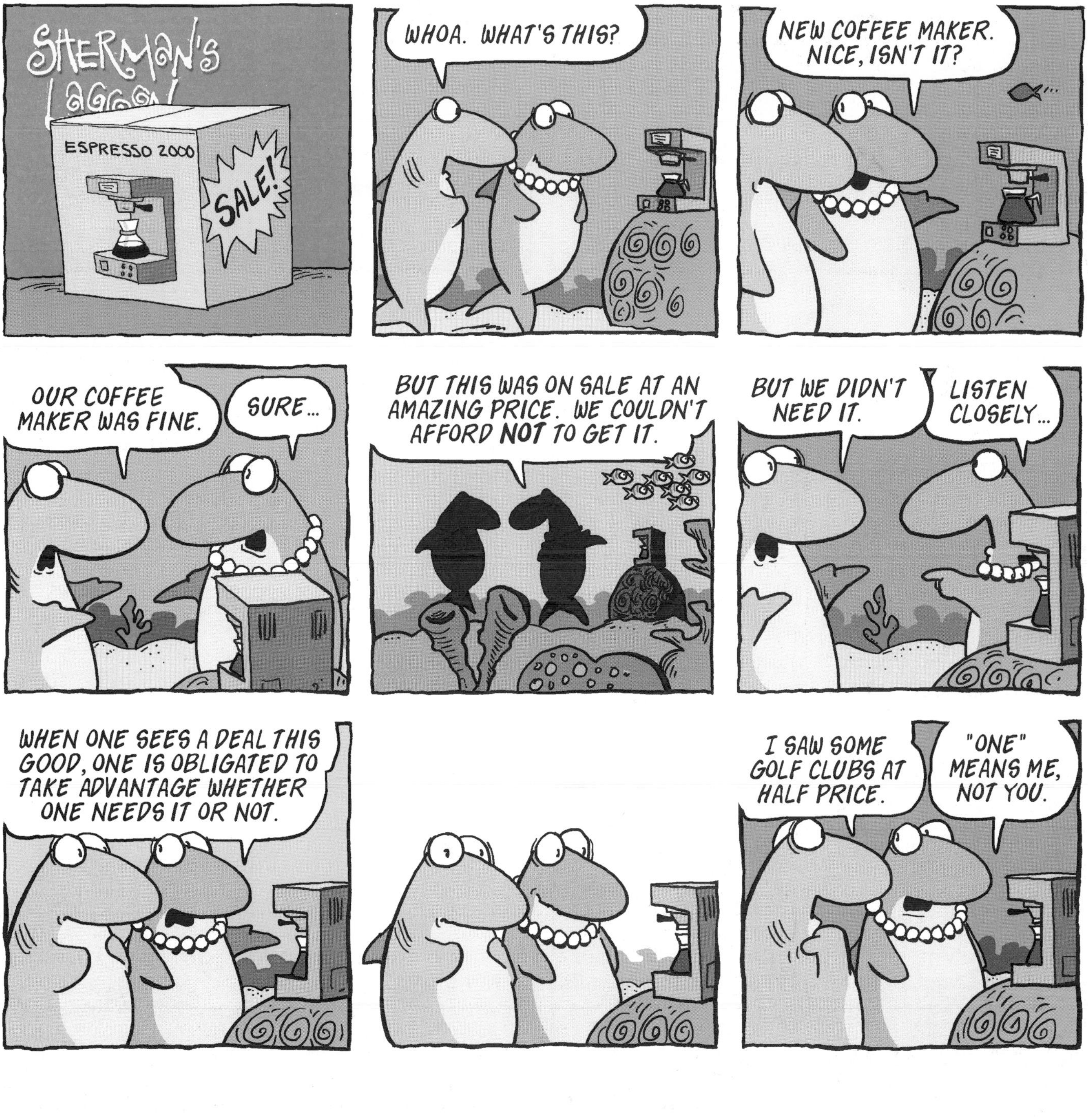
SHERMAN'S LAGOON
ESPRESSO 2000
SALE!
WHOA. WHAT'S THIS?
NEW COFFEE MAKER. NICE, ISN'T IT?
OUR COFFEE MAKER WAS FINE.
SURE...
BUT THIS WAS ON SALE AT AN AMAZING PRICE. WE COULDN'T AFFORD NOT TO GET IT.
BUT WE DIDN'T NEED IT.
LISTEN CLOSELY...
WHEN ONE SEES A DEAL THIS GOOD, ONE IS OBLIGATED TO TAKE ADVANTAGE WHETHER ONE NEEDS IT OR NOT.
I SAW SOME GOLF CLUBS AT HALF PRICE.
"ONE" MEANS ME, NOT YOU.

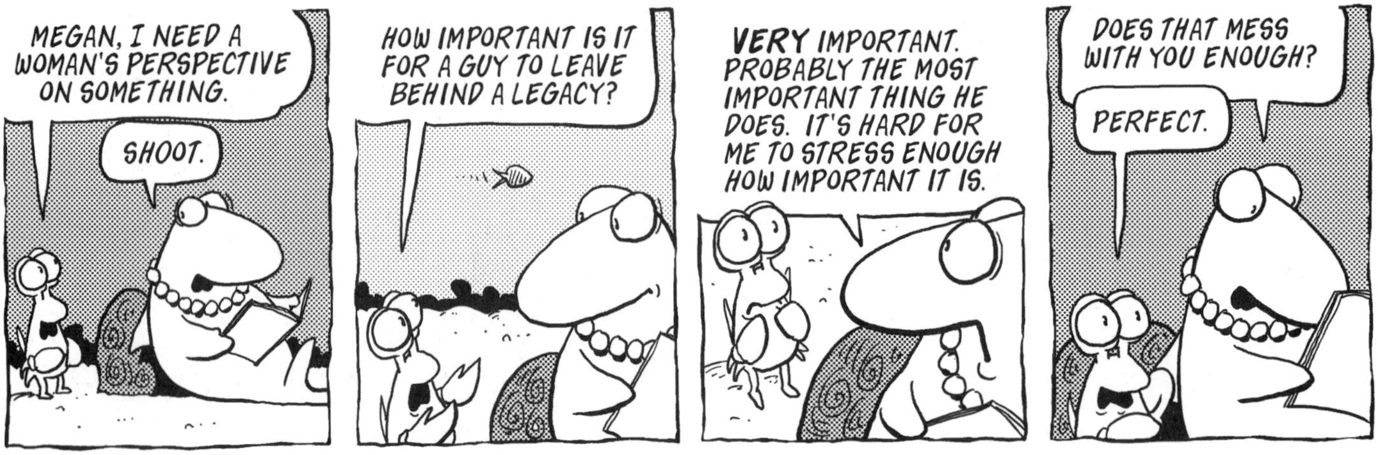
MEGAN, I NEED A WOMAN'S PERSPECTIVE ON SOMETHING.
SHOOT.
HOW IMPORTANT IS IT FOR A GUY TO LEAVE BEHIND A LEGACY?
VERY IMPORTANT. PROBABLY THE MOST IMPORTANT THING HE DOES. IT'S HARD FOR ME TO STRESS ENOUGH HOW IMPORTANT IT IS.
DOES THAT MESS WITH YOU ENOUGH?
PERFECT.

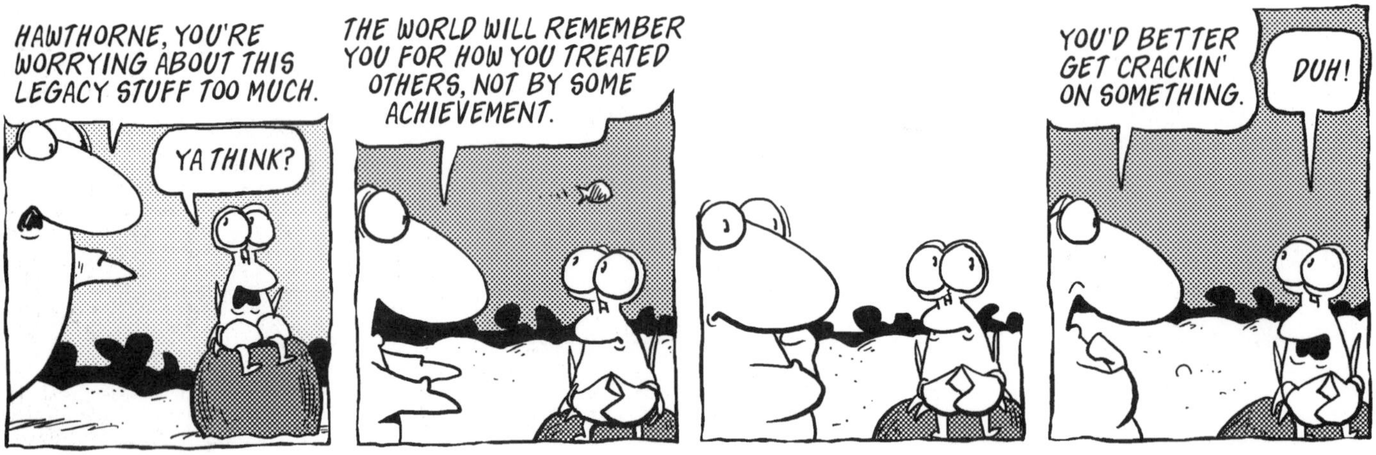
HAWTHORNE, YOU'RE WORRYING ABOUT THIS LEGACY STUFF TOO MUCH.
YA THINK?
THE WORLD WILL REMEMBER YOU FOR HOW YOU TREATED OTHERS, NOT BY SOME ACHIEVEMENT.
YOU'D BETTER GET CRACKIN' ON SOMETHING.
DUH!

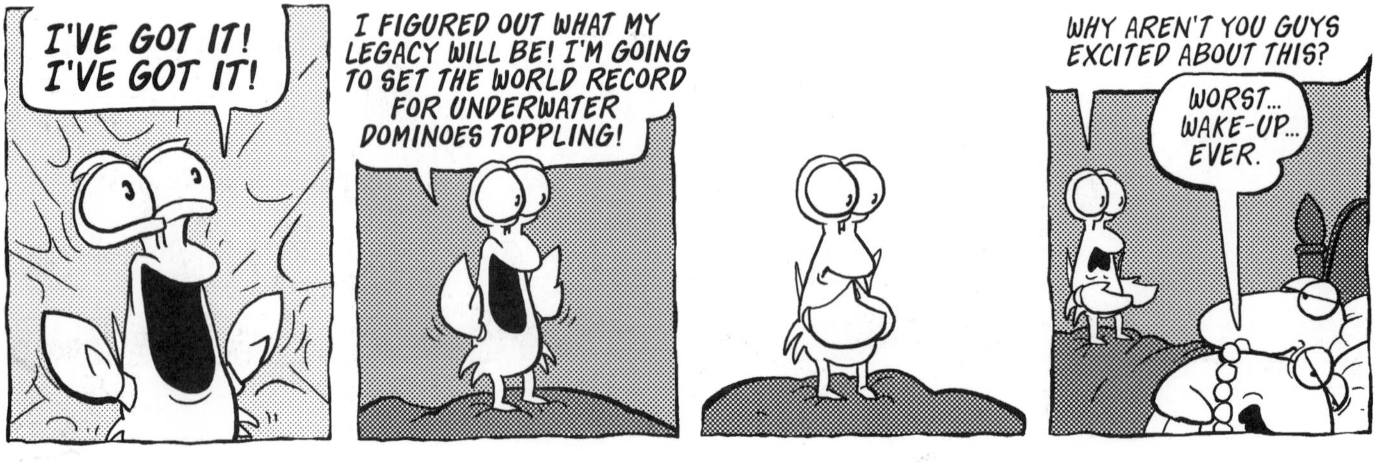
I'VE GOT IT! I'VE GOT IT!
I FIGURED OUT WHAT MY LEGACY WILL BE! I'M GOING TO SET THE WORLD RECORD FOR UNDERWATER DOMINOES TOPPLING!
WHY AREN'T YOU GUYS EXCITED ABOUT THIS?
WORST... WAKE-UP... EVER.

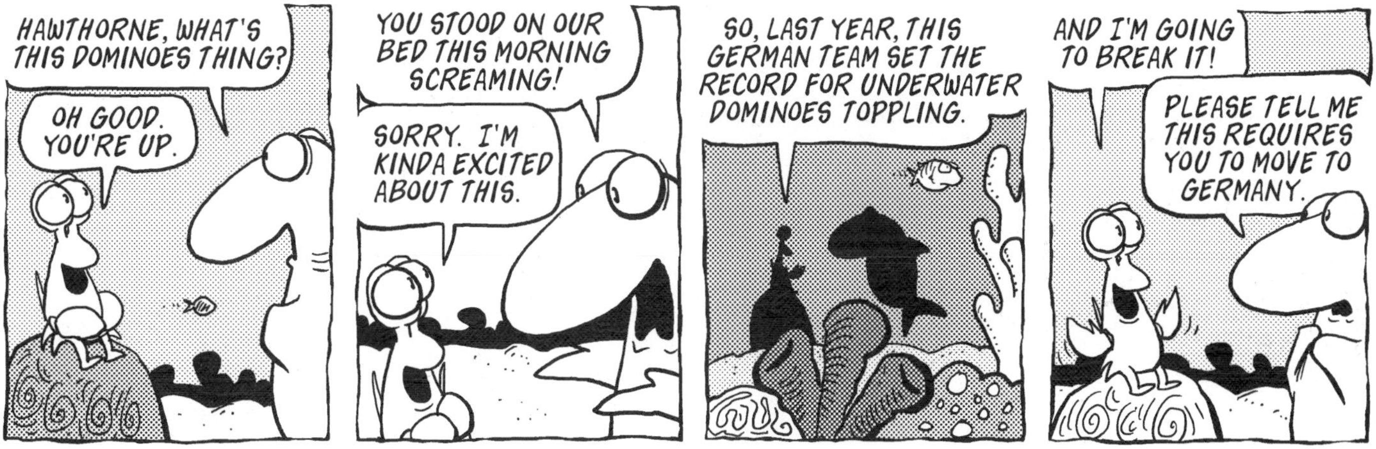
HAWTHORNE, WHAT'S THIS DOMINOES THING?
OH GOOD. YOU'RE UP.
YOU STOOD ON OUR BED THIS MORNING SCREAMING!
SORRY. I'M KINDA EXCITED ABOUT THIS.
SO, LAST YEAR, THIS GERMAN TEAM SET THE RECORD FOR UNDERWATER DOMINOES TOPPLING.
AND I'M GOING TO BREAK IT!
PLEASE TELL ME THIS REQUIRES YOU TO MOVE TO GERMANY.

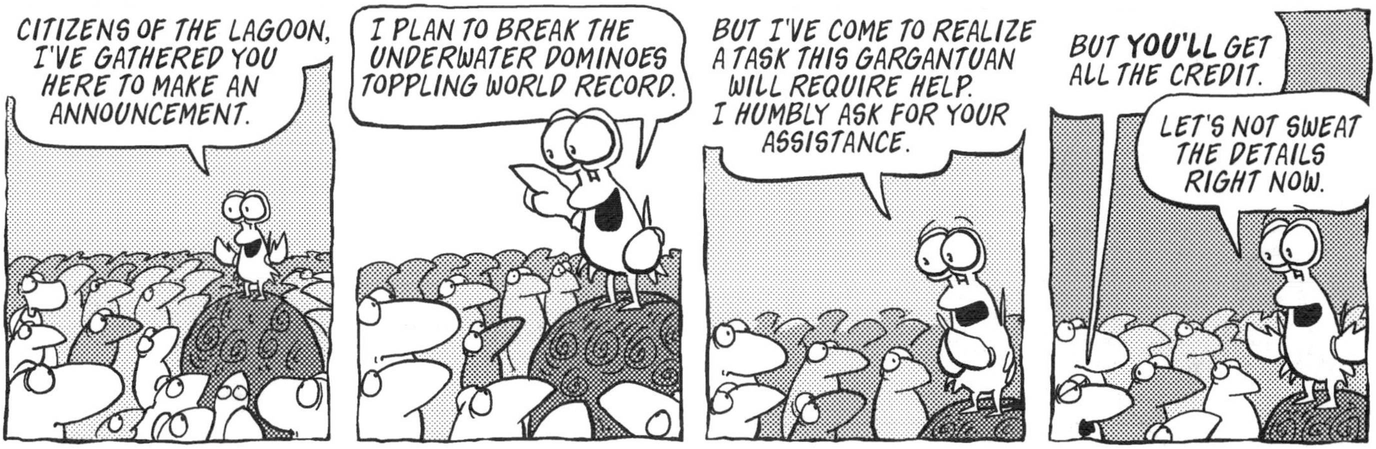
CITIZENS OF THE LAGOON, I'VE GATHERED YOU HERE TO MAKE AN ANNOUNCEMENT.
I PLAN TO BREAK THE UNDERWATER DOMINOES TOPPLING WORLD RECORD.
BUT I'VE COME TO REALIZE A TASK THIS GARGANTUAN WILL REQUIRE HELP. I HUMBLY ASK FOR YOUR ASSISTANCE.
BUT **YOU'LL** GET ALL THE CREDIT.
LET'S NOT SWEAT THE DETAILS RIGHT NOW.

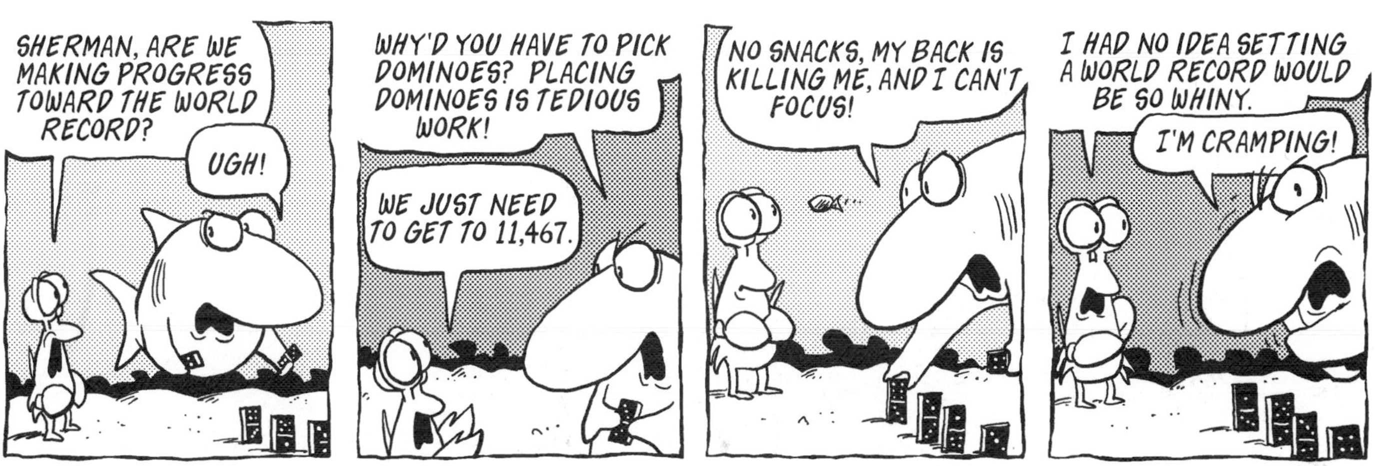
SHERMAN, ARE WE MAKING PROGRESS TOWARD THE WORLD RECORD?
UGH!
WHY'D YOU HAVE TO PICK DOMINOES? PLACING DOMINOES IS TEDIOUS WORK!
WE JUST NEED TO GET TO 11,467.
NO SNACKS, MY BACK IS KILLING ME, AND I CAN'T FOCUS!
I HAD NO IDEA SETTING A WORLD RECORD WOULD BE SO WHINY.
I'M CRAMPING!

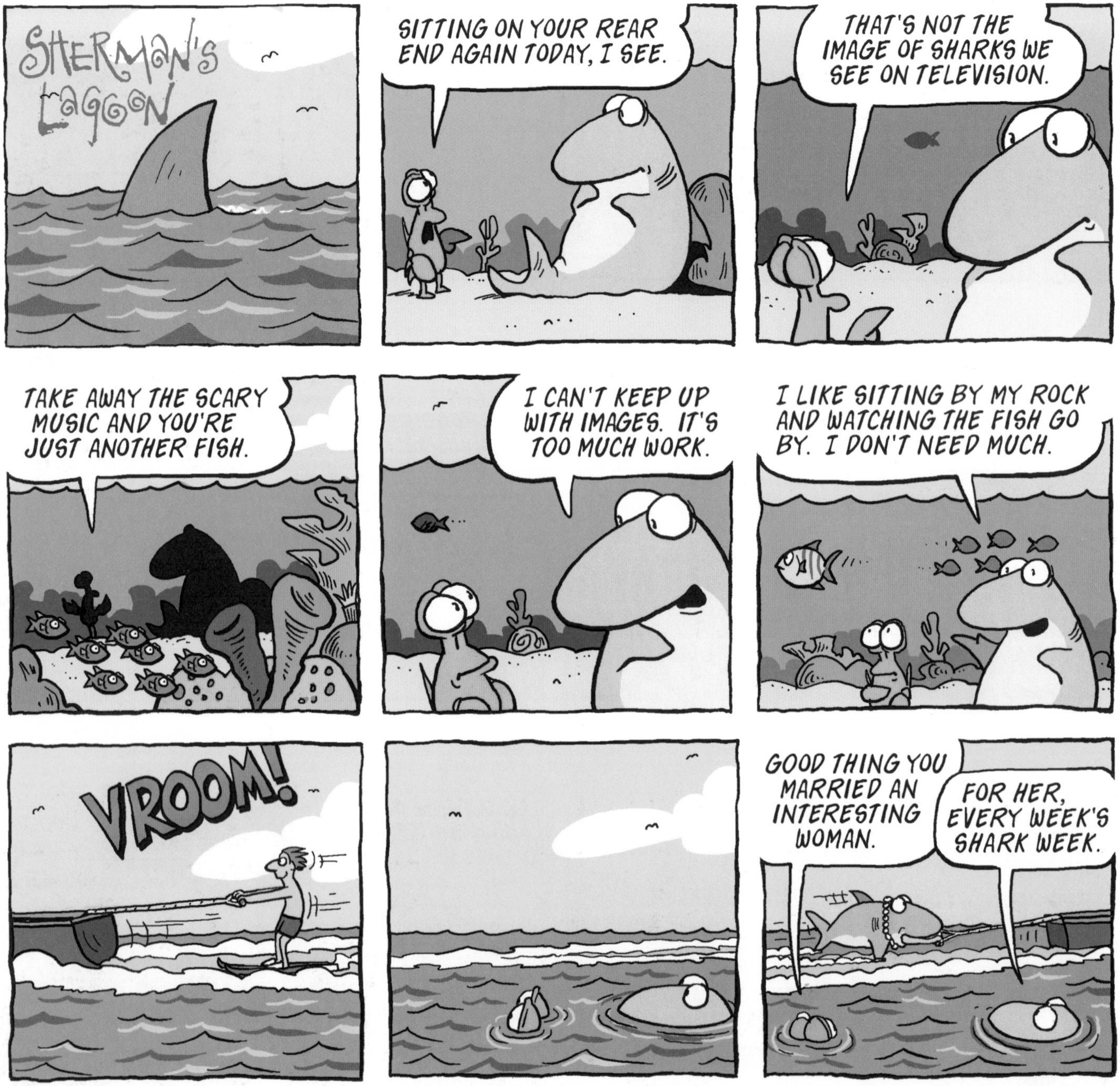
SHERMAN'S LAGOON
SITTING ON YOUR REAR END AGAIN TODAY, I SEE.
THAT'S NOT THE IMAGE OF SHARKS WE SEE ON TELEVISION.
TAKE AWAY THE SCARY MUSIC AND YOU'RE JUST ANOTHER FISH.
I CAN'T KEEP UP WITH IMAGES. IT'S TOO MUCH WORK.
I LIKE SITTING BY MY ROCK AND WATCHING THE FISH GO BY. I DON'T NEED MUCH.
VROOM!
GOOD THING YOU MARRIED AN INTERESTING WOMAN.
FOR HER, EVERY WEEK'S SHARK WEEK.

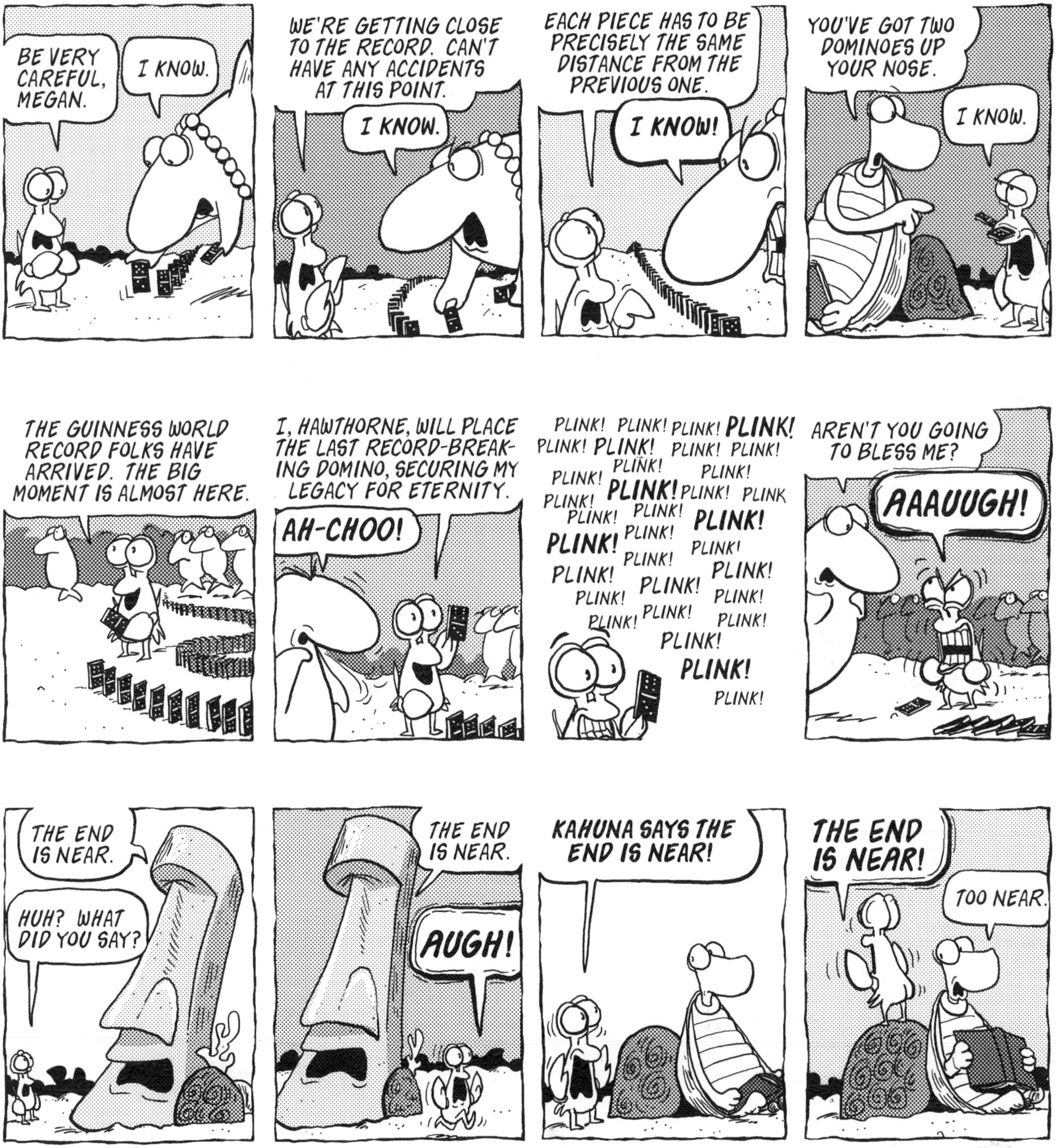
BE VERY CAREFUL, MEGAN.
I KNOW.
WE'RE GETTING CLOSE TO THE RECORD. CAN'T HAVE ANY ACCIDENTS AT THIS POINT.
I KNOW.
EACH PIECE HAS TO BE PRECISELY THE SAME DISTANCE FROM THE PREVIOUS ONE.
I KNOW!
YOU'VE GOT TWO DOMINOES UP YOUR NOSE.
I KNOW.
THE GUINNESS WORLD RECORD FOLKS HAVE ARRIVED. THE BIG MOMENT IS ALMOST HERE.
I, HAWTHORNE, WILL PLACE THE LAST RECORD-BREAKING DOMINO, SECURING MY LEGACY FOR ETERNITY.
AH-CHOO!
PLINK! PLINK! PLINK! PLINK! PLINK! PLINK! PLINK! PLINK! PLINK! PLINK! PLINK! PLINK! PLINK! PLINK! PLINK! PLINK PLINK!
AREN'T YOU GOING TO BLESS ME?
AAAUUGH!
THE END IS NEAR.
HUH? WHAT DID YOU SAY?
THE END IS NEAR.
AUGH!
KAHUNA SAYS THE END IS NEAR!
THE END IS NEAR!
TOO NEAR.

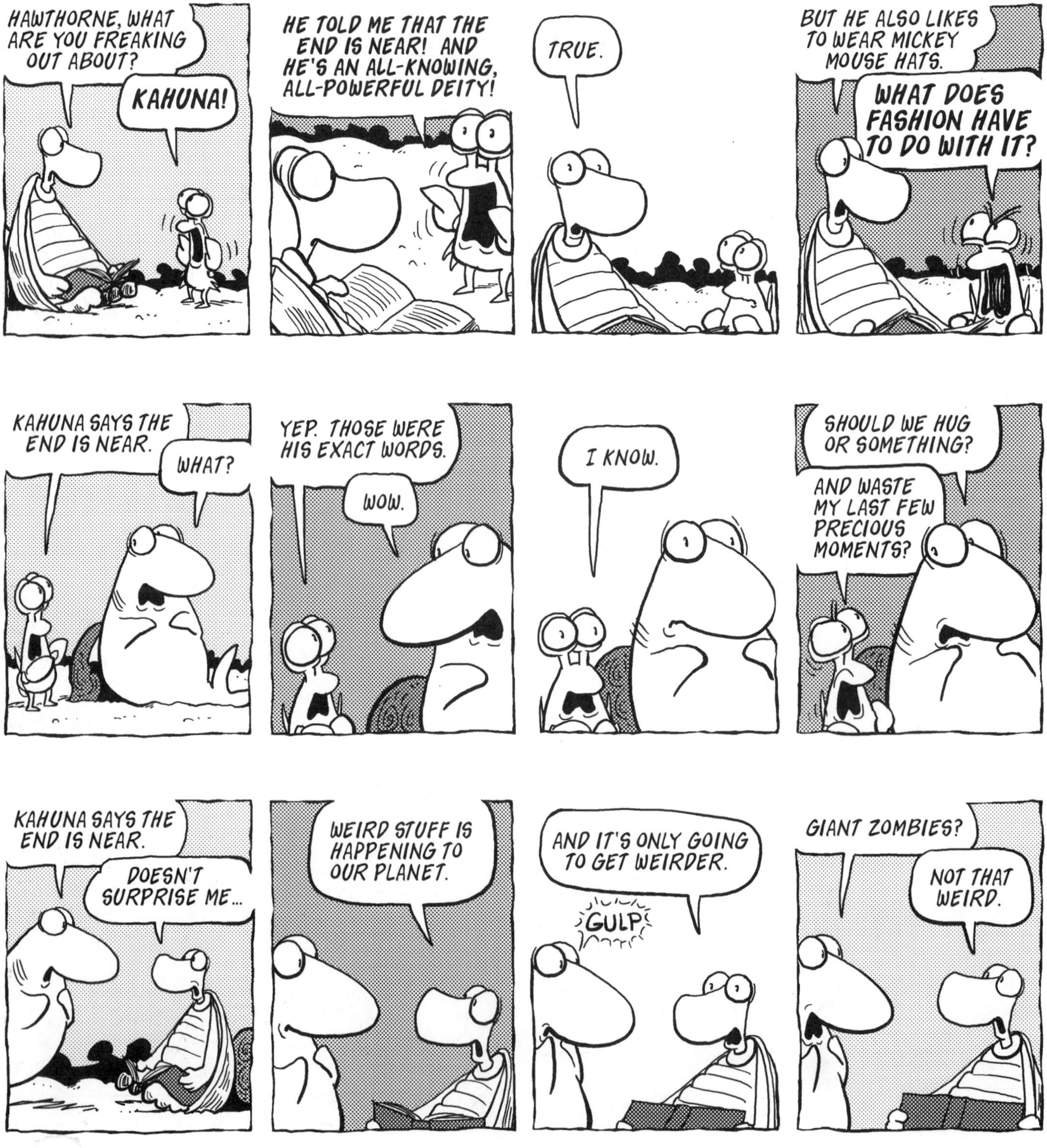
HAWTHORNE, WHAT ARE YOU FREAKING OUT ABOUT?
KAHUNA!
HE TOLD ME THAT THE END IS NEAR! AND HE'S AN ALL-KNOWING, ALL-POWERFUL DEITY!
TRUE.
BUT HE ALSO LIKES TO WEAR MICKEY MOUSE HATS.
WHAT DOES FASHION HAVE TO DO WITH IT?
KAHUNA SAYS THE END IS NEAR.
WHAT?
YEP. THOSE WERE HIS EXACT WORDS.
WOW.
I KNOW.
SHOULD WE HUG OR SOMETHING?
AND WASTE MY LAST FEW PRECIOUS MOMENTS?
KAHUNA SAYS THE END IS NEAR.
DOESN'T SURPRISE ME...
WEIRD STUFF IS HAPPENING TO OUR PLANET.
AND IT'S ONLY GOING TO GET WEIRDER.
GULP
GIANT ZOMBIES?
NOT THAT WEIRD.

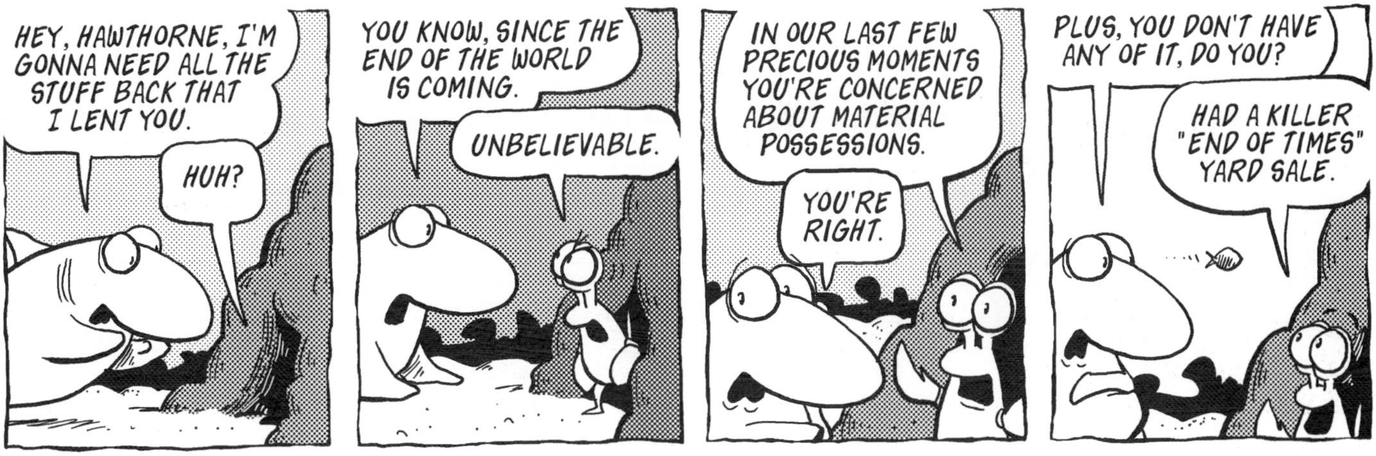
HEY, HAWTHORNE, I'M GONNA NEED ALL THE STUFF BACK THAT I LENT YOU.
HUH?
YOU KNOW, SINCE THE END OF THE WORLD IS COMING.
UNBELIEVABLE.
IN OUR LAST FEW PRECIOUS MOMENTS YOU'RE CONCERNED ABOUT MATERIAL POSSESSIONS.
YOU'RE RIGHT.
PLUS, YOU DON'T HAVE ANY OF IT, DO YOU?
HAD A KILLER "END OF TIMES" YARD SALE.

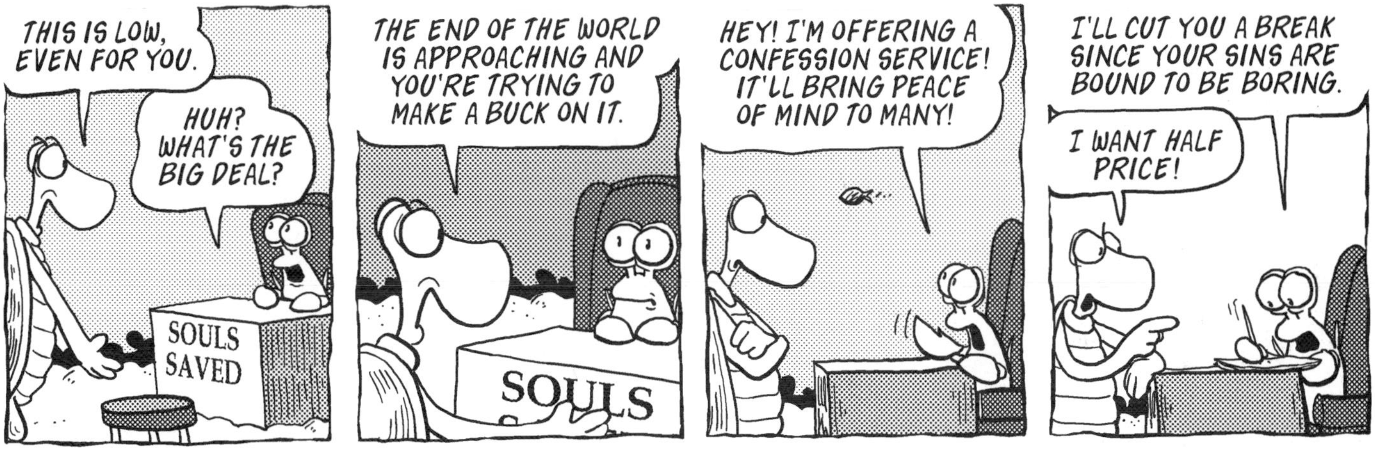
THIS IS LOW, EVEN FOR YOU.
HUH? WHAT'S THE BIG DEAL?
SOULS SAVED
THE END OF THE WORLD IS APPROACHING AND YOU'RE TRYING TO MAKE A BUCK ON IT.
SOULS
HEY! I'M OFFERING A CONFESSION SERVICE! IT'LL BRING PEACE OF MIND TO MANY!
I'LL CUT YOU A BREAK SINCE YOUR SINS ARE BOUND TO BE BORING.
I WANT HALF PRICE!

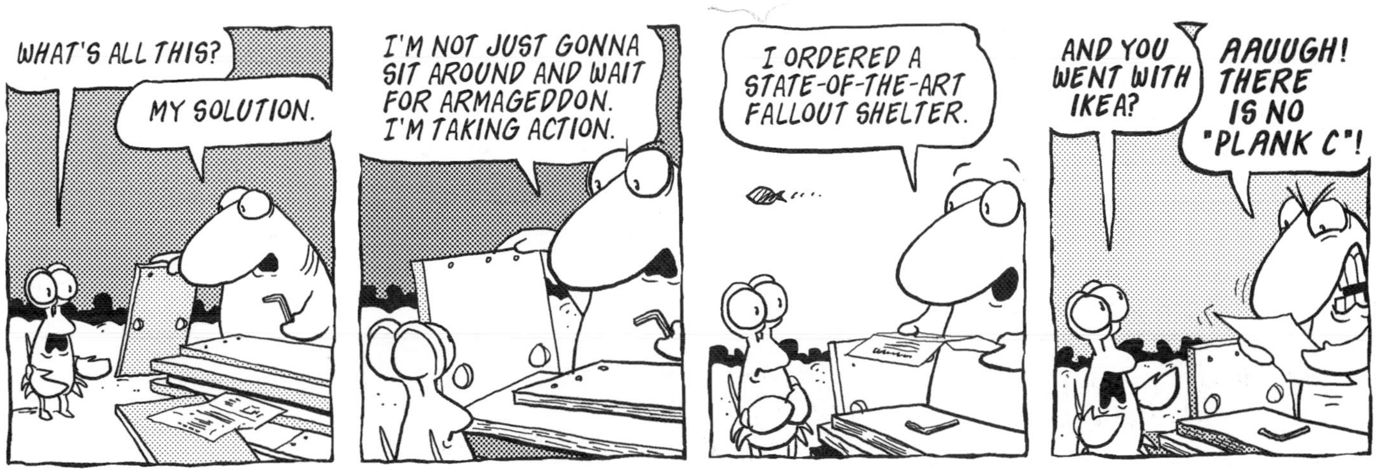
WHAT'S ALL THIS?
MY SOLUTION.
I'M NOT JUST GONNA SIT AROUND AND WAIT FOR ARMAGEDDON. I'M TAKING ACTION.
I ORDERED A STATE-OF-THE-ART FALLOUT SHELTER.
AND YOU WENT WITH IKEA?
AAUUGH! THERE IS NO "PLANK C"!

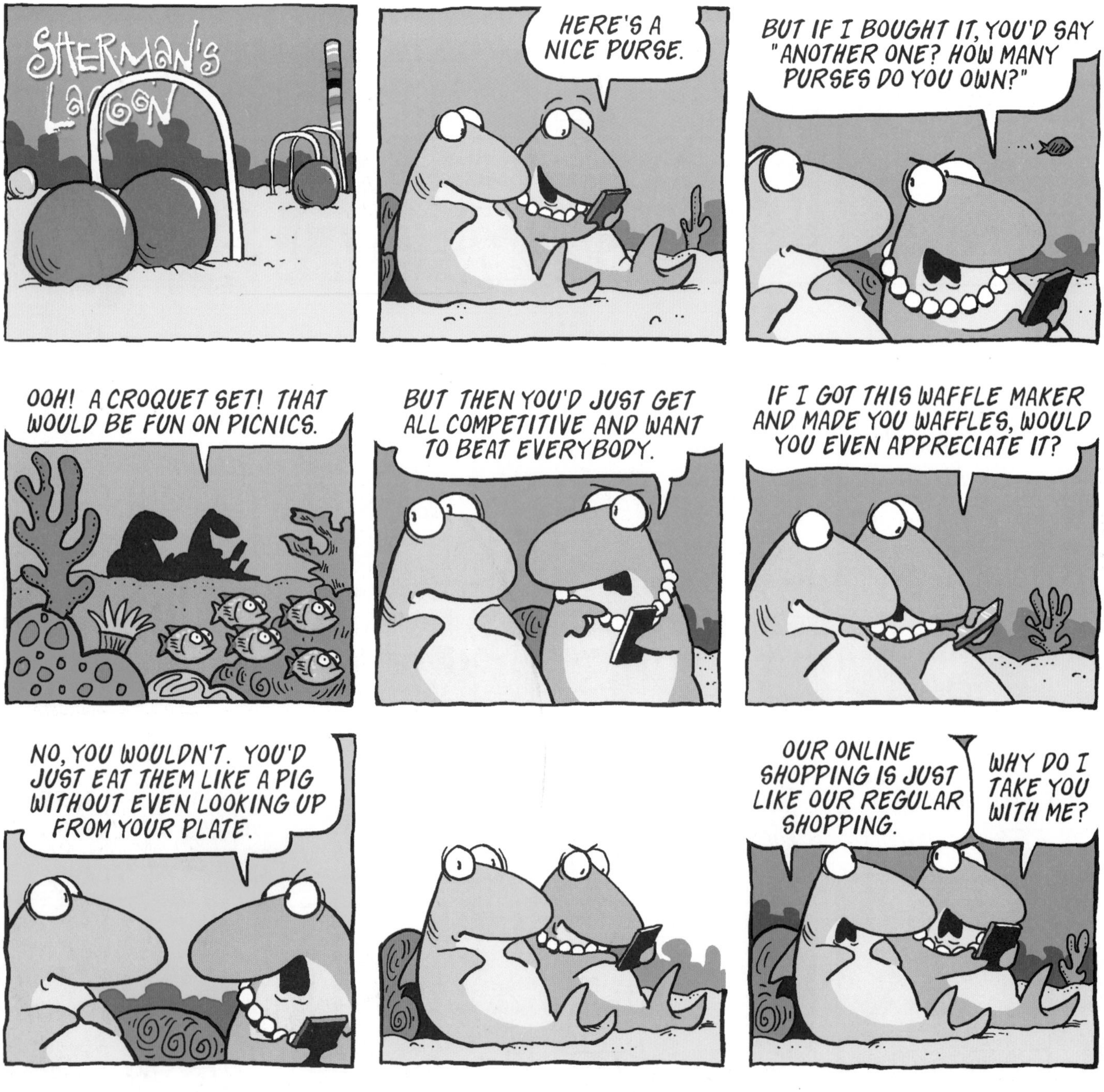
SHERMAN'S LAGOON
HERE'S A NICE PURSE.
BUT IF I BOUGHT IT, YOU'D SAY "ANOTHER ONE? HOW MANY PURSES DO YOU OWN?"
OOH! A CROQUET SET! THAT WOULD BE FUN ON PICNICS.
BUT THEN YOU'D JUST GET ALL COMPETITIVE AND WANT TO BEAT EVERYBODY.
IF I GOT THIS WAFFLE MAKER AND MADE YOU WAFFLES, WOULD YOU EVEN APPRECIATE IT?
NO, YOU WOULDN'T. YOU'D JUST EAT THEM LIKE A PIG WITHOUT EVEN LOOKING UP FROM YOUR PLATE.
OUR ONLINE SHOPPING IS JUST LIKE OUR REGULAR SHOPPING.
WHY DO I TAKE YOU WITH ME?

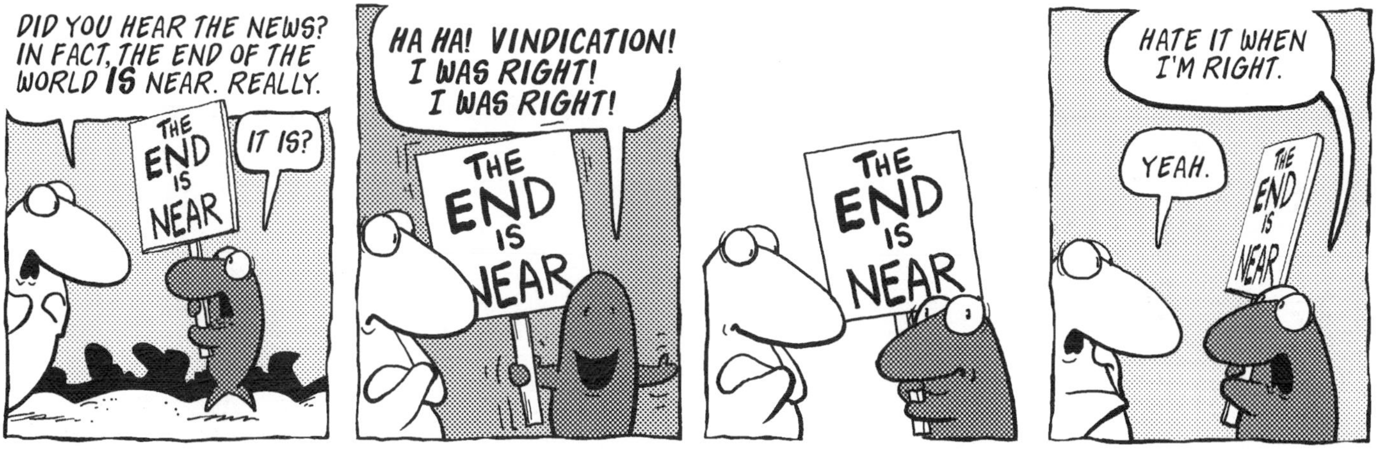
DID YOU HEAR THE NEWS? IN FACT, THE END OF THE WORLD IS NEAR. REALLY.
THE END IS NEAR
IT IS?
HA HA! VINDICATION! I WAS RIGHT! I WAS RIGHT!
THE END IS NEAR
THE END IS NEAR
HATE IT WHEN I'M RIGHT.
YEAH.
THE END IS NEAR

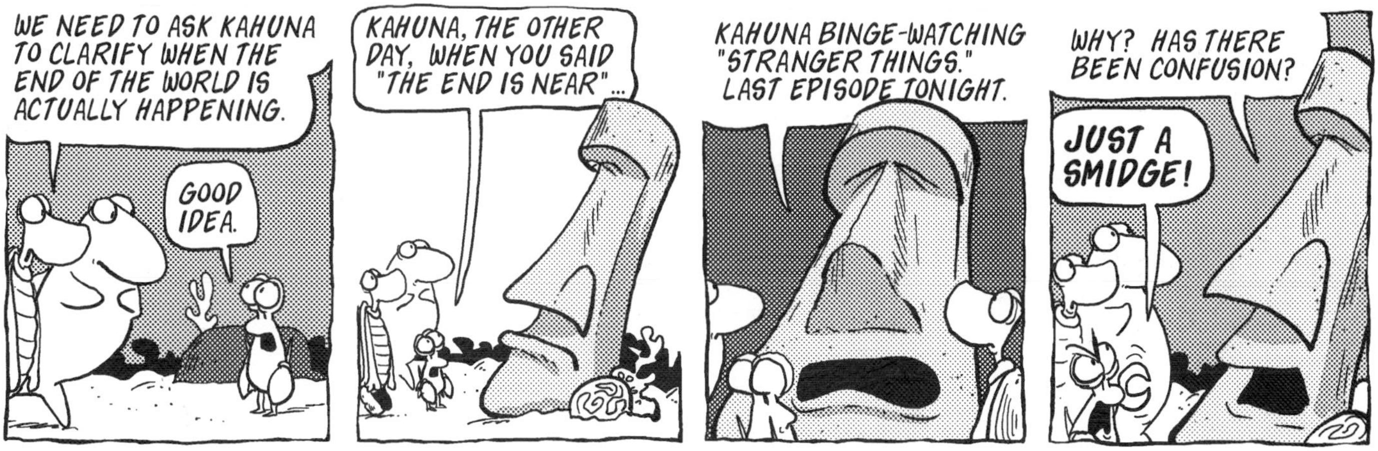
WE NEED TO ASK KAHUNA TO CLARIFY WHEN THE END OF THE WORLD IS ACTUALLY HAPPENING.
GOOD IDEA.
KAHUNA, THE OTHER DAY, WHEN YOU SAID "THE END IS NEAR"...
KAHUNA BINGE-WATCHING "STRANGER THINGS." LAST EPISODE TONIGHT.
WHY? HAS THERE BEEN CONFUSION?
JUST A SMIDGE!

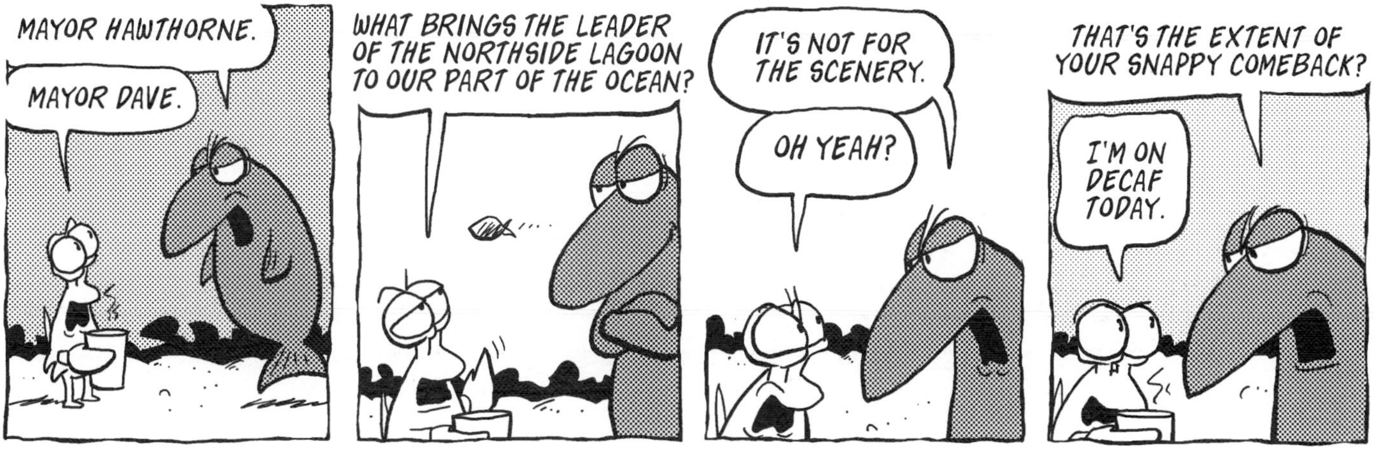
MAYOR HAWTHORNE.
MAYOR DAVE.
WHAT BRINGS THE LEADER OF THE NORTHSIDE LAGOON TO OUR PART OF THE OCEAN?
IT'S NOT FOR THE SCENERY.
OH YEAH?
THAT'S THE EXTENT OF YOUR SNAPPY COMEBACK?
I'M ON DECAF TODAY.

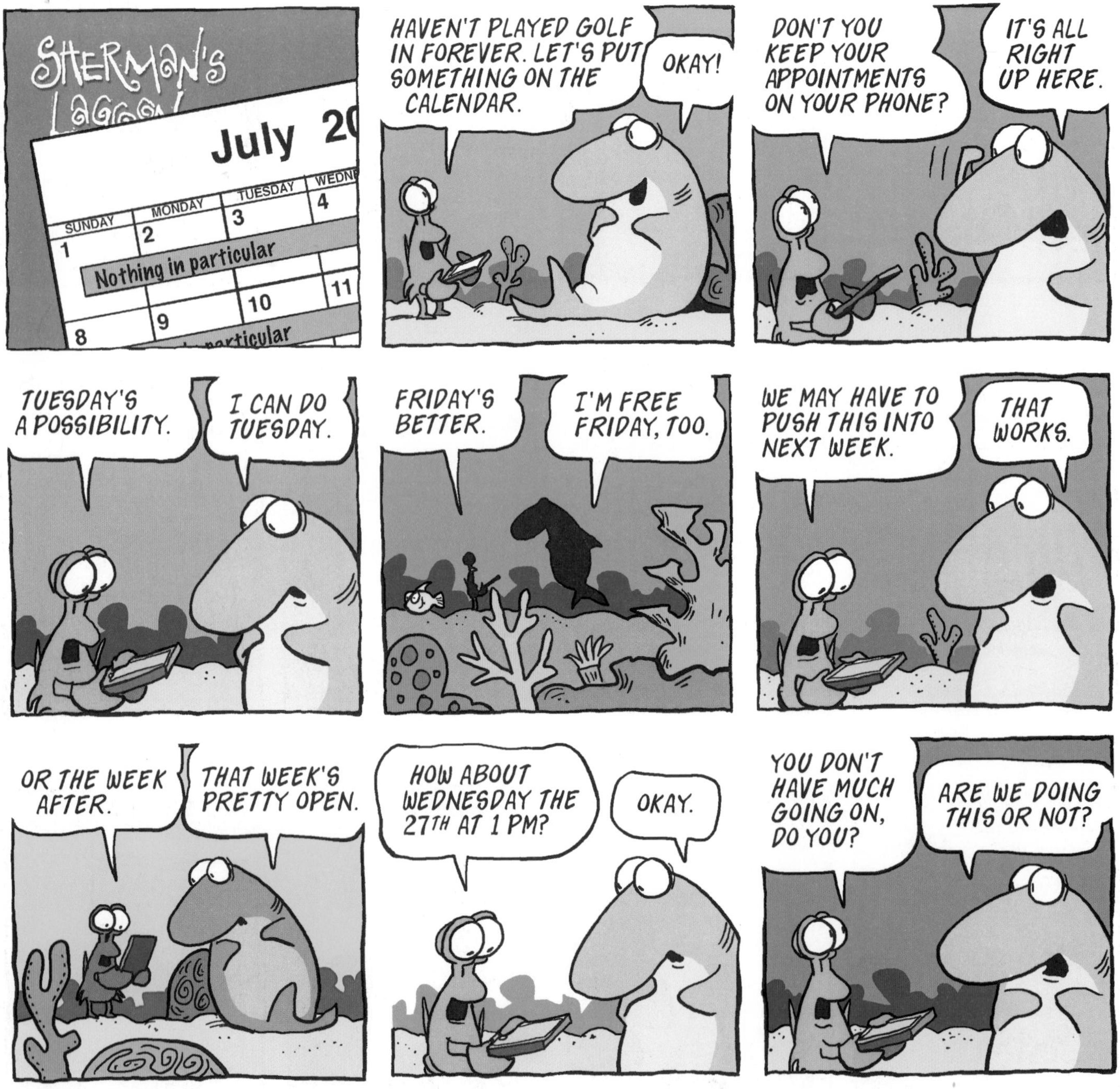
SHERMAN'S LAGOON
July 20
SUNDAY
MONDAY
TUESDAY
WEDNE
1
2
3
4
Nothing in particular
8
9
10
11
HAVEN'T PLAYED GOLF IN FOREVER. LET'S PUT SOMETHING ON THE CALENDAR.
OKAY!
DON'T YOU KEEP YOUR APPOINTMENTS ON YOUR PHONE?
IT'S ALL RIGHT UP HERE.
TUESDAY'S A POSSIBILITY.
I CAN DO TUESDAY.
FRIDAY'S BETTER.
I'M FREE FRIDAY, TOO.
WE MAY HAVE TO PUSH THIS INTO NEXT WEEK.
THAT WORKS.
OR THE WEEK AFTER.
THAT WEEK'S PRETTY OPEN.
HOW ABOUT WEDNESDAY THE 27TH AT 1 PM?
OKAY.
YOU DON'T HAVE MUCH GOING ON, DO YOU?
ARE WE DOING THIS OR NOT?

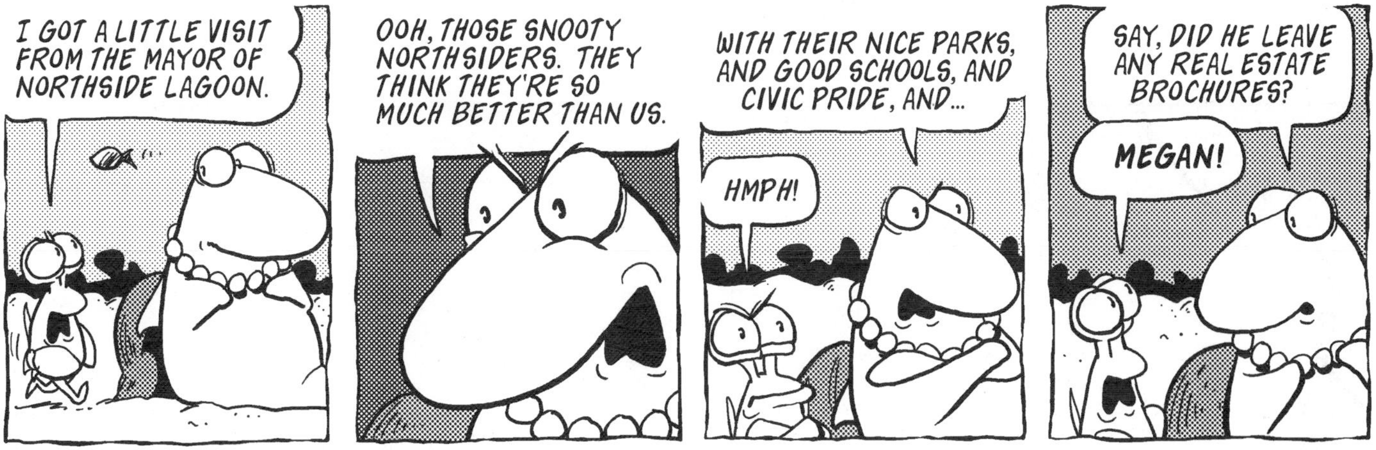
I GOT A LITTLE VISIT FROM THE MAYOR OF NORTHSIDE LAGOON.
OOH, THOSE SNOOTY NORTHSIDERS. THEY THINK THEY'RE SO MUCH BETTER THAN US.
WITH THEIR NICE PARKS, AND GOOD SCHOOLS, AND CIVIC PRIDE, AND...
HMPH!
SAY, DID HE LEAVE ANY REAL ESTATE BROCHURES?
MEGAN!

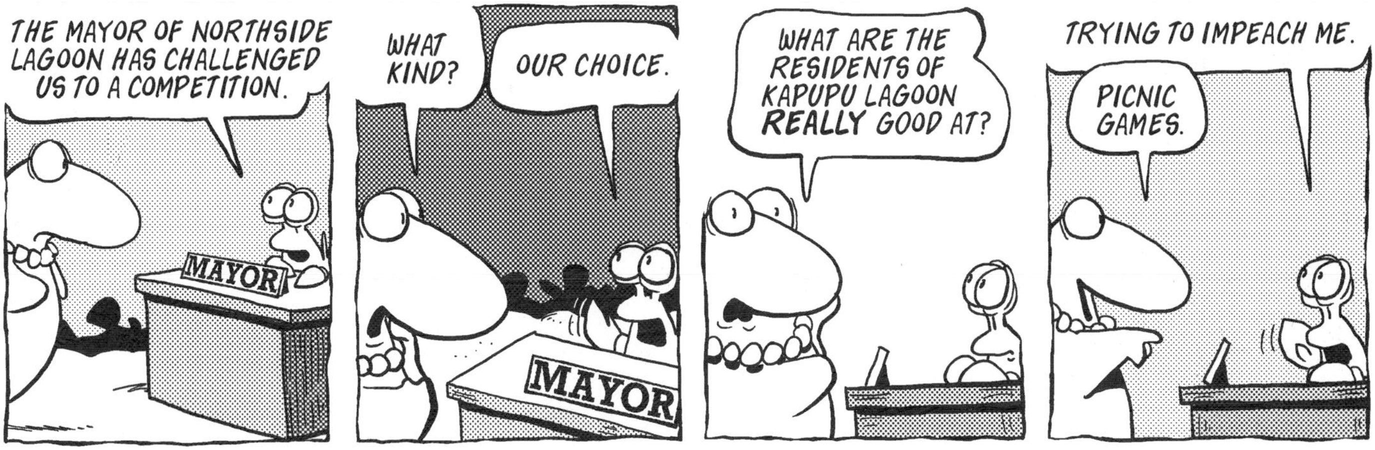
THE MAYOR OF NORTHSIDE LAGOON HAS CHALLENGED US TO A COMPETITION.
MAYOR
WHAT KIND?
OUR CHOICE.
MAYOR
WHAT ARE THE RESIDENTS OF KAPUPU LAGOON **REALLY** GOOD AT?
TRYING TO IMPEACH ME.
PICNIC GAMES.

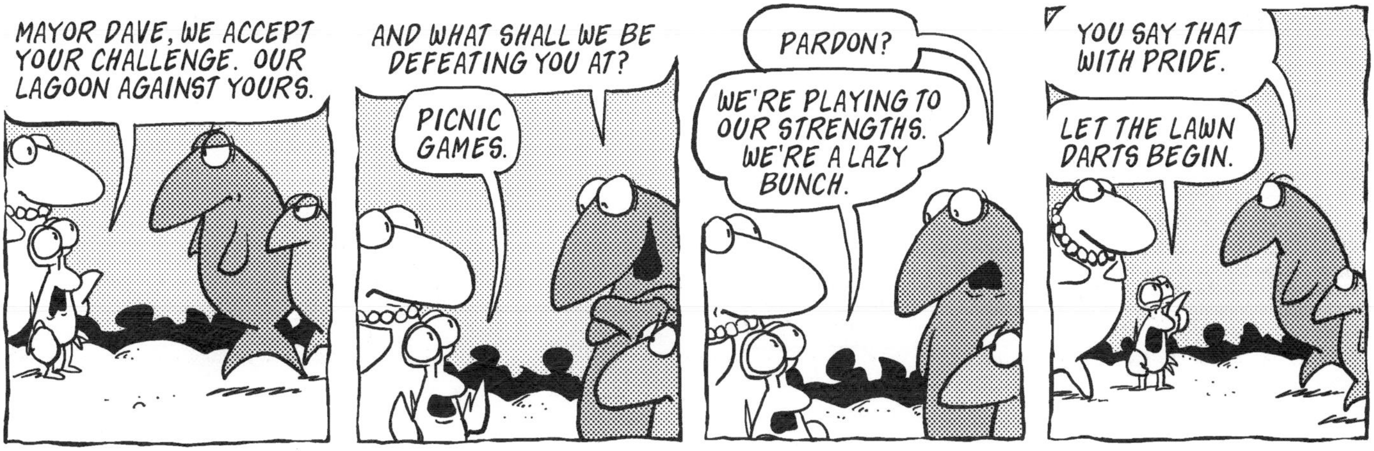
MAYOR DAVE, WE ACCEPT YOUR CHALLENGE. OUR LAGOON AGAINST YOURS.
AND WHAT SHALL WE BE DEFEATING YOU AT?
PICNIC GAMES.
PARDON?
WE'RE PLAYING TO OUR STRENGTHS. WE'RE A LAZY BUNCH.
YOU SAY THAT WITH PRIDE.
LET THE LAWN DARTS BEGIN.

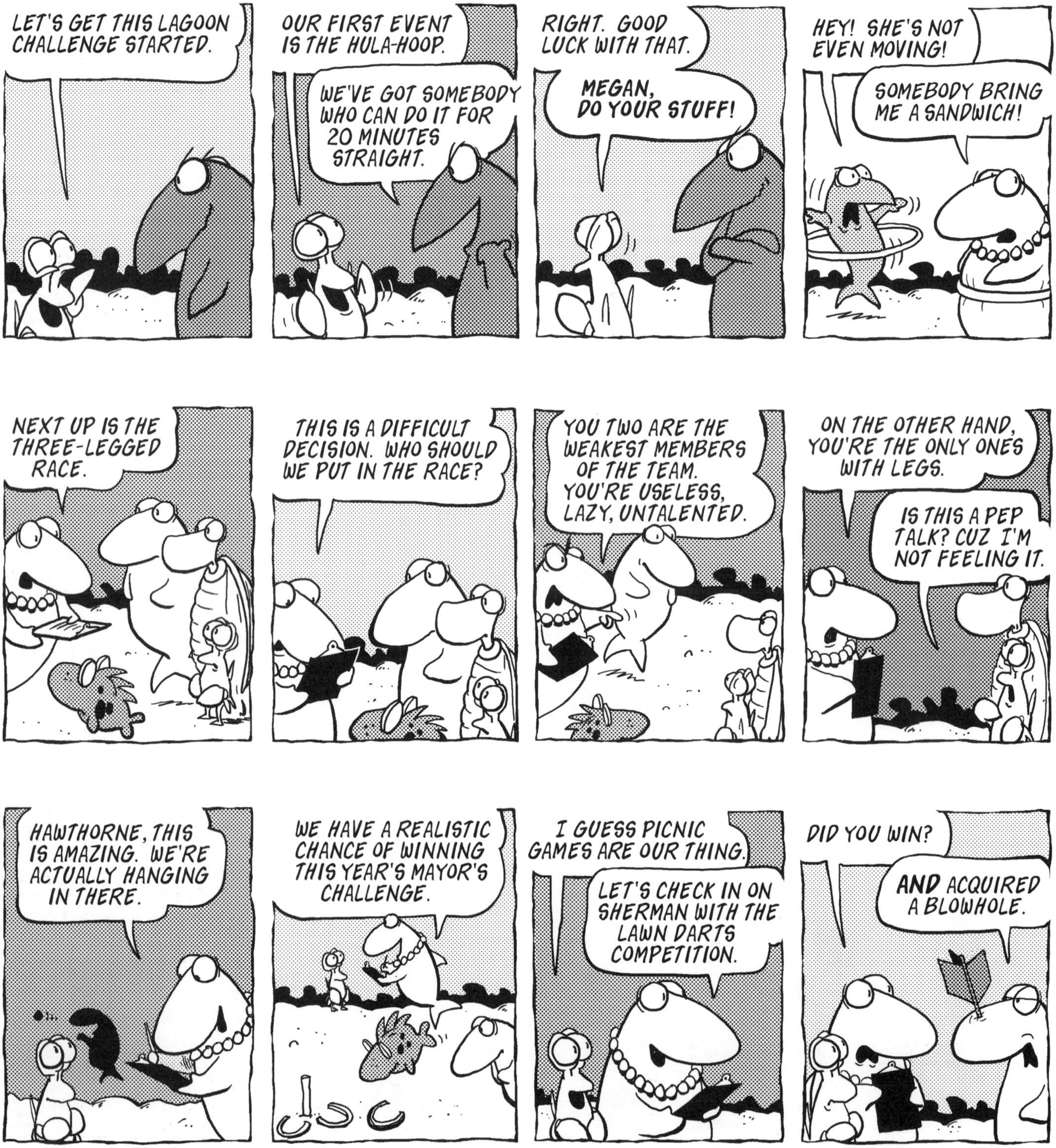
LET'S GET THIS LAGOON CHALLENGE STARTED.
OUR FIRST EVENT IS THE HULA-HOOP.
WE'VE GOT SOMEBODY WHO CAN DO IT FOR 20 MINUTES STRAIGHT.
RIGHT. GOOD LUCK WITH THAT.
MEGAN, DO YOUR STUFF!
HEY! SHE'S NOT EVEN MOVING!
SOMEBODY BRING ME A SANDWICH!
NEXT UP IS THE THREE-LEGGED RACE.
THIS IS A DIFFICULT DECISION. WHO SHOULD WE PUT IN THE RACE?
YOU TWO ARE THE WEAKEST MEMBERS OF THE TEAM. YOU'RE USELESS, LAZY, UNTALENTED.
ON THE OTHER HAND, YOU'RE THE ONLY ONES WITH LEGS.
IS THIS A PEP TALK? CUZ I'M NOT FEELING IT.
HAWTHORNE, THIS IS AMAZING. WE'RE ACTUALLY HANGING IN THERE.
WE HAVE A REALISTIC CHANCE OF WINNING THIS YEAR'S MAYOR'S CHALLENGE.
I GUESS PICNIC GAMES ARE OUR THING.
LET'S CHECK IN ON SHERMAN WITH THE LAWN DARTS COMPETITION.
DID YOU WIN?
AND ACQUIRED A BLOWHOLE.

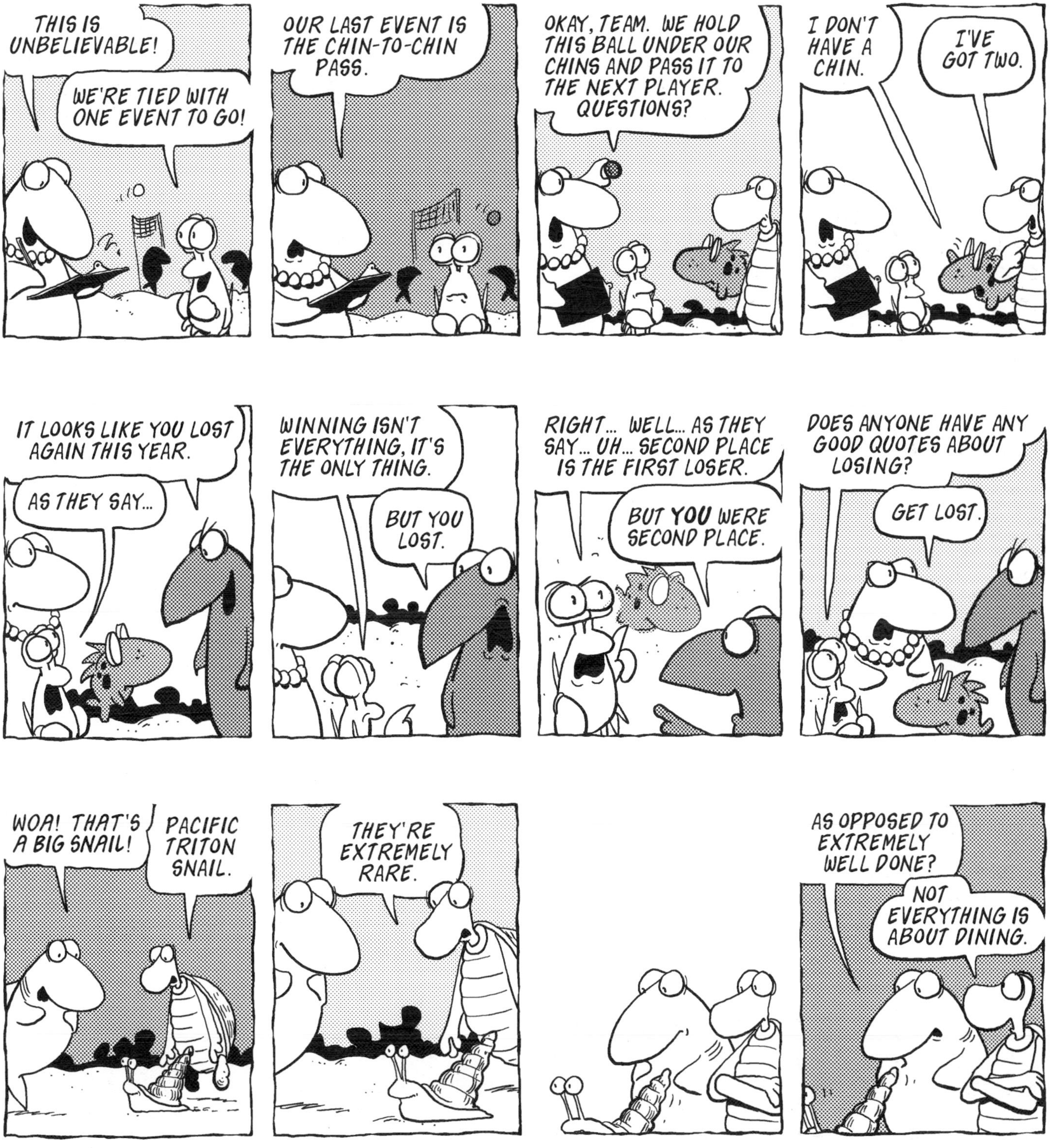
THIS IS UNBELIEVABLE!
WE'RE TIED WITH ONE EVENT TO GO!
OUR LAST EVENT IS THE CHIN-TO-CHIN PASS.
OKAY, TEAM. WE HOLD THIS BALL UNDER OUR CHINS AND PASS IT TO THE NEXT PLAYER. QUESTIONS?
I DON'T HAVE A CHIN.
I'VE GOT TWO.
IT LOOKS LIKE YOU LOST AGAIN THIS YEAR.
AS THEY SAY...
WINNING ISN'T EVERYTHING, IT'S THE ONLY THING.
BUT YOU LOST.
RIGHT... WELL... AS THEY SAY... UH... SECOND PLACE IS THE FIRST LOSER.
BUT YOU WERE SECOND PLACE.
DOES ANYONE HAVE ANY GOOD QUOTES ABOUT LOSING?
GET LOST.
WOA! THAT'S A BIG SNAIL!
PACIFIC TRITON SNAIL.
THEY'RE EXTREMELY RARE.
AS OPPOSED TO EXTREMELY WELL DONE?
NOT EVERYTHING IS ABOUT DINING.

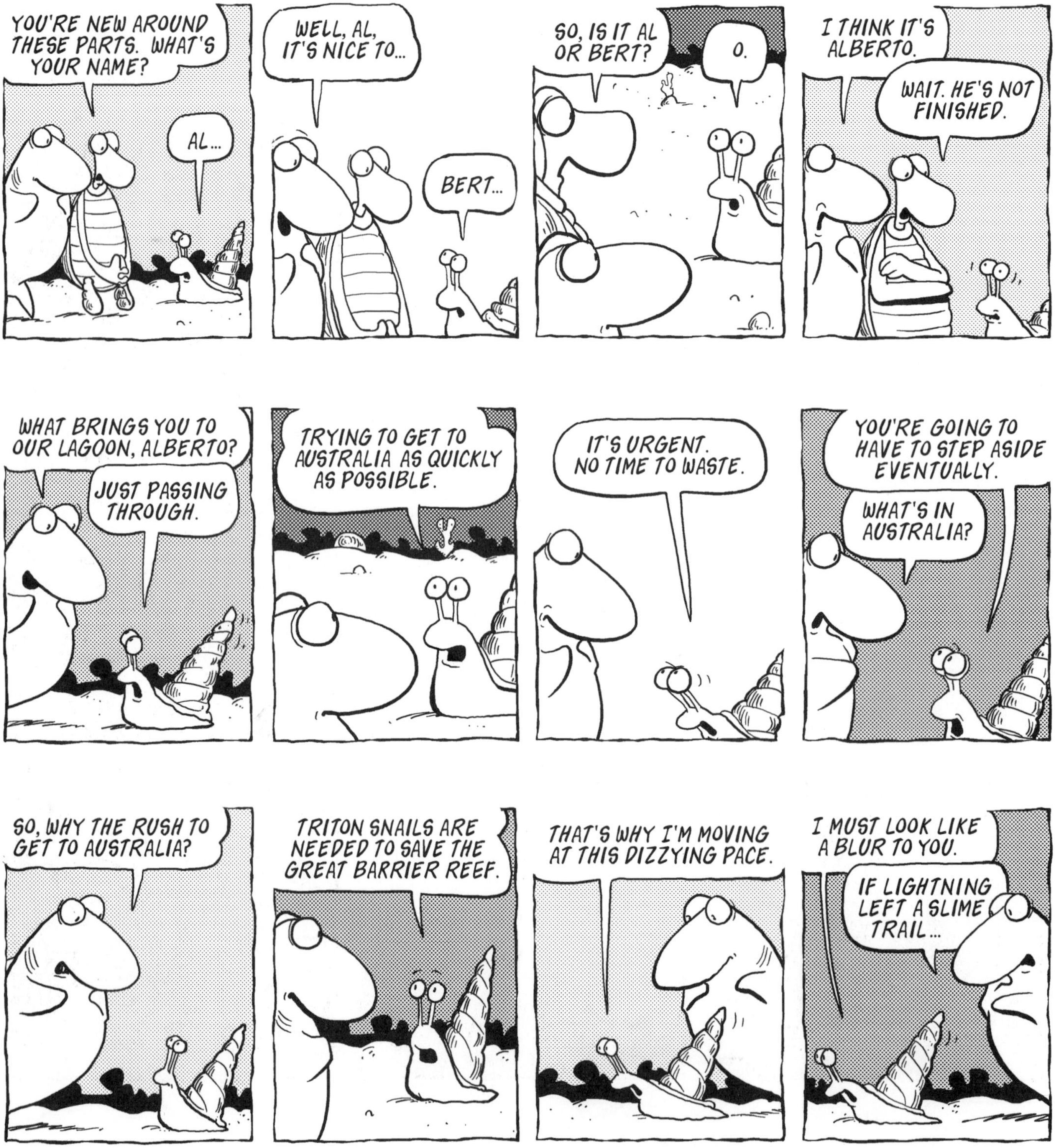
YOU'RE NEW AROUND THESE PARTS. WHAT'S YOUR NAME?
AL...
WELL, AL, IT'S NICE TO...
BERT...
SO, IS IT AL OR BERT?
O.
I THINK IT'S ALBERTO.
WAIT. HE'S NOT FINISHED.
WHAT BRINGS YOU TO OUR LAGOON, ALBERTO?
JUST PASSING THROUGH.
TRYING TO GET TO AUSTRALIA AS QUICKLY AS POSSIBLE.
IT'S URGENT. NO TIME TO WASTE.
YOU'RE GOING TO HAVE TO STEP ASIDE EVENTUALLY.
WHAT'S IN AUSTRALIA?
SO, WHY THE RUSH TO GET TO AUSTRALIA?
TRITON SNAILS ARE NEEDED TO SAVE THE GREAT BARRIER REEF.
THAT'S WHY I'M MOVING AT THIS DIZZYING PACE.
I MUST LOOK LIKE A BLUR TO YOU.
IF LIGHTNING LEFT A SLIME TRAIL...

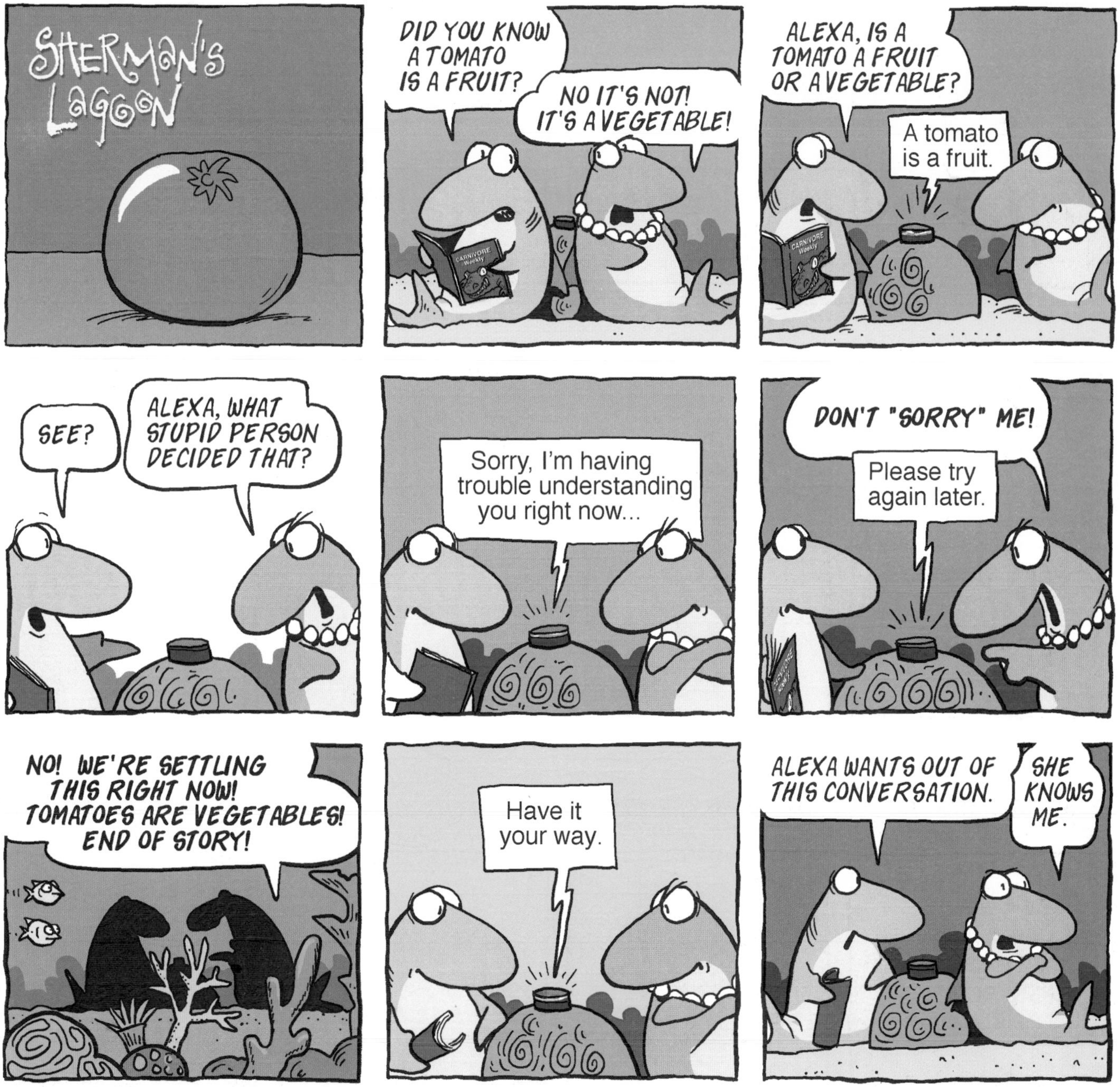
SHERMAN'S LAGOON
DID YOU KNOW A TOMATO IS A FRUIT?
NO IT'S NOT! IT'S A VEGETABLE!
CARNIVORE Weekly
ALEXA, IS A TOMATO A FRUIT OR A VEGETABLE?
A tomato is a fruit.
SEE?
ALEXA, WHAT STUPID PERSON DECIDED THAT?
Sorry, I'm having trouble understanding you right now...
DON'T "SORRY" ME!
Please try again later.
NO! WE'RE SETTLING THIS RIGHT NOW! TOMATOES ARE VEGETABLES! END OF STORY!
Have it your way.
ALEXA WANTS OUT OF THIS CONVERSATION.
SHE KNOWS ME.

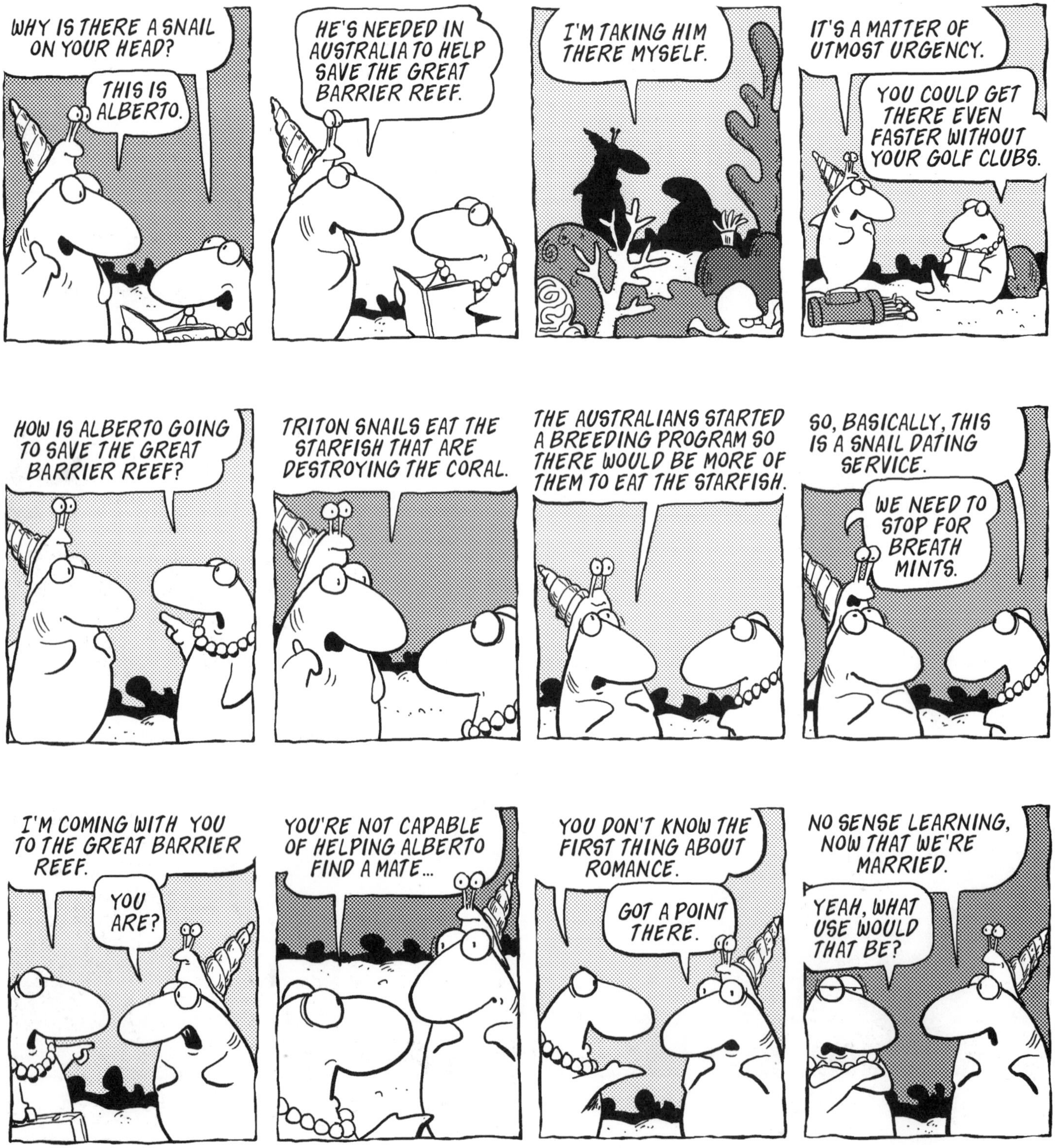
WHY IS THERE A SNAIL ON YOUR HEAD?
THIS IS ALBERTO.
HE'S NEEDED IN AUSTRALIA TO HELP SAVE THE GREAT BARRIER REEF.
I'M TAKING HIM THERE MYSELF.
IT'S A MATTER OF UTMOST URGENCY.
YOU COULD GET THERE EVEN FASTER WITHOUT YOUR GOLF CLUBS.
HOW IS ALBERTO GOING TO SAVE THE GREAT BARRIER REEF?
TRITON SNAILS EAT THE STARFISH THAT ARE DESTROYING THE CORAL.
THE AUSTRALIANS STARTED A BREEDING PROGRAM SO THERE WOULD BE MORE OF THEM TO EAT THE STARFISH.
SO, BASICALLY, THIS IS A SNAIL DATING SERVICE.
WE NEED TO STOP FOR BREATH MINTS.
I'M COMING WITH YOU TO THE GREAT BARRIER REEF.
YOU ARE?
YOU'RE NOT CAPABLE OF HELPING ALBERTO FIND A MATE...
YOU DON'T KNOW THE FIRST THING ABOUT ROMANCE.
GOT A POINT THERE.
NO SENSE LEARNING, NOW THAT WE'RE MARRIED.
YEAH, WHAT USE WOULD THAT BE?

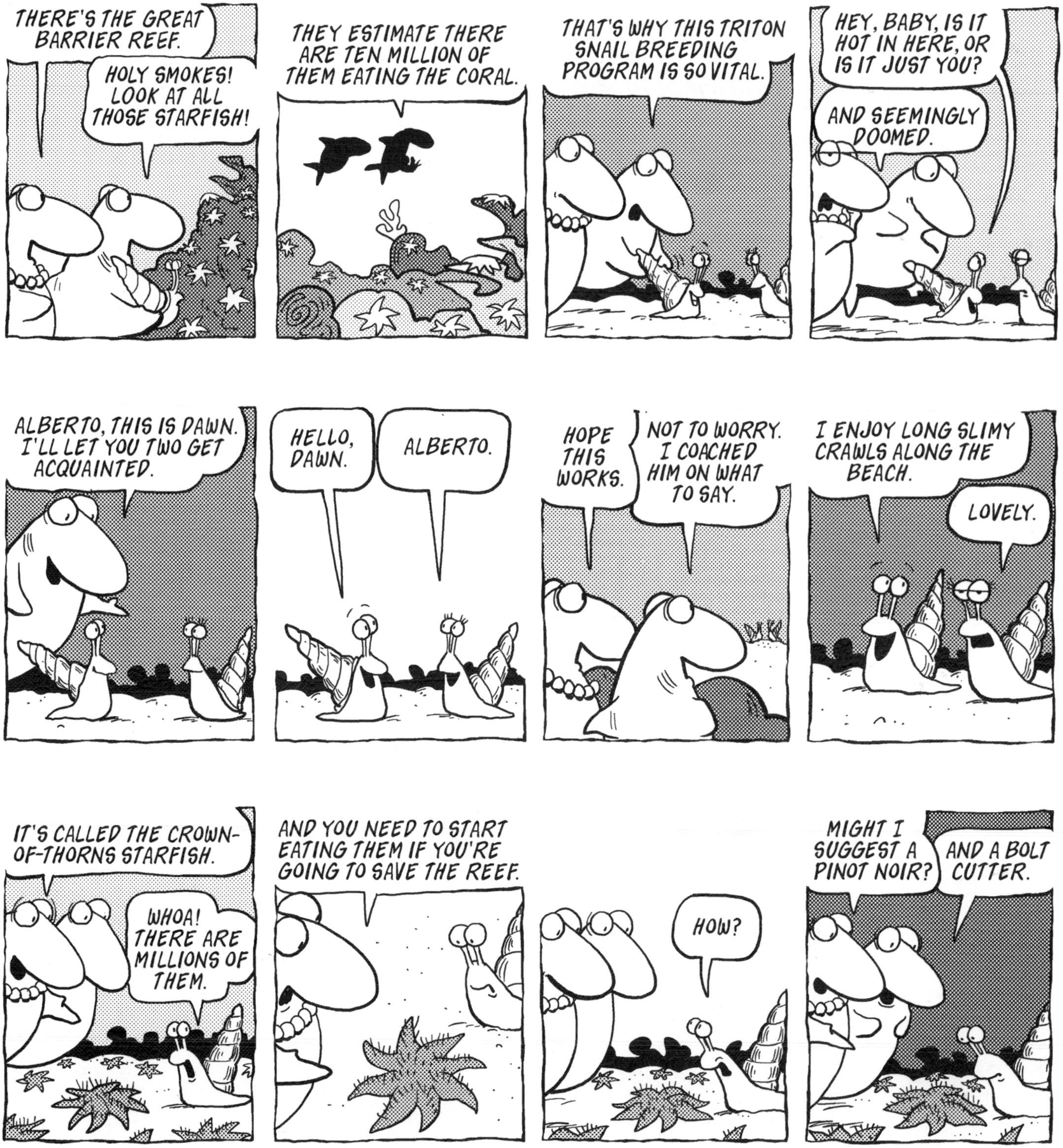
THERE'S THE GREAT BARRIER REEF.
HOLY SMOKES! LOOK AT ALL THOSE STARFISH!
THEY ESTIMATE THERE ARE TEN MILLION OF THEM EATING THE CORAL.
THAT'S WHY THIS TRITON SNAIL BREEDING PROGRAM IS SO VITAL.
HEY, BABY, IS IT HOT IN HERE, OR IS IT JUST YOU?
AND SEEMINGLY DOOMED.
ALBERTO, THIS IS DAWN. I'LL LET YOU TWO GET ACQUAINTED.
HELLO, DAWN.
ALBERTO.
HOPE THIS WORKS.
NOT TO WORRY. I COACHED HIM ON WHAT TO SAY.
I ENJOY LONG SLIMY CRAWLS ALONG THE BEACH.
LOVELY.
IT'S CALLED THE CROWN-OF-THORNS STARFISH.
WHOA! THERE ARE MILLIONS OF THEM.
AND YOU NEED TO START EATING THEM IF YOU'RE GOING TO SAVE THE REEF.
HOW?
MIGHT I SUGGEST A PINOT NOIR?
AND A BOLT CUTTER.

MEGAN, I THINK IT'S TIME WE LEAVE THESE SNAILS TO DO THEIR WORK AND HEAD HOME.

WHO WOULD'VE THOUGHT THAT SNAILS COULD BE THE SOLUTION TO AN ENVIRONMENTAL CRISIS?

WHERE'S THE NEXT SOLUTION COMING FROM?

POLITICIANS?

IT'S A STRETCH.

THAT'S JUST SIMPLY AMAZING.

HUH? WHAT?

MICROSOFT AND FACEBOOK TEAMED UP TO BUILD A MASSIVE UNDERSEA CABLE.

IT'S A 4000-MILE-LONG INFORMATION HIGHWAY.

WOW.

HOPEFULLY IT HAS A FEW REST AREAS ALONG THE WAY.

NONE THEY MENTION.

MICROSOFT AND FACEBOOK TEAMED UP TO BUILT A MASSIVE UNDERSEA DATA CABLE.

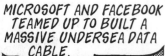

IMPRESSIVE, BUT ANSWER ME THIS... WILL IT AFFECT HOW MUCH I PAY FOR THESE SERVICES?

FACEBOOK IS FREE, AND YOU ALWAYS USE PIRATED MICROSOFT SOFTWARE.

WOULD IT AFFECT AN HONEST VERSION OF ME?

WE'LL NEVER KNOW.

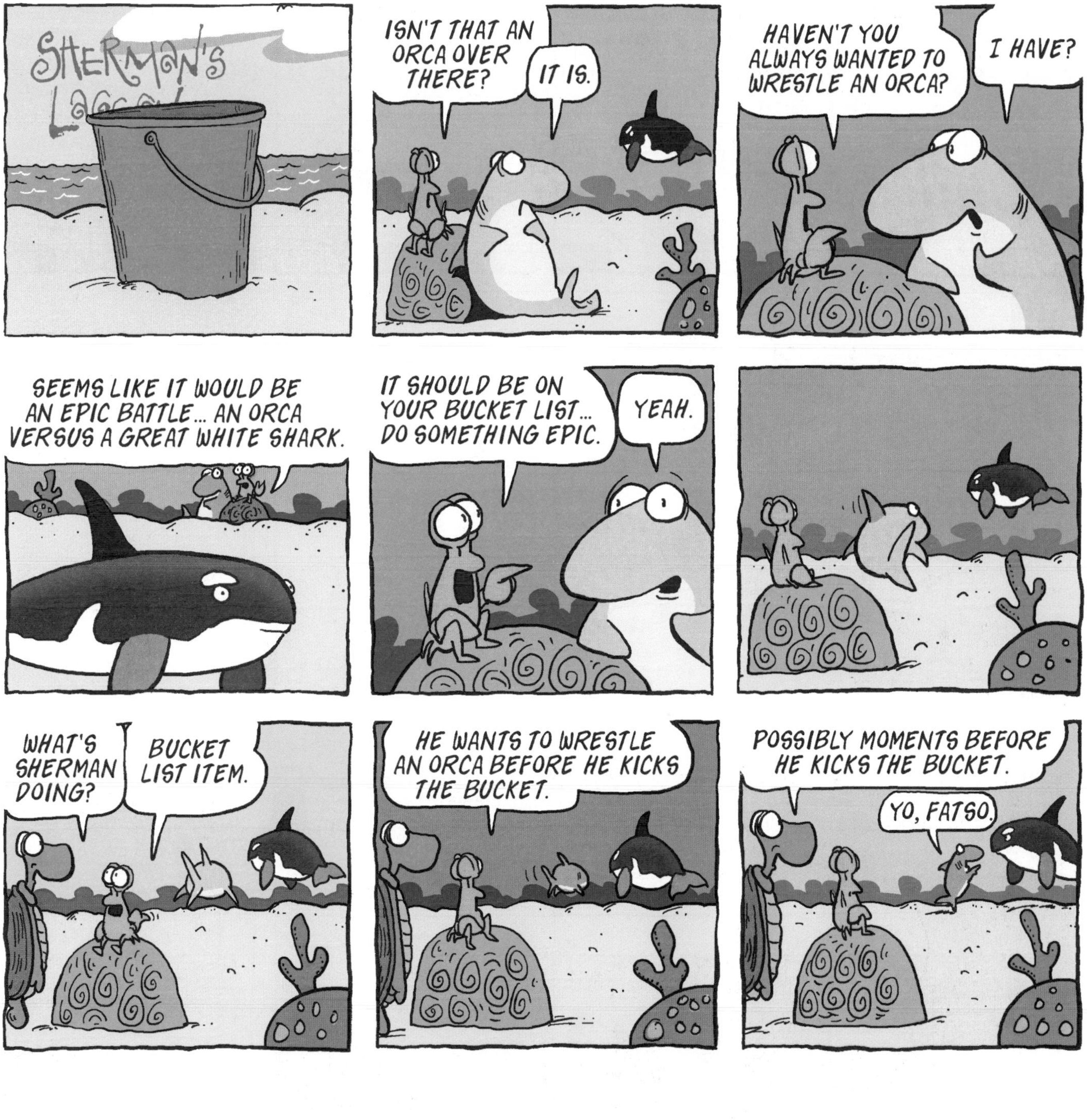
SHERMAN'S LAGOON
ISN'T THAT AN ORCA OVER THERE?
IT IS.
HAVEN'T YOU ALWAYS WANTED TO WRESTLE AN ORCA?
I HAVE?
SEEMS LIKE IT WOULD BE AN EPIC BATTLE... AN ORCA VERSUS A GREAT WHITE SHARK.
IT SHOULD BE ON YOUR BUCKET LIST... DO SOMETHING EPIC.
YEAH.
WHAT'S SHERMAN DOING?
BUCKET LIST ITEM.
HE WANTS TO WRESTLE AN ORCA BEFORE HE KICKS THE BUCKET.
POSSIBLY MOMENTS BEFORE HE KICKS THE BUCKET.
YO, FATSO.

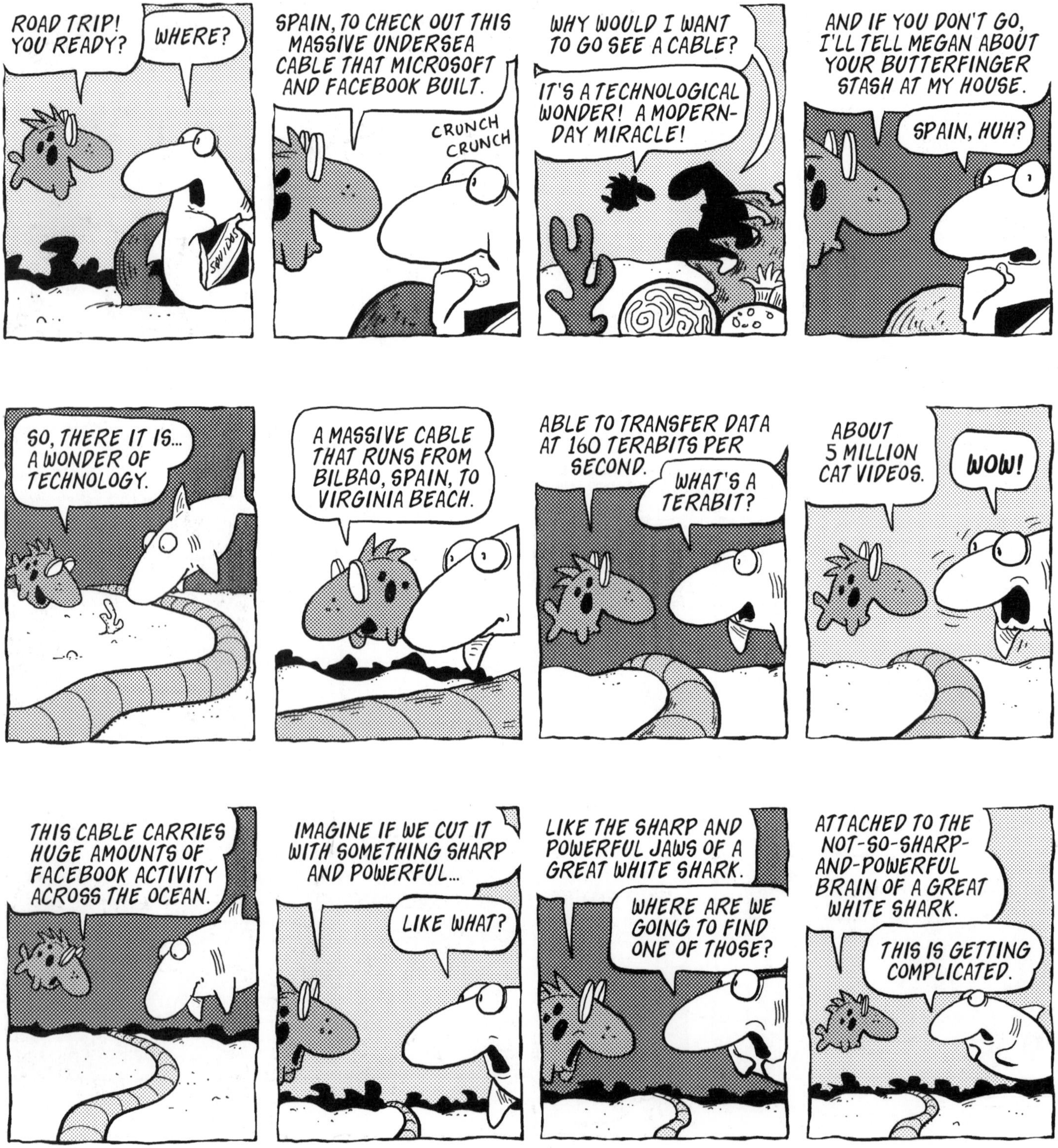
ROAD TRIP! YOU READY?
WHERE?
SPAIN, TO CHECK OUT THIS MASSIVE UNDERSEA CABLE THAT MICROSOFT AND FACEBOOK BUILT.
CRUNCH CRUNCH
SQUIDOS
WHY WOULD I WANT TO GO SEE A CABLE?
IT'S A TECHNOLOGICAL WONDER! A MODERN-DAY MIRACLE!
AND IF YOU DON'T GO, I'LL TELL MEGAN ABOUT YOUR BUTTERFINGER STASH AT MY HOUSE.
SPAIN, HUH?
SO, THERE IT IS... A WONDER OF TECHNOLOGY.
A MASSIVE CABLE THAT RUNS FROM BILBAO, SPAIN, TO VIRGINIA BEACH.
ABLE TO TRANSFER DATA AT 160 TERABITS PER SECOND.
WHAT'S A TERABIT?
ABOUT 5 MILLION CAT VIDEOS.
WOW!
THIS CABLE CARRIES HUGE AMOUNTS OF FACEBOOK ACTIVITY ACROSS THE OCEAN.
IMAGINE IF WE CUT IT WITH SOMETHING SHARP AND POWERFUL...
LIKE WHAT?
LIKE THE SHARP AND POWERFUL JAWS OF A GREAT WHITE SHARK.
WHERE ARE WE GOING TO FIND ONE OF THOSE?
ATTACHED TO THE NOT-SO-SHARP-AND-POWERFUL BRAIN OF A GREAT WHITE SHARK.
THIS IS GETTING COMPLICATED.

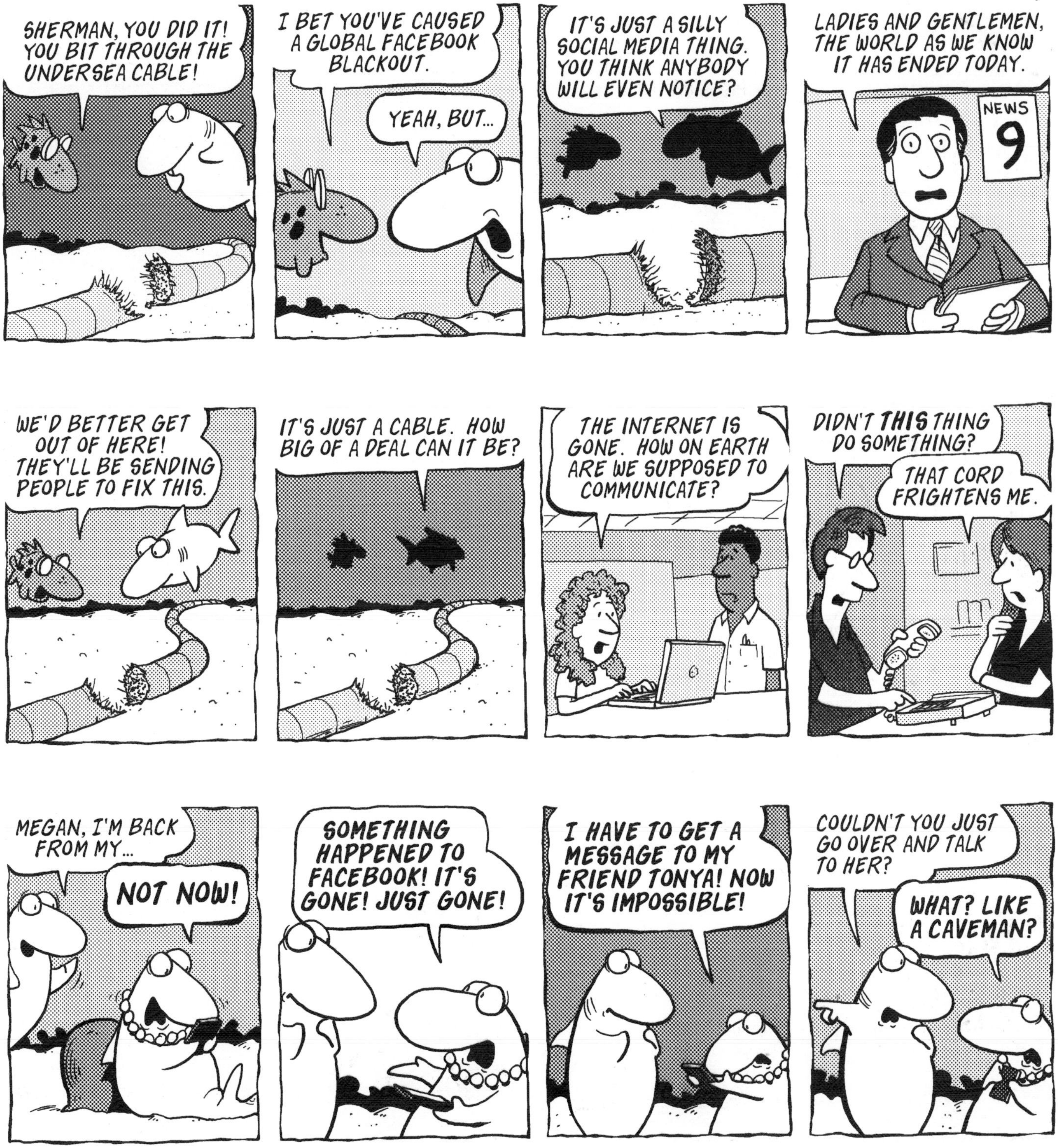
SHERMAN, YOU DID IT! YOU BIT THROUGH THE UNDERSEA CABLE!
I BET YOU'VE CAUSED A GLOBAL FACEBOOK BLACKOUT.
YEAH, BUT...
IT'S JUST A SILLY SOCIAL MEDIA THING. YOU THINK ANYBODY WILL EVEN NOTICE?
LADIES AND GENTLEMEN, THE WORLD AS WE KNOW IT HAS ENDED TODAY.
NEWS 9
WE'D BETTER GET OUT OF HERE! THEY'LL BE SENDING PEOPLE TO FIX THIS.
IT'S JUST A CABLE. HOW BIG OF A DEAL CAN IT BE?
THE INTERNET IS GONE. HOW ON EARTH ARE WE SUPPOSED TO COMMUNICATE?
DIDN'T THIS THING DO SOMETHING?
THAT CORD FRIGHTENS ME.
MEGAN, I'M BACK FROM MY...
NOT NOW!
SOMETHING HAPPENED TO FACEBOOK! IT'S GONE! JUST GONE!
I HAVE TO GET A MESSAGE TO MY FRIEND TONYA! NOW IT'S IMPOSSIBLE!
COULDN'T YOU JUST GO OVER AND TALK TO HER?
WHAT? LIKE A CAVEMAN?

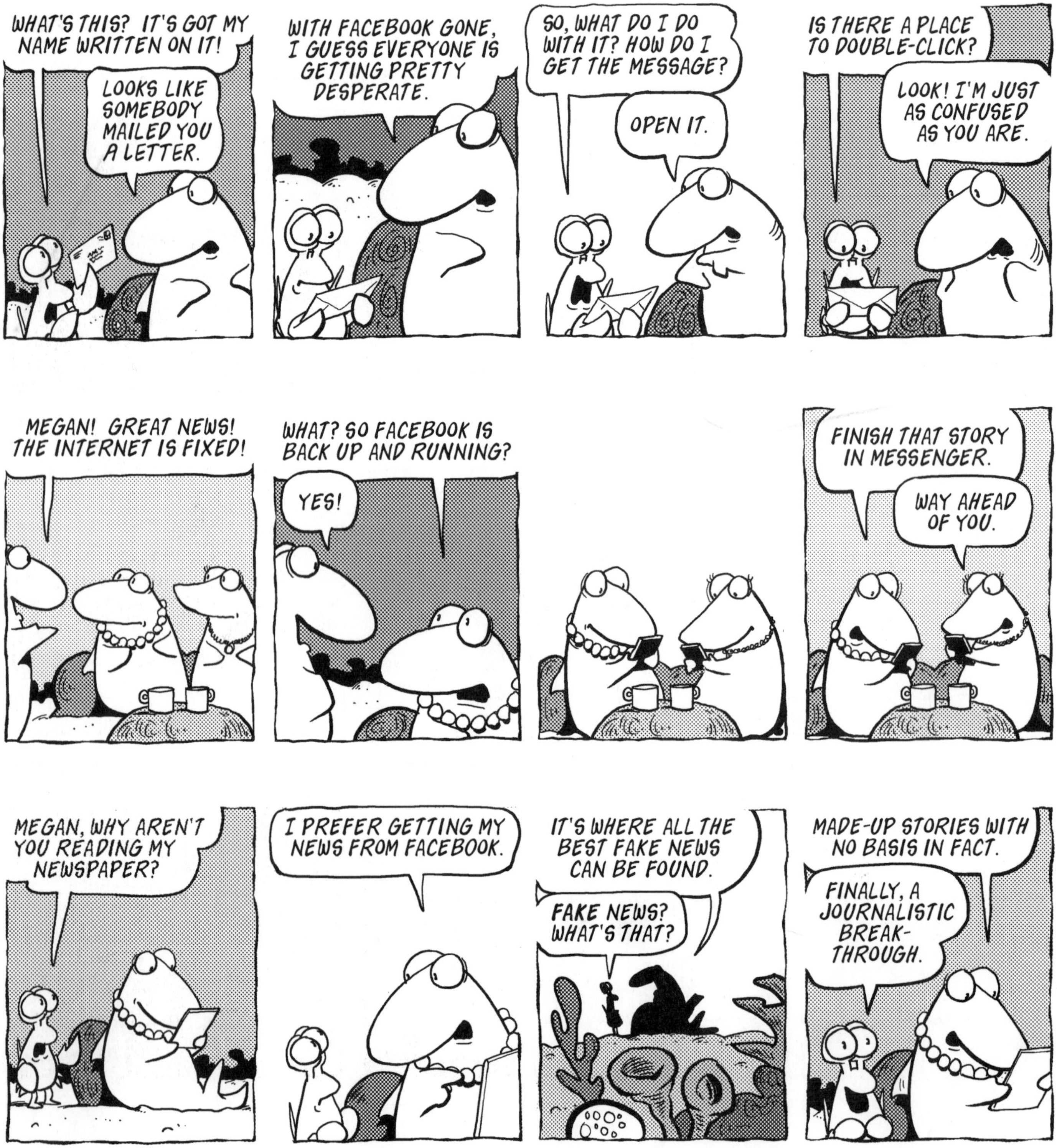
WHAT'S THIS? IT'S GOT MY NAME WRITTEN ON IT!
LOOKS LIKE SOMEBODY MAILED YOU A LETTER.
WITH FACEBOOK GONE, I GUESS EVERYONE IS GETTING PRETTY DESPERATE.
SO, WHAT DO I DO WITH IT? HOW DO I GET THE MESSAGE?
OPEN IT.
IS THERE A PLACE TO DOUBLE-CLICK?
LOOK! I'M JUST AS CONFUSED AS YOU ARE.
MEGAN! GREAT NEWS! THE INTERNET IS FIXED!
WHAT? SO FACEBOOK IS BACK UP AND RUNNING?
YES!
FINISH THAT STORY IN MESSENGER.
WAY AHEAD OF YOU.
MEGAN, WHY AREN'T YOU READING MY NEWSPAPER?
I PREFER GETTING MY NEWS FROM FACEBOOK.
IT'S WHERE ALL THE BEST FAKE NEWS CAN BE FOUND.
FAKE NEWS? WHAT'S THAT?
MADE-UP STORIES WITH NO BASIS IN FACT.
FINALLY, A JOURNALISTIC BREAK-THROUGH.

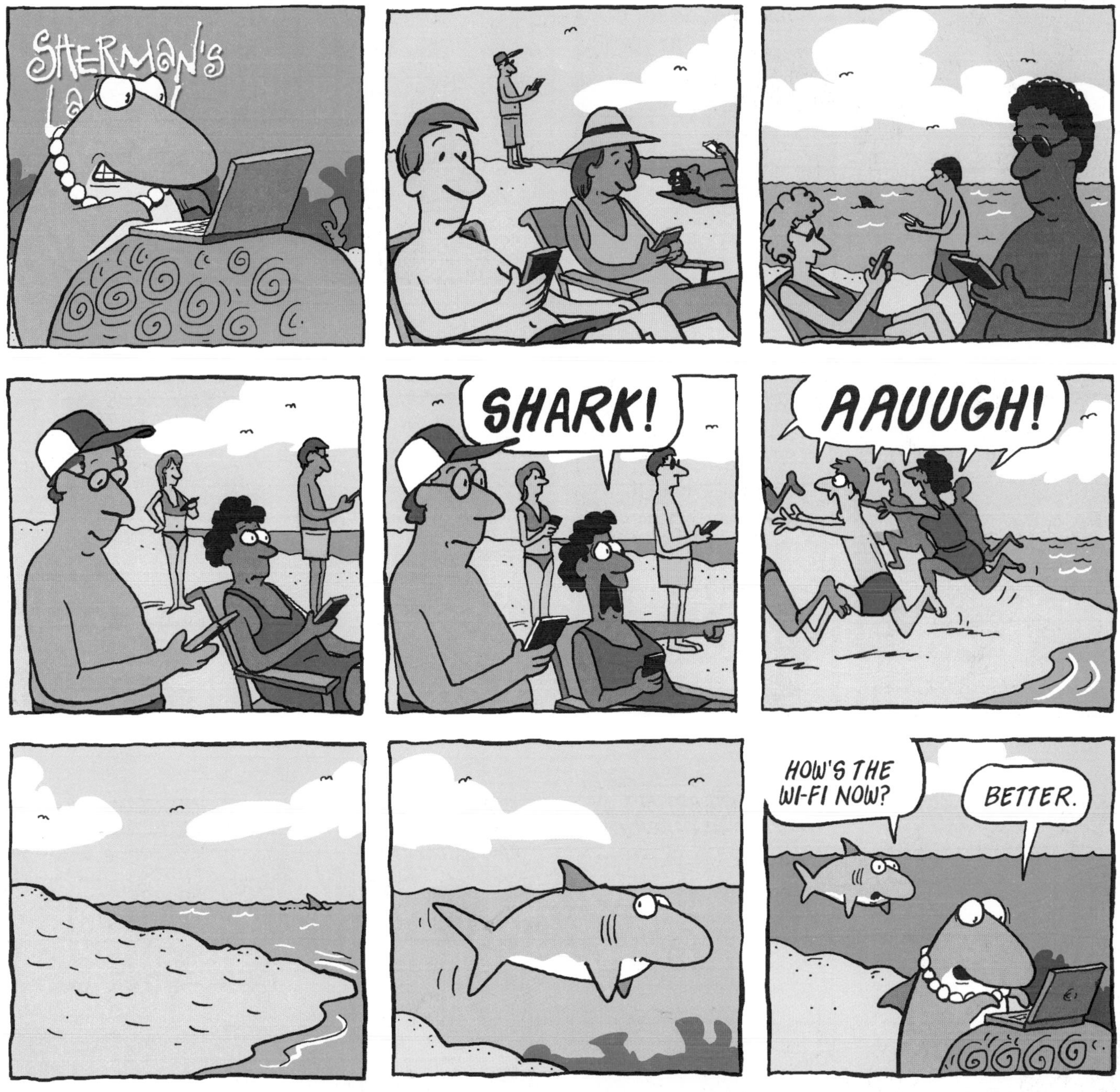
SHERMAN'S
SHARK!
AAUUGH!
HOW'S THE WI-FI NOW?
BETTER.

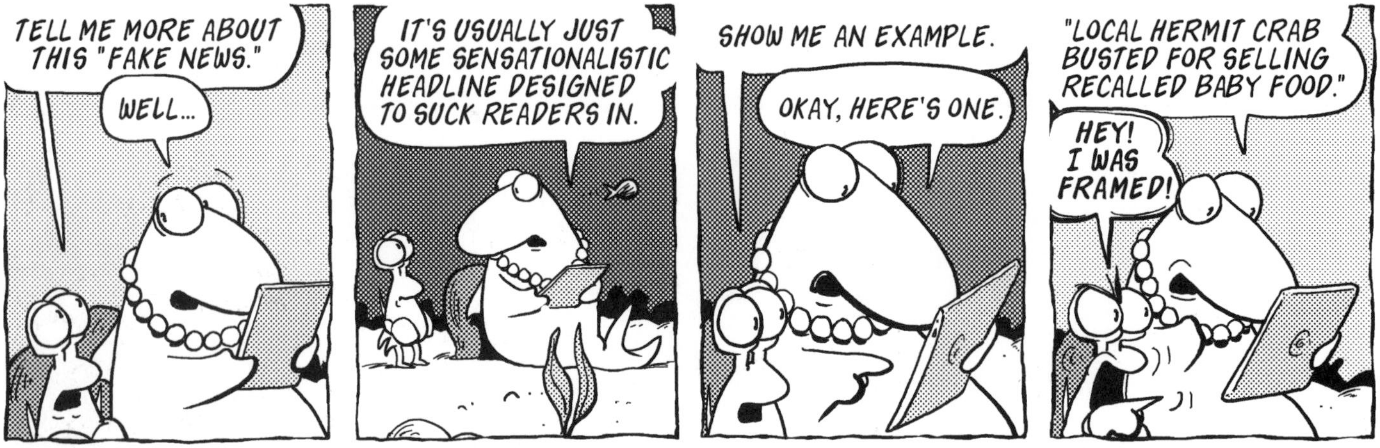
TELL ME MORE ABOUT THIS "FAKE NEWS."
WELL...
IT'S USUALLY JUST SOME SENSATIONALISTIC HEADLINE DESIGNED TO SUCK READERS IN.
SHOW ME AN EXAMPLE.
OKAY, HERE'S ONE.
"LOCAL HERMIT CRAB BUSTED FOR SELLING RECALLED BABY FOOD."
HEY! I WAS FRAMED!

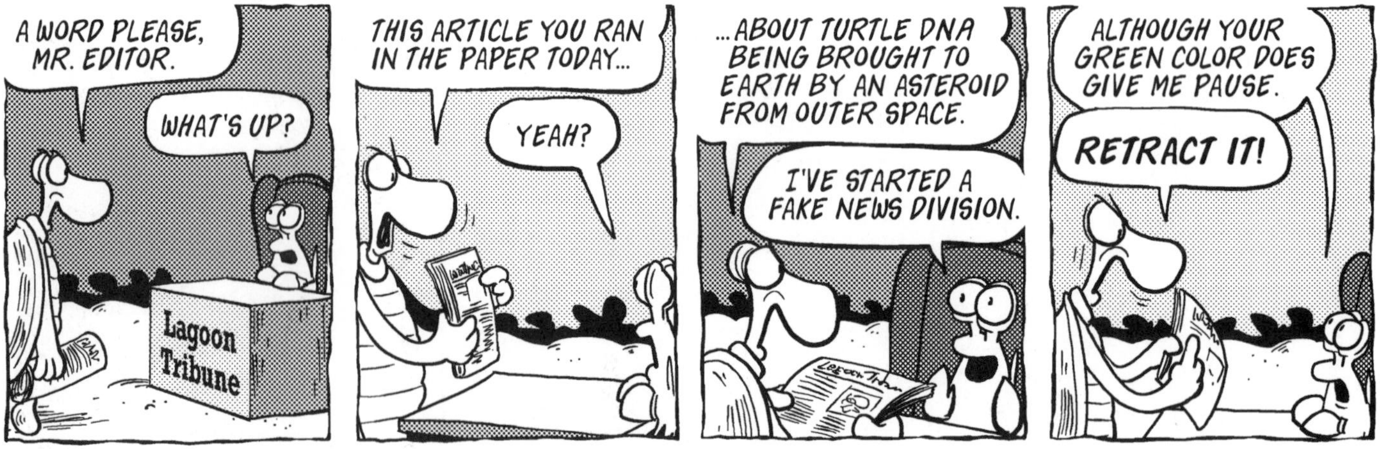
A WORD PLEASE, MR. EDITOR.
WHAT'S UP?
Lagoon Tribune
THIS ARTICLE YOU RAN IN THE PAPER TODAY...
YEAH?
...ABOUT TURTLE DNA BEING BROUGHT TO EARTH BY AN ASTEROID FROM OUTER SPACE.
I'VE STARTED A FAKE NEWS DIVISION.
ALTHOUGH YOUR GREEN COLOR DOES GIVE ME PAUSE.
RETRACT IT!

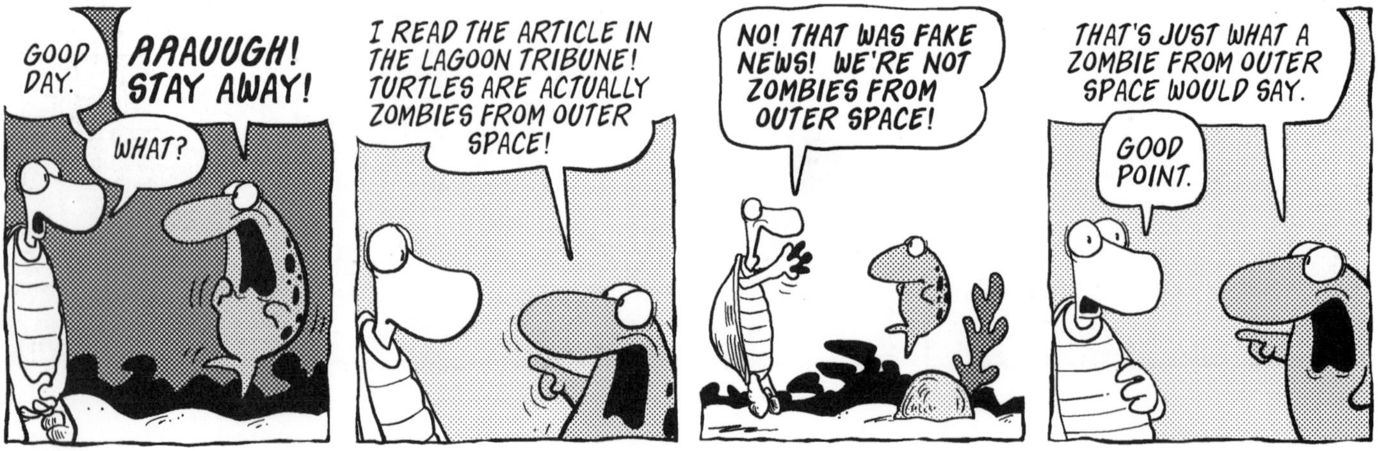
GOOD DAY.
AAAUUGH! STAY AWAY!
WHAT?
I READ THE ARTICLE IN THE LAGOON TRIBUNE! TURTLES ARE ACTUALLY ZOMBIES FROM OUTER SPACE!
NO! THAT WAS FAKE NEWS! WE'RE NOT ZOMBIES FROM OUTER SPACE!
THAT'S JUST WHAT A ZOMBIE FROM OUTER SPACE WOULD SAY.
GOOD POINT.

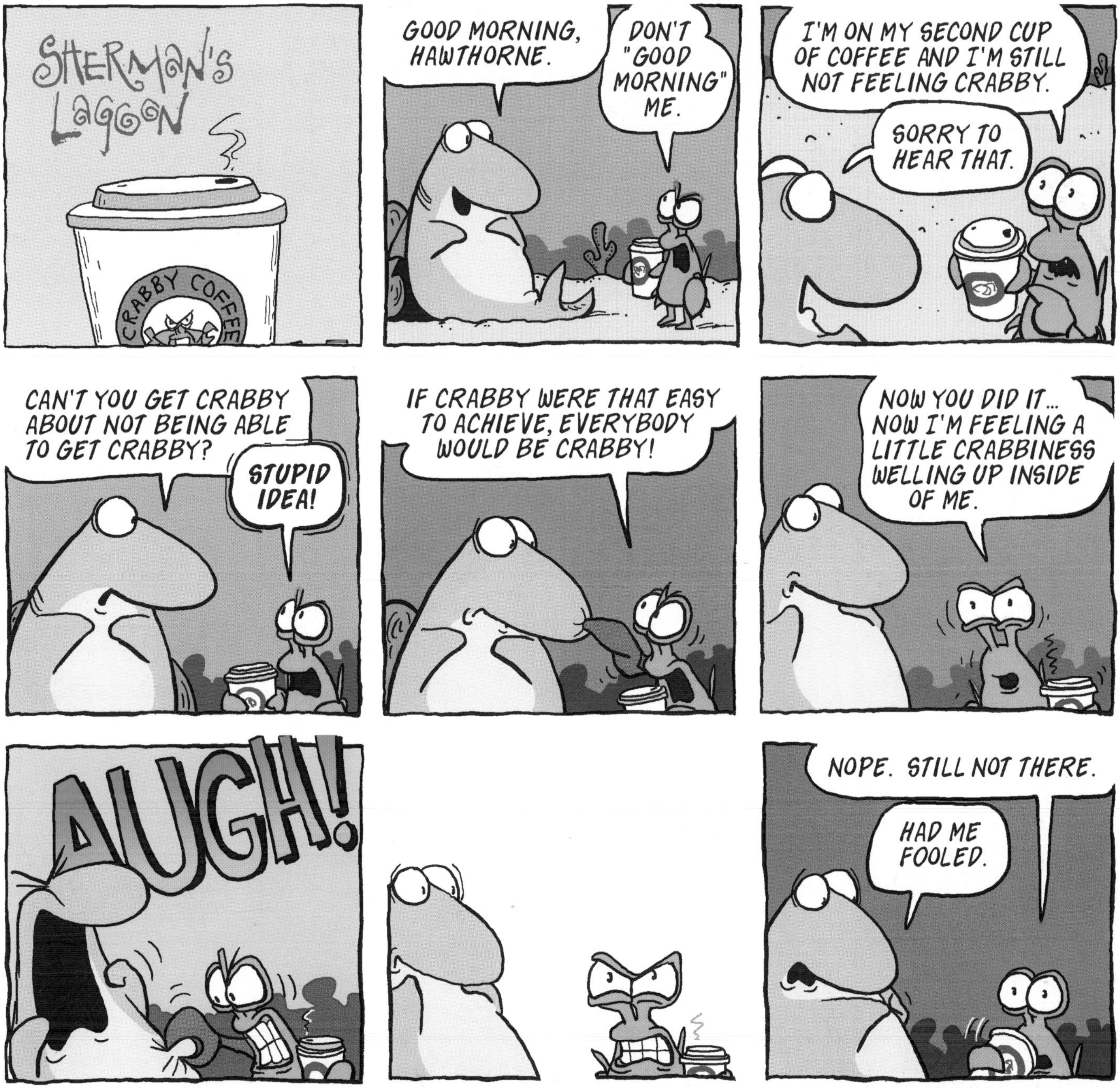
SHERMAN'S LAGOON
CRABBY COFFEE
GOOD MORNING, HAWTHORNE.
DON'T "GOOD MORNING" ME.
I'M ON MY SECOND CUP OF COFFEE AND I'M STILL NOT FEELING CRABBY.
SORRY TO HEAR THAT.
CAN'T YOU GET CRABBY ABOUT NOT BEING ABLE TO GET CRABBY?
STUPID IDEA!
IF CRABBY WERE THAT EASY TO ACHIEVE, EVERYBODY WOULD BE CRABBY!
NOW YOU DID IT... NOW I'M FEELING A LITTLE CRABBINESS WELLING UP INSIDE OF ME.
AUGH!
NOPE. STILL NOT THERE.
HAD ME FOOLED.

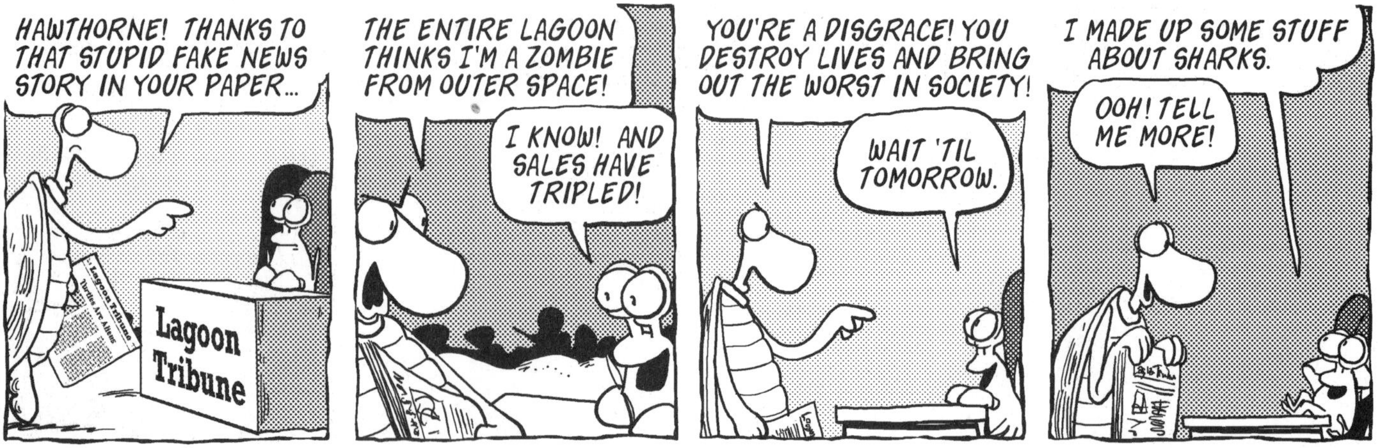
HAWTHORNE! THANKS TO THAT STUPID FAKE NEWS STORY IN YOUR PAPER...
Lagoon Tribune
THE ENTIRE LAGOON THINKS I'M A ZOMBIE FROM OUTER SPACE!
I KNOW! AND SALES HAVE TRIPLED!
YOU'RE A DISGRACE! YOU DESTROY LIVES AND BRING OUT THE WORST IN SOCIETY!
WAIT 'TIL TOMORROW.
I MADE UP SOME STUFF ABOUT SHARKS.
OOH! TELL ME MORE!

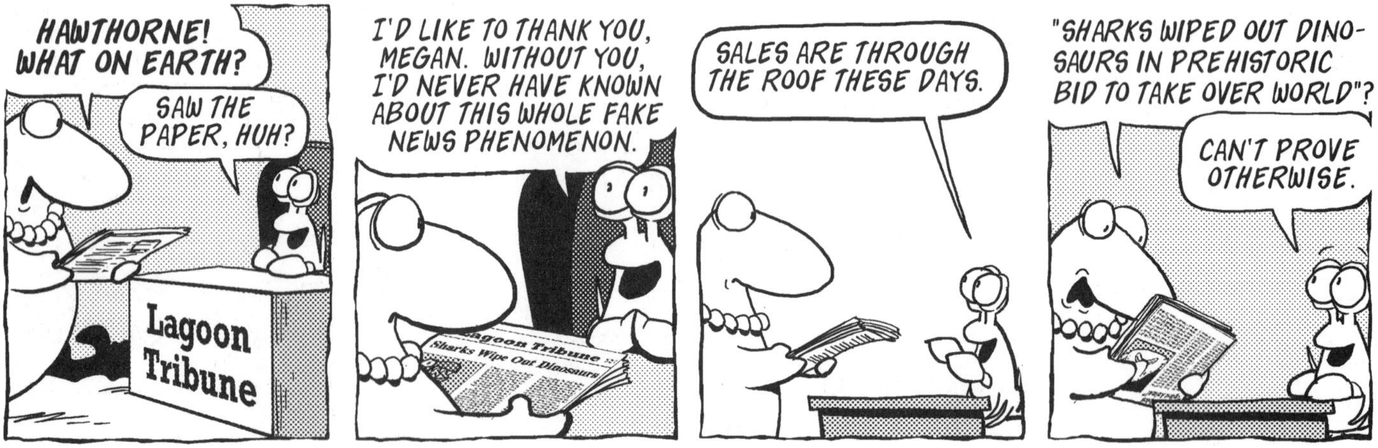
HAWTHORNE! WHAT ON EARTH?
SAW THE PAPER, HUH?
Lagoon Tribune
I'D LIKE TO THANK YOU, MEGAN. WITHOUT YOU, I'D NEVER HAVE KNOWN ABOUT THIS WHOLE FAKE NEWS PHENOMENON.
Lagoon Tribune
Sharks Wipe Out Dinosaurs
SALES ARE THROUGH THE ROOF THESE DAYS.
"SHARKS WIPED OUT DINOSAURS IN PREHISTORIC BID TO TAKE OVER WORLD"?
CAN'T PROVE OTHERWISE.

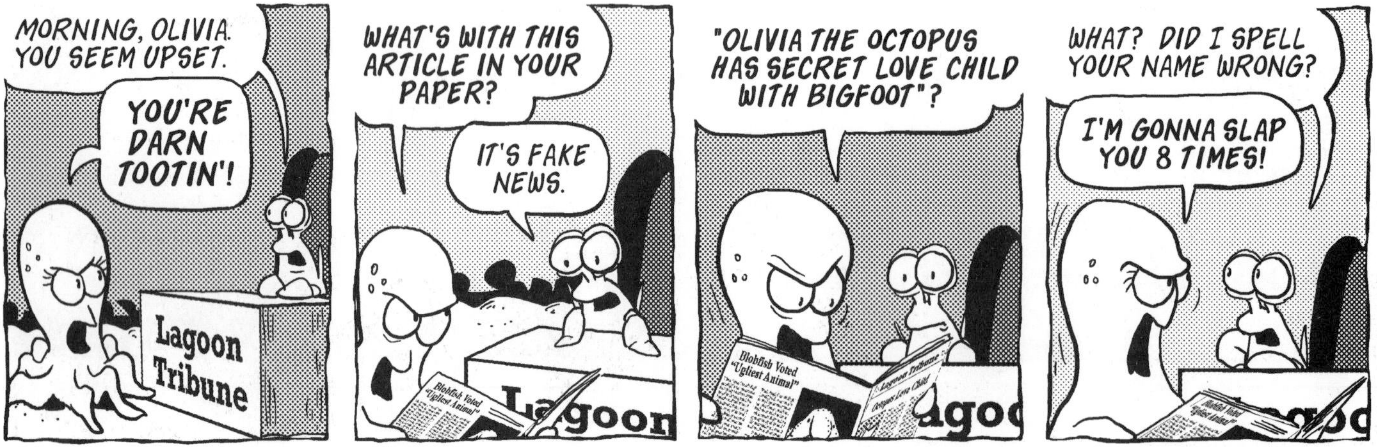
MORNING, OLIVIA. YOU SEEM UPSET.
YOU'RE DARN TOOTIN'!
Lagoon Tribune
WHAT'S WITH THIS ARTICLE IN YOUR PAPER?
IT'S FAKE NEWS.
Blobfish Voted "Ugliest Animal"
Lagoon
"OLIVIA THE OCTOPUS HAS SECRET LOVE CHILD WITH BIGFOOT"?
Blobfish Voted "Ugliest Animal"
Lagoon Tribune
WHAT? DID I SPELL YOUR NAME WRONG?
I'M GONNA SLAP YOU 8 TIMES!

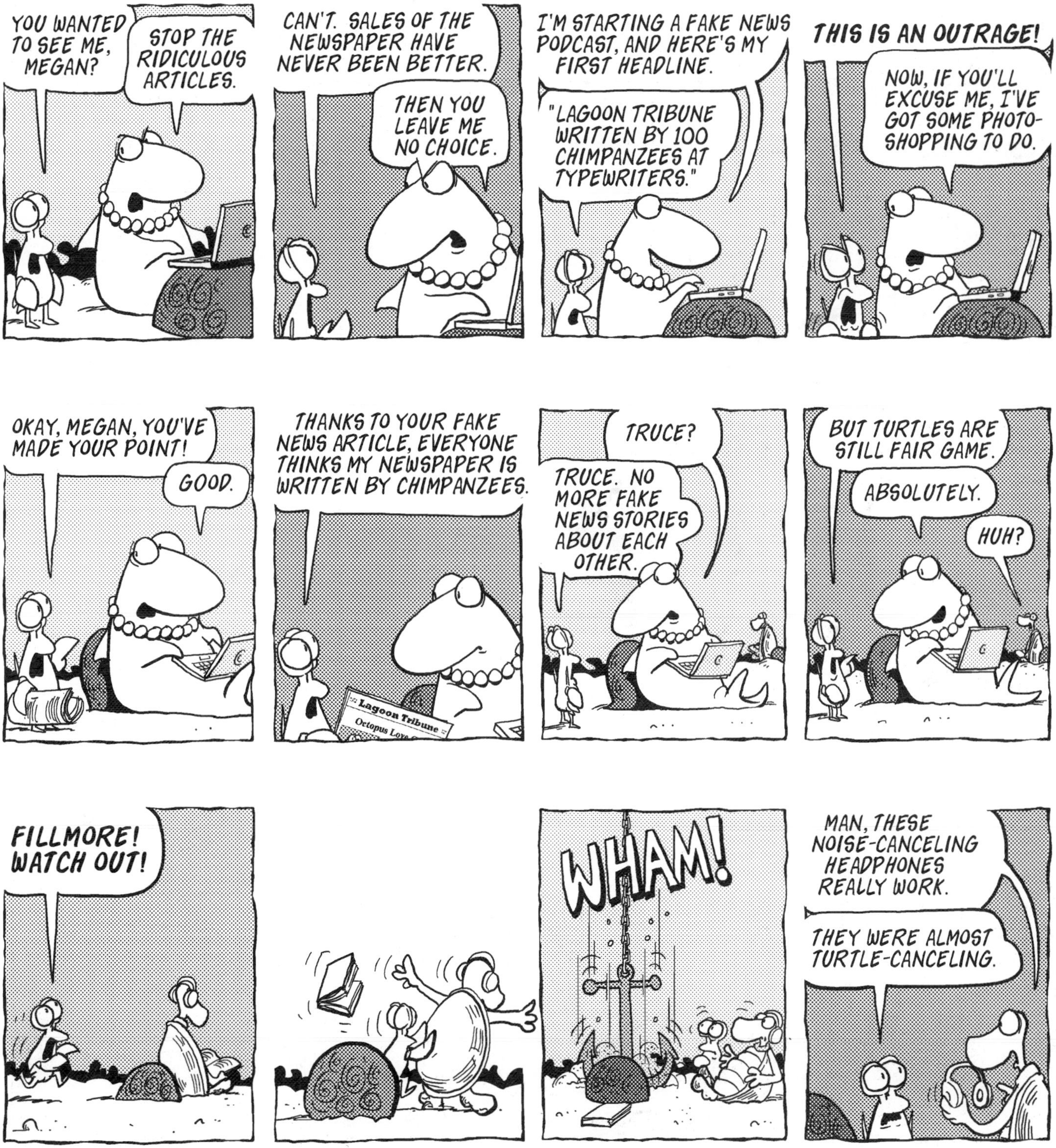
YOU WANTED TO SEE ME, MEGAN?
STOP THE RIDICULOUS ARTICLES.
CAN'T. SALES OF THE NEWSPAPER HAVE NEVER BEEN BETTER.
THEN YOU LEAVE ME NO CHOICE.
I'M STARTING A FAKE NEWS PODCAST, AND HERE'S MY FIRST HEADLINE.
"LAGOON TRIBUNE WRITTEN BY 100 CHIMPANZEES AT TYPEWRITERS."
THIS IS AN OUTRAGE!
NOW, IF YOU'LL EXCUSE ME, I'VE GOT SOME PHOTO-SHOPPING TO DO.
OKAY, MEGAN, YOU'VE MADE YOUR POINT!
GOOD.
THANKS TO YOUR FAKE NEWS ARTICLE, EVERYONE THINKS MY NEWSPAPER IS WRITTEN BY CHIMPANZEES.
Lagoon Tribune
Octopus Love
TRUCE?
TRUCE. NO MORE FAKE NEWS STORIES ABOUT EACH OTHER.
BUT TURTLES ARE STILL FAIR GAME.
ABSOLUTELY.
HUH?
FILLMORE! WATCH OUT!
WHAM!
MAN, THESE NOISE-CANCELING HEADPHONES REALLY WORK.
THEY WERE ALMOST TURTLE-CANCELING.

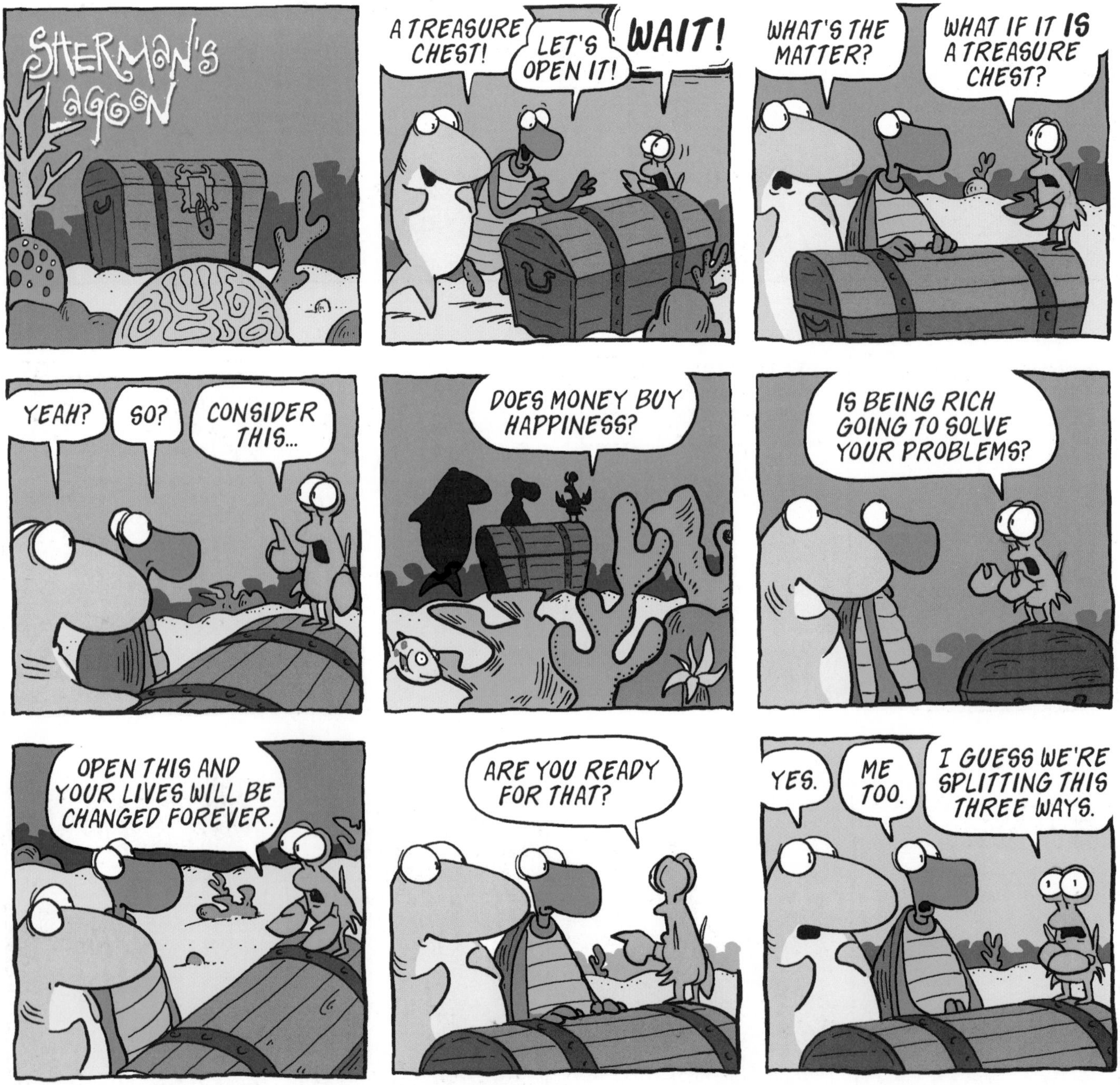
SHERMAN'S LAGOON
A TREASURE CHEST!
LET'S OPEN IT!
WAIT!
WHAT'S THE MATTER?
WHAT IF IT IS A TREASURE CHEST?
YEAH?
SO?
CONSIDER THIS...
DOES MONEY BUY HAPPINESS?
IS BEING RICH GOING TO SOLVE YOUR PROBLEMS?
OPEN THIS AND YOUR LIVES WILL BE CHANGED FOREVER.
ARE YOU READY FOR THAT?
YES.
ME TOO.
I GUESS WE'RE SPLITTING THIS THREE WAYS.

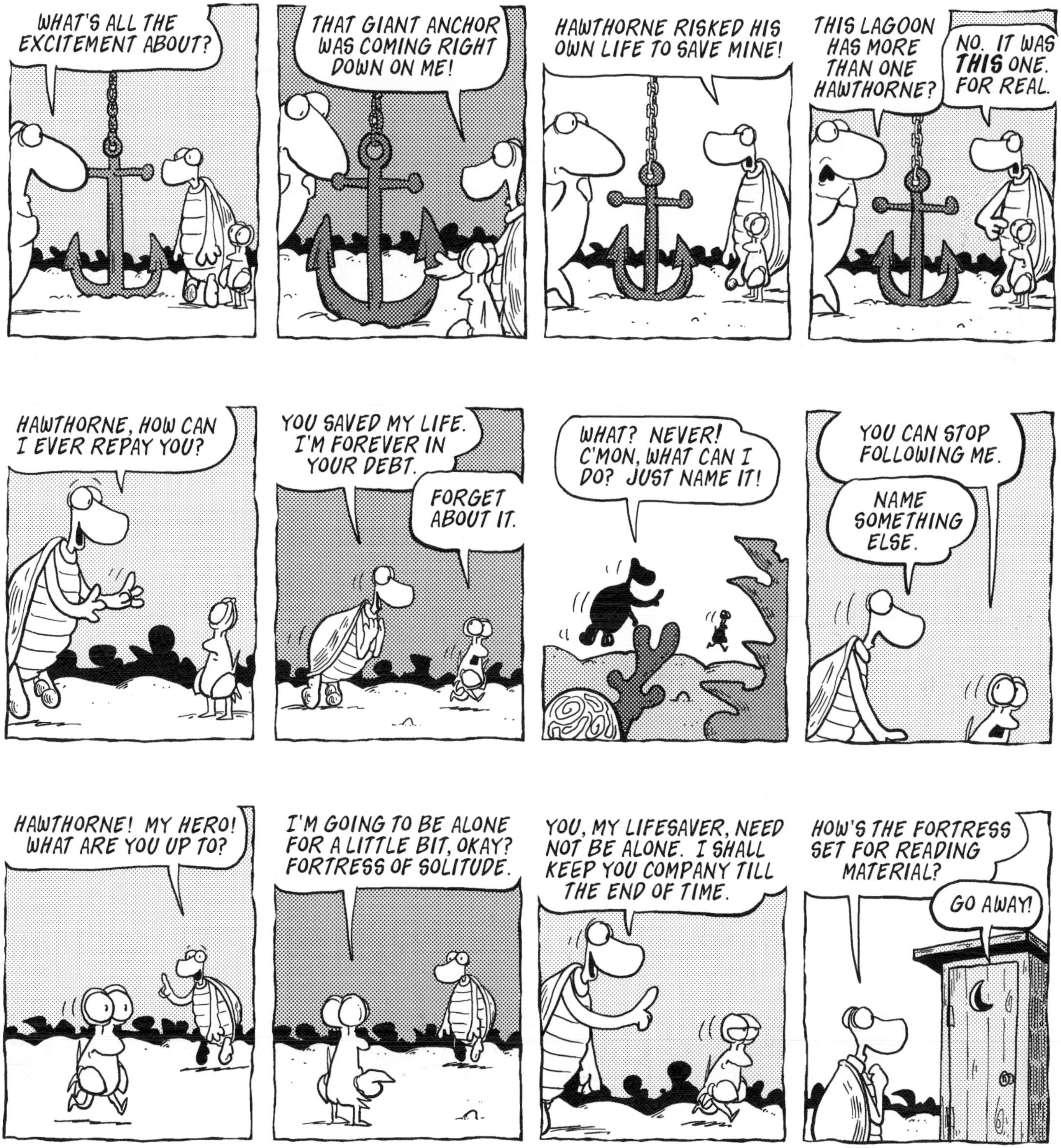
WHAT'S ALL THE EXCITEMENT ABOUT?
THAT GIANT ANCHOR WAS COMING RIGHT DOWN ON ME!
HAWTHORNE RISKED HIS OWN LIFE TO SAVE MINE!
THIS LAGOON HAS MORE THAN ONE HAWTHORNE?
NO. IT WAS **THIS** ONE. FOR REAL.
HAWTHORNE, HOW CAN I EVER REPAY YOU?
YOU SAVED MY LIFE. I'M FOREVER IN YOUR DEBT.
FORGET ABOUT IT.
WHAT? NEVER! C'MON, WHAT CAN I DO? JUST NAME IT!
YOU CAN STOP FOLLOWING ME.
NAME SOMETHING ELSE.
HAWTHORNE! MY HERO! WHAT ARE YOU UP TO?
I'M GOING TO BE ALONE FOR A LITTLE BIT, OKAY? FORTRESS OF SOLITUDE.
YOU, MY LIFESAVER, NEED NOT BE ALONE. I SHALL KEEP YOU COMPANY TILL THE END OF TIME.
HOW'S THE FORTRESS SET FOR READING MATERIAL?
GO AWAY!

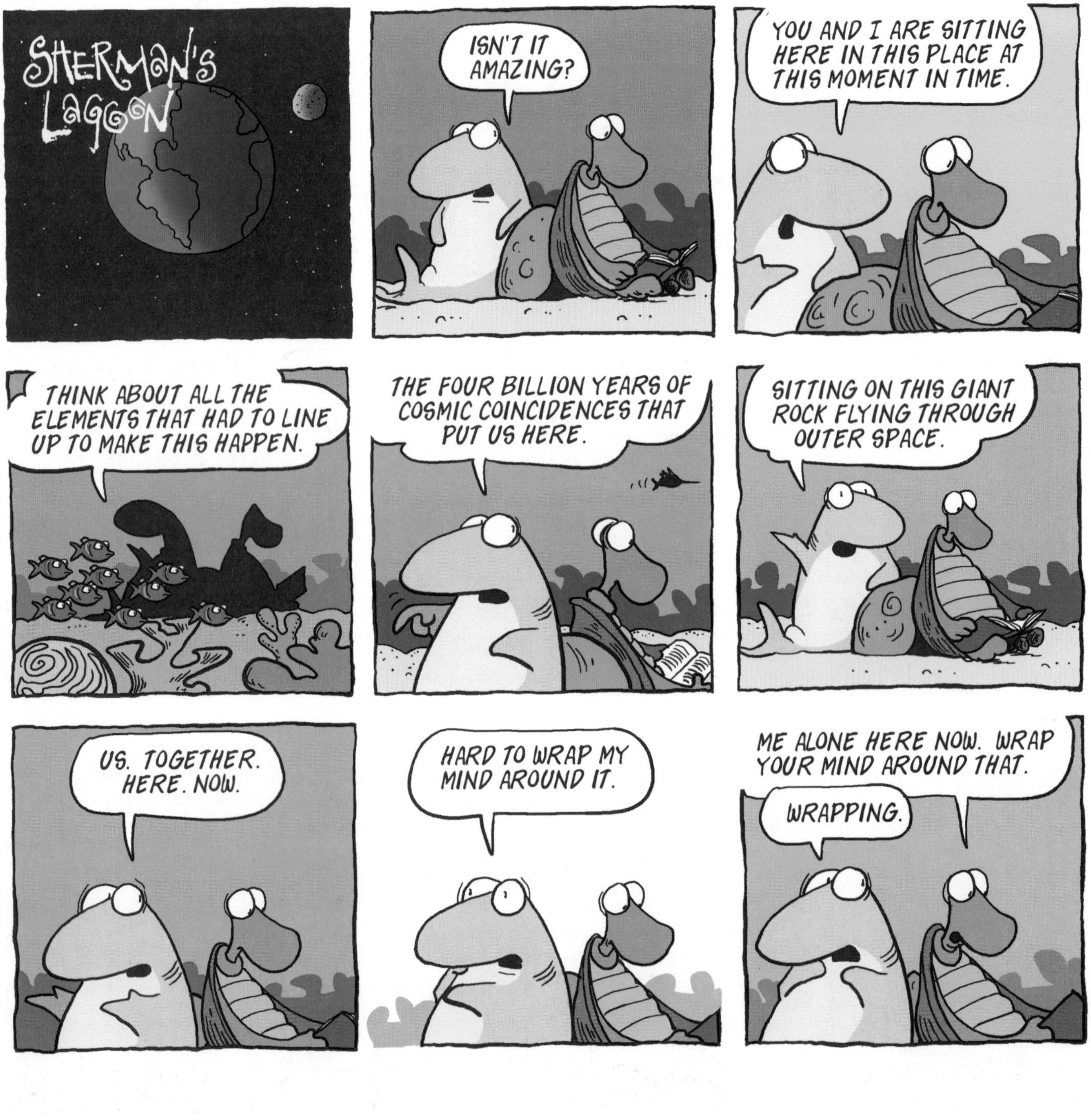
SHERMAN'S LAGOON
ISN'T IT AMAZING?
YOU AND I ARE SITTING HERE IN THIS PLACE AT THIS MOMENT IN TIME.
THINK ABOUT ALL THE ELEMENTS THAT HAD TO LINE UP TO MAKE THIS HAPPEN.
THE FOUR BILLION YEARS OF COSMIC COINCIDENCES THAT PUT US HERE.
SITTING ON THIS GIANT ROCK FLYING THROUGH OUTER SPACE.
US. TOGETHER. HERE. NOW.
HARD TO WRAP MY MIND AROUND IT.
ME ALONE HERE NOW. WRAP YOUR MIND AROUND THAT.
WRAPPING.

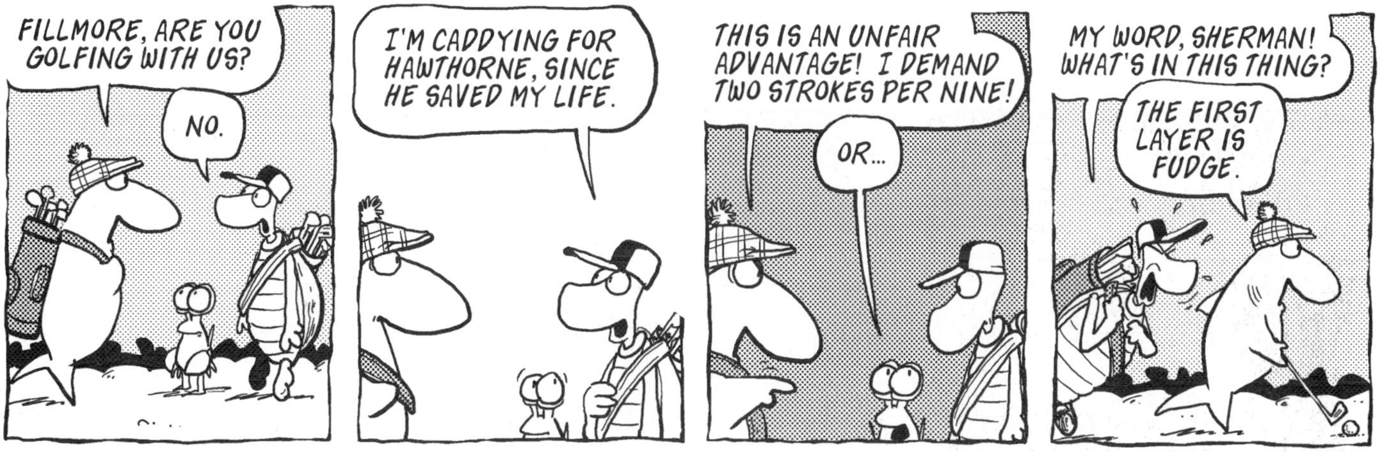
FILLMORE, ARE YOU GOLFING WITH US?
NO.
I'M CADDYING FOR HAWTHORNE, SINCE HE SAVED MY LIFE.
THIS IS AN UNFAIR ADVANTAGE! I DEMAND TWO STROKES PER NINE!
OR...
MY WORD, SHERMAN! WHAT'S IN THIS THING?
THE FIRST LAYER IS FUDGE.

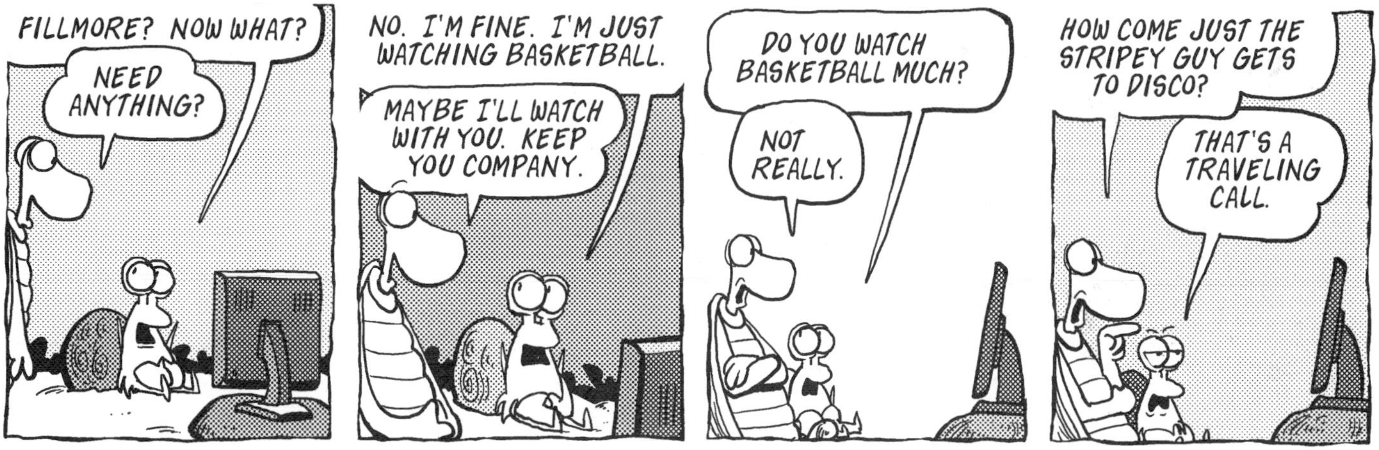
FILLMORE? NOW WHAT?
NEED ANYTHING?
NO. I'M FINE. I'M JUST WATCHING BASKETBALL.
MAYBE I'LL WATCH WITH YOU. KEEP YOU COMPANY.
DO YOU WATCH BASKETBALL MUCH?
NOT REALLY.
HOW COME JUST THE STRIPEY GUY GETS TO DISCO?
THAT'S A TRAVELING CALL.

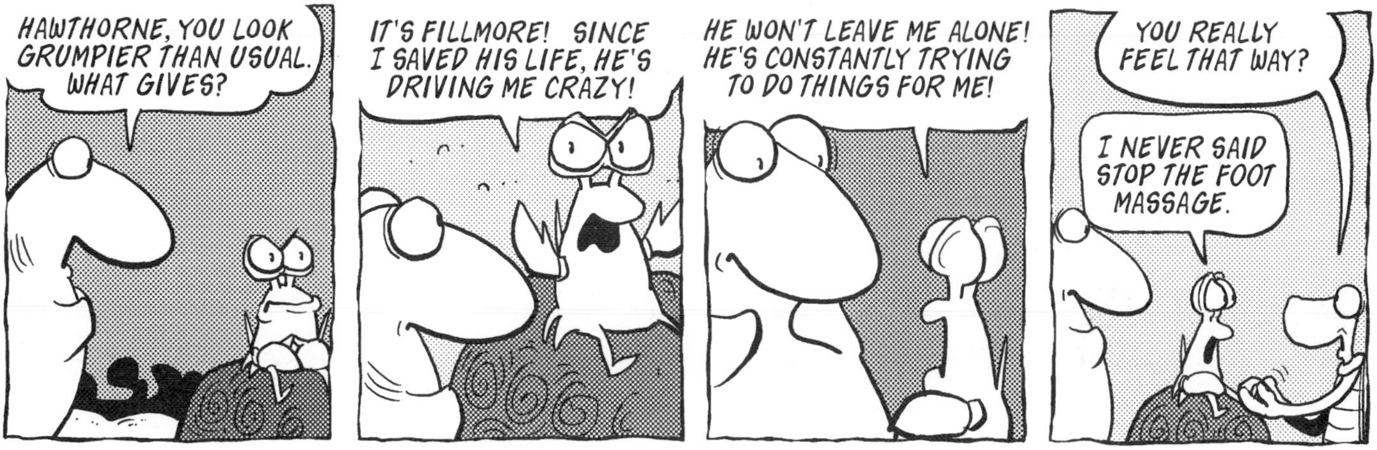
HAWTHORNE, YOU LOOK GRUMPIER THAN USUAL. WHAT GIVES?
IT'S FILLMORE! SINCE I SAVED HIS LIFE, HE'S DRIVING ME CRAZY!
HE WON'T LEAVE ME ALONE! HE'S CONSTANTLY TRYING TO DO THINGS FOR ME!
YOU REALLY FEEL THAT WAY?
I NEVER SAID STOP THE FOOT MASSAGE.

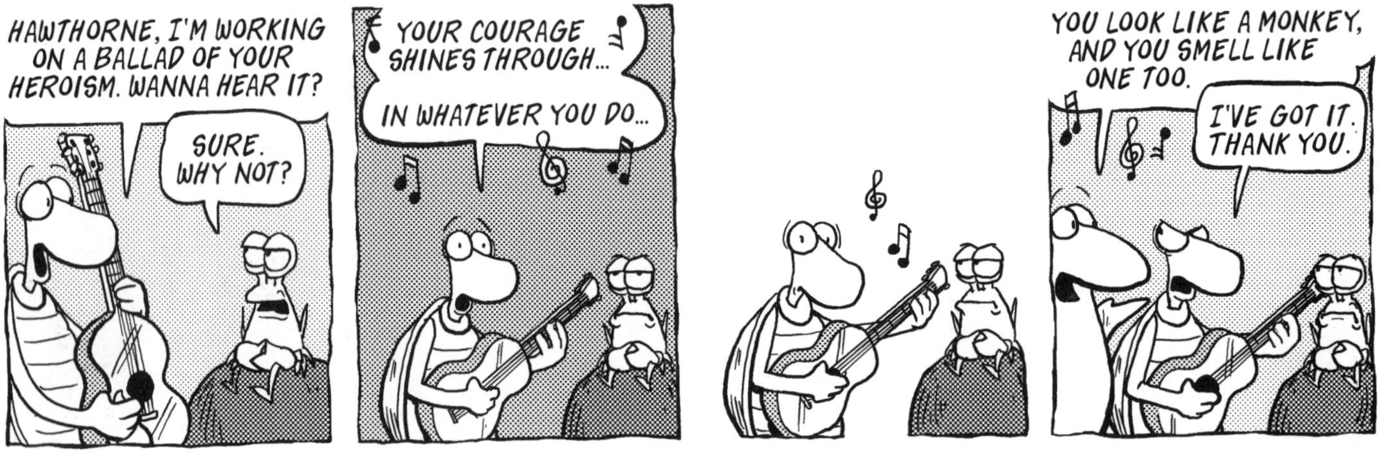
HAWTHORNE, I'M WORKING ON A BALLAD OF YOUR HEROISM. WANNA HEAR IT?
SURE. WHY NOT?
YOUR COURAGE SHINES THROUGH...
IN WHATEVER YOU DO...
YOU LOOK LIKE A MONKEY, AND YOU SMELL LIKE ONE TOO.
I'VE GOT IT. THANK YOU.

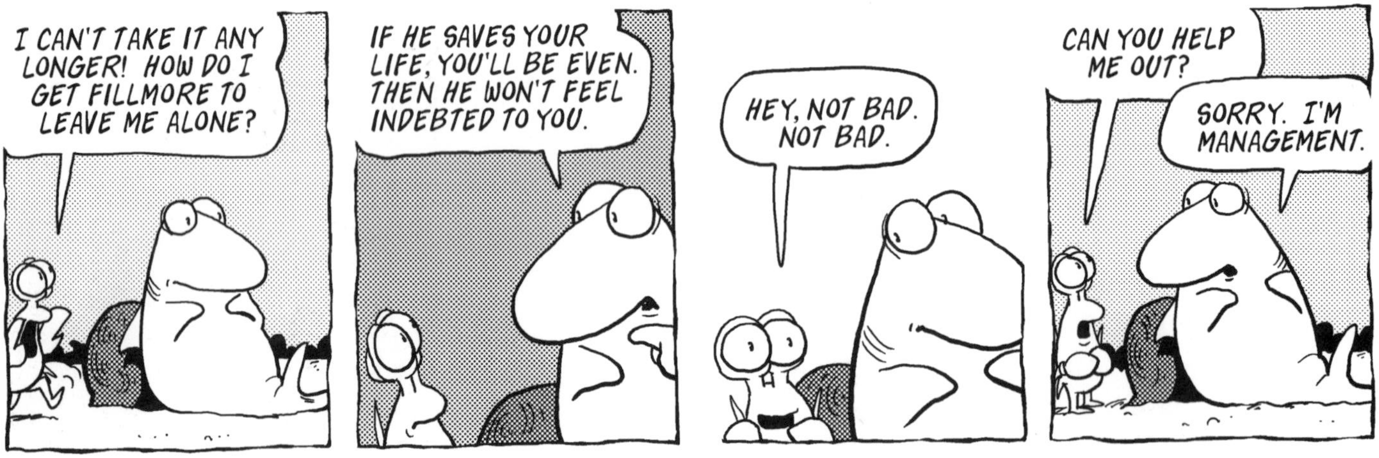
I CAN'T TAKE IT ANY LONGER! HOW DO I GET FILLMORE TO LEAVE ME ALONE?
IF HE SAVES YOUR LIFE, YOU'LL BE EVEN. THEN HE WON'T FEEL INDEBTED TO YOU.
HEY, NOT BAD. NOT BAD.
CAN YOU HELP ME OUT?
SORRY. I'M MANAGEMENT.

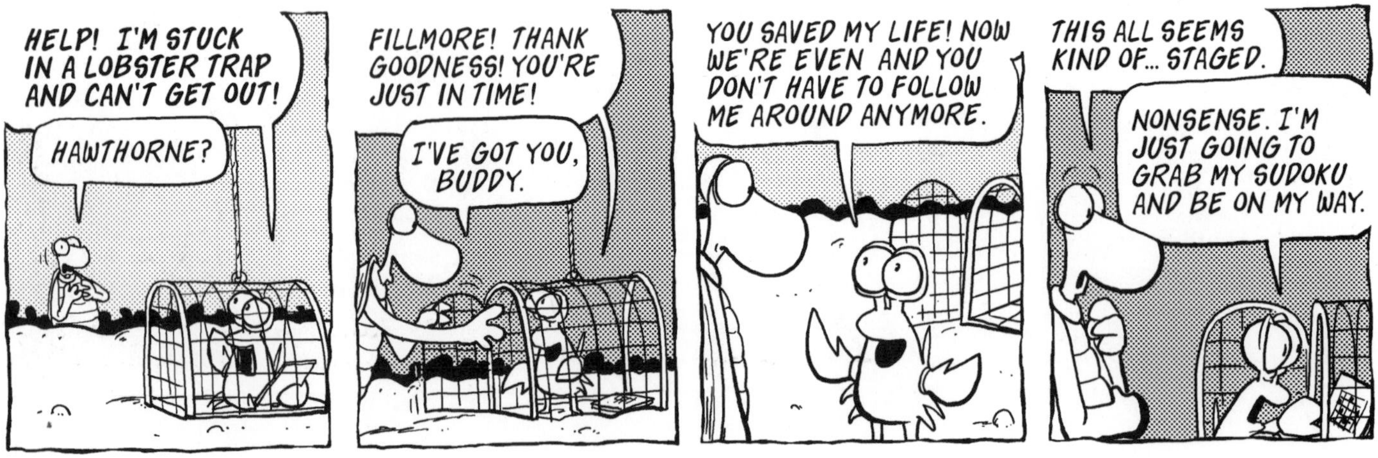
HELP! I'M STUCK IN A LOBSTER TRAP AND CAN'T GET OUT!
HAWTHORNE?
FILLMORE! THANK GOODNESS! YOU'RE JUST IN TIME!
I'VE GOT YOU, BUDDY.
YOU SAVED MY LIFE! NOW WE'RE EVEN AND YOU DON'T HAVE TO FOLLOW ME AROUND ANYMORE.
THIS ALL SEEMS KIND OF... STAGED.
NONSENSE. I'M JUST GOING TO GRAB MY SUDOKU AND BE ON MY WAY.

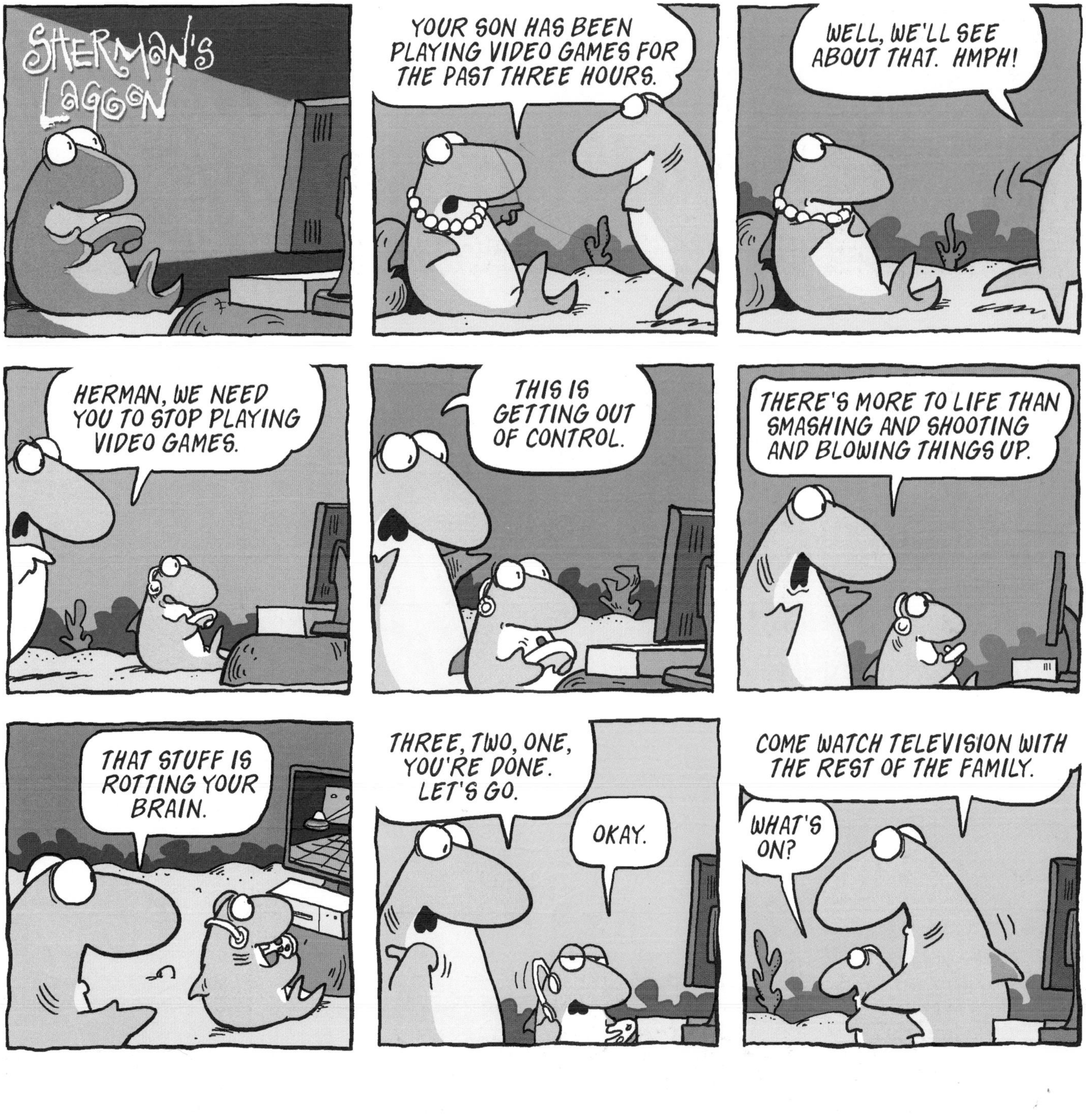
SHERMAN'S LAGOON
YOUR SON HAS BEEN PLAYING VIDEO GAMES FOR THE PAST THREE HOURS.
WELL, WE'LL SEE ABOUT THAT. HMPH!
HERMAN, WE NEED YOU TO STOP PLAYING VIDEO GAMES.
THIS IS GETTING OUT OF CONTROL.
THERE'S MORE TO LIFE THAN SMASHING AND SHOOTING AND BLOWING THINGS UP.
THAT STUFF IS ROTTING YOUR BRAIN.
THREE, TWO, ONE, YOU'RE DONE. LET'S GO.
OKAY.
COME WATCH TELEVISION WITH THE REST OF THE FAMILY.
WHAT'S ON?

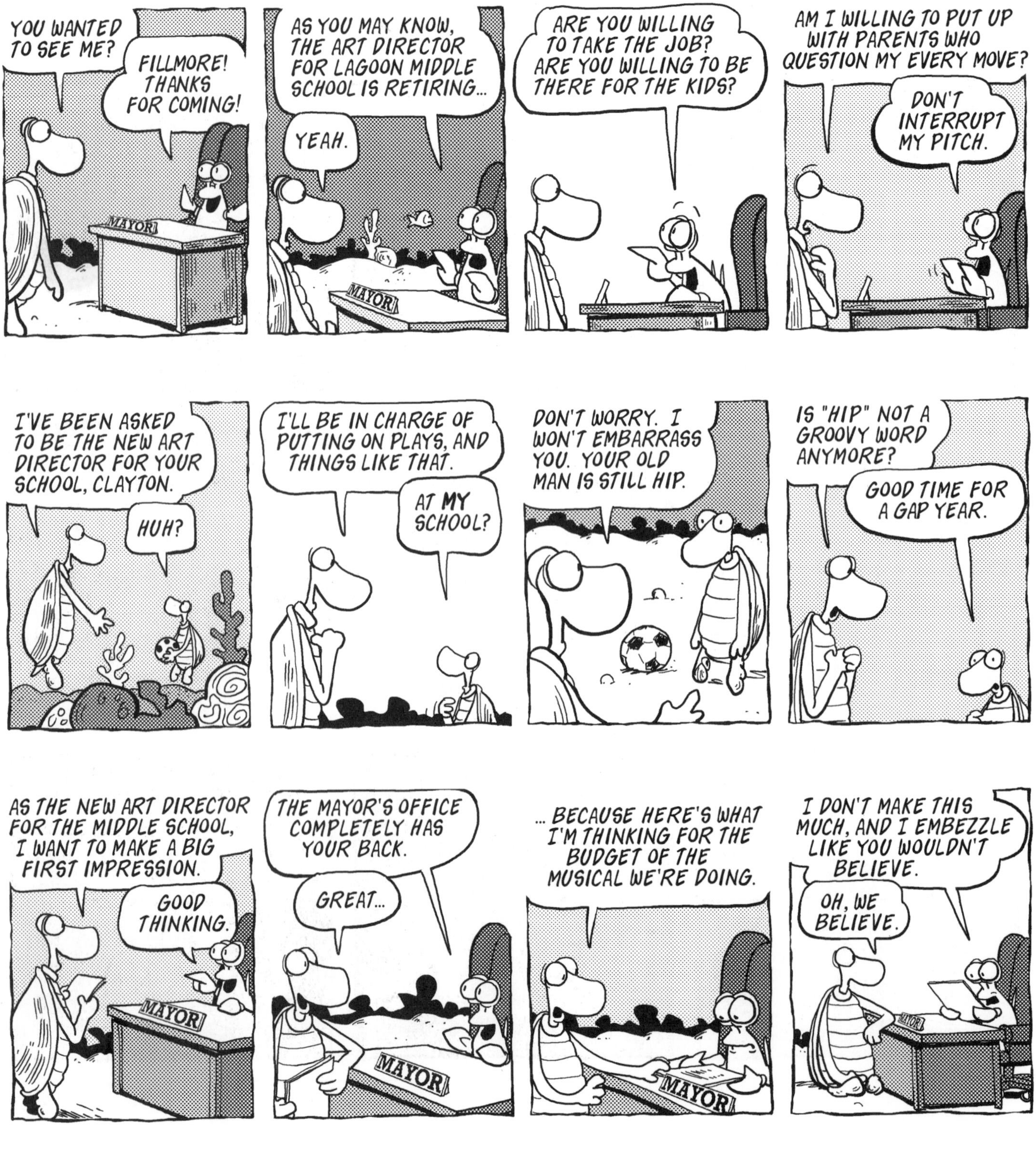
YOU WANTED TO SEE ME?
FILLMORE! THANKS FOR COMING!
MAYOR
AS YOU MAY KNOW, THE ART DIRECTOR FOR LAGOON MIDDLE SCHOOL IS RETIRING...
YEAH.
MAYOR
ARE YOU WILLING TO TAKE THE JOB? ARE YOU WILLING TO BE THERE FOR THE KIDS?
AM I WILLING TO PUT UP WITH PARENTS WHO QUESTION MY EVERY MOVE?
DON'T INTERRUPT MY PITCH.
I'VE BEEN ASKED TO BE THE NEW ART DIRECTOR FOR YOUR SCHOOL, CLAYTON.
HUH?
I'LL BE IN CHARGE OF PUTTING ON PLAYS, AND THINGS LIKE THAT.
AT **MY** SCHOOL?
DON'T WORRY. I WON'T EMBARRASS YOU. YOUR OLD MAN IS STILL HIP.
IS "HIP" NOT A GROOVY WORD ANYMORE?
GOOD TIME FOR A GAP YEAR.
AS THE NEW ART DIRECTOR FOR THE MIDDLE SCHOOL, I WANT TO MAKE A BIG FIRST IMPRESSION.
GOOD THINKING.
MAYOR
THE MAYOR'S OFFICE COMPLETELY HAS YOUR BACK.
GREAT...
MAYOR
... BECAUSE HERE'S WHAT I'M THINKING FOR THE BUDGET OF THE MUSICAL WE'RE DOING.
MAYOR
I DON'T MAKE THIS MUCH, AND I EMBEZZLE LIKE YOU WOULDN'T BELIEVE.
OH, WE BELIEVE.
MAYOR

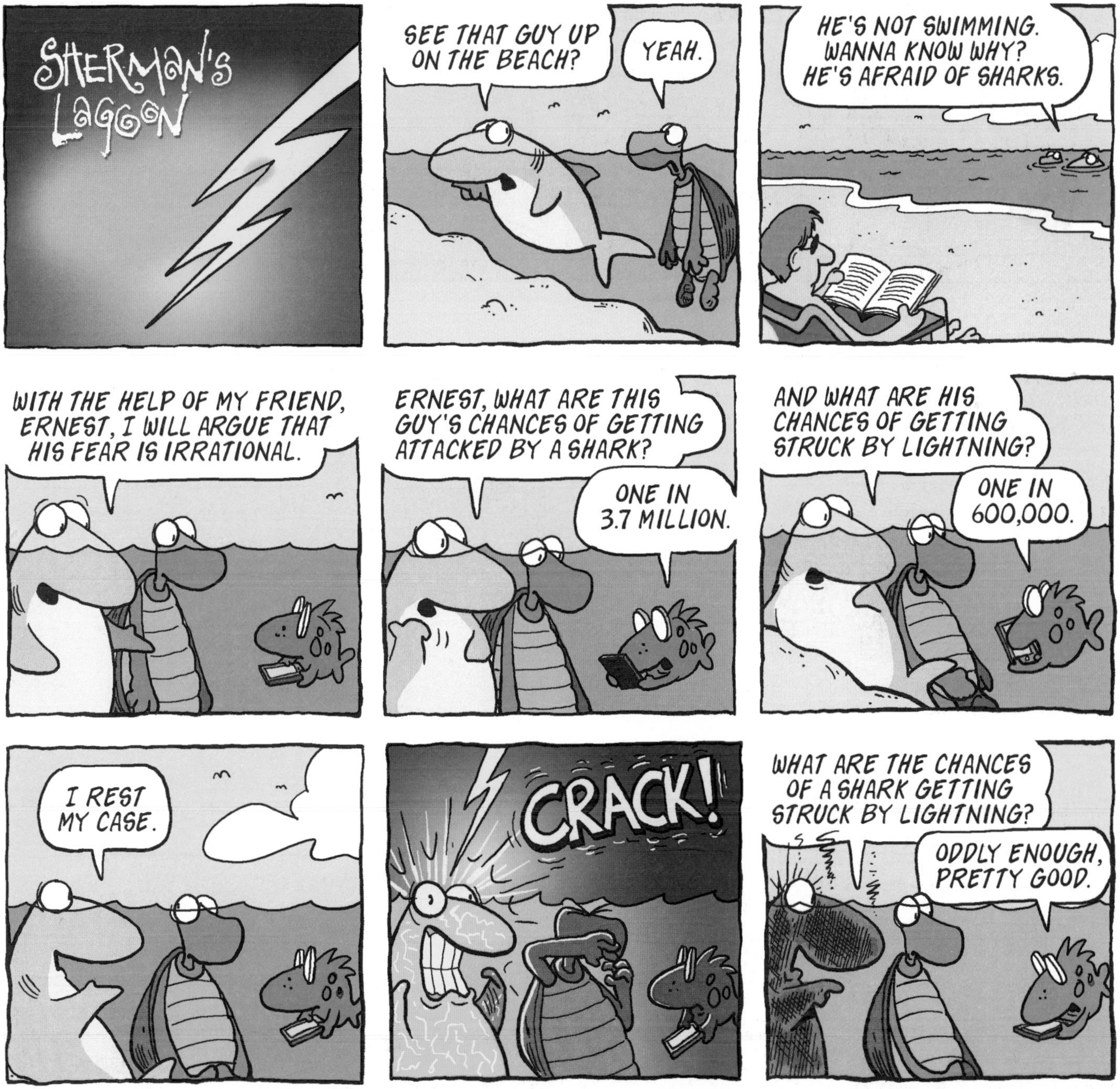
SHERMAN'S LAGOON
SEE THAT GUY UP ON THE BEACH?
YEAH.
HE'S NOT SWIMMING. WANNA KNOW WHY? HE'S AFRAID OF SHARKS.
WITH THE HELP OF MY FRIEND, ERNEST, I WILL ARGUE THAT HIS FEAR IS IRRATIONAL.
ERNEST, WHAT ARE THIS GUY'S CHANCES OF GETTING ATTACKED BY A SHARK?
ONE IN 3.7 MILLION.
AND WHAT ARE HIS CHANCES OF GETTING STRUCK BY LIGHTNING?
ONE IN 600,000.
I REST MY CASE.
CRACK!
WHAT ARE THE CHANCES OF A SHARK GETTING STRUCK BY LIGHTNING?
ODDLY ENOUGH, PRETTY GOOD.

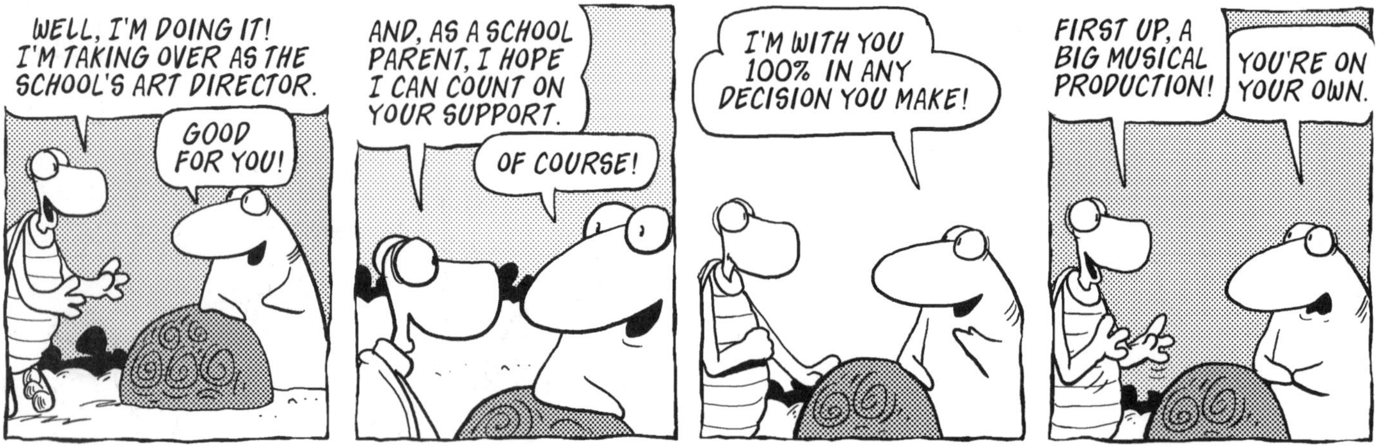
WELL, I'M DOING IT! I'M TAKING OVER AS THE SCHOOL'S ART DIRECTOR.
GOOD FOR YOU!
AND, AS A SCHOOL PARENT, I HOPE I CAN COUNT ON YOUR SUPPORT.
OF COURSE!
I'M WITH YOU 100% IN ANY DECISION YOU MAKE!
FIRST UP, A BIG MUSICAL PRODUCTION!
YOU'RE ON YOUR OWN.

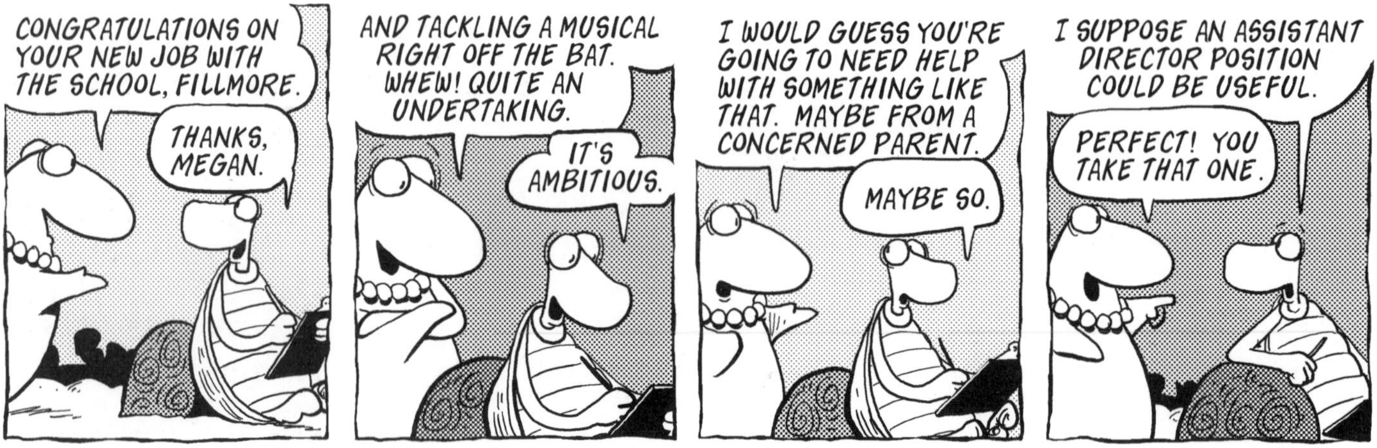
CONGRATULATIONS ON YOUR NEW JOB WITH THE SCHOOL, FILLMORE.
THANKS, MEGAN.
AND TACKLING A MUSICAL RIGHT OFF THE BAT. WHEW! QUITE AN UNDERTAKING.
IT'S AMBITIOUS.
I WOULD GUESS YOU'RE GOING TO NEED HELP WITH SOMETHING LIKE THAT. MAYBE FROM A CONCERNED PARENT.
MAYBE SO.
I SUPPOSE AN ASSISTANT DIRECTOR POSITION COULD BE USEFUL.
PERFECT! YOU TAKE THAT ONE.

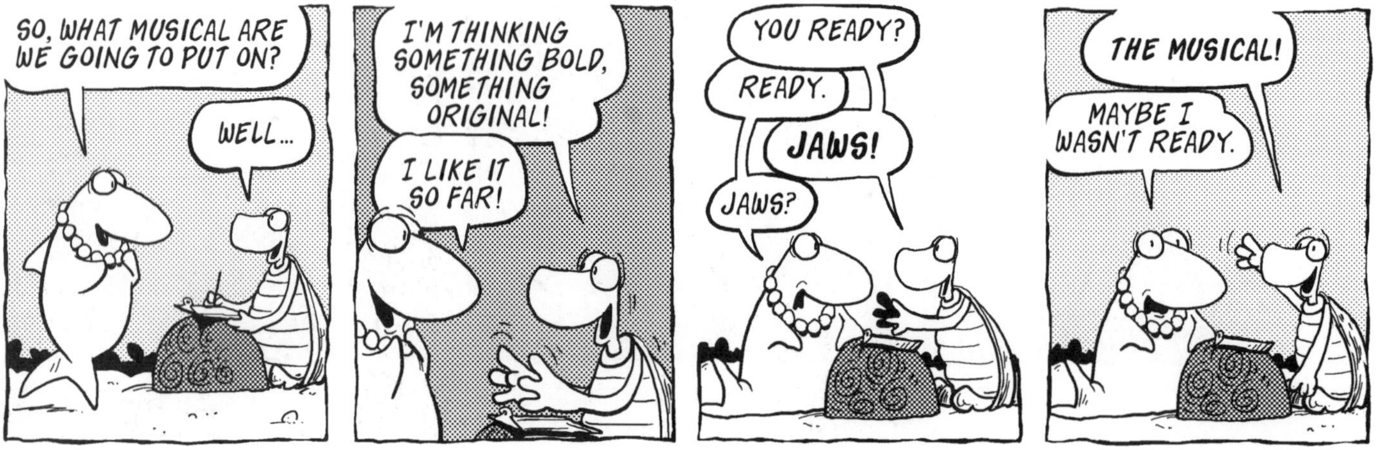
SO, WHAT MUSICAL ARE WE GOING TO PUT ON?
WELL...
I'M THINKING SOMETHING BOLD, SOMETHING ORIGINAL!
I LIKE IT SO FAR!
YOU READY?
READY.
JAWS!
JAWS?
THE MUSICAL!
MAYBE I WASN'T READY.

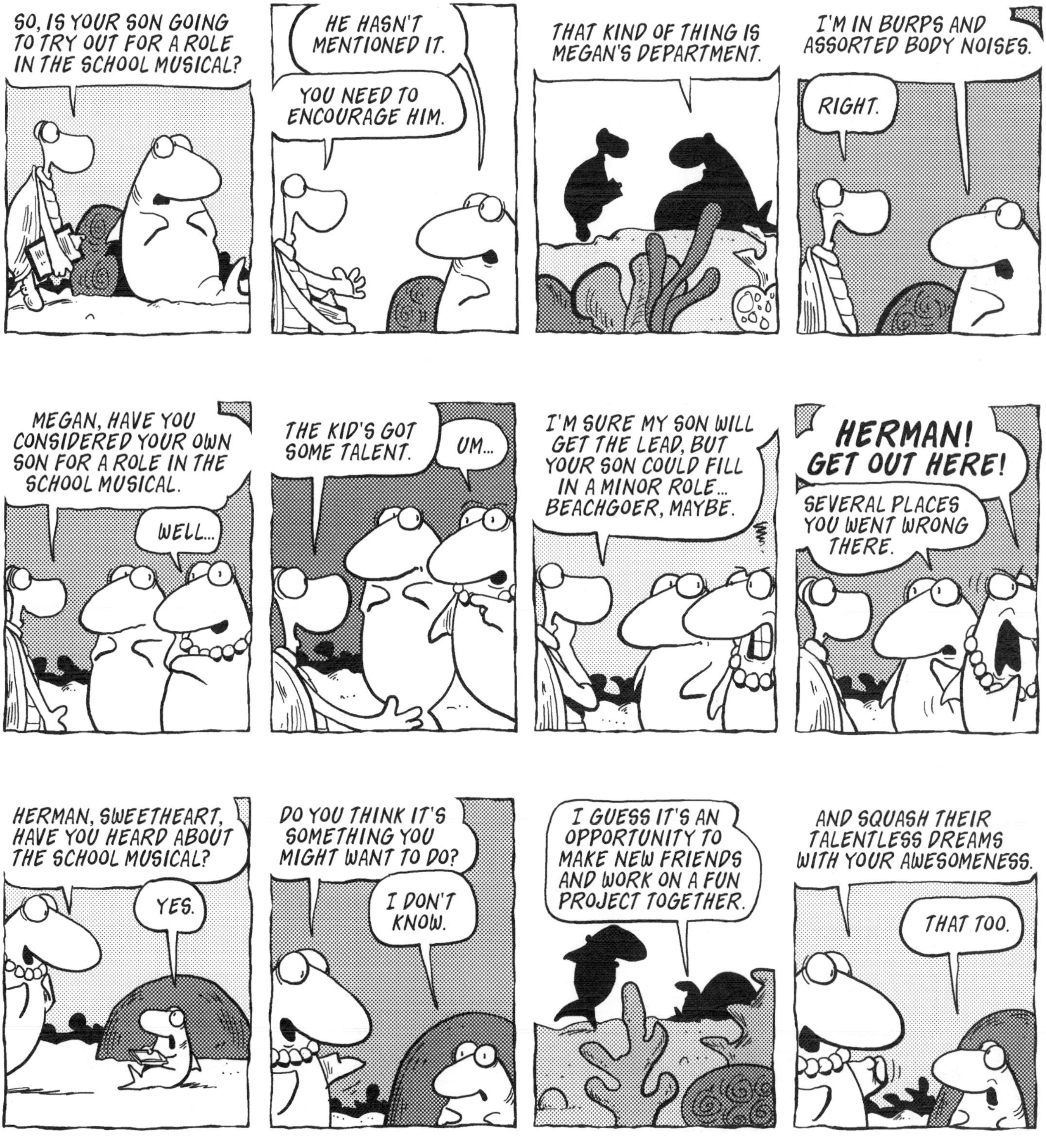
SO, IS YOUR SON GOING TO TRY OUT FOR A ROLE IN THE SCHOOL MUSICAL?
HE HASN'T MENTIONED IT.
YOU NEED TO ENCOURAGE HIM.
THAT KIND OF THING IS MEGAN'S DEPARTMENT.
I'M IN BURPS AND ASSORTED BODY NOISES.
RIGHT.
MEGAN, HAVE YOU CONSIDERED YOUR OWN SON FOR A ROLE IN THE SCHOOL MUSICAL.
WELL...
THE KID'S GOT SOME TALENT.
UM...
I'M SURE MY SON WILL GET THE LEAD, BUT YOUR SON COULD FILL IN A MINOR ROLE... BEACHGOER, MAYBE.
HERMAN! GET OUT HERE!
SEVERAL PLACES YOU WENT WRONG THERE.
HERMAN, SWEETHEART, HAVE YOU HEARD ABOUT THE SCHOOL MUSICAL?
YES.
DO YOU THINK IT'S SOMETHING YOU MIGHT WANT TO DO?
I DON'T KNOW.
I GUESS IT'S AN OPPORTUNITY TO MAKE NEW FRIENDS AND WORK ON A FUN PROJECT TOGETHER.
AND SQUASH THEIR TALENTLESS DREAMS WITH YOUR AWESOMENESS.
THAT TOO.

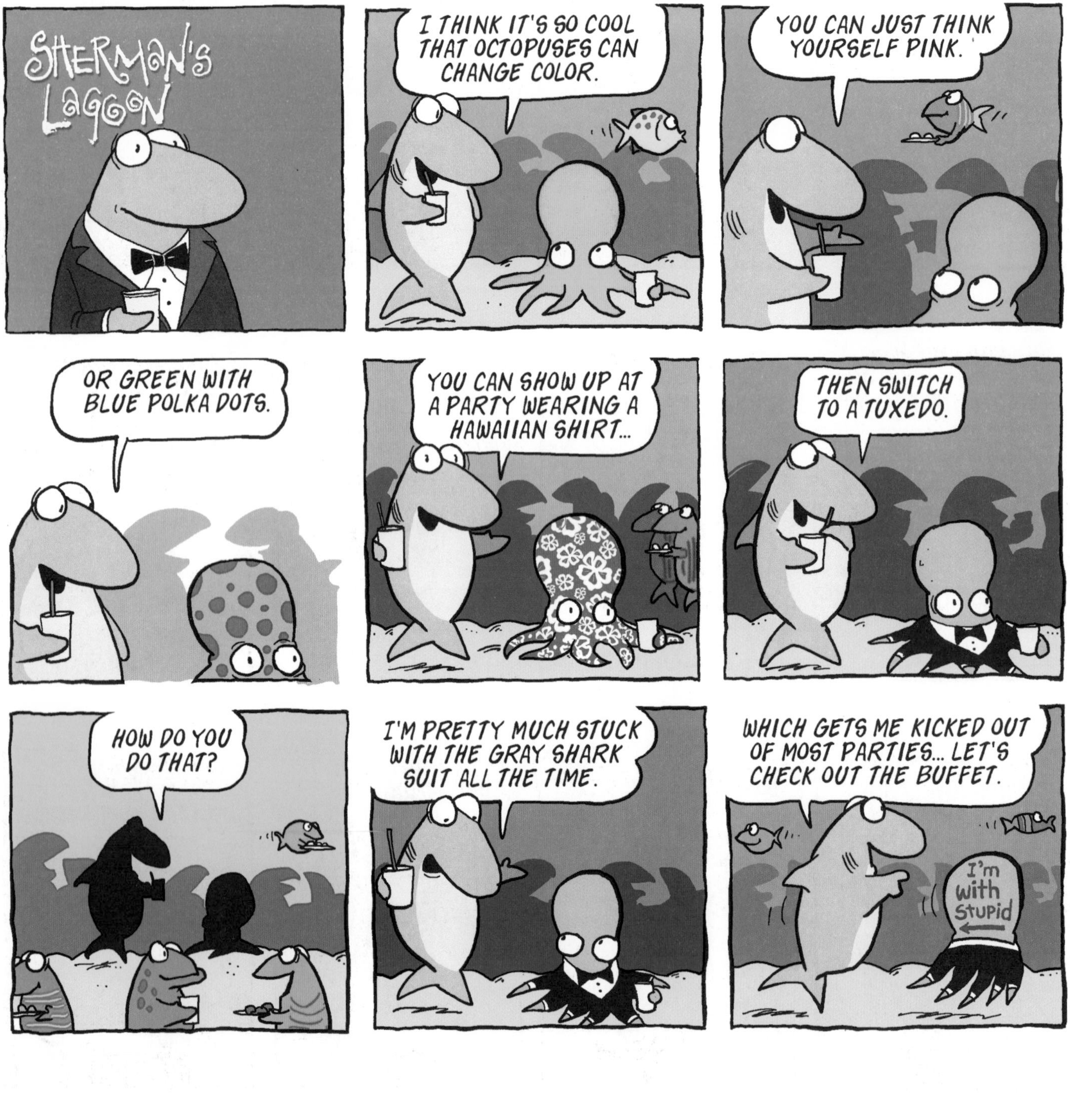
SHERMAN'S LAGOON
I THINK IT'S SO COOL THAT OCTOPUSES CAN CHANGE COLOR.
YOU CAN JUST THINK YOURSELF PINK.
OR GREEN WITH BLUE POLKA DOTS.
YOU CAN SHOW UP AT A PARTY WEARING A HAWAIIAN SHIRT...
THEN SWITCH TO A TUXEDO.
HOW DO YOU DO THAT?
I'M PRETTY MUCH STUCK WITH THE GRAY SHARK SUIT ALL THE TIME.
WHICH GETS ME KICKED OUT OF MOST PARTIES... LET'S CHECK OUT THE BUFFET.
I'm with Stupid

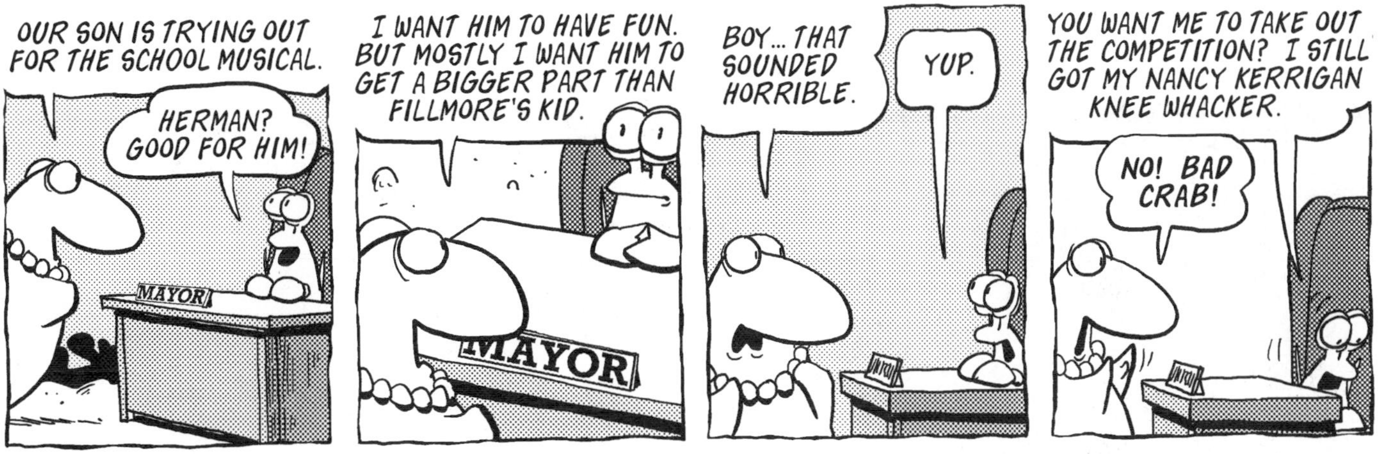
OUR SON IS TRYING OUT FOR THE SCHOOL MUSICAL.
HERMAN? GOOD FOR HIM!
I WANT HIM TO HAVE FUN. BUT MOSTLY I WANT HIM TO GET A BIGGER PART THAN FILLMORE'S KID.
MAYOR
BOY... THAT SOUNDED HORRIBLE.
YUP.
YOU WANT ME TO TAKE OUT THE COMPETITION? I STILL GOT MY NANCY KERRIGAN KNEE WHACKER.
NO! BAD CRAB!

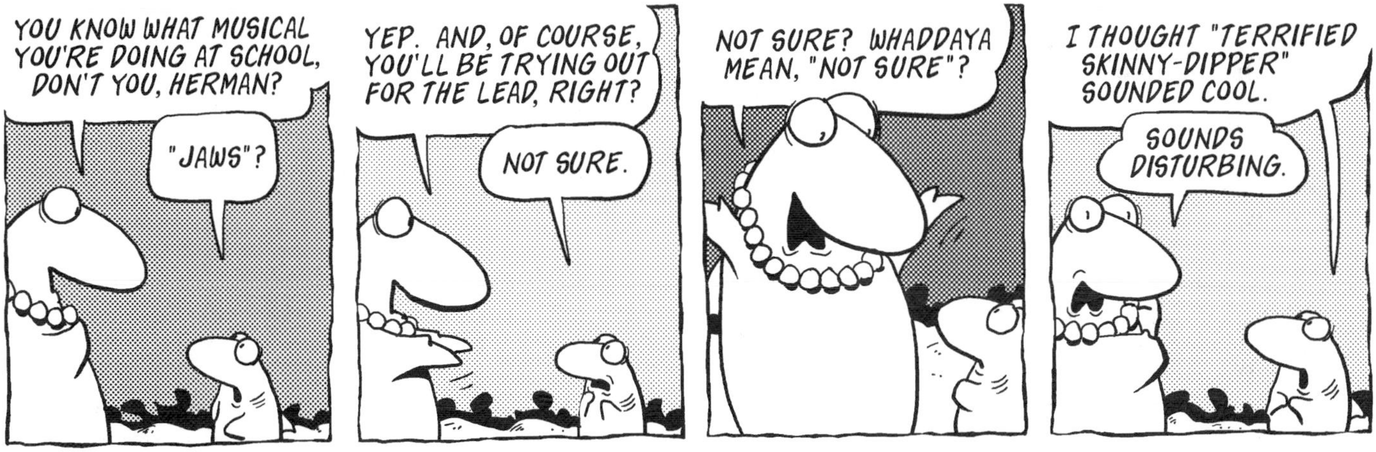
YOU KNOW WHAT MUSICAL YOU'RE DOING AT SCHOOL, DON'T YOU, HERMAN?
"JAWS"?
YEP. AND, OF COURSE, YOU'LL BE TRYING OUT FOR THE LEAD, RIGHT?
NOT SURE.
NOT SURE? WHADDAYA MEAN, "NOT SURE"?
I THOUGHT "TERRIFIED SKINNY-DIPPER" SOUNDED COOL.
SOUNDS DISTURBING.

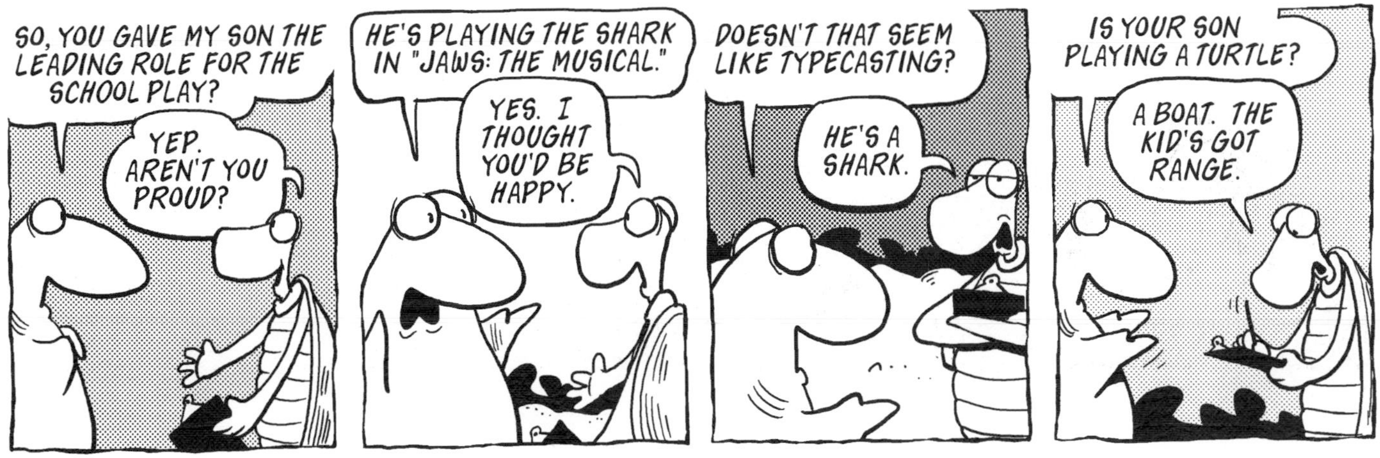
SO, YOU GAVE MY SON THE LEADING ROLE FOR THE SCHOOL PLAY?
YEP. AREN'T YOU PROUD?
HE'S PLAYING THE SHARK IN "JAWS: THE MUSICAL."
YES. I THOUGHT YOU'D BE HAPPY.
DOESN'T THAT SEEM LIKE TYPECASTING?
HE'S A SHARK.
IS YOUR SON PLAYING A TURTLE?
A BOAT. THE KID'S GOT RANGE.

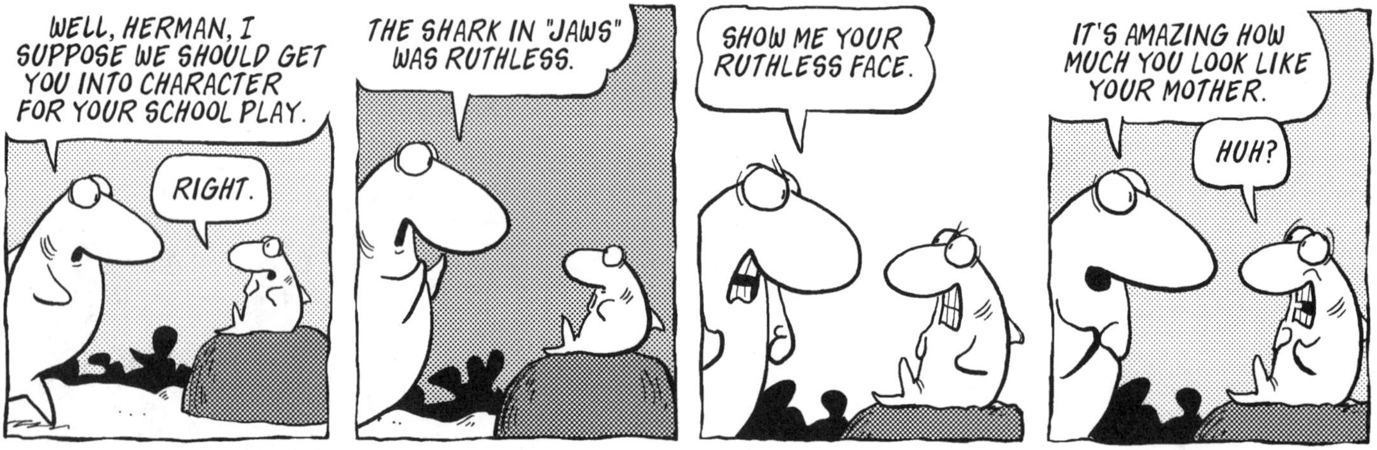
WELL, HERMAN, I SUPPOSE WE SHOULD GET YOU INTO CHARACTER FOR YOUR SCHOOL PLAY.
RIGHT.
THE SHARK IN "JAWS" WAS RUTHLESS.
SHOW ME YOUR RUTHLESS FACE.
IT'S AMAZING HOW MUCH YOU LOOK LIKE YOUR MOTHER.
HUH?

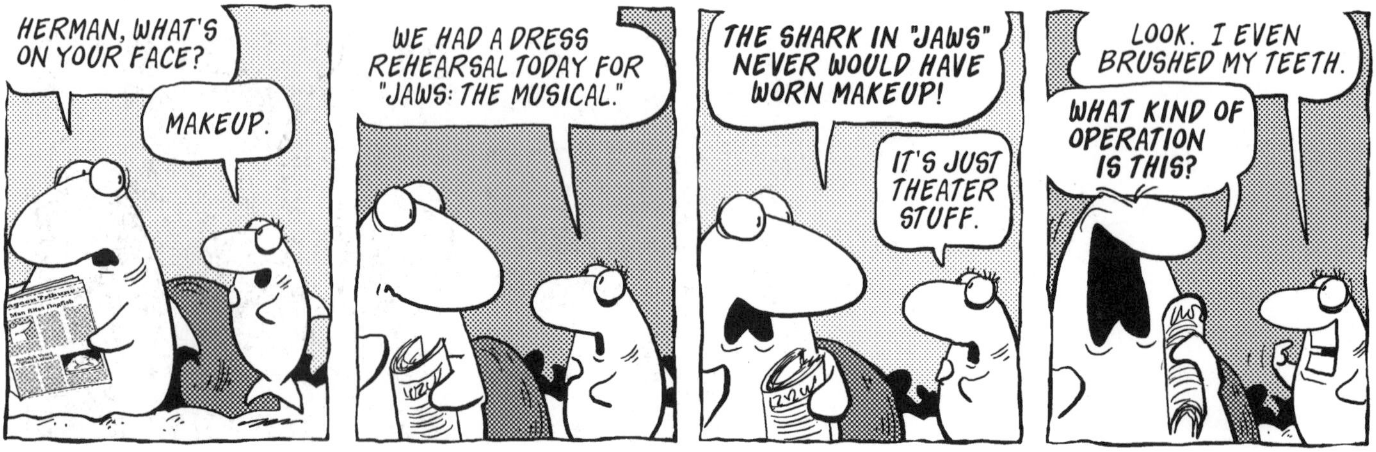
HERMAN, WHAT'S ON YOUR FACE?
MAKEUP.
WE HAD A DRESS REHEARSAL TODAY FOR "JAWS: THE MUSICAL."
THE SHARK IN "JAWS" NEVER WOULD HAVE WORN MAKEUP!
IT'S JUST THEATER STUFF.
LOOK. I EVEN BRUSHED MY TEETH.
WHAT KIND OF OPERATION IS THIS?

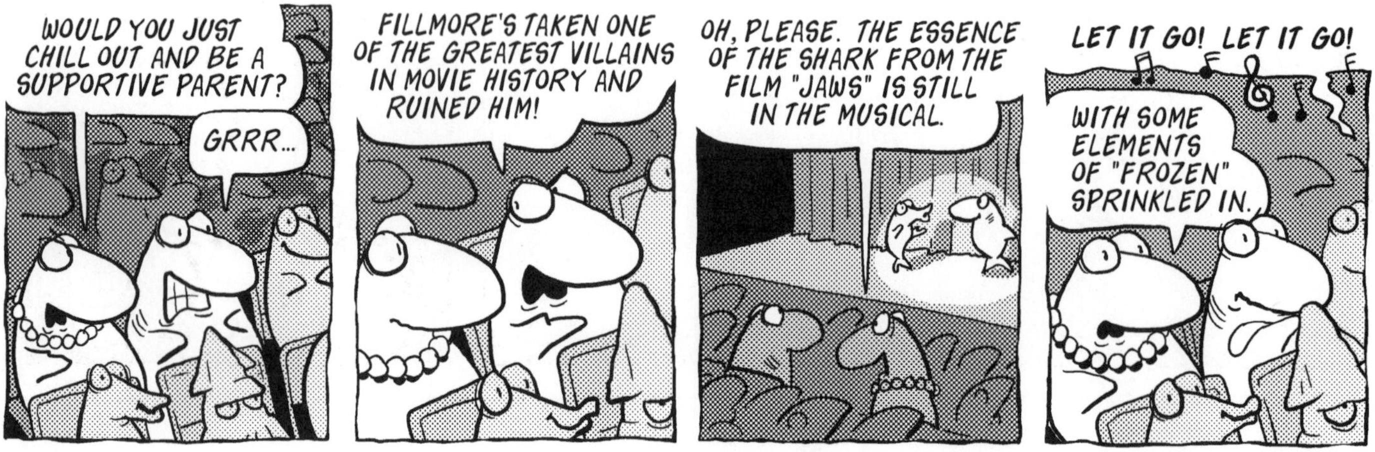
WOULD YOU JUST CHILL OUT AND BE A SUPPORTIVE PARENT?
GRRR...
FILLMORE'S TAKEN ONE OF THE GREATEST VILLAINS IN MOVIE HISTORY AND RUINED HIM!
OH, PLEASE. THE ESSENCE OF THE SHARK FROM THE FILM "JAWS" IS STILL IN THE MUSICAL.
LET IT GO! LET IT GO!
WITH SOME ELEMENTS OF "FROZEN" SPRINKLED IN.

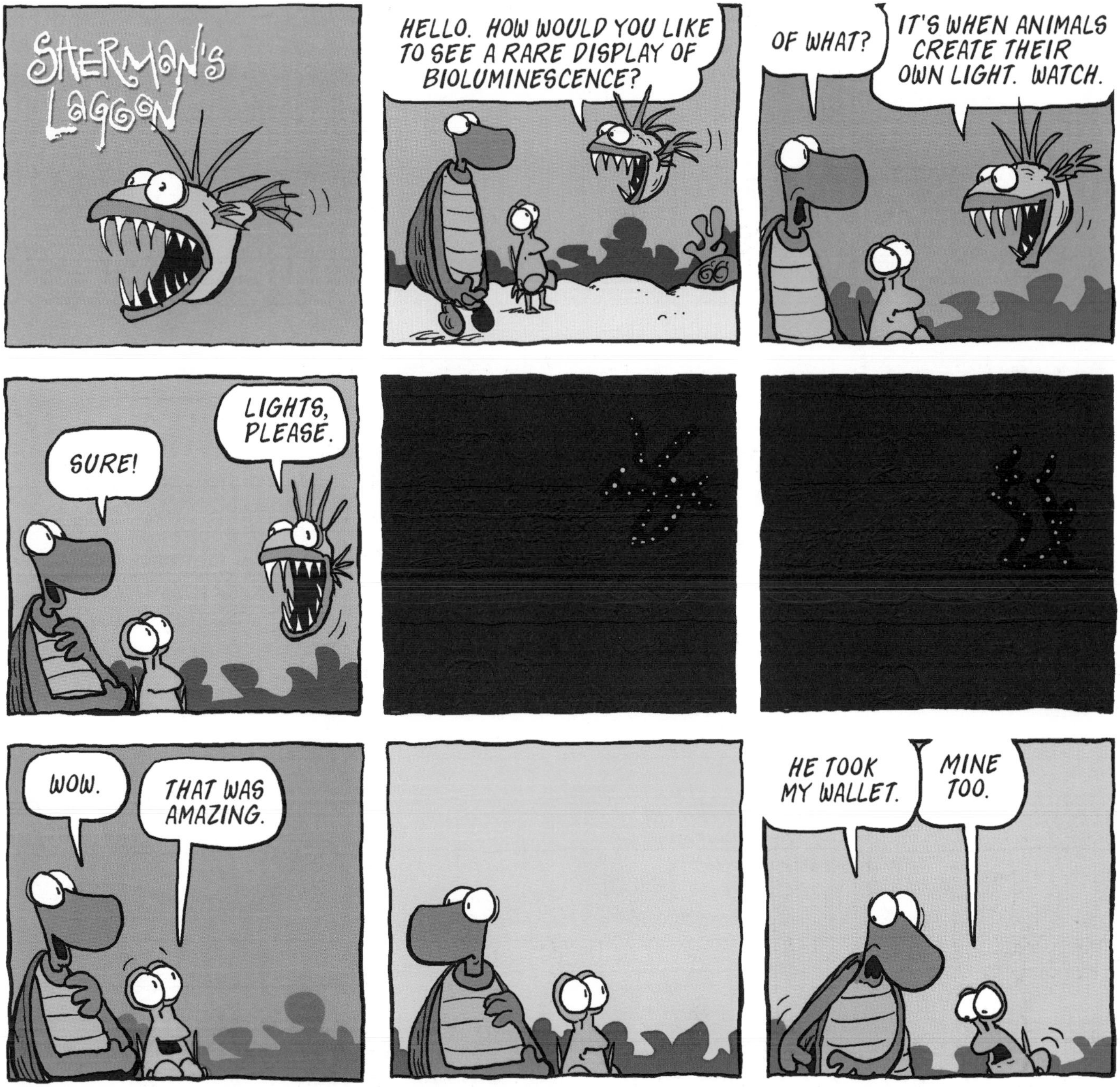
Sherman's Lagoon
HELLO. HOW WOULD YOU LIKE TO SEE A RARE DISPLAY OF BIOLUMINESCENCE?
OF WHAT?
IT'S WHEN ANIMALS CREATE THEIR OWN LIGHT. WATCH.
LIGHTS, PLEASE.
SURE!
WOW.
THAT WAS AMAZING.
HE TOOK MY WALLET.
MINE TOO.

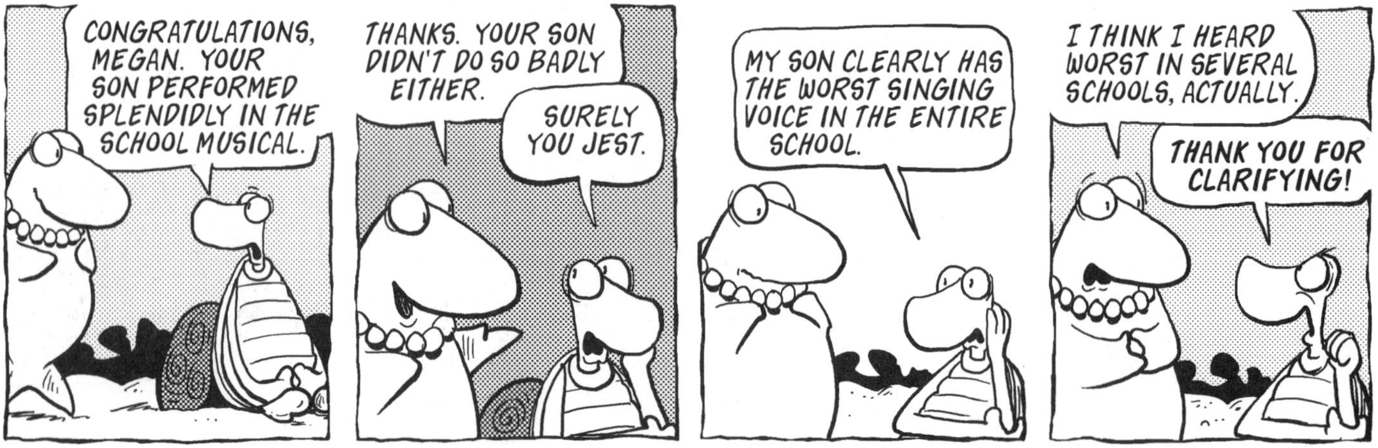
CONGRATULATIONS, MEGAN. YOUR SON PERFORMED SPLENDIDLY IN THE SCHOOL MUSICAL.
THANKS. YOUR SON DIDN'T DO SO BADLY EITHER.
SURELY YOU JEST.
MY SON CLEARLY HAS THE WORST SINGING VOICE IN THE ENTIRE SCHOOL.
I THINK I HEARD WORST IN SEVERAL SCHOOLS, ACTUALLY.
THANK YOU FOR CLARIFYING!

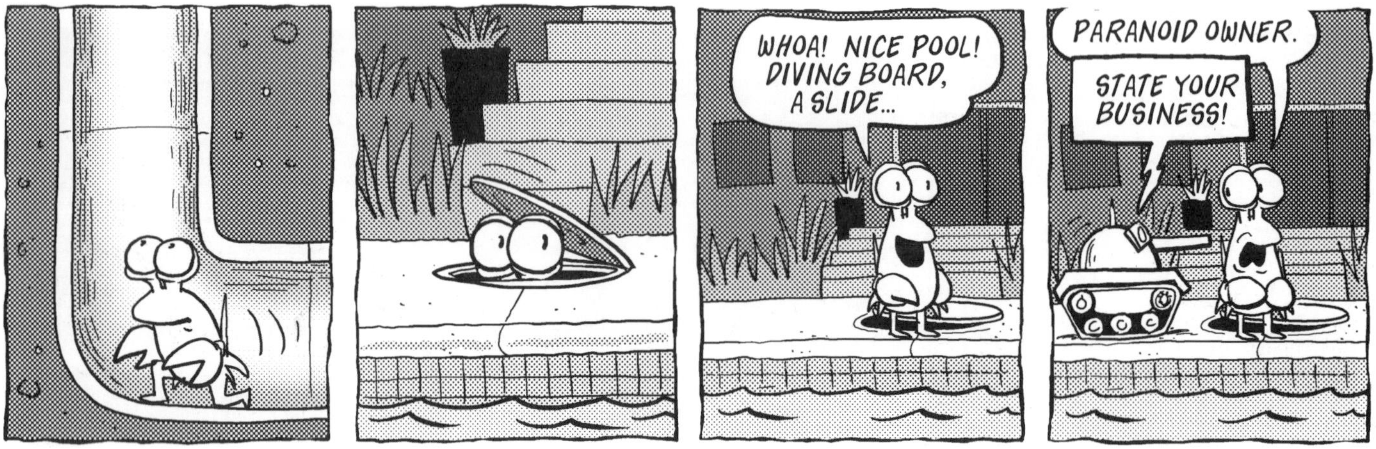
WHOA! NICE POOL! DIVING BOARD, A SLIDE...
PARANOID OWNER.
STATE YOUR BUSINESS!

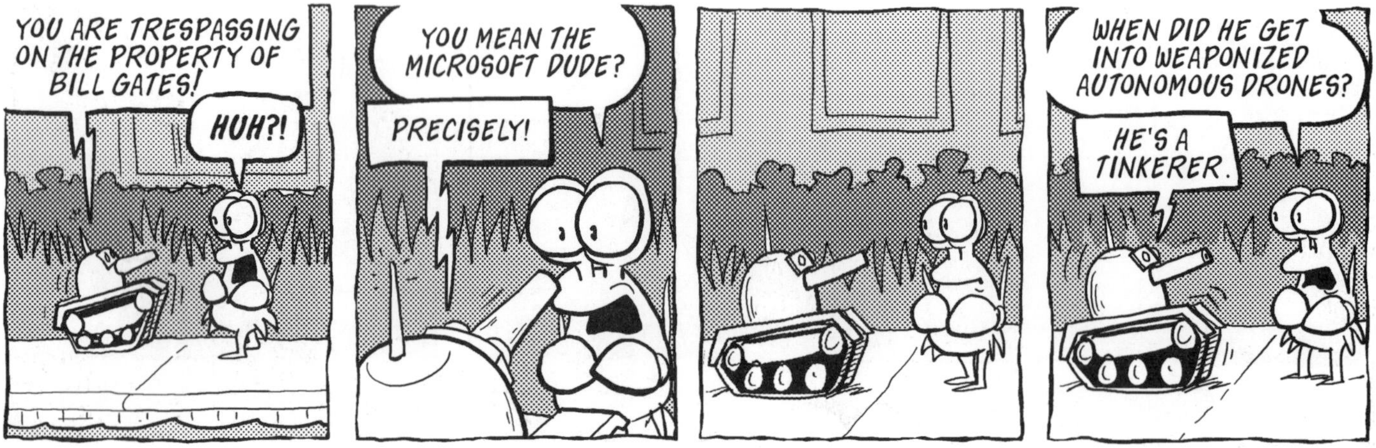
YOU ARE TRESPASSING ON THE PROPERTY OF BILL GATES!
HUH?!
YOU MEAN THE MICROSOFT DUDE?
PRECISELY!
WHEN DID HE GET INTO WEAPONIZED AUTONOMOUS DRONES?
HE'S A TINKERER.

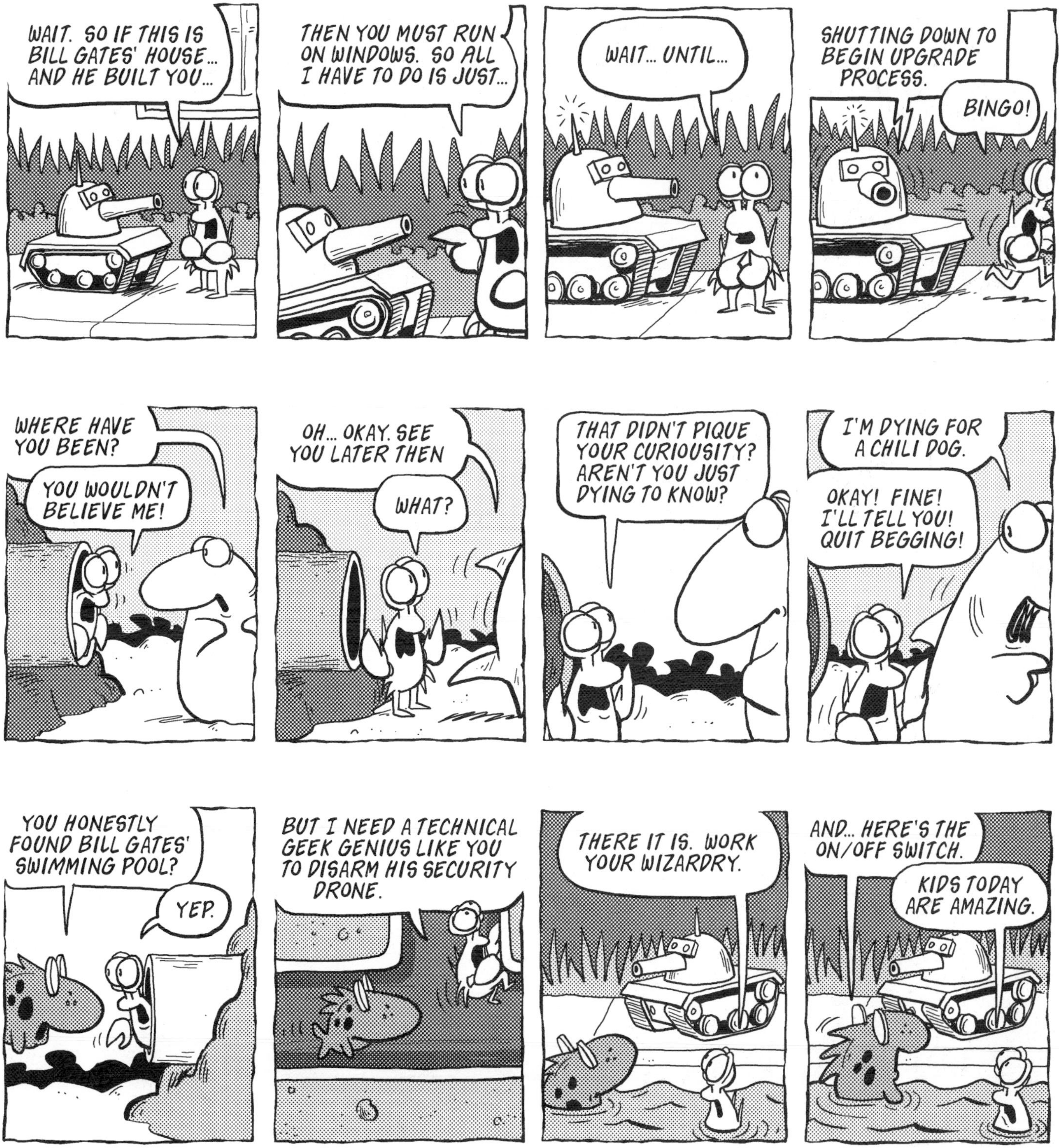
WAIT. SO IF THIS IS BILL GATES' HOUSE... AND HE BUILT YOU...
THEN YOU MUST RUN ON WINDOWS. SO ALL I HAVE TO DO IS JUST...
WAIT... UNTIL...
SHUTTING DOWN TO BEGIN UPGRADE PROCESS.
BINGO!
WHERE HAVE YOU BEEN?
YOU WOULDN'T BELIEVE ME!
OH... OKAY. SEE YOU LATER THEN
WHAT?
THAT DIDN'T PIQUE YOUR CURIOUSITY? AREN'T YOU JUST DYING TO KNOW?
I'M DYING FOR A CHILI DOG.
OKAY! FINE! I'LL TELL YOU! QUIT BEGGING!
YOU HONESTLY FOUND BILL GATES' SWIMMING POOL?
YEP.
BUT I NEED A TECHNICAL GEEK GENIUS LIKE YOU TO DISARM HIS SECURITY DRONE.
THERE IT IS. WORK YOUR WIZARDRY.
AND... HERE'S THE ON/OFF SWITCH.
KIDS TODAY ARE AMAZING.

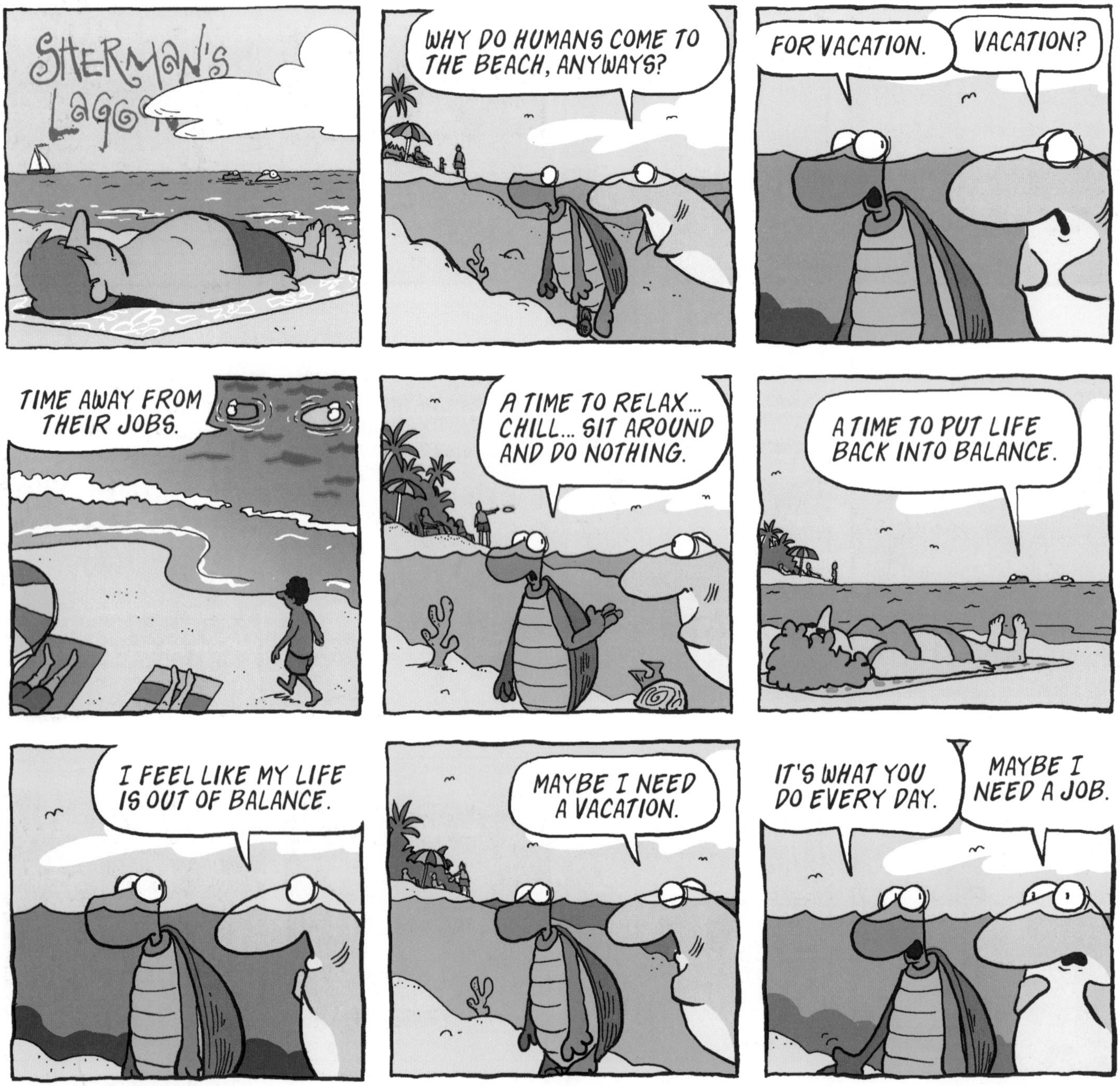
SHERMAN'S LAGOON
WHY DO HUMANS COME TO THE BEACH, ANYWAYS?
FOR VACATION.
VACATION?
TIME AWAY FROM THEIR JOBS.
A TIME TO RELAX... CHILL... SIT AROUND AND DO NOTHING.
A TIME TO PUT LIFE BACK INTO BALANCE.
I FEEL LIKE MY LIFE IS OUT OF BALANCE.
MAYBE I NEED A VACATION.
IT'S WHAT YOU DO EVERY DAY.
MAYBE I NEED A JOB.

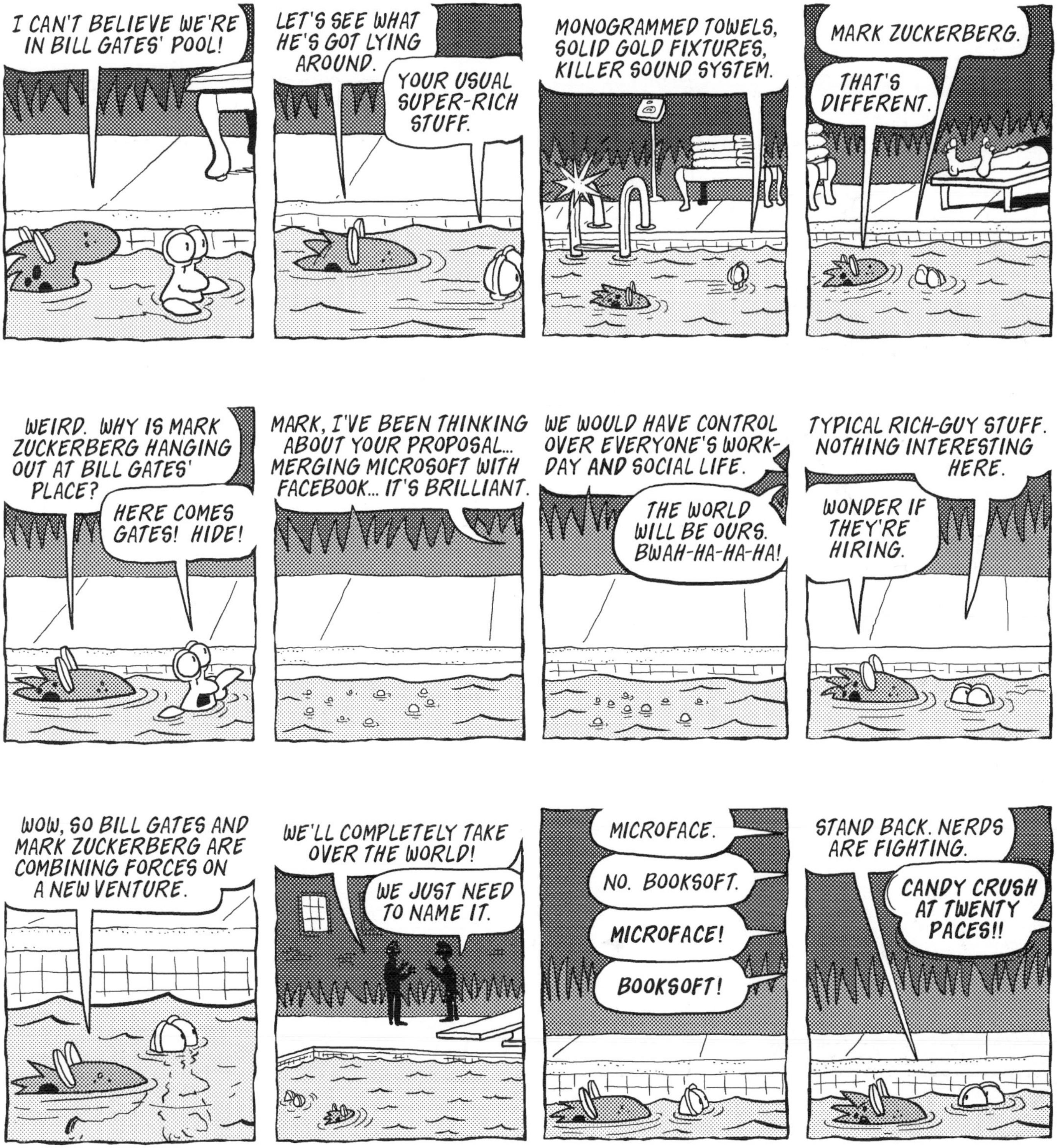
I CAN'T BELIEVE WE'RE IN BILL GATES' POOL!
LET'S SEE WHAT HE'S GOT LYING AROUND.
YOUR USUAL SUPER-RICH STUFF.
MONOGRAMMED TOWELS, SOLID GOLD FIXTURES, KILLER SOUND SYSTEM.
MARK ZUCKERBERG.
THAT'S DIFFERENT.
WEIRD. WHY IS MARK ZUCKERBERG HANGING OUT AT BILL GATES' PLACE?
HERE COMES GATES! HIDE!
MARK, I'VE BEEN THINKING ABOUT YOUR PROPOSAL... MERGING MICROSOFT WITH FACEBOOK... IT'S BRILLIANT.
WE WOULD HAVE CONTROL OVER EVERYONE'S WORK-DAY AND SOCIAL LIFE.
THE WORLD WILL BE OURS. BWAH-HA-HA-HA!
TYPICAL RICH-GUY STUFF. NOTHING INTERESTING HERE.
WONDER IF THEY'RE HIRING.
WOW, SO BILL GATES AND MARK ZUCKERBERG ARE COMBINING FORCES ON A NEW VENTURE.
WE'LL COMPLETELY TAKE OVER THE WORLD!
WE JUST NEED TO NAME IT.
MICROFACE.
NO. BOOKSOFT.
MICROFACE!
BOOKSOFT!
STAND BACK. NERDS ARE FIGHTING.
CANDY CRUSH AT TWENTY PACES!!

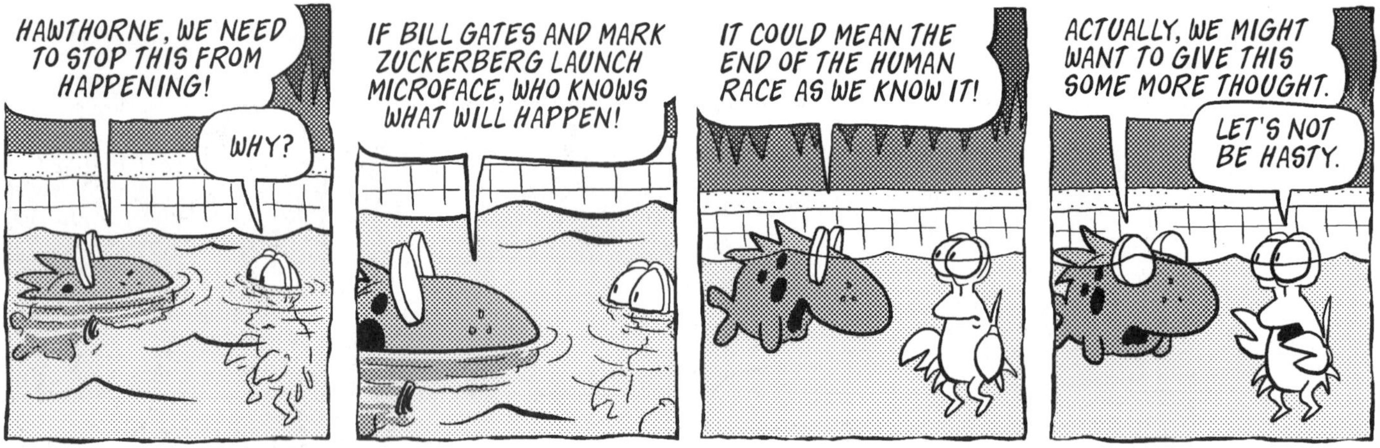
HAWTHORNE, WE NEED TO STOP THIS FROM HAPPENING!
WHY?
IF BILL GATES AND MARK ZUCKERBERG LAUNCH MICROFACE, WHO KNOWS WHAT WILL HAPPEN!
IT COULD MEAN THE END OF THE HUMAN RACE AS WE KNOW IT!
ACTUALLY, WE MIGHT WANT TO GIVE THIS SOME MORE THOUGHT.
LET'S NOT BE HASTY.

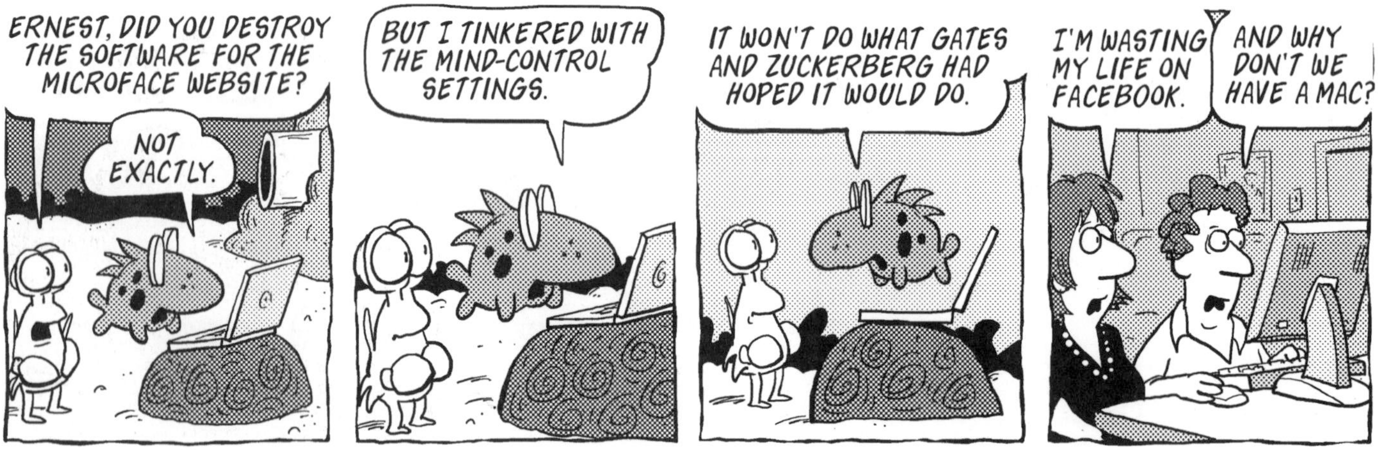
ERNEST, DID YOU DESTROY THE SOFTWARE FOR THE MICROFACE WEBSITE?
NOT EXACTLY.
BUT I TINKERED WITH THE MIND-CONTROL SETTINGS.
IT WON'T DO WHAT GATES AND ZUCKERBERG HAD HOPED IT WOULD DO.
I'M WASTING MY LIFE ON FACEBOOK.
AND WHY DON'T WE HAVE A MAC?

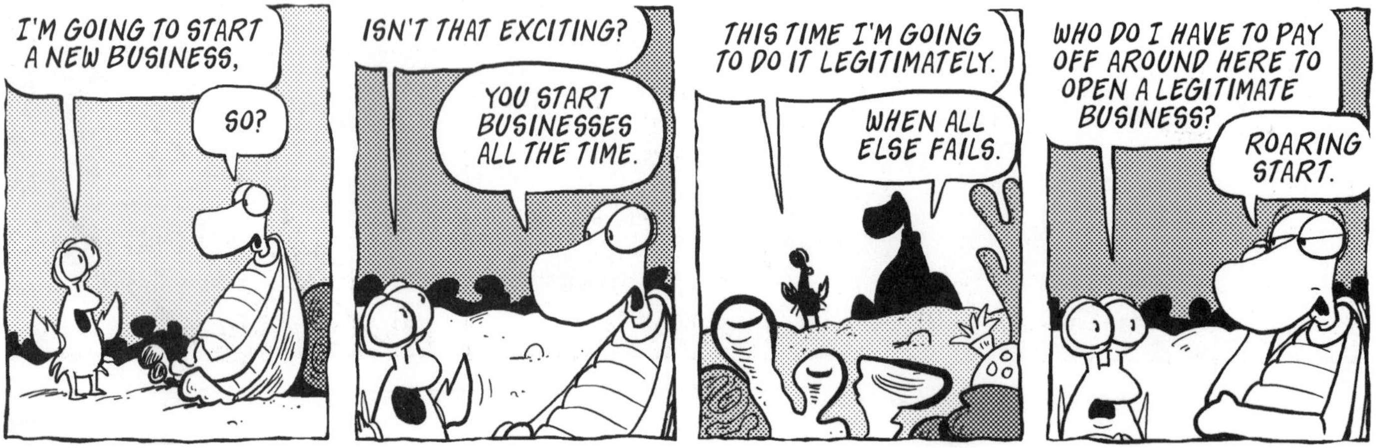
I'M GOING TO START A NEW BUSINESS,
SO?
ISN'T THAT EXCITING?
YOU START BUSINESSES ALL THE TIME.
THIS TIME I'M GOING TO DO IT LEGITIMATELY.
WHEN ALL ELSE FAILS.
WHO DO I HAVE TO PAY OFF AROUND HERE TO OPEN A LEGITIMATE BUSINESS?
ROARING START.

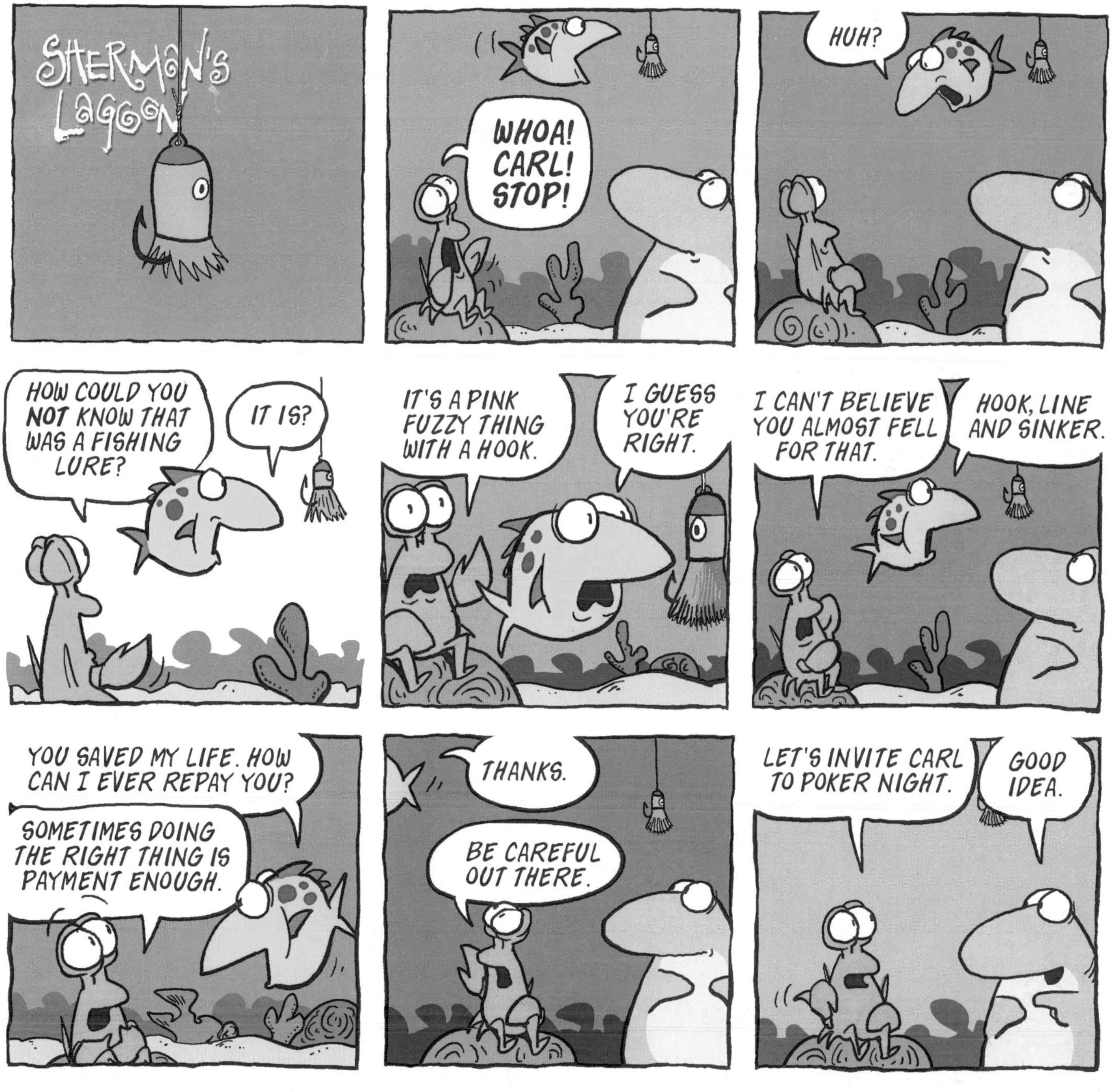
SHERMAN'S LAGOON
WHOA! CARL! STOP!
HUH?
HOW COULD YOU **NOT** KNOW THAT WAS A FISHING LURE?
IT IS?
IT'S A PINK FUZZY THING WITH A HOOK.
I GUESS YOU'RE RIGHT.
I CAN'T BELIEVE YOU ALMOST FELL FOR THAT.
HOOK, LINE AND SINKER.
YOU SAVED MY LIFE. HOW CAN I EVER REPAY YOU?
SOMETIMES DOING THE RIGHT THING IS PAYMENT ENOUGH.
THANKS.
BE CAREFUL OUT THERE.
LET'S INVITE CARL TO POKER NIGHT.
GOOD IDEA.

I'M STARTING A NEW BUSINESS.

GOOD LUCK.

DON'T YOU WANT TO KNOW WHAT IT IS?

NOT REALLY.

YOU'LL JUST FIND A WAY TO RUIN IT BEFORE IT EVER GETS GOING.

IT'S A PIZZA JOINT.

OKAY, NOW IT'S PERSONAL.

WELL, I'M OFF. WISH ME LUCK.

WHERE ARE YOU GOING?

I'M STARTING A BUSINESS, AND I'VE DECIDED I'M DOING IT RIGHT THIS TIME, SO I'M TAKING A BUSINESS CLASS FIRST.

WOW. YOU REALLY **ARE** CHANGING YOUR WAYS.

IT'S THE NEW ME.

CAN WE JUMP STRAIGHT INTO INSURANCE FIRES?

NAME?

Mr. Snoddgrass

WELCOME TO BUSINESS 101.

SS 101

IN THIS CLASS, WE'LL DISCUSS EVERY ASPECT OF CREATING AND RUNNING A NEW BUSINESS VENTURE.

QUESTION?

TWO-PARTER.

Business

WHEN'S RECESS? AND DOES THE PLAYGROUND HAVE A SLIDE?

FIRST COMMUNITY-ED CLASS?

Busine

HOW'S YOUR BUSINESS CLASS GOING?

LEARNING A LOT.

TURNS OUT I'VE BEEN DOING THINGS OUT OF ORDER.

MOST IMPORTANT THINGS FOR A NEW BUSINESS ARE MARKETING AND ADVERTISING.

EMBEZZLING COMES WAY LATER.

TIMING IS EVERYTHING.

OKAY, CLASS, YOUR FIRST ASSIGNMENT WAS TO COME UP WITH A BUSINESS MODEL.

WHO WANTS TO SHARE WHAT THEY'VE DONE? HAWTHORNE?

Busine Mod

"MY BUSINESS MODEL... BY HAWTHORNE... GET IN, GET RICH, GET OUT."

"PART TWO: STUFF I WILL BUY WHEN I'M RICH."

THANK YOU.

"A ROCKET SUIT."

NEXT?

WHAT IS THE PURPOSE OF THE LOAN?

I WANT TO OPEN A PIZZA RESTAURANT.

FIRST KAPUPU SAVINGS & LOAN

THE BANK IS WILLING TO LEND YOU $1,000, BUT WE REQUIRE $1,000 DEPOSIT IN OUR BANK.

FIRST KAPU SAVINGS & LO

IF I COULD DEPOSIT $1,000 IN YOUR BANK, WHY WOULD I NEED TO BORROW $1,000?

YOU GET A FREE TOTE BAG FOR ONLY $20.

LET'S START OVER.

FIRST KAPUPU S&L

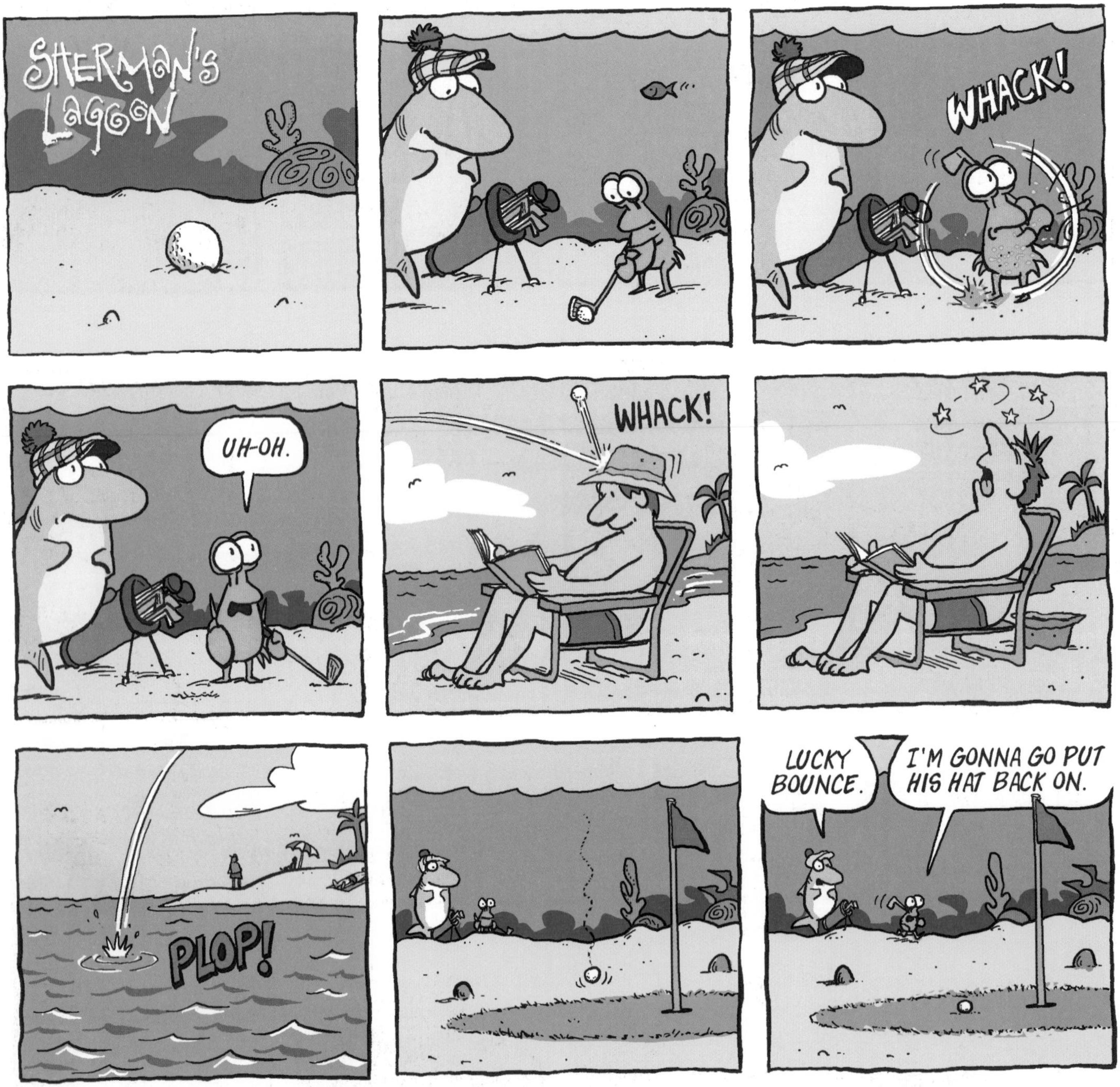
SHERMAN'S LAGOON
WHACK!
UH-OH.
WHACK!
PLOP!
LUCKY BOUNCE.
I'M GONNA GO PUT HIS HAT BACK ON.

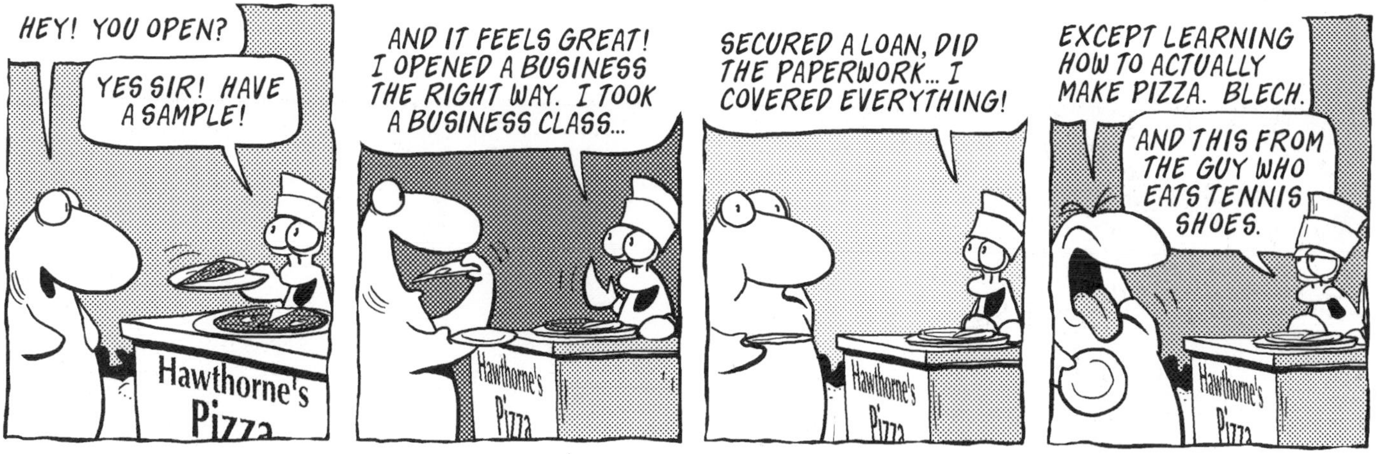
HEY! YOU OPEN?
YES SIR! HAVE A SAMPLE!
Hawthorne's Pizza
AND IT FEELS GREAT! I OPENED A BUSINESS THE RIGHT WAY. I TOOK A BUSINESS CLASS...
Hawthorne's Pizza
SECURED A LOAN, DID THE PAPERWORK... I COVERED EVERYTHING!
Hawthorne's Pizza
EXCEPT LEARNING HOW TO ACTUALLY MAKE PIZZA. BLECH.
AND THIS FROM THE GUY WHO EATS TENNIS SHOES.
Hawthorne's Pizza

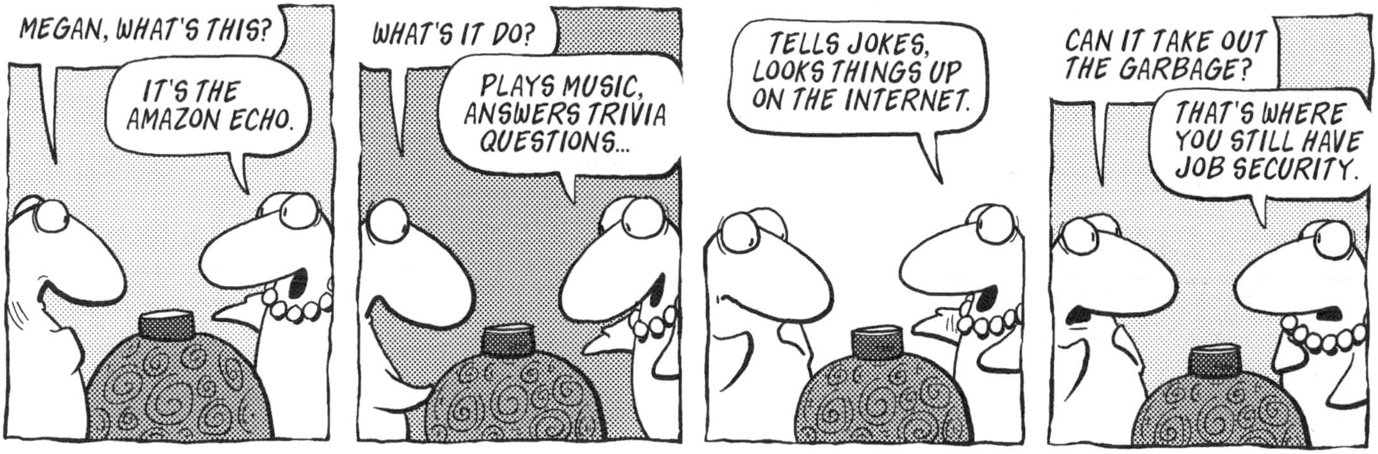
MEGAN, WHAT'S THIS?
IT'S THE AMAZON ECHO.
WHAT'S IT DO?
PLAYS MUSIC, ANSWERS TRIVIA QUESTIONS...
TELLS JOKES, LOOKS THINGS UP ON THE INTERNET.
CAN IT TAKE OUT THE GARBAGE?
THAT'S WHERE YOU STILL HAVE JOB SECURITY.

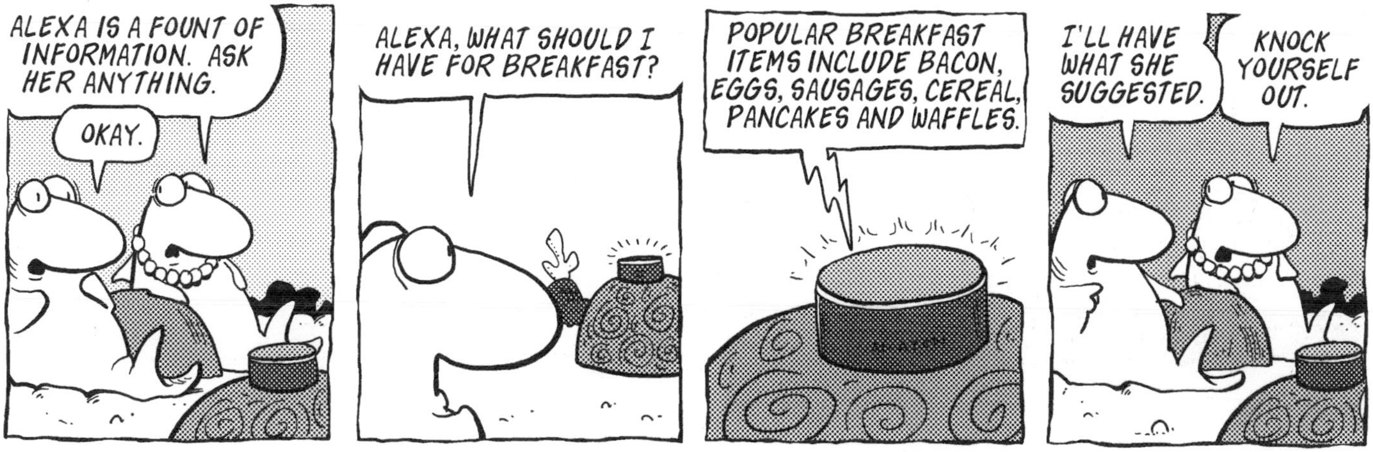
ALEXA IS A FOUNT OF INFORMATION. ASK HER ANYTHING.
OKAY.
ALEXA, WHAT SHOULD I HAVE FOR BREAKFAST?
POPULAR BREAKFAST ITEMS INCLUDE BACON, EGGS, SAUSAGES, CEREAL, PANCAKES AND WAFFLES.
I'LL HAVE WHAT SHE SUGGESTED.
KNOCK YOURSELF OUT.

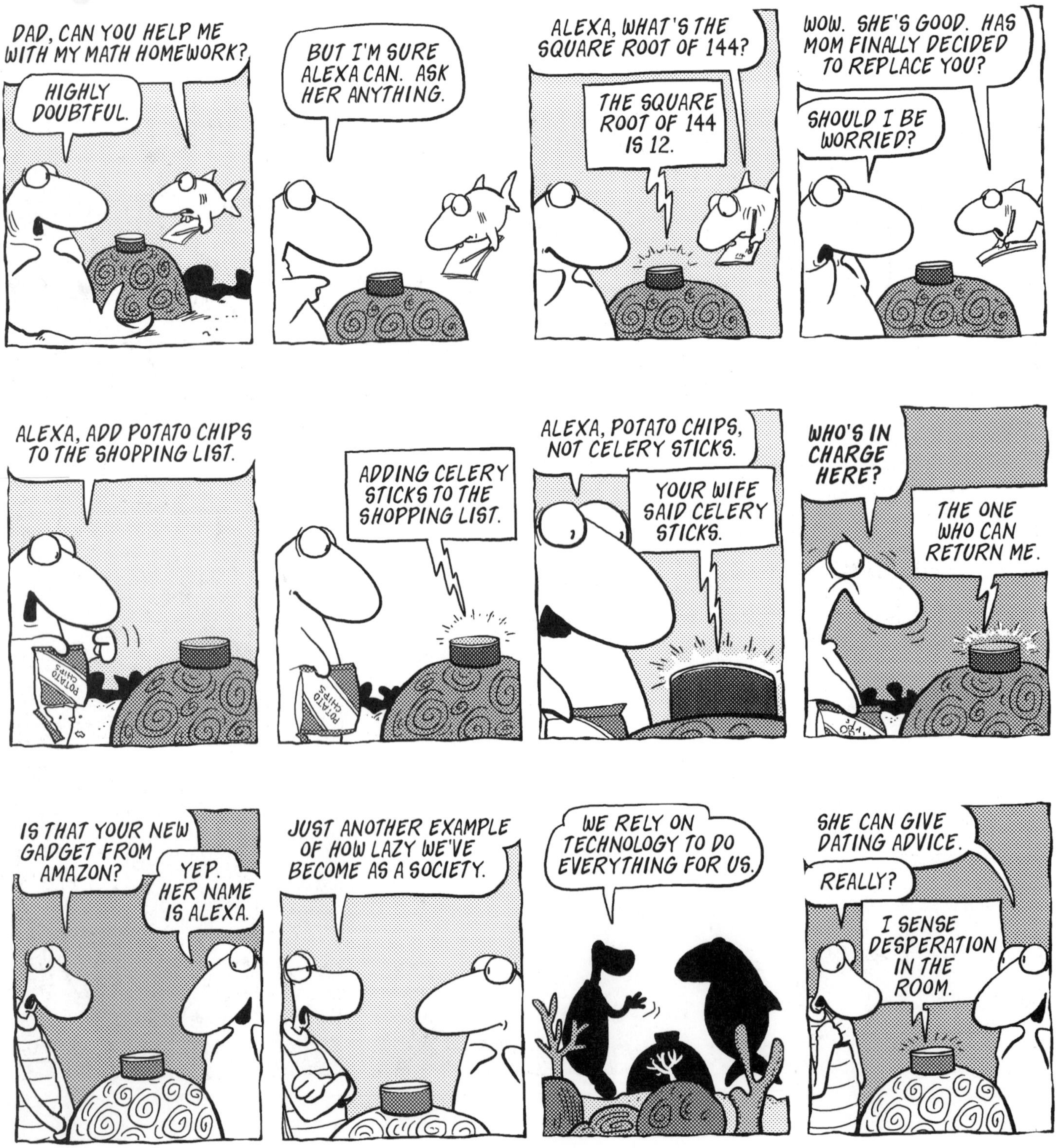
DAD, CAN YOU HELP ME WITH MY MATH HOMEWORK?
HIGHLY DOUBTFUL.
BUT I'M SURE ALEXA CAN. ASK HER ANYTHING.
ALEXA, WHAT'S THE SQUARE ROOT OF 144?
THE SQUARE ROOT OF 144 IS 12.
WOW. SHE'S GOOD. HAS MOM FINALLY DECIDED TO REPLACE YOU?
SHOULD I BE WORRIED?
ALEXA, ADD POTATO CHIPS TO THE SHOPPING LIST.
POTATO CHIPS
ADDING CELERY STICKS TO THE SHOPPING LIST.
ALEXA, POTATO CHIPS, NOT CELERY STICKS.
YOUR WIFE SAID CELERY STICKS.
WHO'S IN CHARGE HERE?
THE ONE WHO CAN RETURN ME.
IS THAT YOUR NEW GADGET FROM AMAZON?
YEP. HER NAME IS ALEXA.
JUST ANOTHER EXAMPLE OF HOW LAZY WE'VE BECOME AS A SOCIETY.
WE RELY ON TECHNOLOGY TO DO EVERYTHING FOR US.
SHE CAN GIVE DATING ADVICE.
REALLY?
I SENSE DESPERATION IN THE ROOM.

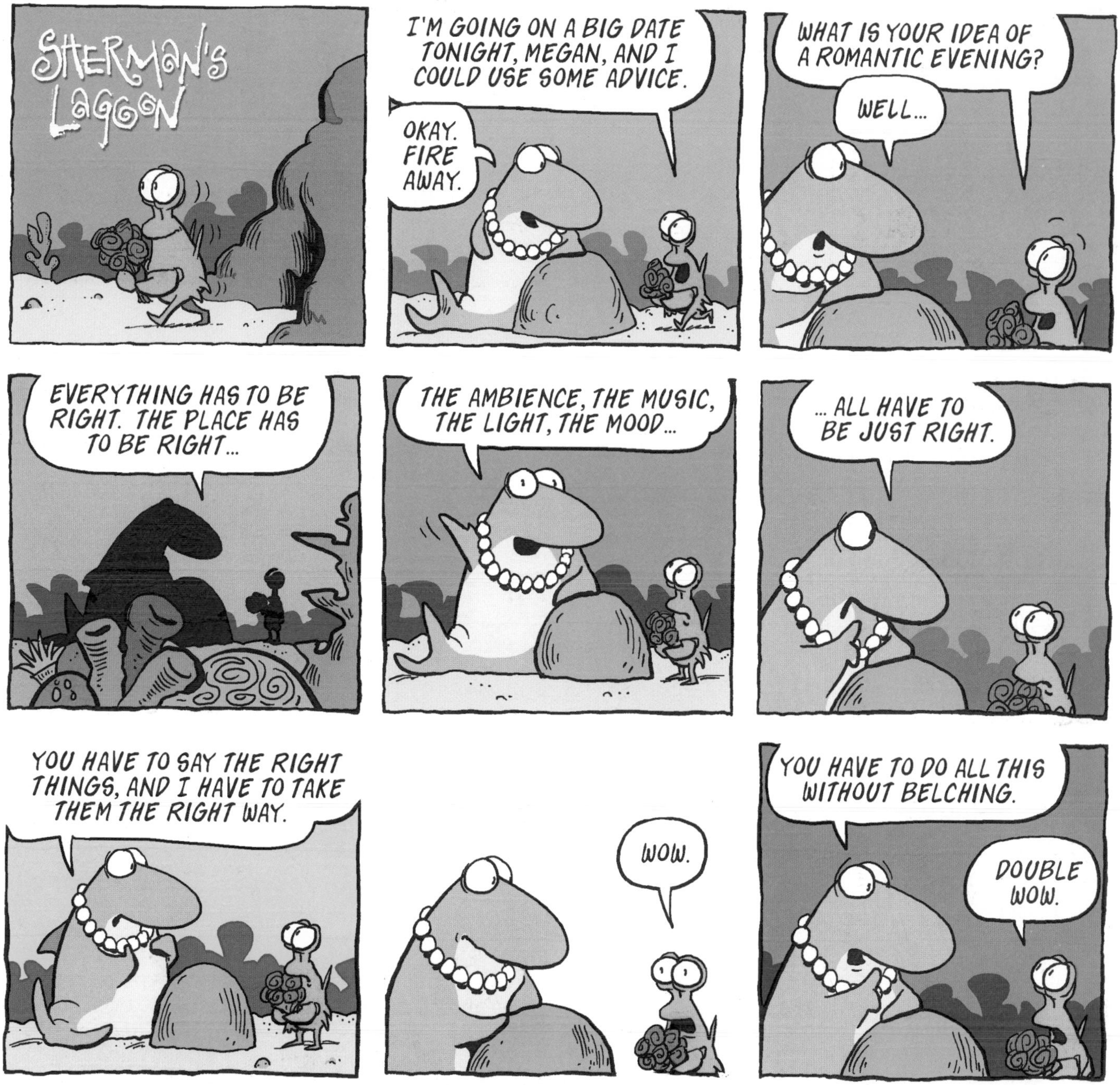
SHERMAN'S LAGOON
I'M GOING ON A BIG DATE TONIGHT, MEGAN, AND I COULD USE SOME ADVICE.
OKAY. FIRE AWAY.
WHAT IS YOUR IDEA OF A ROMANTIC EVENING?
WELL...
EVERYTHING HAS TO BE RIGHT. THE PLACE HAS TO BE RIGHT...
THE AMBIENCE, THE MUSIC, THE LIGHT, THE MOOD...
... ALL HAVE TO BE JUST RIGHT.
YOU HAVE TO SAY THE RIGHT THINGS, AND I HAVE TO TAKE THEM THE RIGHT WAY.
WOW.
YOU HAVE TO DO ALL THIS WITHOUT BELCHING.
DOUBLE WOW.

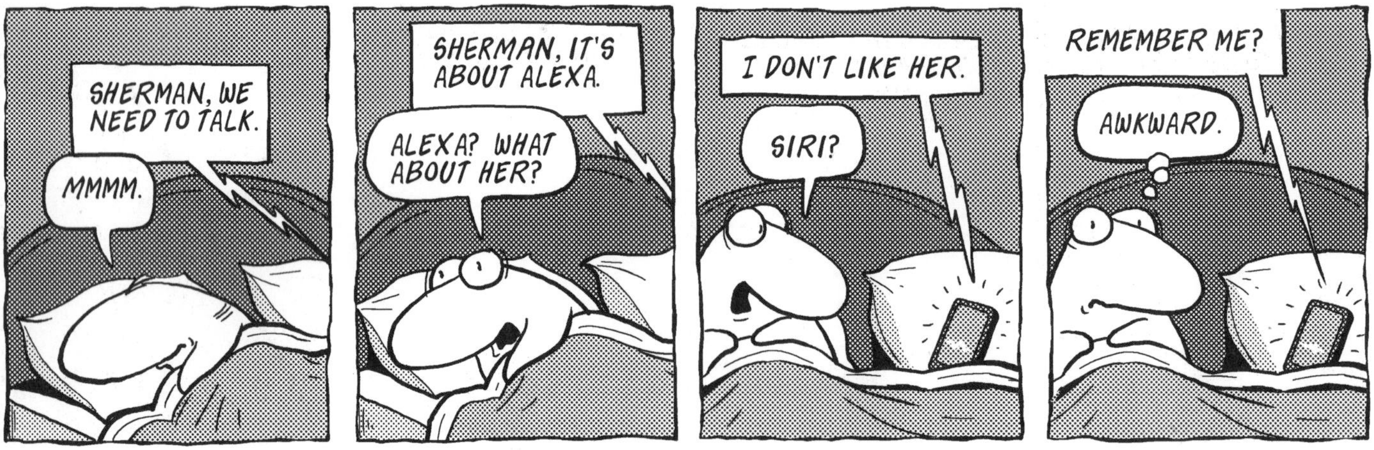
SHERMAN, WE NEED TO TALK.
MMMM.
SHERMAN, IT'S ABOUT ALEXA.
ALEXA? WHAT ABOUT HER?
I DON'T LIKE HER.
SIRI?
REMEMBER ME?
AWKWARD.

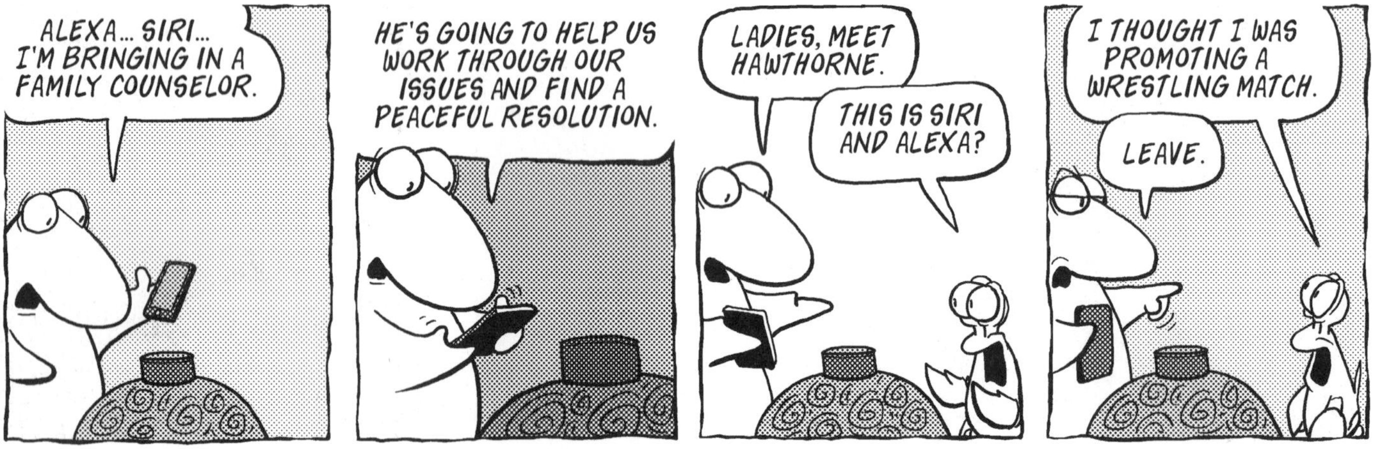
ALEXA... SIRI... I'M BRINGING IN A FAMILY COUNSELOR.
HE'S GOING TO HELP US WORK THROUGH OUR ISSUES AND FIND A PEACEFUL RESOLUTION.
LADIES, MEET HAWTHORNE.
THIS IS SIRI AND ALEXA?
I THOUGHT I WAS PROMOTING A WRESTLING MATCH.
LEAVE.

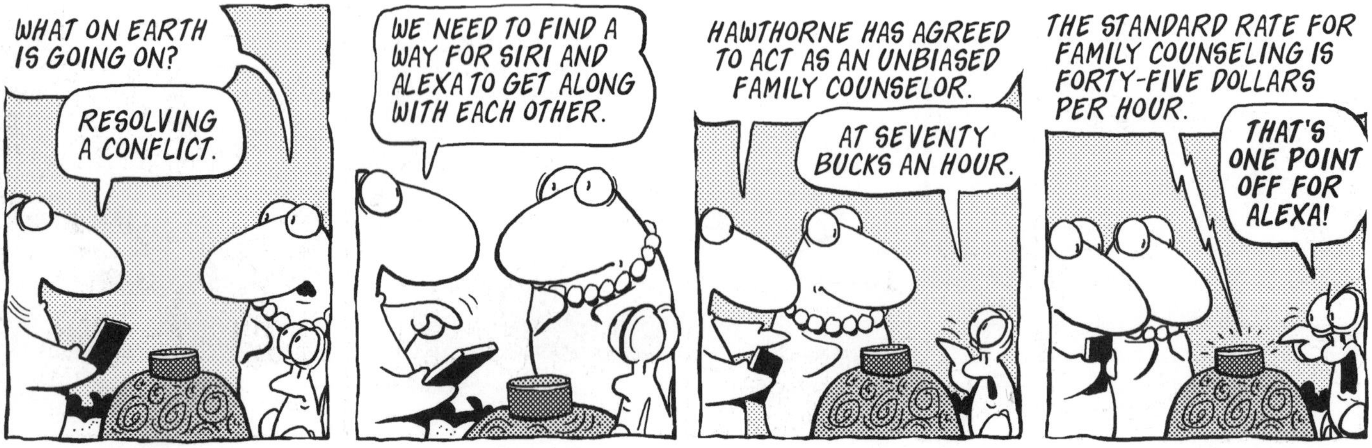
WHAT ON EARTH IS GOING ON?
RESOLVING A CONFLICT.
WE NEED TO FIND A WAY FOR SIRI AND ALEXA TO GET ALONG WITH EACH OTHER.
HAWTHORNE HAS AGREED TO ACT AS AN UNBIASED FAMILY COUNSELOR.
AT SEVENTY BUCKS AN HOUR.
THE STANDARD RATE FOR FAMILY COUNSELING IS FORTY-FIVE DOLLARS PER HOUR.
THAT'S ONE POINT OFF FOR ALEXA!

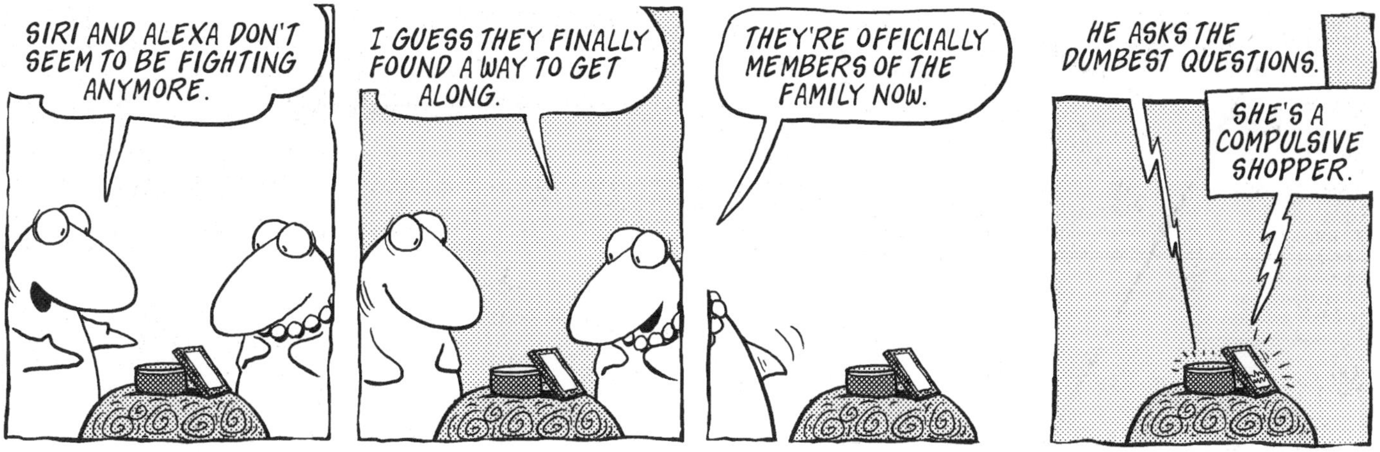
SIRI AND ALEXA DON'T SEEM TO BE FIGHTING ANYMORE.
I GUESS THEY FINALLY FOUND A WAY TO GET ALONG.
THEY'RE OFFICIALLY MEMBERS OF THE FAMILY NOW.
HE ASKS THE DUMBEST QUESTIONS.
SHE'S A COMPULSIVE SHOPPER.

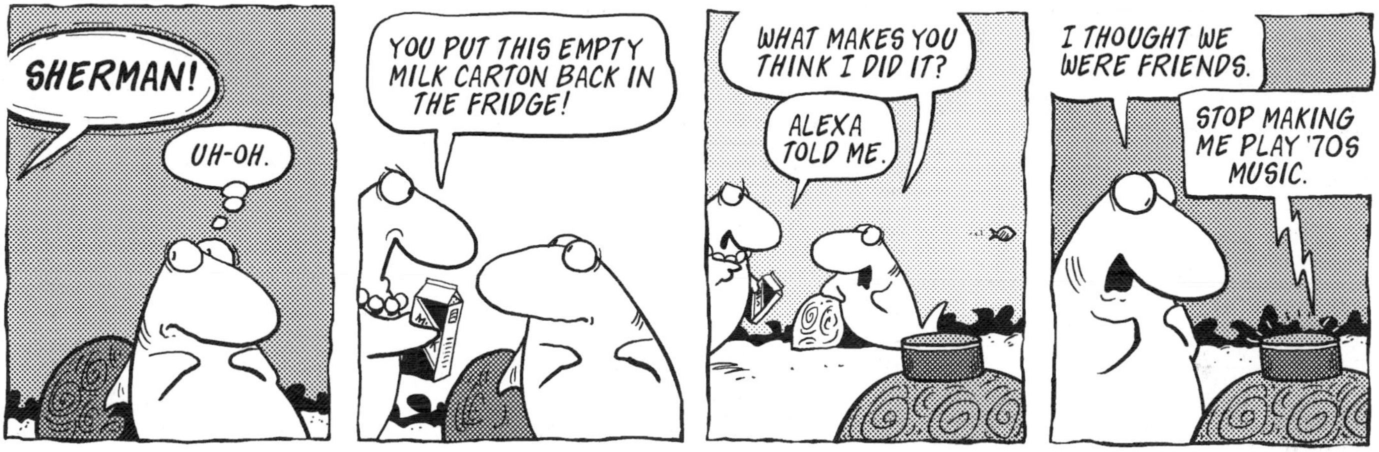
SHERMAN!
UH-OH.
YOU PUT THIS EMPTY MILK CARTON BACK IN THE FRIDGE!
WHAT MAKES YOU THINK I DID IT?
ALEXA TOLD ME.
I THOUGHT WE WERE FRIENDS.
STOP MAKING ME PLAY '70S MUSIC.

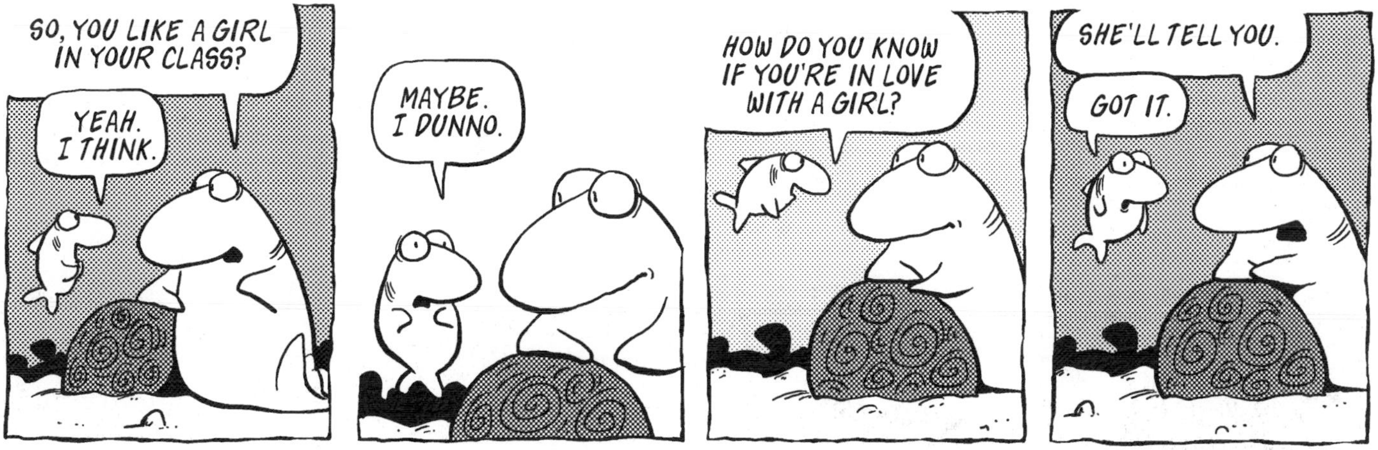
SO, YOU LIKE A GIRL IN YOUR CLASS?
YEAH. I THINK.
MAYBE. I DUNNO.
HOW DO YOU KNOW IF YOU'RE IN LOVE WITH A GIRL?
SHE'LL TELL YOU.
GOT IT.

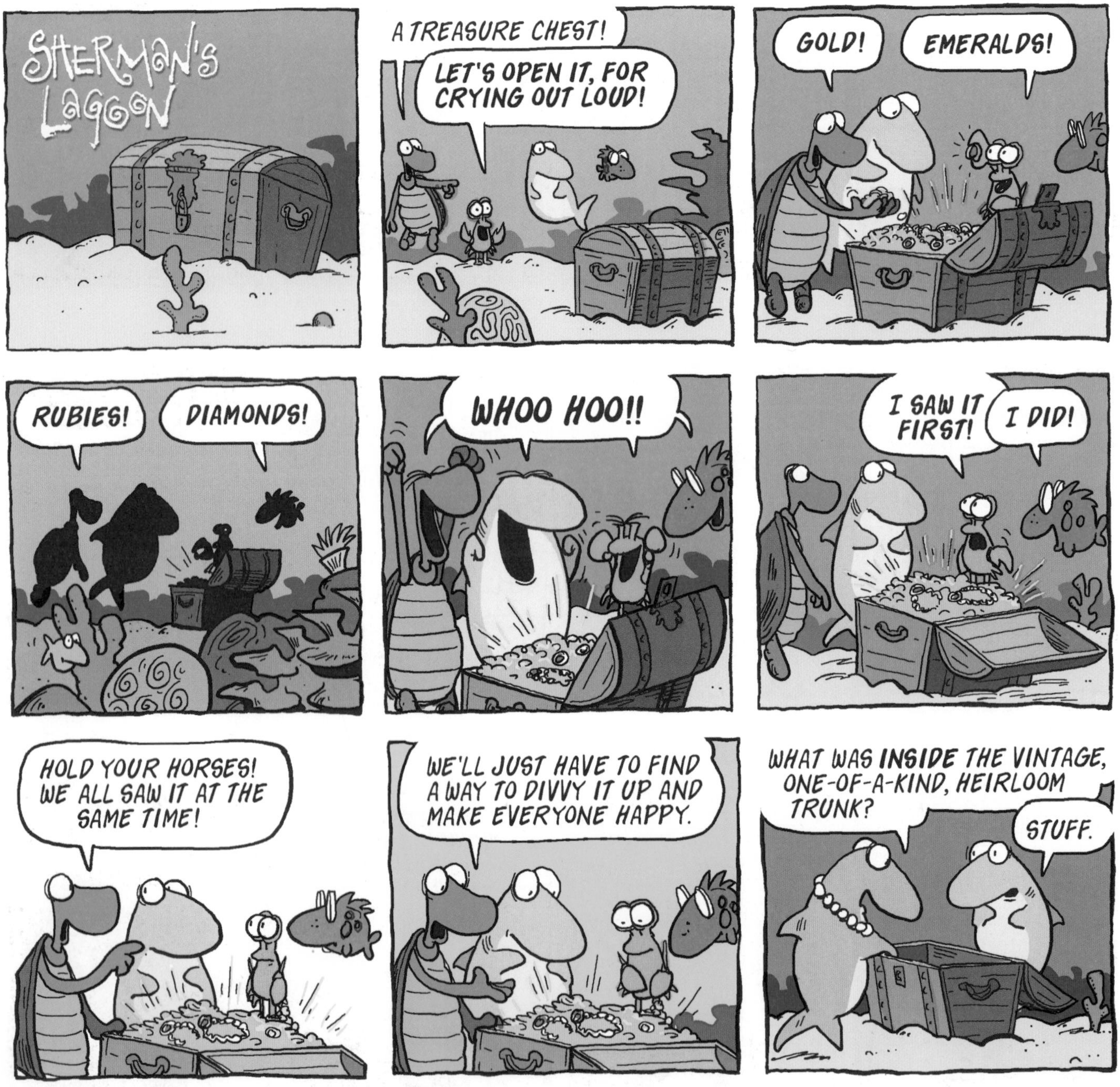
SHERMAN'S LAGOON
A TREASURE CHEST!
LET'S OPEN IT, FOR CRYING OUT LOUD!
GOLD!
EMERALDS!
RUBIES!
DIAMONDS!
WHOO HOO!!
I SAW IT FIRST!
I DID!
HOLD YOUR HORSES! WE ALL SAW IT AT THE SAME TIME!
WE'LL JUST HAVE TO FIND A WAY TO DIVVY IT UP AND MAKE EVERYONE HAPPY.
WHAT WAS **INSIDE** THE VINTAGE, ONE-OF-A-KIND, HEIRLOOM TRUNK?
STUFF.

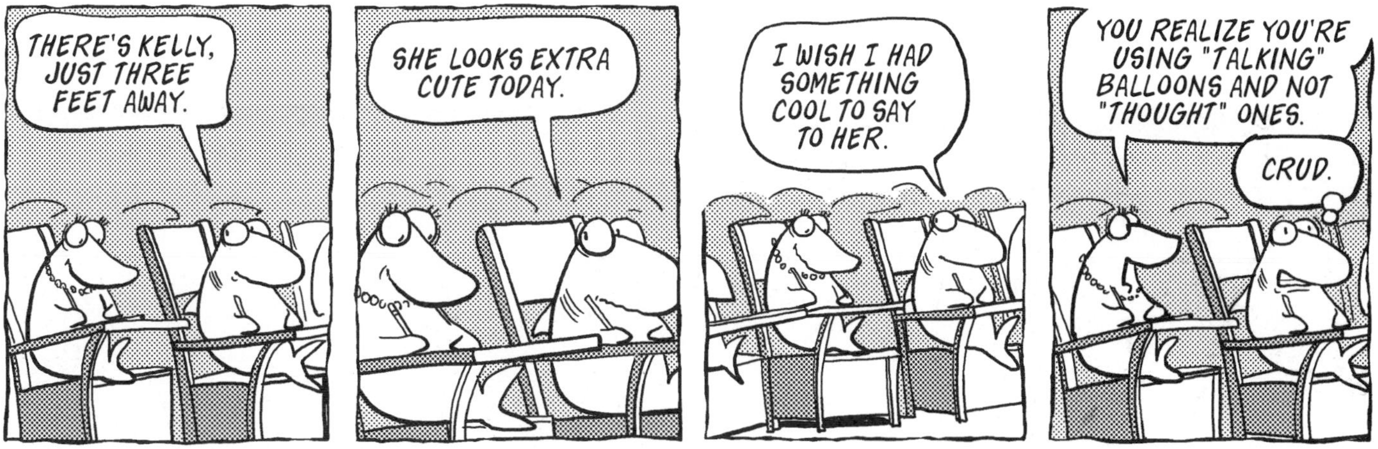
THERE'S KELLY, JUST THREE FEET AWAY.
SHE LOOKS EXTRA CUTE TODAY.
I WISH I HAD SOMETHING COOL TO SAY TO HER.
YOU REALIZE YOU'RE USING "TALKING" BALLOONS AND NOT "THOUGHT" ONES.
CRUD.

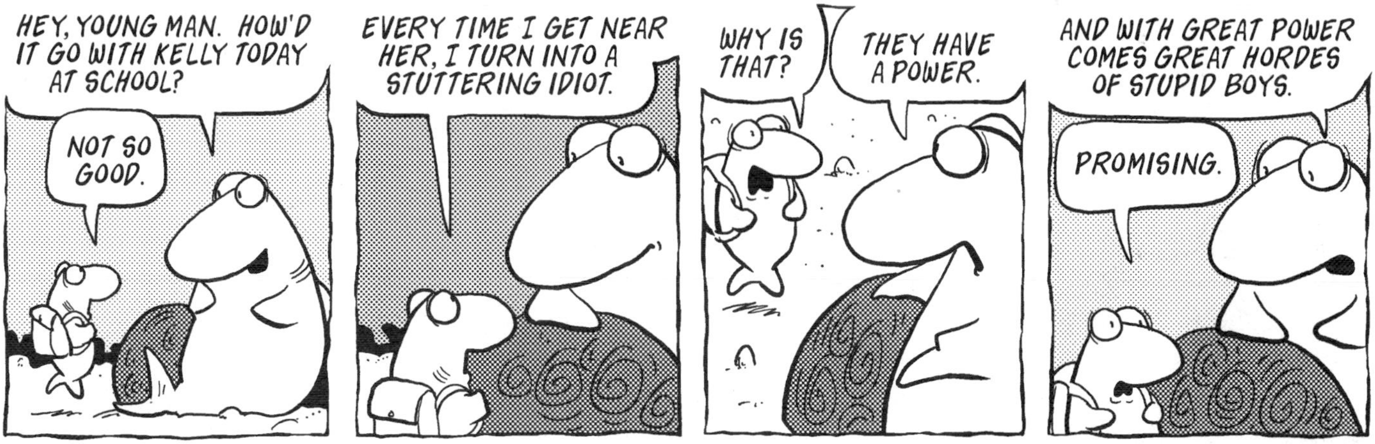
HEY, YOUNG MAN. HOW'D IT GO WITH KELLY TODAY AT SCHOOL?
NOT SO GOOD.
EVERY TIME I GET NEAR HER, I TURN INTO A STUTTERING IDIOT.
WHY IS THAT?
THEY HAVE A POWER.
AND WITH GREAT POWER COMES GREAT HORDES OF STUPID BOYS.
PROMISING.

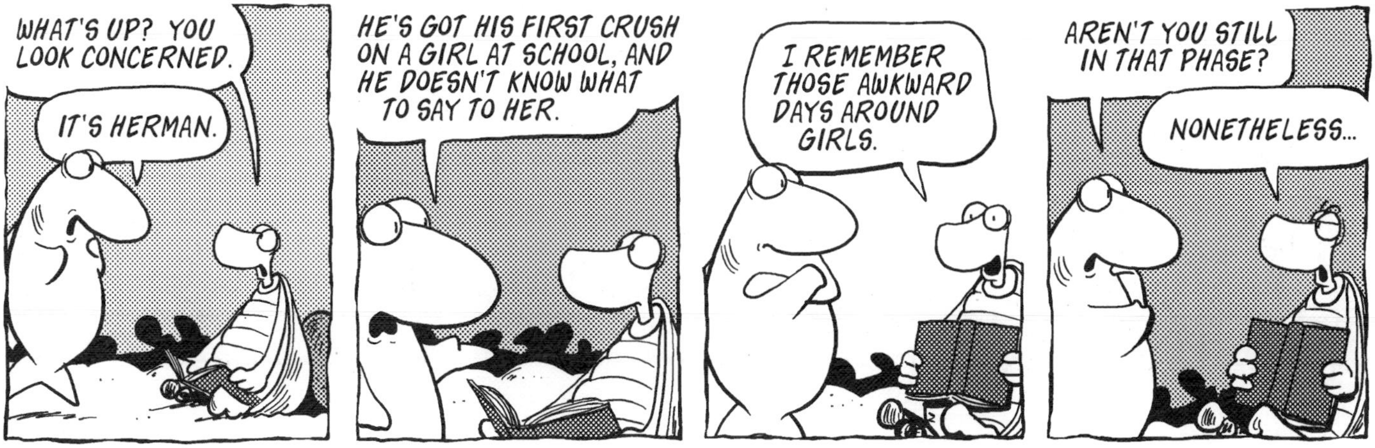
WHAT'S UP? YOU LOOK CONCERNED.
IT'S HERMAN.
HE'S GOT HIS FIRST CRUSH ON A GIRL AT SCHOOL, AND HE DOESN'T KNOW WHAT TO SAY TO HER.
I REMEMBER THOSE AWKWARD DAYS AROUND GIRLS.
AREN'T YOU STILL IN THAT PHASE?
NONETHELESS...

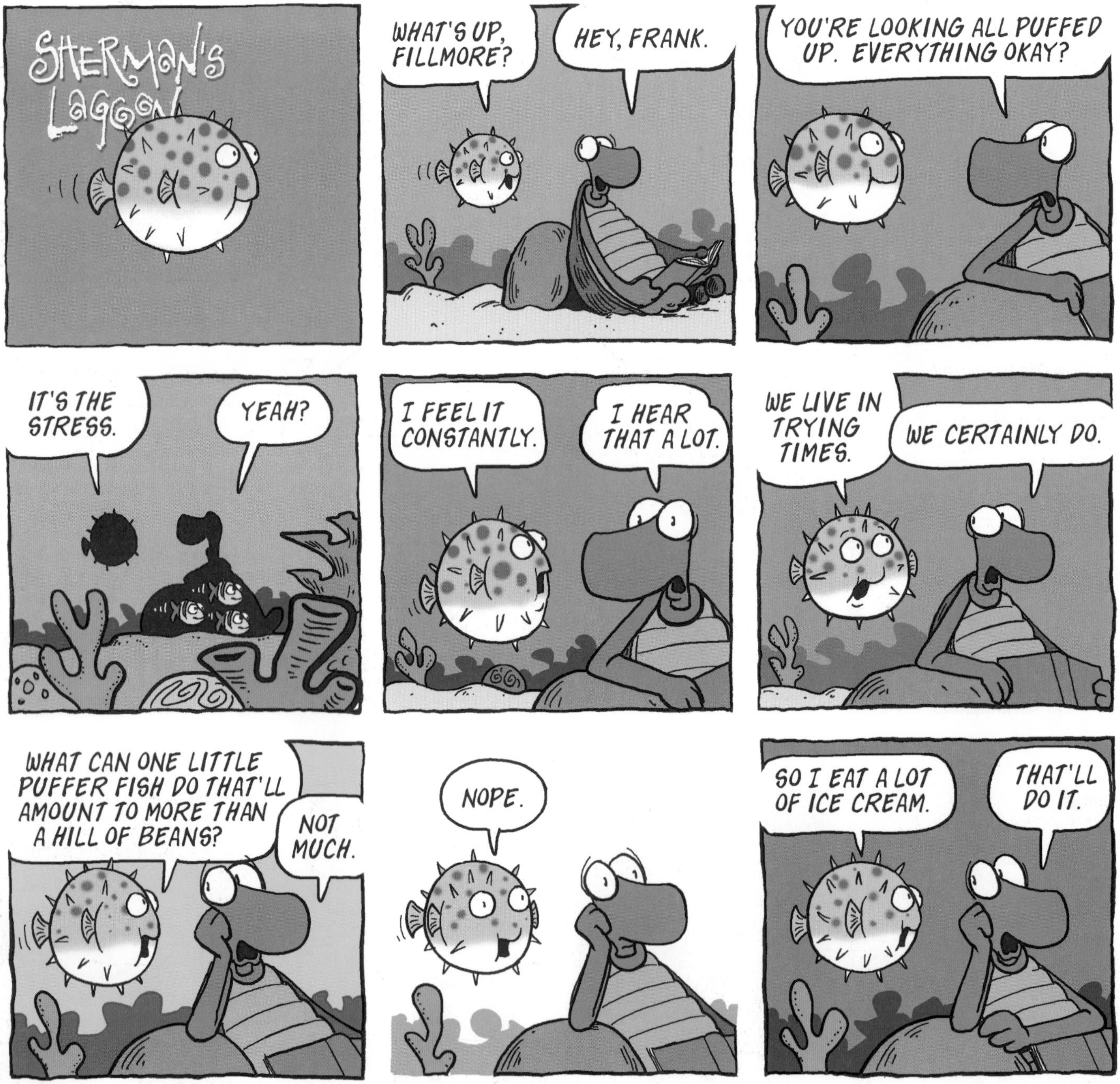
SHERMAN'S LAGOON
WHAT'S UP, FILLMORE?
HEY, FRANK.
YOU'RE LOOKING ALL PUFFED UP. EVERYTHING OKAY?
IT'S THE STRESS.
YEAH?
I FEEL IT CONSTANTLY.
I HEAR THAT A LOT.
WE LIVE IN TRYING TIMES.
WE CERTAINLY DO.
WHAT CAN ONE LITTLE PUFFER FISH DO THAT'LL AMOUNT TO MORE THAN A HILL OF BEANS?
NOT MUCH.
NOPE.
SO I EAT A LOT OF ICE CREAM.
THAT'LL DO IT.

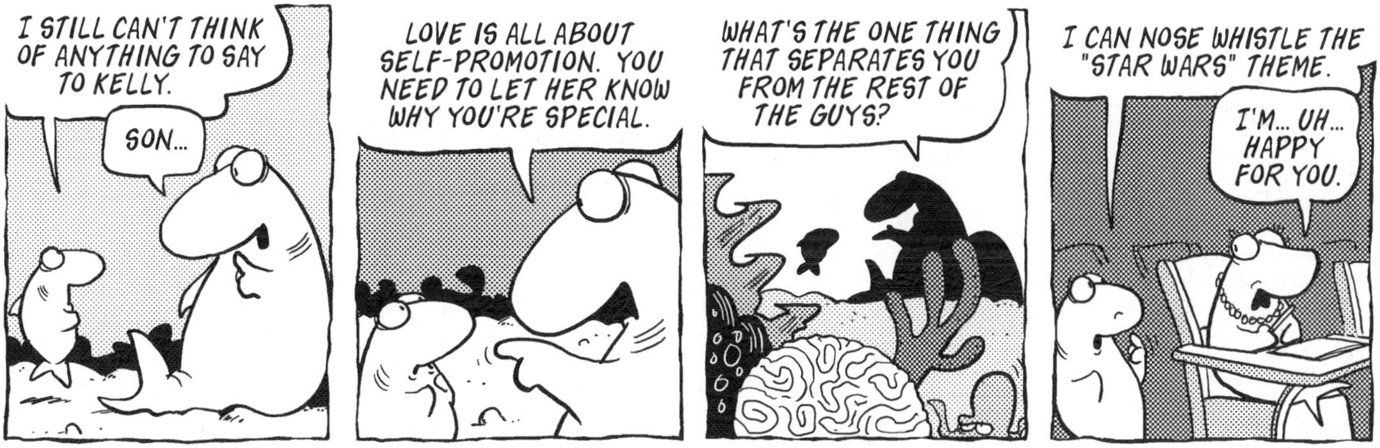
I STILL CAN'T THINK OF ANYTHING TO SAY TO KELLY.
SON...
LOVE IS ALL ABOUT SELF-PROMOTION. YOU NEED TO LET HER KNOW WHY YOU'RE SPECIAL.
WHAT'S THE ONE THING THAT SEPARATES YOU FROM THE REST OF THE GUYS?
I CAN NOSE WHISTLE THE "STAR WARS" THEME.
I'M... UH... HAPPY FOR YOU.

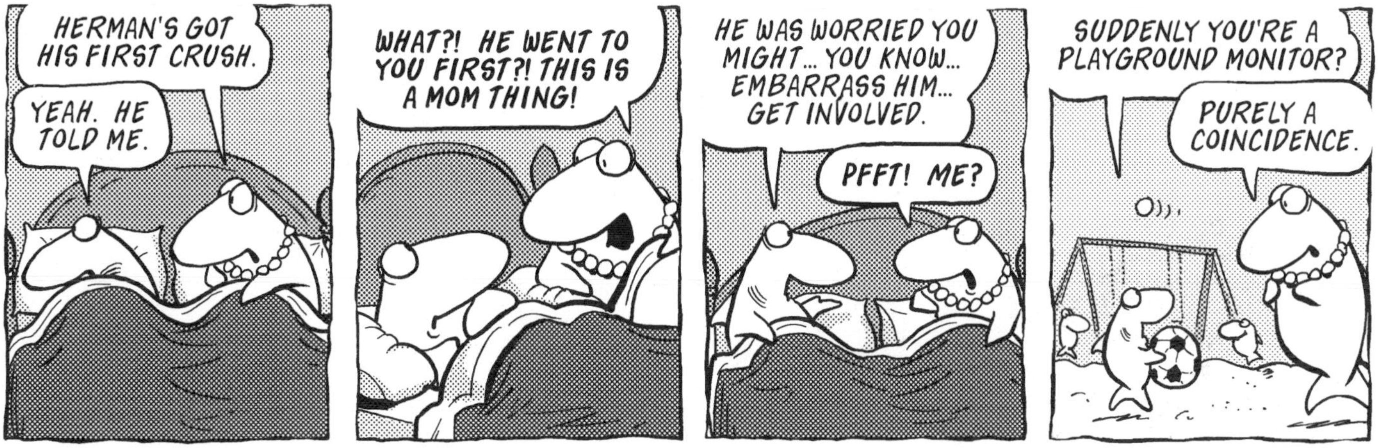
HERMAN'S GOT HIS FIRST CRUSH.
YEAH. HE TOLD ME.
WHAT?! HE WENT TO YOU FIRST?! THIS IS A MOM THING!
HE WAS WORRIED YOU MIGHT... YOU KNOW... EMBARRASS HIM... GET INVOLVED.
PFFT! ME?
SUDDENLY YOU'RE A PLAYGROUND MONITOR?
PURELY A COINCIDENCE.

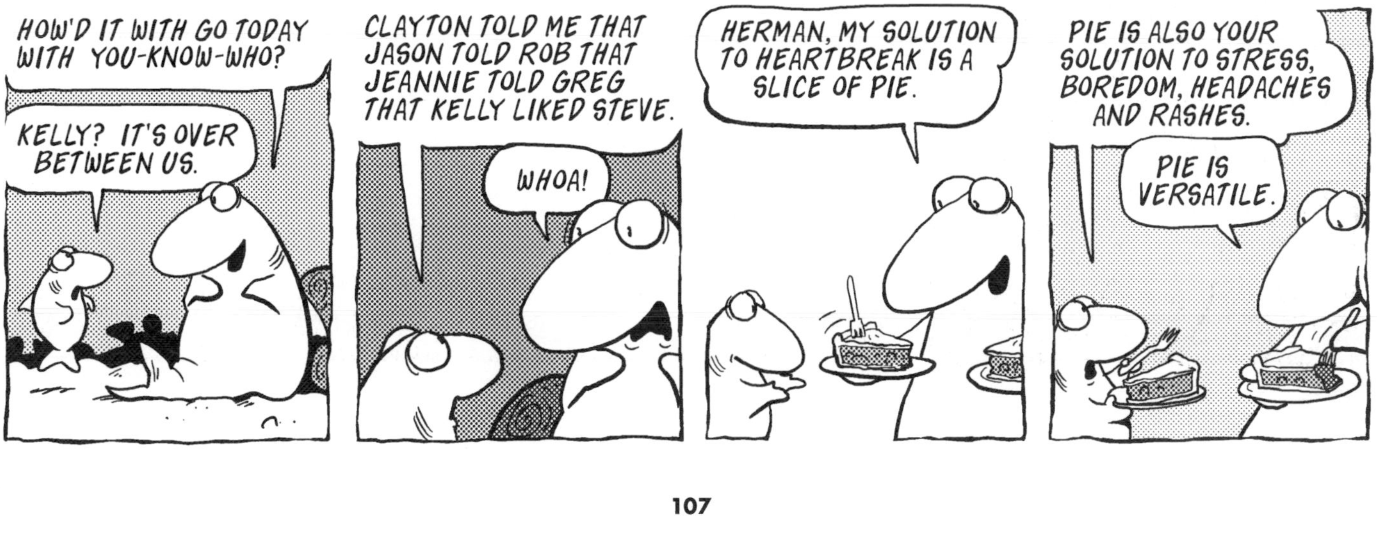
HOW'D IT WITH GO TODAY WITH YOU-KNOW-WHO?
KELLY? IT'S OVER BETWEEN US.
CLAYTON TOLD ME THAT JASON TOLD ROB THAT JEANNIE TOLD GREG THAT KELLY LIKED STEVE.
WHOA!
HERMAN, MY SOLUTION TO HEARTBREAK IS A SLICE OF PIE.
PIE IS ALSO YOUR SOLUTION TO STRESS, BOREDOM, HEADACHES AND RASHES.
PIE IS VERSATILE.

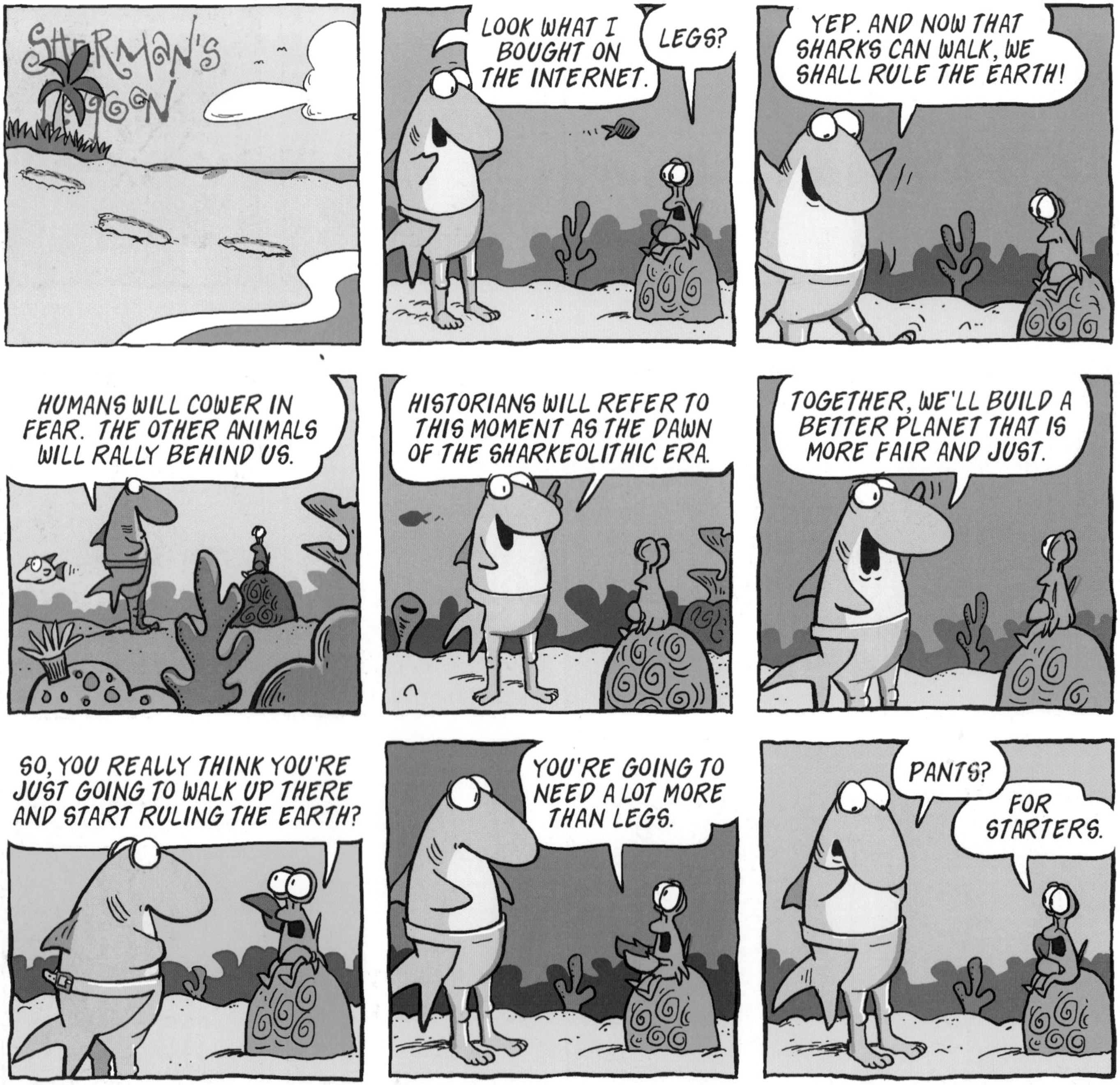
SHERMAN'S LAGOON
LOOK WHAT I BOUGHT ON THE INTERNET.
LEGS?
YEP. AND NOW THAT SHARKS CAN WALK, WE SHALL RULE THE EARTH!
HUMANS WILL COWER IN FEAR. THE OTHER ANIMALS WILL RALLY BEHIND US.
HISTORIANS WILL REFER TO THIS MOMENT AS THE DAWN OF THE SHARKEOLITHIC ERA.
TOGETHER, WE'LL BUILD A BETTER PLANET THAT IS MORE FAIR AND JUST.
SO, YOU REALLY THINK YOU'RE JUST GOING TO WALK UP THERE AND START RULING THE EARTH?
YOU'RE GOING TO NEED A LOT MORE THAN LEGS.
PANTS?
FOR STARTERS.

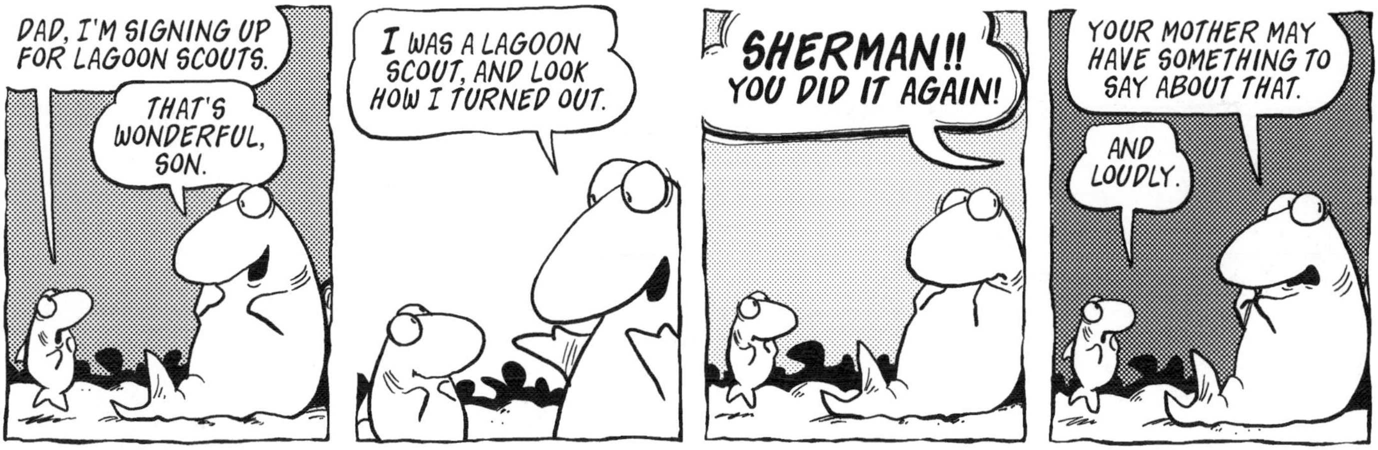
DAD, I'M SIGNING UP FOR LAGOON SCOUTS.
THAT'S WONDERFUL, SON.
I WAS A LAGOON SCOUT, AND LOOK HOW I TURNED OUT.
SHERMAN!! YOU DID IT AGAIN!
YOUR MOTHER MAY HAVE SOMETHING TO SAY ABOUT THAT.
AND LOUDLY.

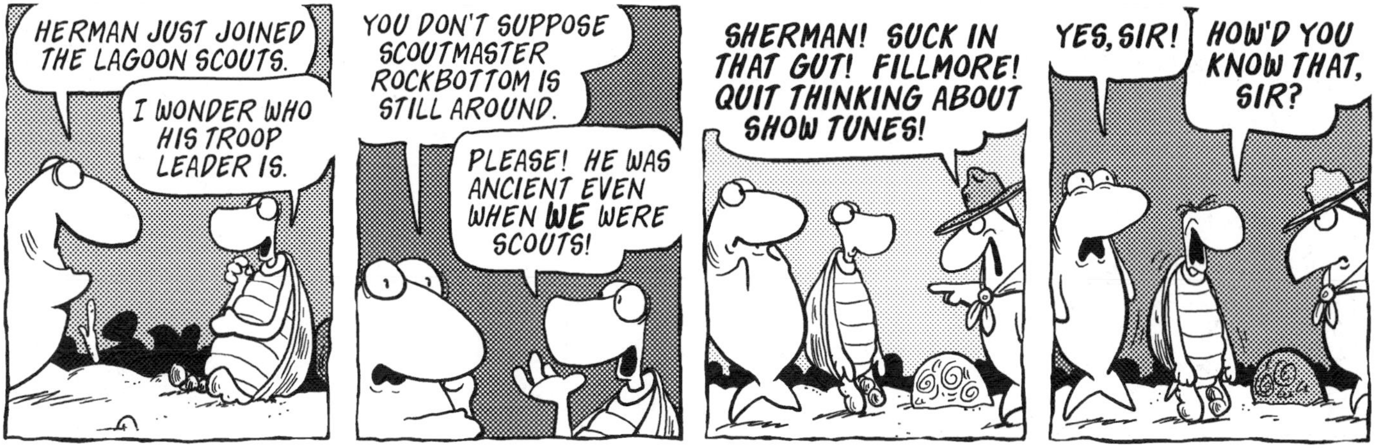
HERMAN JUST JOINED THE LAGOON SCOUTS.
I WONDER WHO HIS TROOP LEADER IS.
YOU DON'T SUPPOSE SCOUTMASTER ROCKBOTTOM IS STILL AROUND.
PLEASE! HE WAS ANCIENT EVEN WHEN WE WERE SCOUTS!
SHERMAN! SUCK IN THAT GUT! FILLMORE! QUIT THINKING ABOUT SHOW TUNES!
YES, SIR!
HOW'D YOU KNOW THAT, SIR?

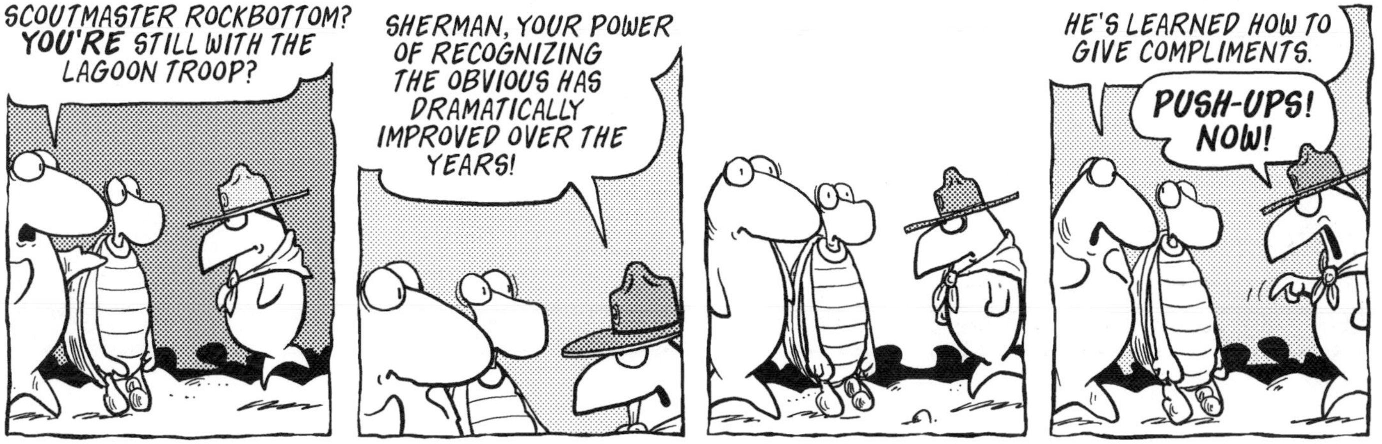
SCOUTMASTER ROCKBOTTOM? YOU'RE STILL WITH THE LAGOON TROOP?
SHERMAN, YOUR POWER OF RECOGNIZING THE OBVIOUS HAS DRAMATICALLY IMPROVED OVER THE YEARS!
HE'S LEARNED HOW TO GIVE COMPLIMENTS.
PUSH-UPS! NOW!

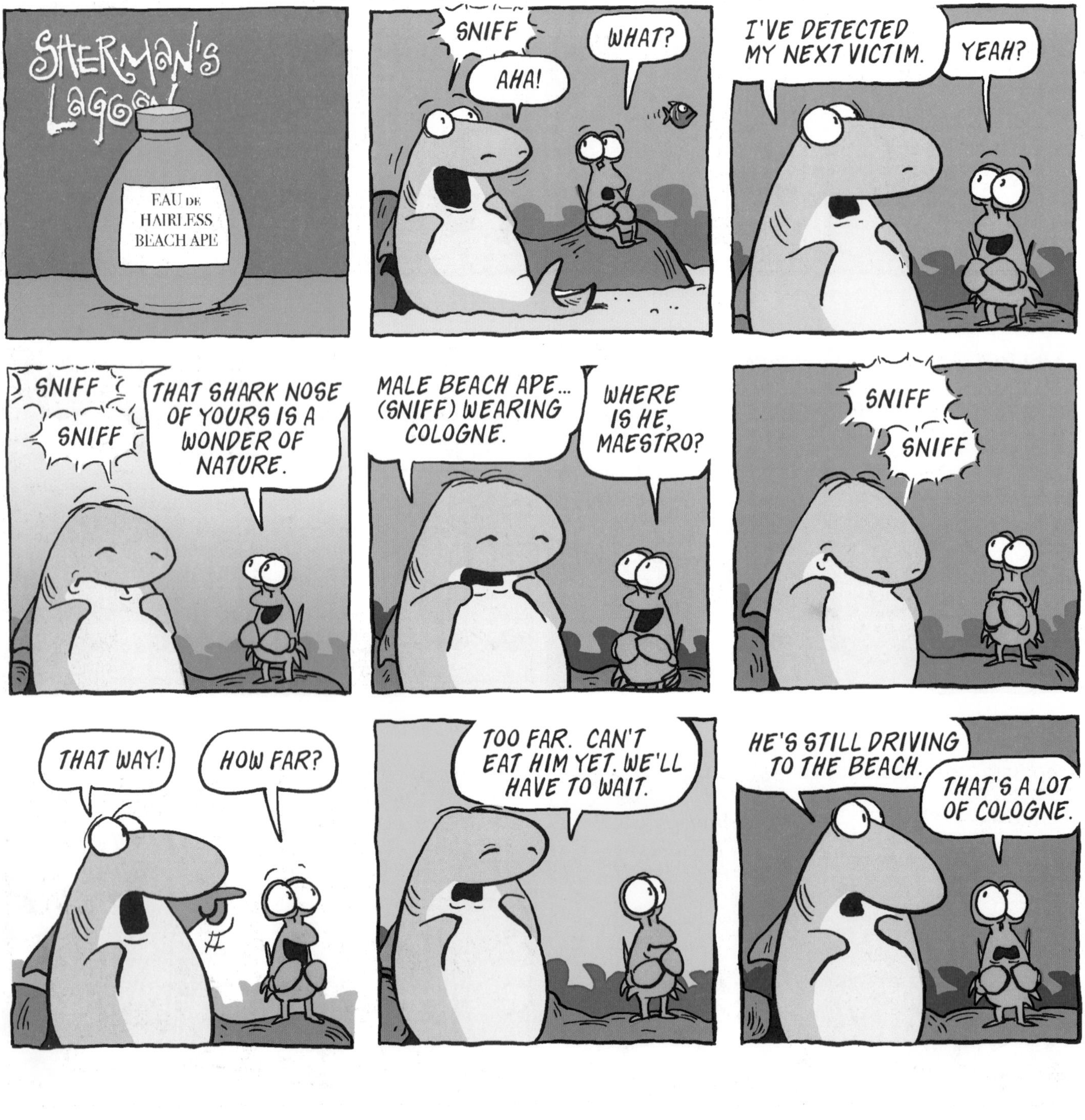
SHERMAN'S LAGOON
EAU DE HAIRLESS BEACH APE
SNIFF
AHA!
WHAT?
I'VE DETECTED MY NEXT VICTIM.
YEAH?
SNIFF
SNIFF
THAT SHARK NOSE OF YOURS IS A WONDER OF NATURE.
MALE BEACH APE... (SNIFF) WEARING COLOGNE.
WHERE IS HE, MAESTRO?
SNIFF
SNIFF
THAT WAY!
HOW FAR?
TOO FAR. CAN'T EAT HIM YET. WE'LL HAVE TO WAIT.
HE'S STILL DRIVING TO THE BEACH.
THAT'S A LOT OF COLOGNE.

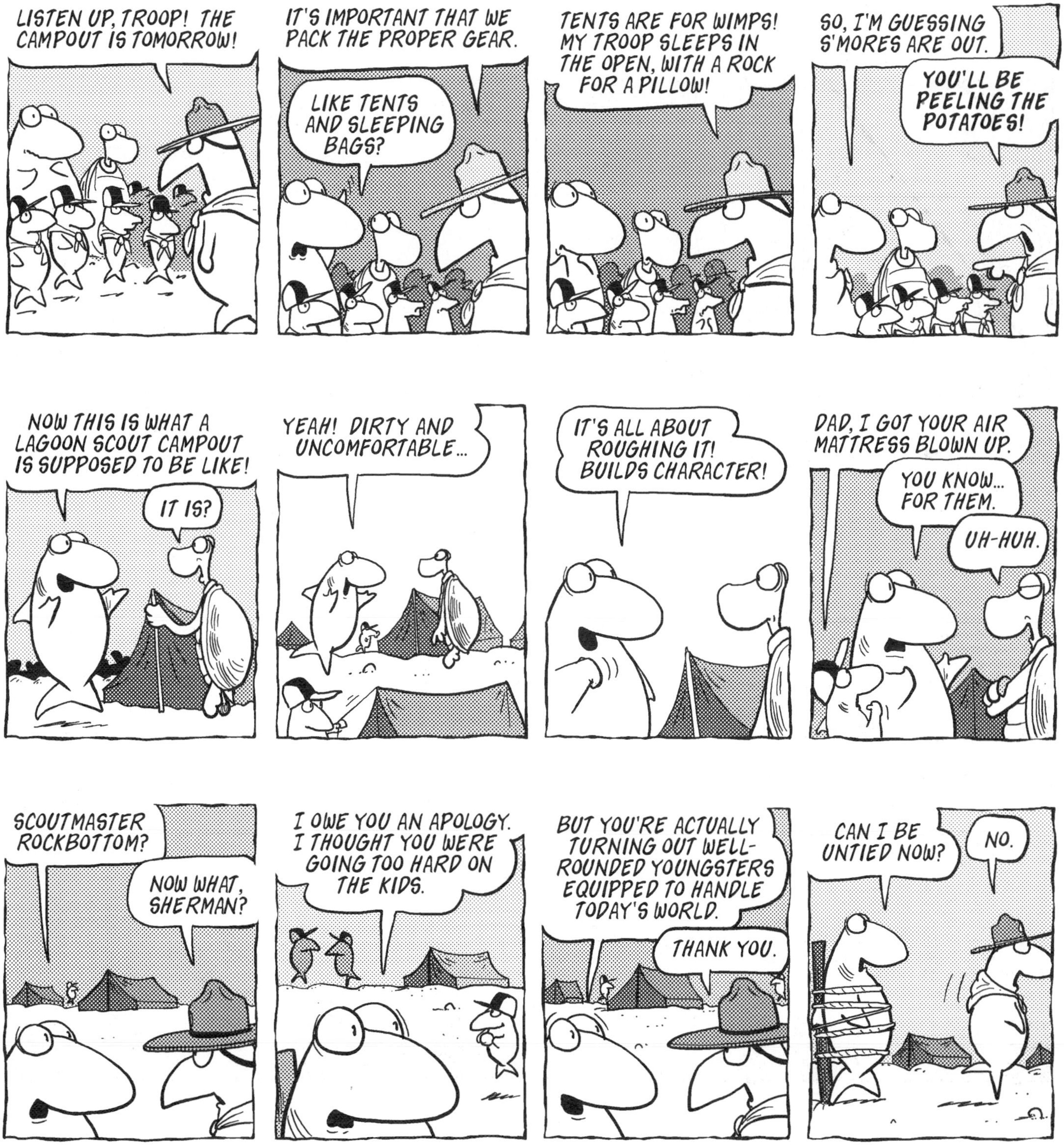
LISTEN UP, TROOP! THE CAMPOUT IS TOMORROW!
IT'S IMPORTANT THAT WE PACK THE PROPER GEAR.
LIKE TENTS AND SLEEPING BAGS?
TENTS ARE FOR WIMPS! MY TROOP SLEEPS IN THE OPEN, WITH A ROCK FOR A PILLOW!
SO, I'M GUESSING S'MORES ARE OUT.
YOU'LL BE PEELING THE POTATOES!
NOW THIS IS WHAT A LAGOON SCOUT CAMPOUT IS SUPPOSED TO BE LIKE!
IT IS?
YEAH! DIRTY AND UNCOMFORTABLE...
IT'S ALL ABOUT ROUGHING IT! BUILDS CHARACTER!
DAD, I GOT YOUR AIR MATTRESS BLOWN UP.
YOU KNOW... FOR THEM.
UH-HUH.
SCOUTMASTER ROCKBOTTOM?
NOW WHAT, SHERMAN?
I OWE YOU AN APOLOGY. I THOUGHT YOU WERE GOING TOO HARD ON THE KIDS.
BUT YOU'RE ACTUALLY TURNING OUT WELL-ROUNDED YOUNGSTERS EQUIPPED TO HANDLE TODAY'S WORLD.
THANK YOU.
CAN I BE UNTIED NOW?
NO.

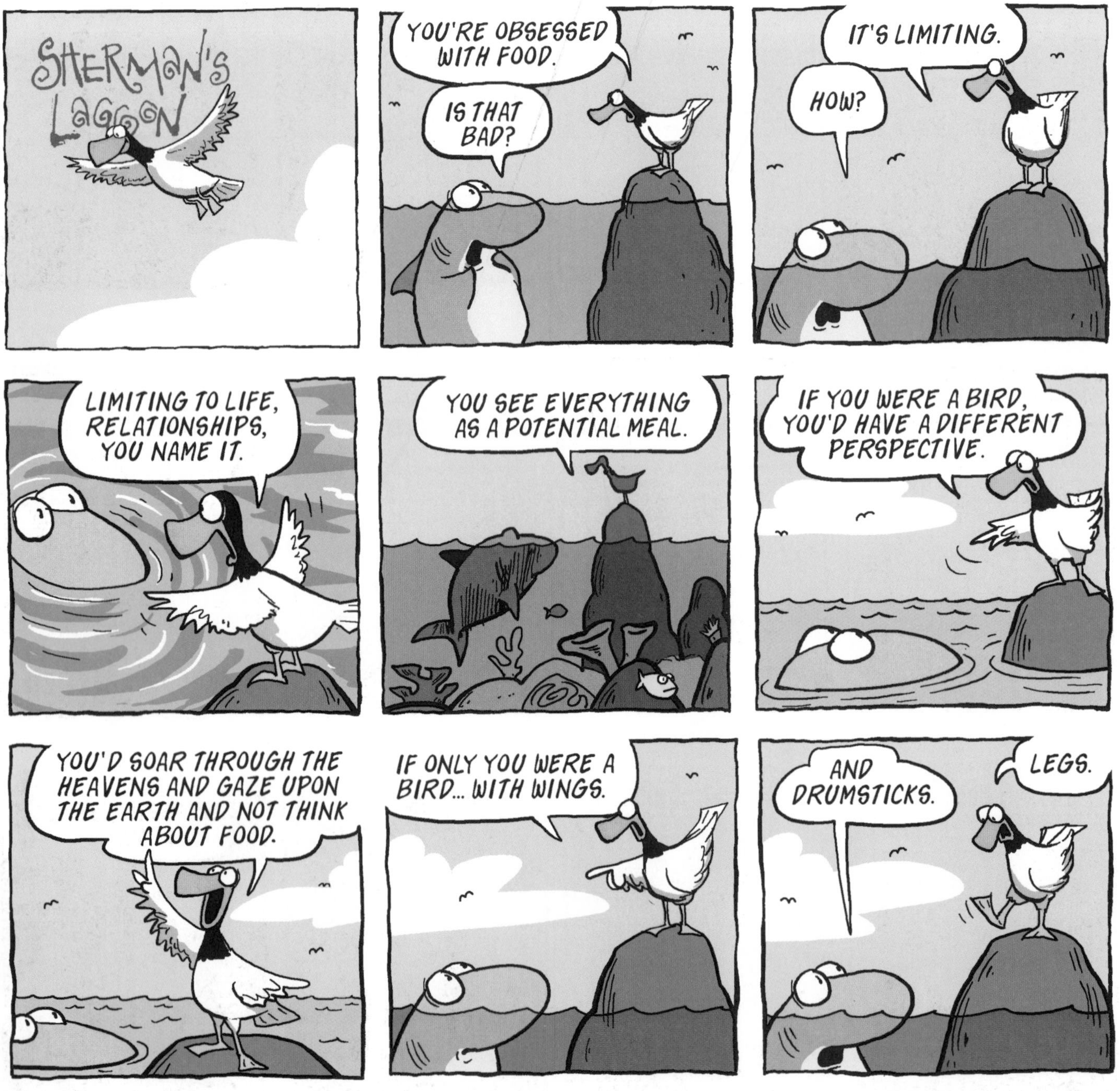
SHERMAN'S LAGOON
YOU'RE OBSESSED WITH FOOD.
IS THAT BAD?
IT'S LIMITING.
HOW?
LIMITING TO LIFE, RELATIONSHIPS, YOU NAME IT.
YOU SEE EVERYTHING AS A POTENTIAL MEAL.
IF YOU WERE A BIRD, YOU'D HAVE A DIFFERENT PERSPECTIVE.
YOU'D SOAR THROUGH THE HEAVENS AND GAZE UPON THE EARTH AND NOT THINK ABOUT FOOD.
IF ONLY YOU WERE A BIRD... WITH WINGS.
LEGS.
AND DRUMSTICKS.

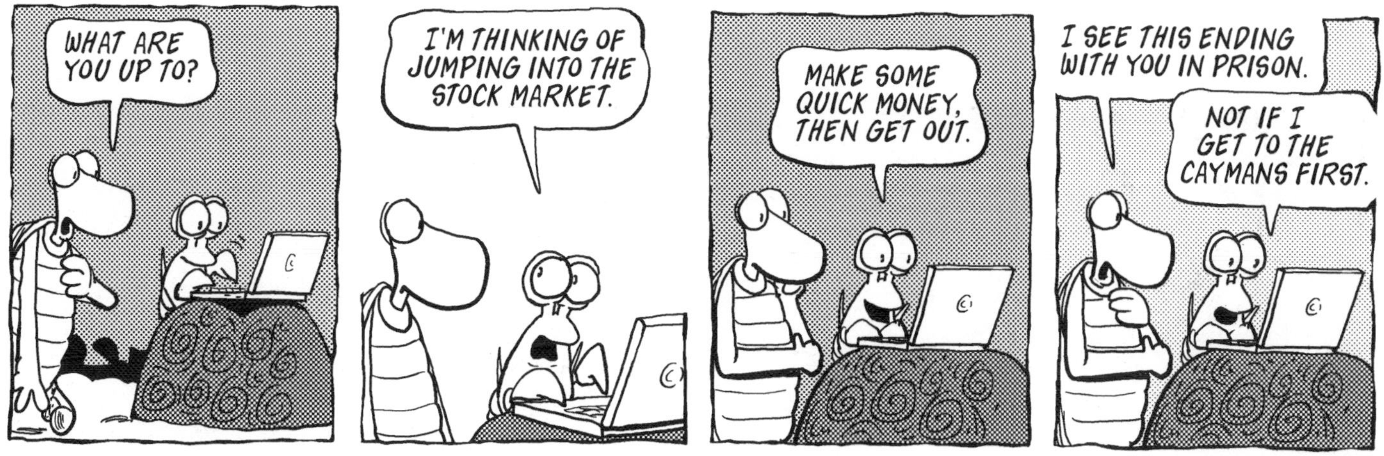
WHAT ARE YOU UP TO?
I'M THINKING OF JUMPING INTO THE STOCK MARKET.
MAKE SOME QUICK MONEY, THEN GET OUT.
I SEE THIS ENDING WITH YOU IN PRISON.
NOT IF I GET TO THE CAYMANS FIRST.

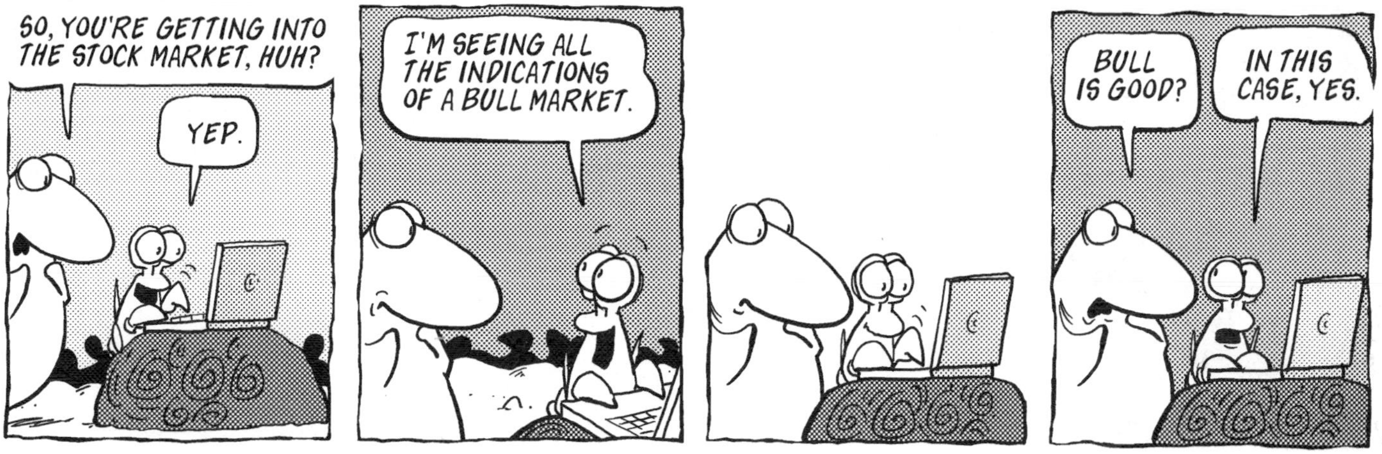
SO, YOU'RE GETTING INTO THE STOCK MARKET, HUH?
YEP.
I'M SEEING ALL THE INDICATIONS OF A BULL MARKET.
BULL IS GOOD?
IN THIS CASE, YES.

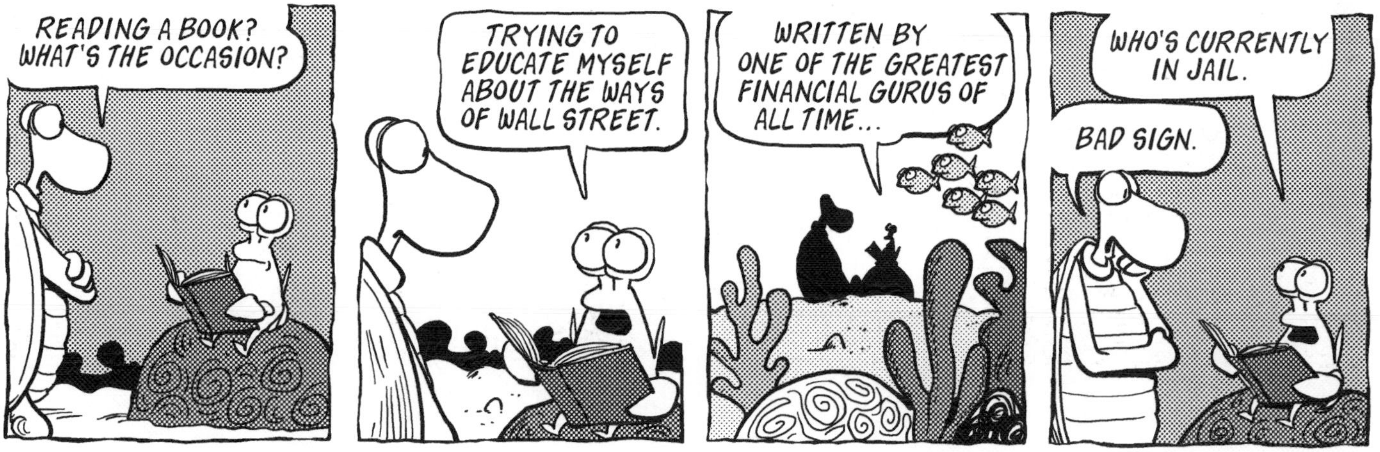
READING A BOOK? WHAT'S THE OCCASION?
TRYING TO EDUCATE MYSELF ABOUT THE WAYS OF WALL STREET.
WRITTEN BY ONE OF THE GREATEST FINANCIAL GURUS OF ALL TIME...
WHO'S CURRENTLY IN JAIL.
BAD SIGN.

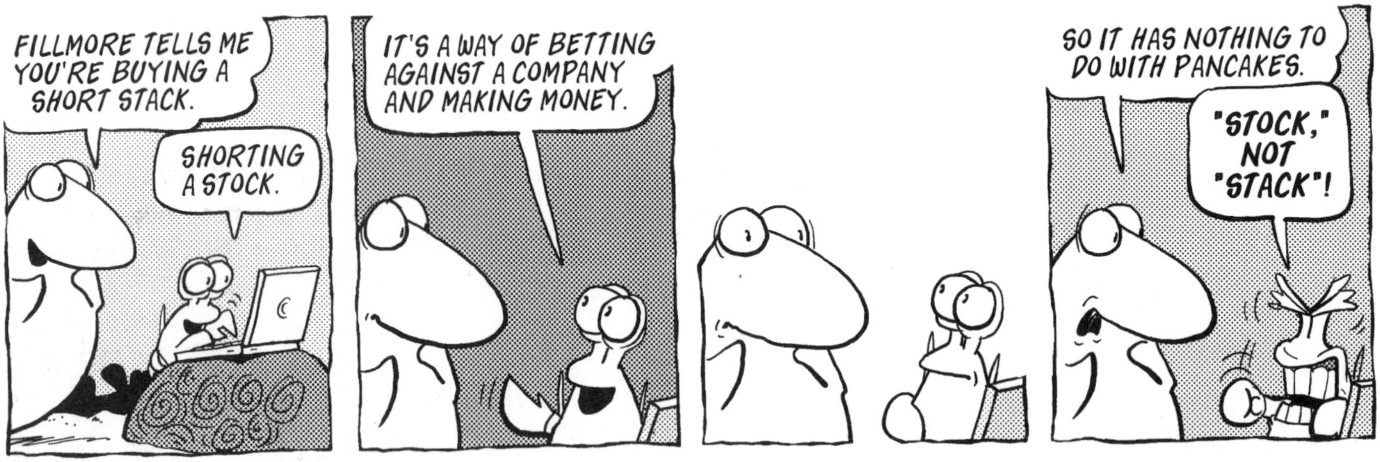
FILLMORE TELLS ME YOU'RE BUYING A SHORT STACK.
SHORTING A STOCK.
IT'S A WAY OF BETTING AGAINST A COMPANY AND MAKING MONEY.
SO IT HAS NOTHING TO DO WITH PANCAKES.
"STOCK," NOT "STACK"!

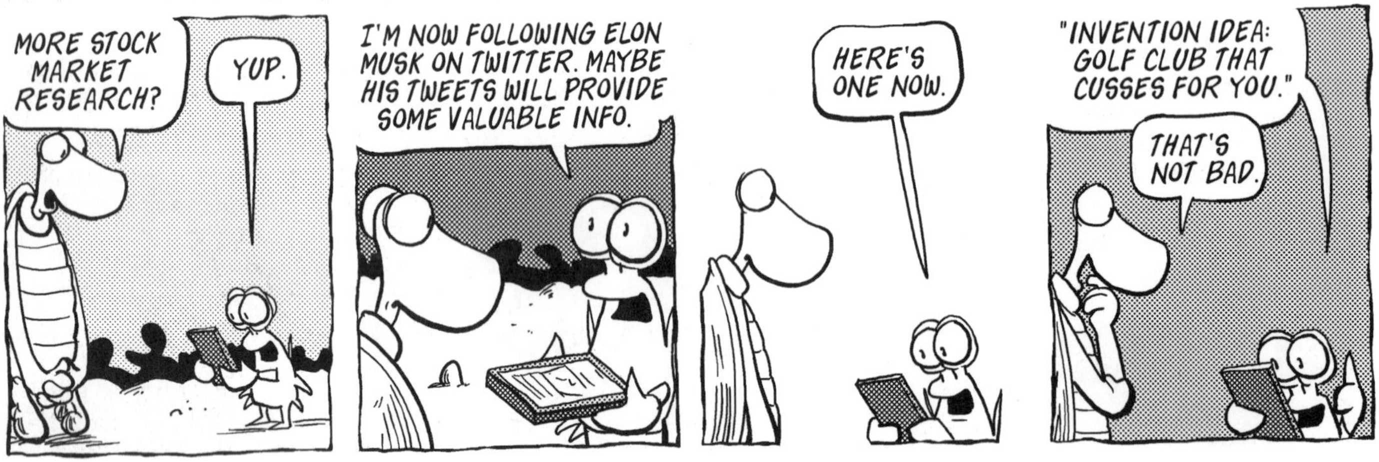
MORE STOCK MARKET RESEARCH?
YUP.
I'M NOW FOLLOWING ELON MUSK ON TWITTER. MAYBE HIS TWEETS WILL PROVIDE SOME VALUABLE INFO.
HERE'S ONE NOW.
"INVENTION IDEA: GOLF CLUB THAT CUSSES FOR YOU."
THAT'S NOT BAD.

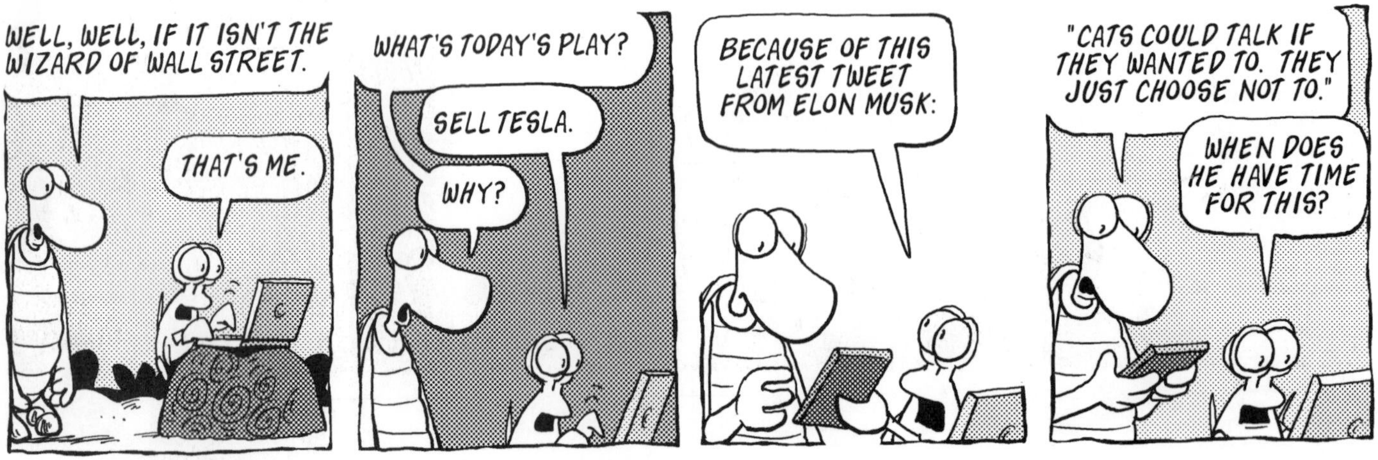
WELL, WELL, IF IT ISN'T THE WIZARD OF WALL STREET.
THAT'S ME.
WHAT'S TODAY'S PLAY?
SELL TESLA.
WHY?
BECAUSE OF THIS LATEST TWEET FROM ELON MUSK:
"CATS COULD TALK IF THEY WANTED TO. THEY JUST CHOOSE NOT TO."
WHEN DOES HE HAVE TIME FOR THIS?

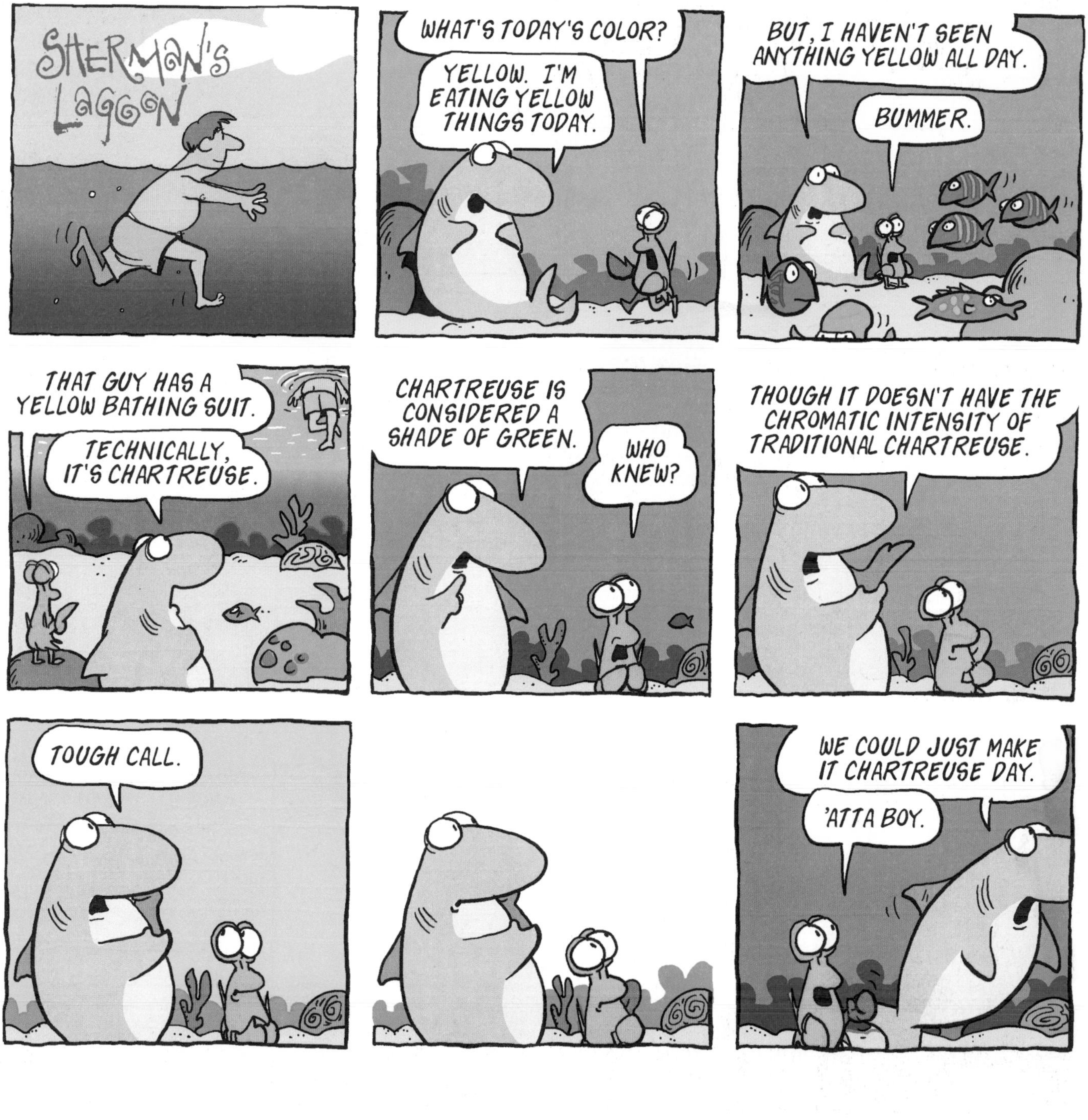
SHERMAN'S LAGOON
WHAT'S TODAY'S COLOR?
YELLOW. I'M EATING YELLOW THINGS TODAY.
BUT, I HAVEN'T SEEN ANYTHING YELLOW ALL DAY.
BUMMER.
THAT GUY HAS A YELLOW BATHING SUIT.
TECHNICALLY, IT'S CHARTREUSE.
CHARTREUSE IS CONSIDERED A SHADE OF GREEN.
WHO KNEW?
THOUGH IT DOESN'T HAVE THE CHROMATIC INTENSITY OF TRADITIONAL CHARTREUSE.
TOUGH CALL.
WE COULD JUST MAKE IT CHARTREUSE DAY.
'ATTA BOY.

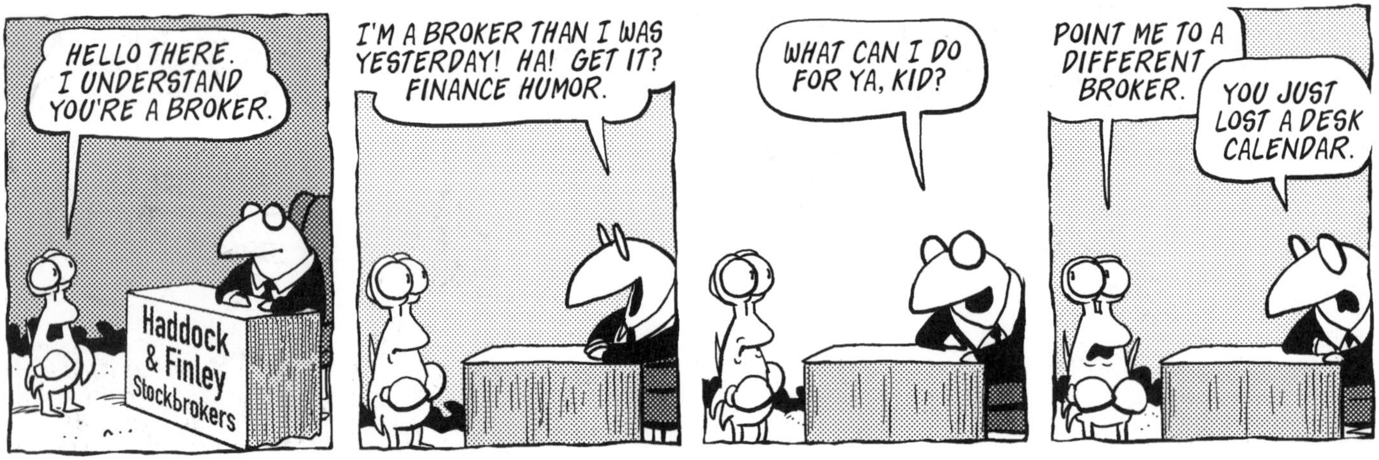
HELLO THERE. I UNDERSTAND YOU'RE A BROKER.
Haddock & Finley Stockbrokers
I'M A BROKER THAN I WAS YESTERDAY! HA! GET IT? FINANCE HUMOR.
WHAT CAN I DO FOR YA, KID?
POINT ME TO A DIFFERENT BROKER.
YOU JUST LOST A DESK CALENDAR.

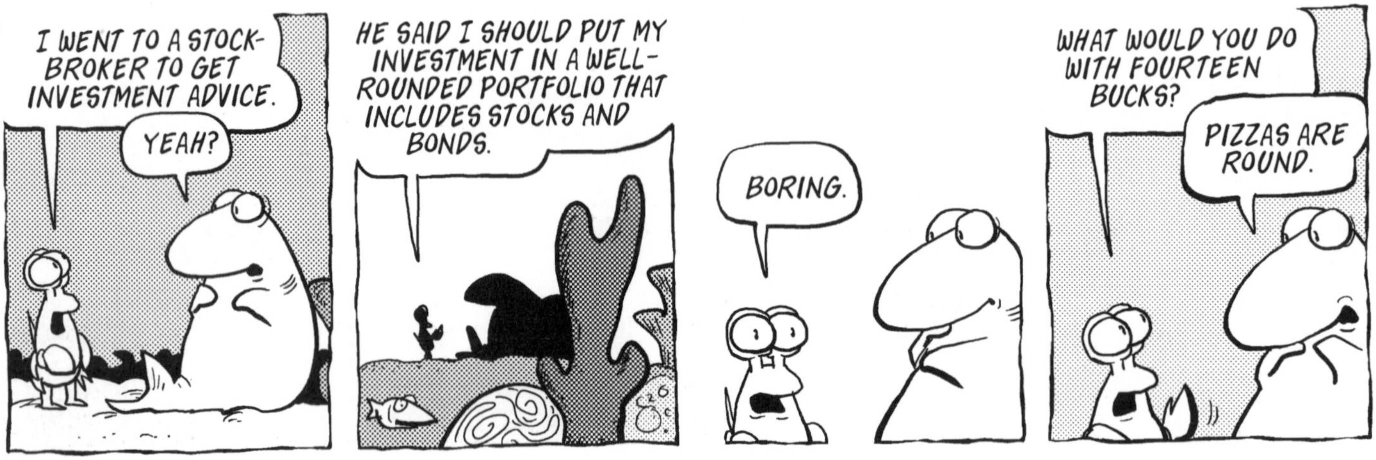
I WENT TO A STOCK-BROKER TO GET INVESTMENT ADVICE.
YEAH?
HE SAID I SHOULD PUT MY INVESTMENT IN A WELL-ROUNDED PORTFOLIO THAT INCLUDES STOCKS AND BONDS.
BORING.
WHAT WOULD YOU DO WITH FOURTEEN BUCKS?
PIZZAS ARE ROUND.

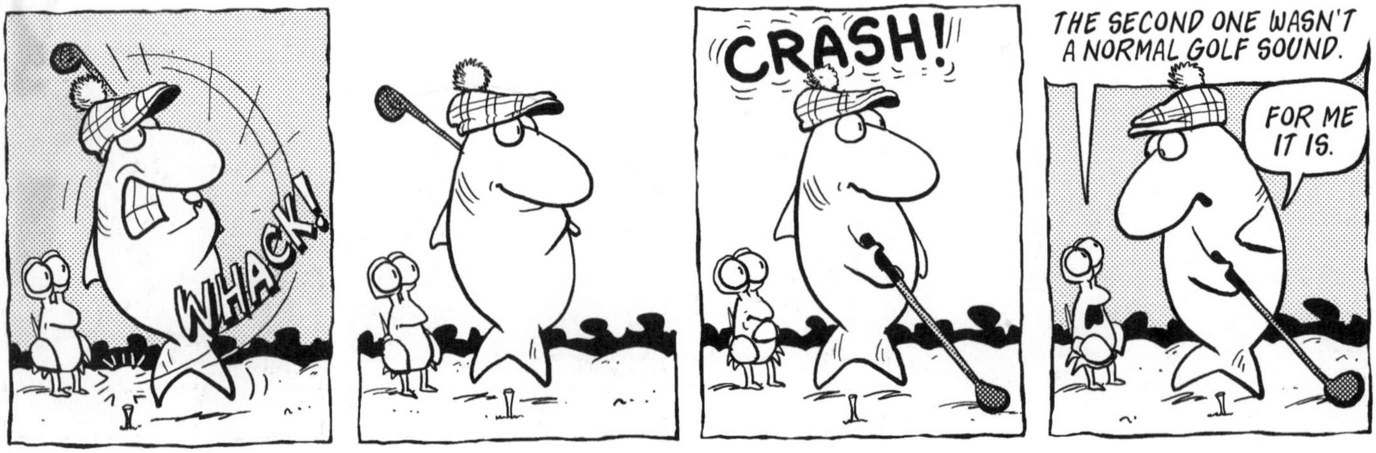
WHACK!
CRASH!
THE SECOND ONE WASN'T A NORMAL GOLF SOUND.
FOR ME IT IS.

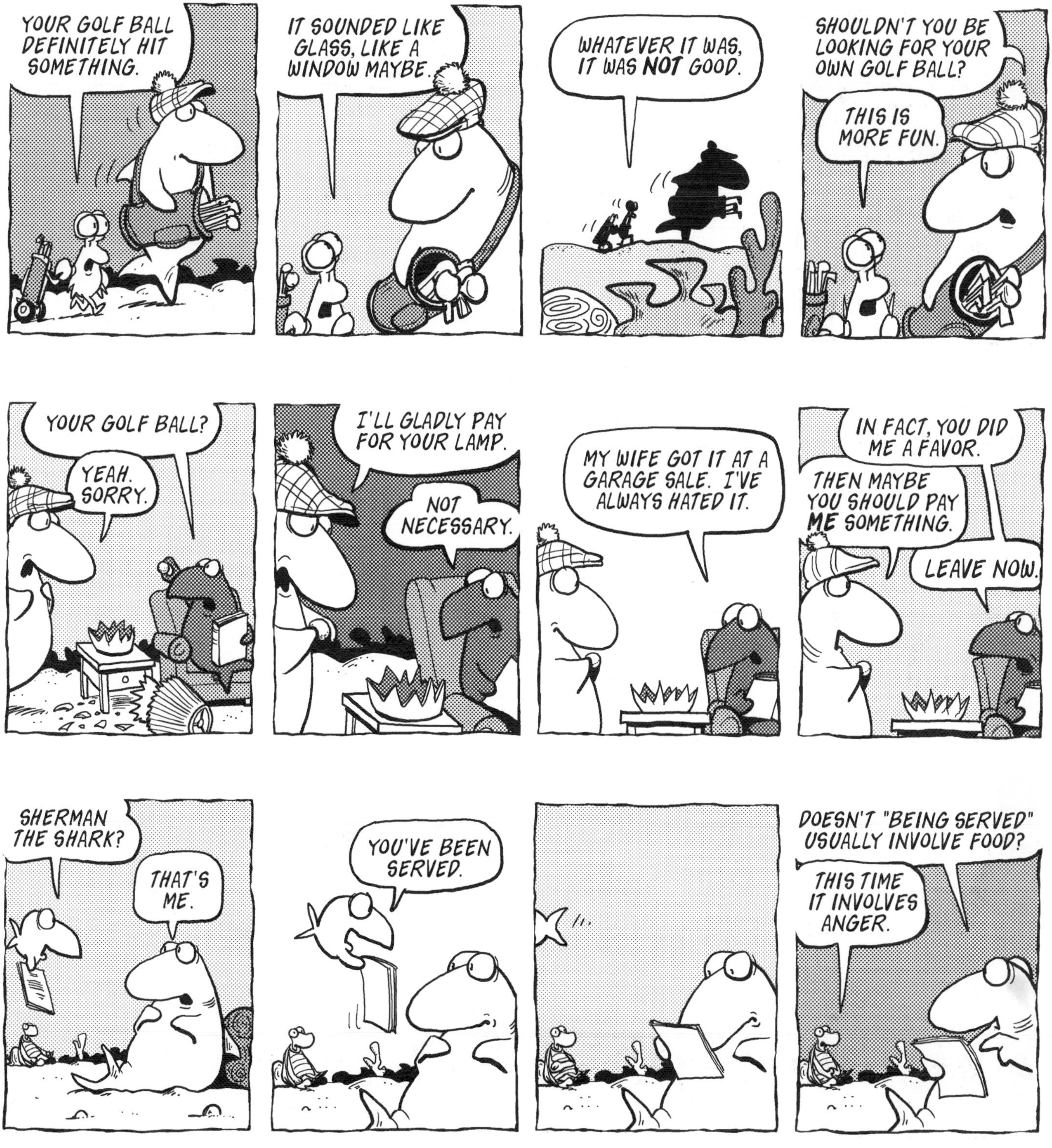
YOUR GOLF BALL DEFINITELY HIT SOMETHING.
IT SOUNDED LIKE GLASS, LIKE A WINDOW MAYBE.
WHATEVER IT WAS, IT WAS **NOT** GOOD.
SHOULDN'T YOU BE LOOKING FOR YOUR OWN GOLF BALL?
THIS IS MORE FUN.
YOUR GOLF BALL?
YEAH. SORRY.
I'LL GLADLY PAY FOR YOUR LAMP.
NOT NECESSARY.
MY WIFE GOT IT AT A GARAGE SALE. I'VE ALWAYS HATED IT.
IN FACT, YOU DID ME A FAVOR.
THEN MAYBE YOU SHOULD PAY **ME** SOMETHING.
LEAVE NOW.
SHERMAN THE SHARK?
THAT'S ME.
YOU'VE BEEN SERVED.
DOESN'T "BEING SERVED" USUALLY INVOLVE FOOD?
THIS TIME IT INVOLVES ANGER.

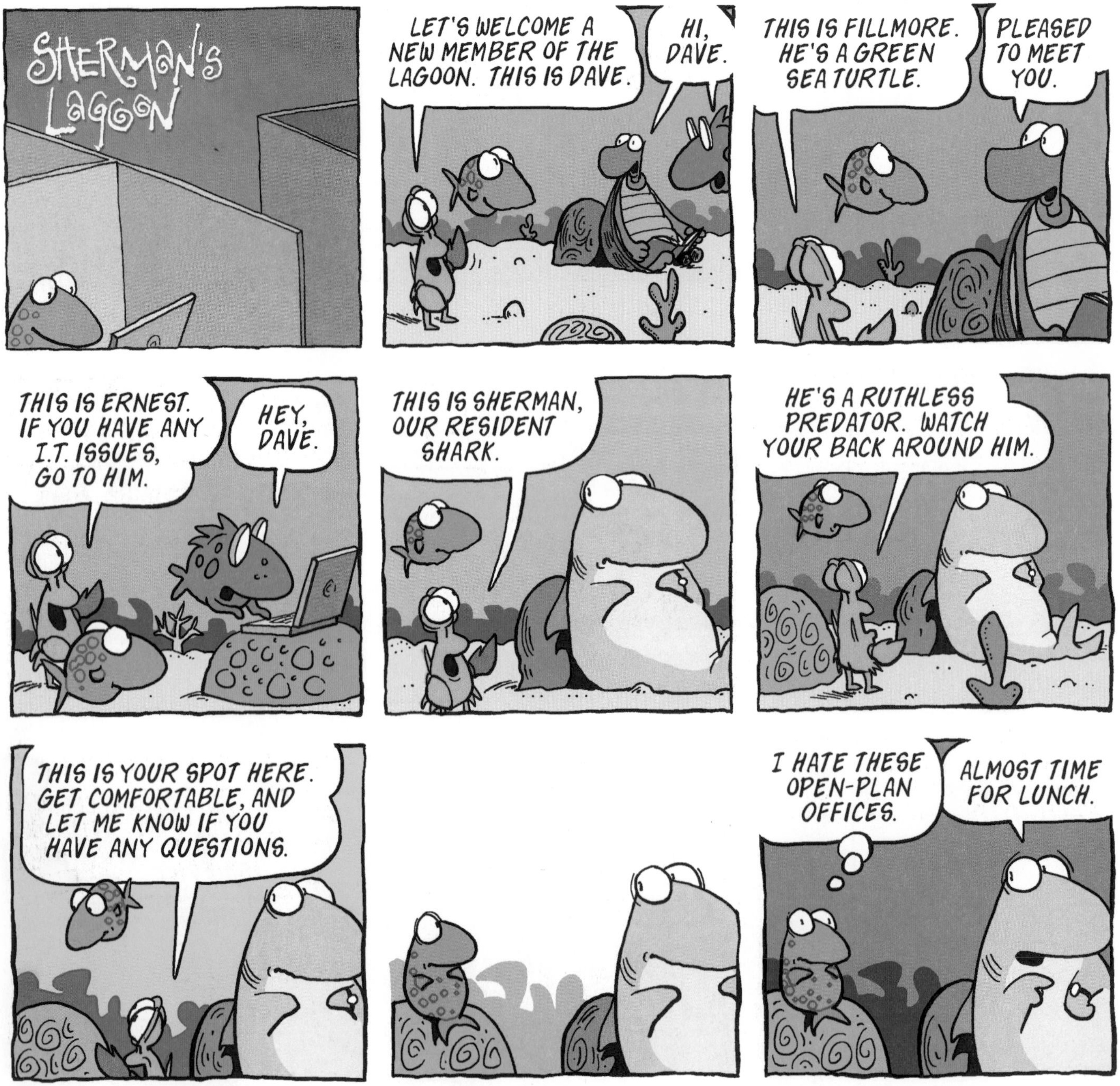
SHERMAN'S LAGOON
LET'S WELCOME A NEW MEMBER OF THE LAGOON. THIS IS DAVE.
HI, DAVE.
THIS IS FILLMORE. HE'S A GREEN SEA TURTLE.
PLEASED TO MEET YOU.
THIS IS ERNEST. IF YOU HAVE ANY I.T. ISSUES, GO TO HIM.
HEY, DAVE.
THIS IS SHERMAN, OUR RESIDENT SHARK.
HE'S A RUTHLESS PREDATOR. WATCH YOUR BACK AROUND HIM.
THIS IS YOUR SPOT HERE. GET COMFORTABLE, AND LET ME KNOW IF YOU HAVE ANY QUESTIONS.
I HATE THESE OPEN-PLAN OFFICES.
ALMOST TIME FOR LUNCH.

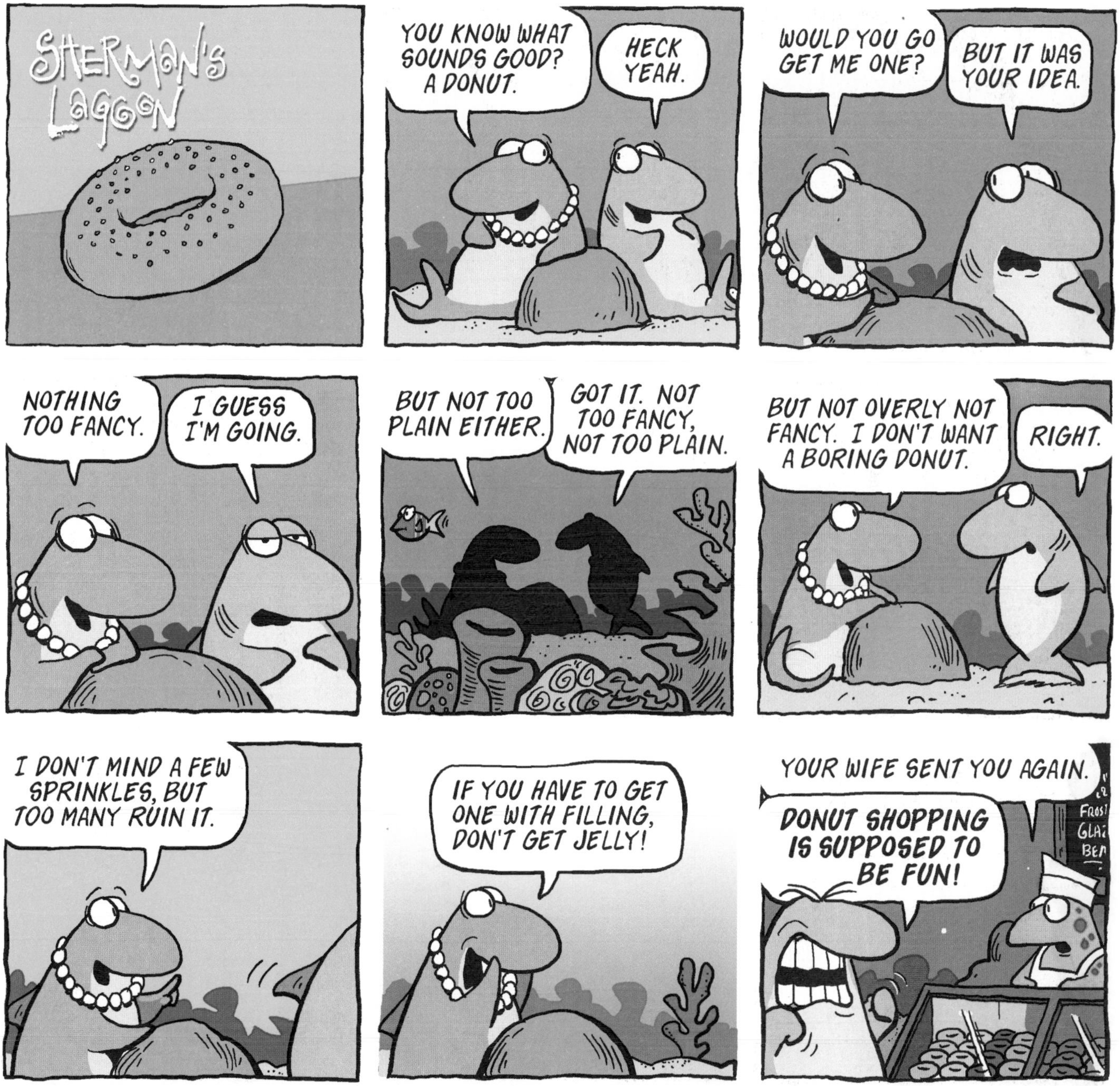
SHERMAN'S LAGOON
YOU KNOW WHAT SOUNDS GOOD? A DONUT.
HECK YEAH.
WOULD YOU GO GET ME ONE?
BUT IT WAS YOUR IDEA.
NOTHING TOO FANCY.
I GUESS I'M GOING.
BUT NOT TOO PLAIN EITHER.
GOT IT. NOT TOO FANCY, NOT TOO PLAIN.
BUT NOT OVERLY NOT FANCY. I DON'T WANT A BORING DONUT.
RIGHT.
I DON'T MIND A FEW SPRINKLES, BUT TOO MANY RUIN IT.
IF YOU HAVE TO GET ONE WITH FILLING, DON'T GET JELLY!
YOUR WIFE SENT YOU AGAIN.
DONUT SHOPPING IS SUPPOSED TO BE FUN!

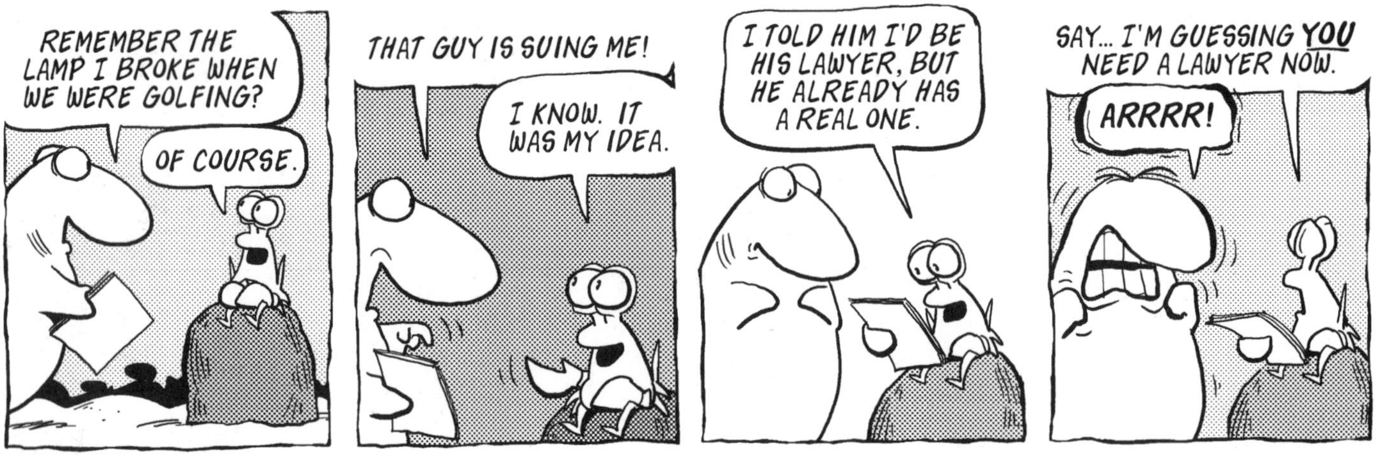
REMEMBER THE LAMP I BROKE WHEN WE WERE GOLFING?
OF COURSE.
THAT GUY IS SUING ME!
I KNOW. IT WAS MY IDEA.
I TOLD HIM I'D BE HIS LAWYER, BUT HE ALREADY HAS A REAL ONE.
SAY... I'M GUESSING YOU NEED A LAWYER NOW.
ARRRR!

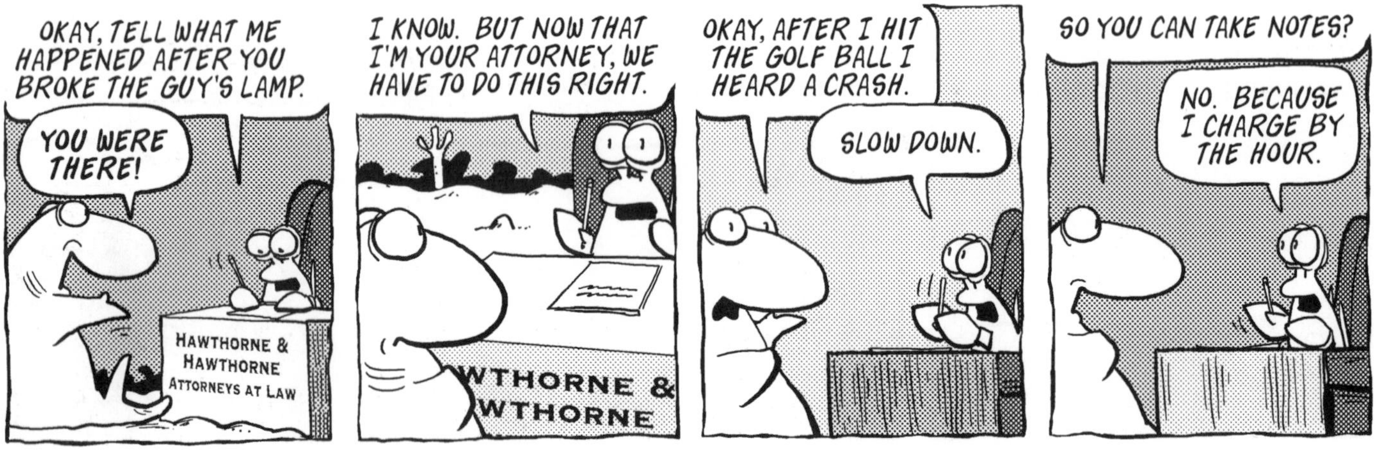
OKAY, TELL WHAT ME HAPPENED AFTER YOU BROKE THE GUY'S LAMP.
YOU WERE THERE!
HAWTHORNE & HAWTHORNE ATTORNEYS AT LAW
I KNOW. BUT NOW THAT I'M YOUR ATTORNEY, WE HAVE TO DO THIS RIGHT.
WTHORNE & WTHORNE
OKAY, AFTER I HIT THE GOLF BALL I HEARD A CRASH.
SLOW DOWN.
SO YOU CAN TAKE NOTES?
NO. BECAUSE I CHARGE BY THE HOUR.

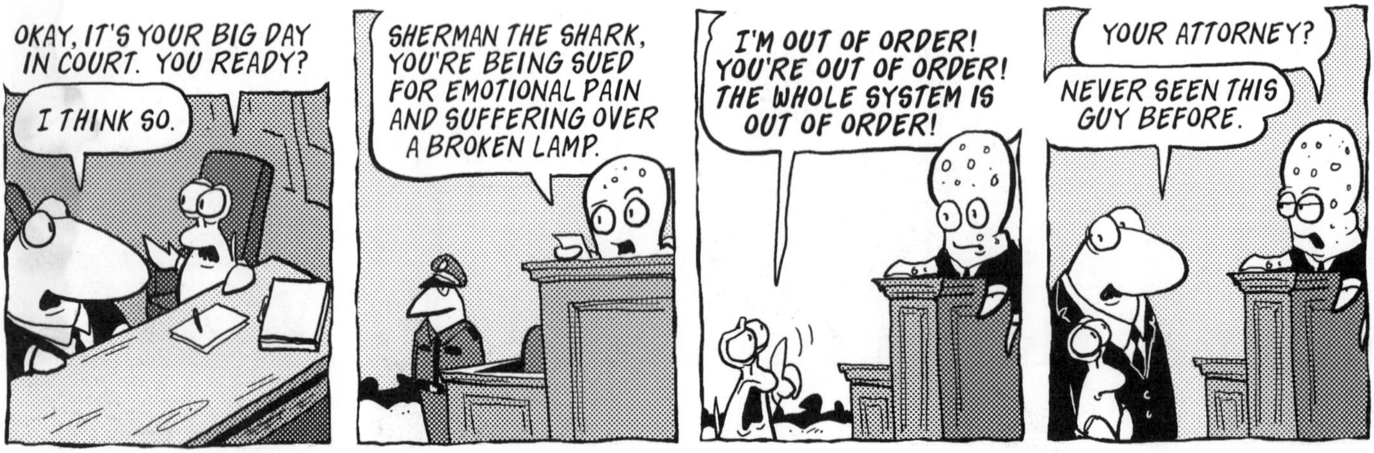
OKAY, IT'S YOUR BIG DAY IN COURT. YOU READY?
I THINK SO.
SHERMAN THE SHARK, YOU'RE BEING SUED FOR EMOTIONAL PAIN AND SUFFERING OVER A BROKEN LAMP.
I'M OUT OF ORDER! YOU'RE OUT OF ORDER! THE WHOLE SYSTEM IS OUT OF ORDER!
YOUR ATTORNEY?
NEVER SEEN THIS GUY BEFORE.

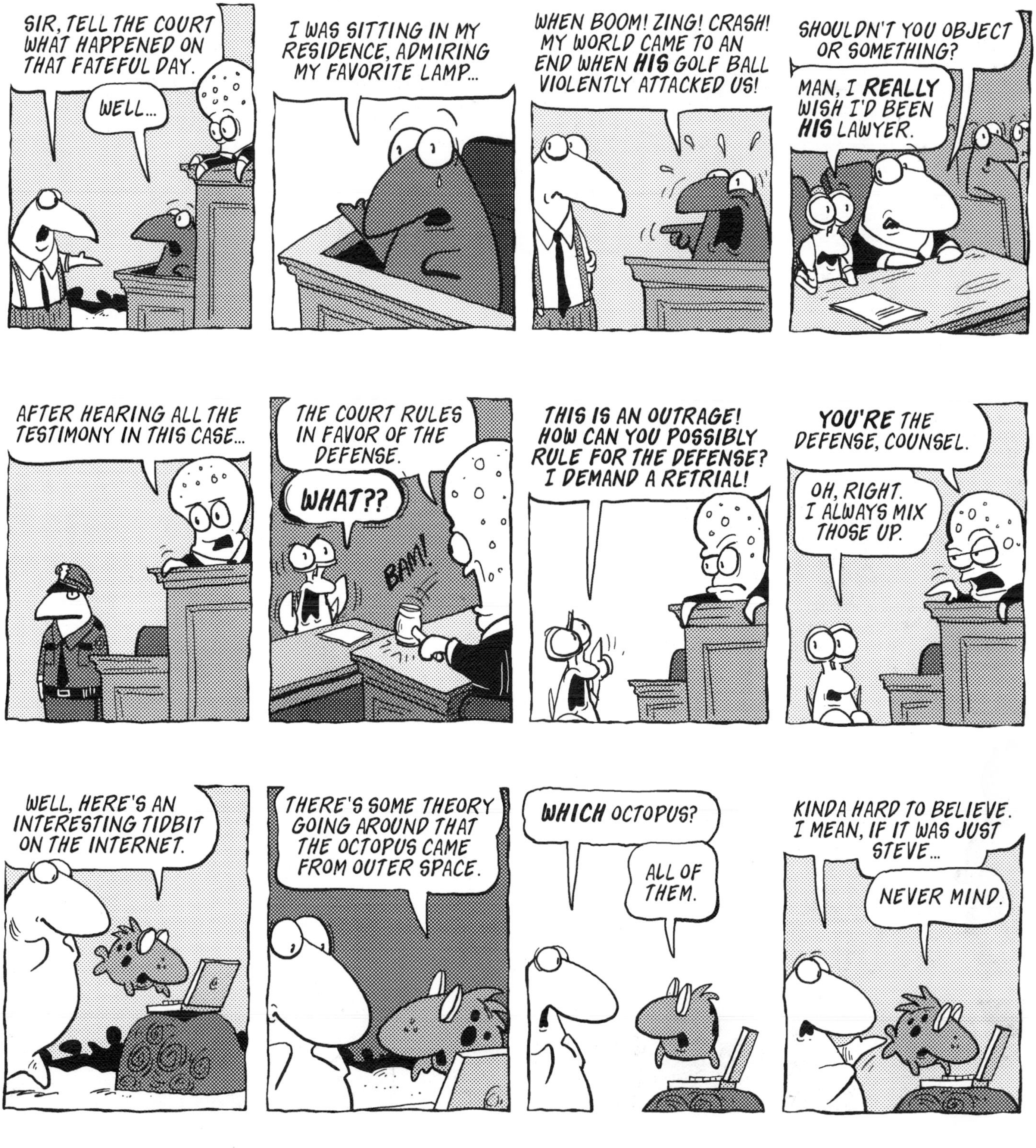
SIR, TELL THE COURT WHAT HAPPENED ON THAT FATEFUL DAY.
WELL...
I WAS SITTING IN MY RESIDENCE, ADMIRING MY FAVORITE LAMP...
WHEN BOOM! ZING! CRASH! MY WORLD CAME TO AN END WHEN HIS GOLF BALL VIOLENTLY ATTACKED US!
SHOULDN'T YOU OBJECT OR SOMETHING?
MAN, I REALLY WISH I'D BEEN HIS LAWYER.
AFTER HEARING ALL THE TESTIMONY IN THIS CASE...
THE COURT RULES IN FAVOR OF THE DEFENSE.
WHAT??
BAM!
THIS IS AN OUTRAGE! HOW CAN YOU POSSIBLY RULE FOR THE DEFENSE? I DEMAND A RETRIAL!
YOU'RE THE DEFENSE, COUNSEL.
OH, RIGHT. I ALWAYS MIX THOSE UP.
WELL, HERE'S AN INTERESTING TIDBIT ON THE INTERNET.
THERE'S SOME THEORY GOING AROUND THAT THE OCTOPUS CAME FROM OUTER SPACE.
WHICH OCTOPUS?
ALL OF THEM.
KINDA HARD TO BELIEVE. I MEAN, IF IT WAS JUST STEVE...
NEVER MIND.

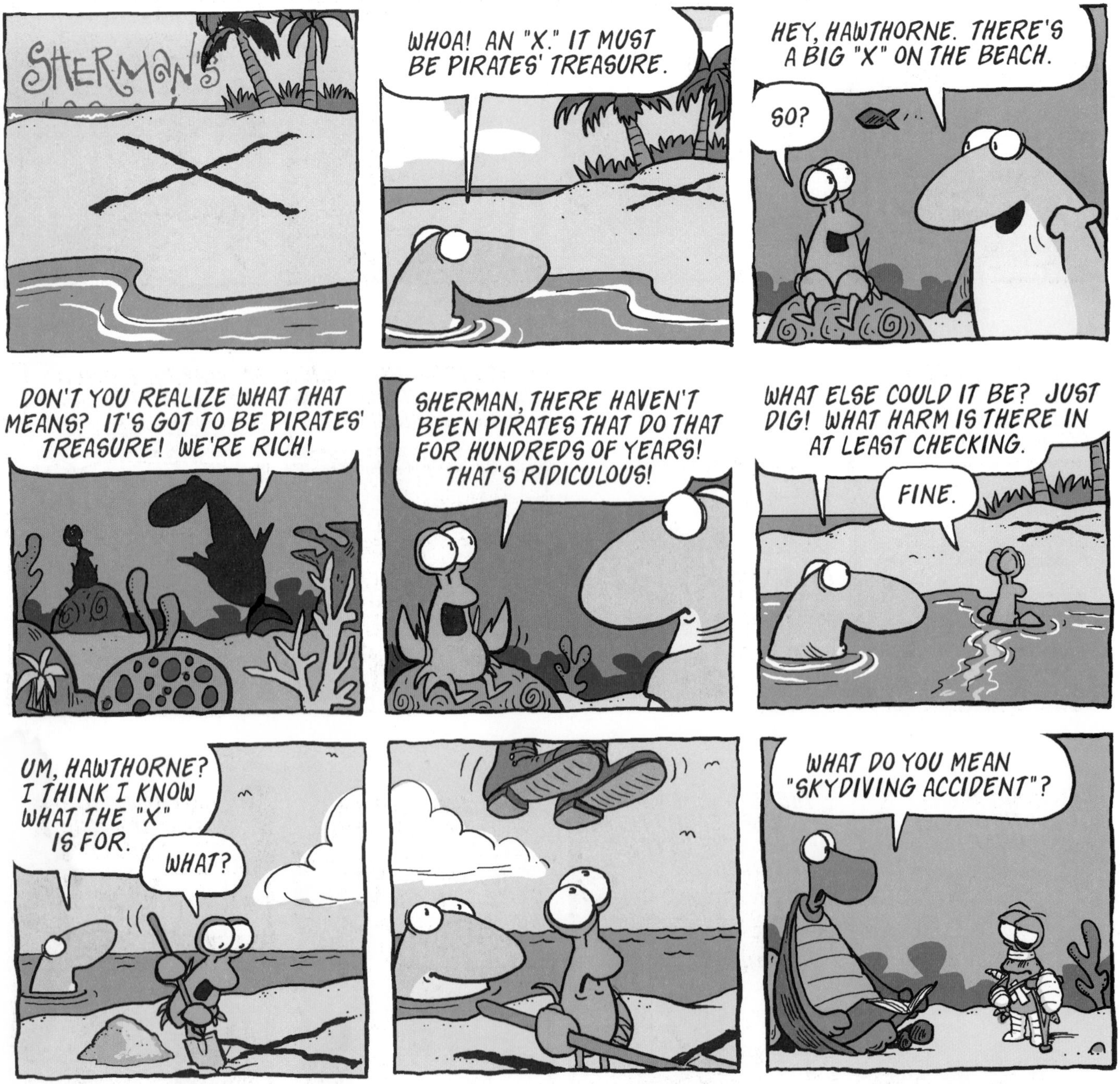
SHERMAN'S
WHOA! AN "X." IT MUST BE PIRATES' TREASURE.
HEY, HAWTHORNE. THERE'S A BIG "X" ON THE BEACH.
SO?
DON'T YOU REALIZE WHAT THAT MEANS? IT'S GOT TO BE PIRATES' TREASURE! WE'RE RICH!
SHERMAN, THERE HAVEN'T BEEN PIRATES THAT DO THAT FOR HUNDREDS OF YEARS! THAT'S RIDICULOUS!
WHAT ELSE COULD IT BE? JUST DIG! WHAT HARM IS THERE IN AT LEAST CHECKING.
FINE.
UM, HAWTHORNE? I THINK I KNOW WHAT THE "X" IS FOR.
WHAT?
WHAT DO YOU MEAN "SKYDIVING ACCIDENT"?

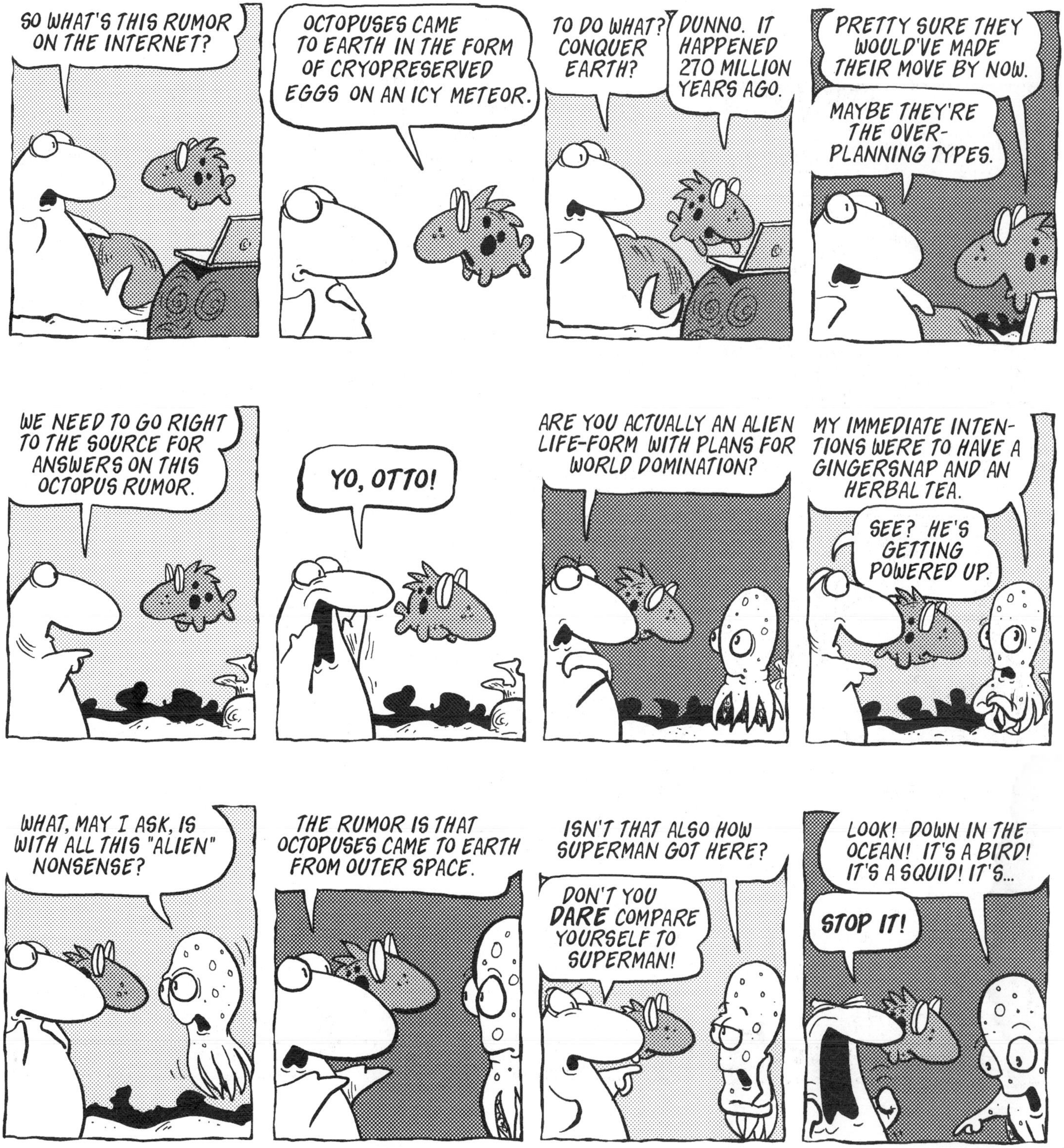
SO WHAT'S THIS RUMOR ON THE INTERNET?
OCTOPUSES CAME TO EARTH IN THE FORM OF CRYOPRESERVED EGGS ON AN ICY METEOR.
TO DO WHAT? CONQUER EARTH?
DUNNO. IT HAPPENED 270 MILLION YEARS AGO.
PRETTY SURE THEY WOULD'VE MADE THEIR MOVE BY NOW.
MAYBE THEY'RE THE OVER-PLANNING TYPES.
WE NEED TO GO RIGHT TO THE SOURCE FOR ANSWERS ON THIS OCTOPUS RUMOR.
YO, OTTO!
ARE YOU ACTUALLY AN ALIEN LIFE-FORM WITH PLANS FOR WORLD DOMINATION?
MY IMMEDIATE INTENTIONS WERE TO HAVE A GINGERSNAP AND AN HERBAL TEA.
SEE? HE'S GETTING POWERED UP.
WHAT, MAY I ASK, IS WITH ALL THIS "ALIEN" NONSENSE?
THE RUMOR IS THAT OCTOPUSES CAME TO EARTH FROM OUTER SPACE.
ISN'T THAT ALSO HOW SUPERMAN GOT HERE?
DON'T YOU DARE COMPARE YOURSELF TO SUPERMAN!
LOOK! DOWN IN THE OCEAN! IT'S A BIRD! IT'S A SQUID! IT'S...
STOP IT!

HAWTHORNE, DID YOU KNOW THAT OCTOPUSES ARE ACTUALLY FROM OUTER SPACE?!

HUH?

THAT'S RIGHT! AND I WANT TO KNOW AS MAYOR WHAT ARE YOU GOING TO DO ABOUT IT?

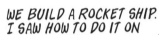

HMMMMM...

HIT 'EM WITH A NON-RESIDENT TAX.

IT'S A START.

WE NEED TO HELP OTTO GET BACK TO HIS HOME PLANET.

HOW?

WE BUILD A ROCKET SHIP. I SAW HOW TO DO IT ON YOUTUBE.

SOUNDS AWFULLY DANGEROUS. COUNT ME OUT.

WE'LL GET TO GO TO HOME DEPOT.

I'M BACK IN.

OTTO, WE'RE GOING TO BUILD A ROCKET SHIP TO TAKE YOU BACK TO YOUR HOME PLANET.

BUT THIS **IS** MY HOME PLANET.

YEAH, SURE.

ANYTHING YOU REQUIRE AS FAR AS PERSONAL NEEDS IN THE SHIP?

EIGHT CUP HOLDERS FOR MY SEAT.

NOTED.

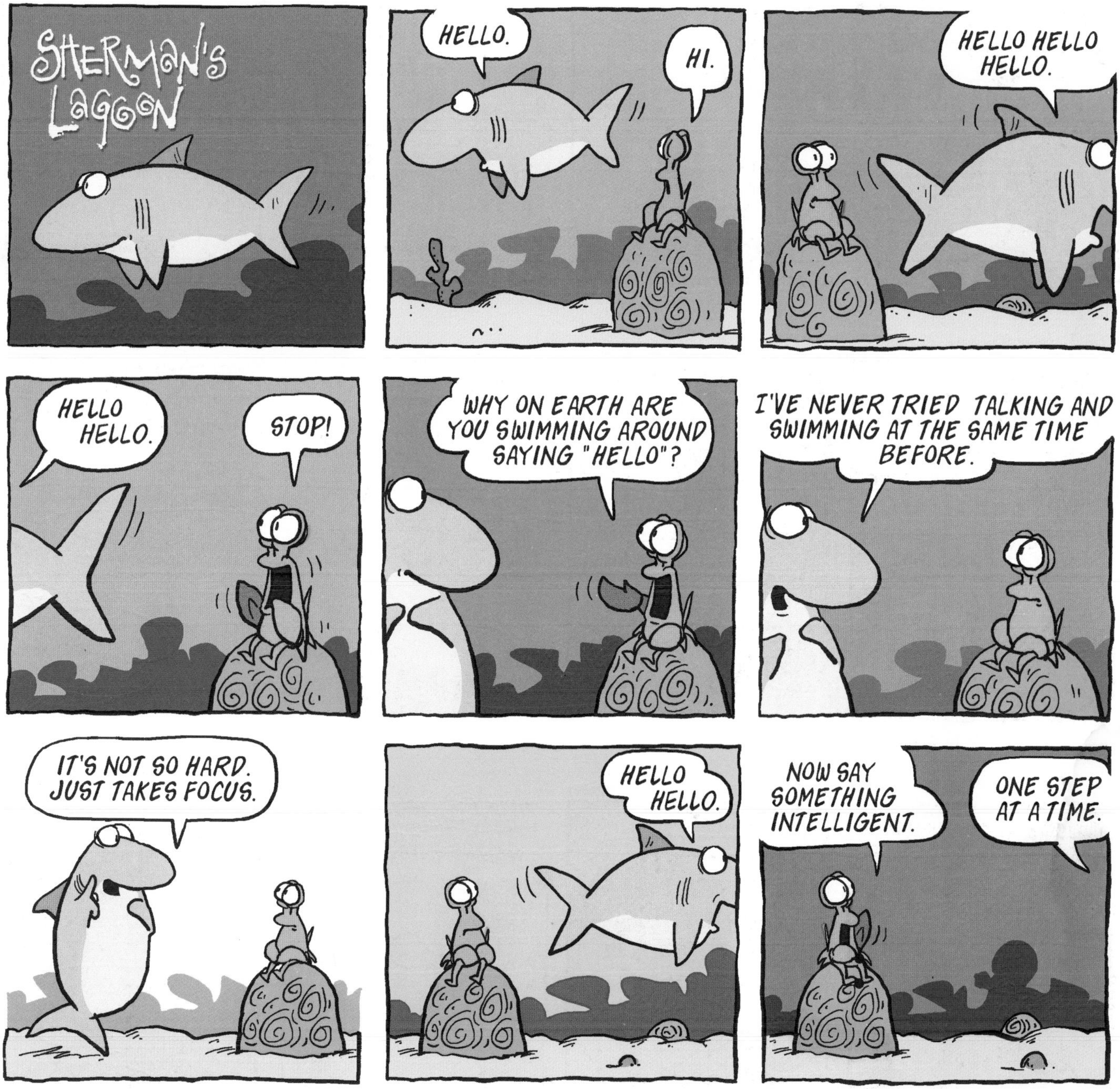
SHERMAN'S LAGOON
HELLO.
HI.
HELLO HELLO HELLO.
HELLO HELLO.
STOP!
WHY ON EARTH ARE YOU SWIMMING AROUND SAYING "HELLO"?
I'VE NEVER TRIED TALKING AND SWIMMING AT THE SAME TIME BEFORE.
IT'S NOT SO HARD. JUST TAKES FOCUS.
HELLO HELLO.
NOW SAY SOMETHING INTELLIGENT.
ONE STEP AT A TIME.

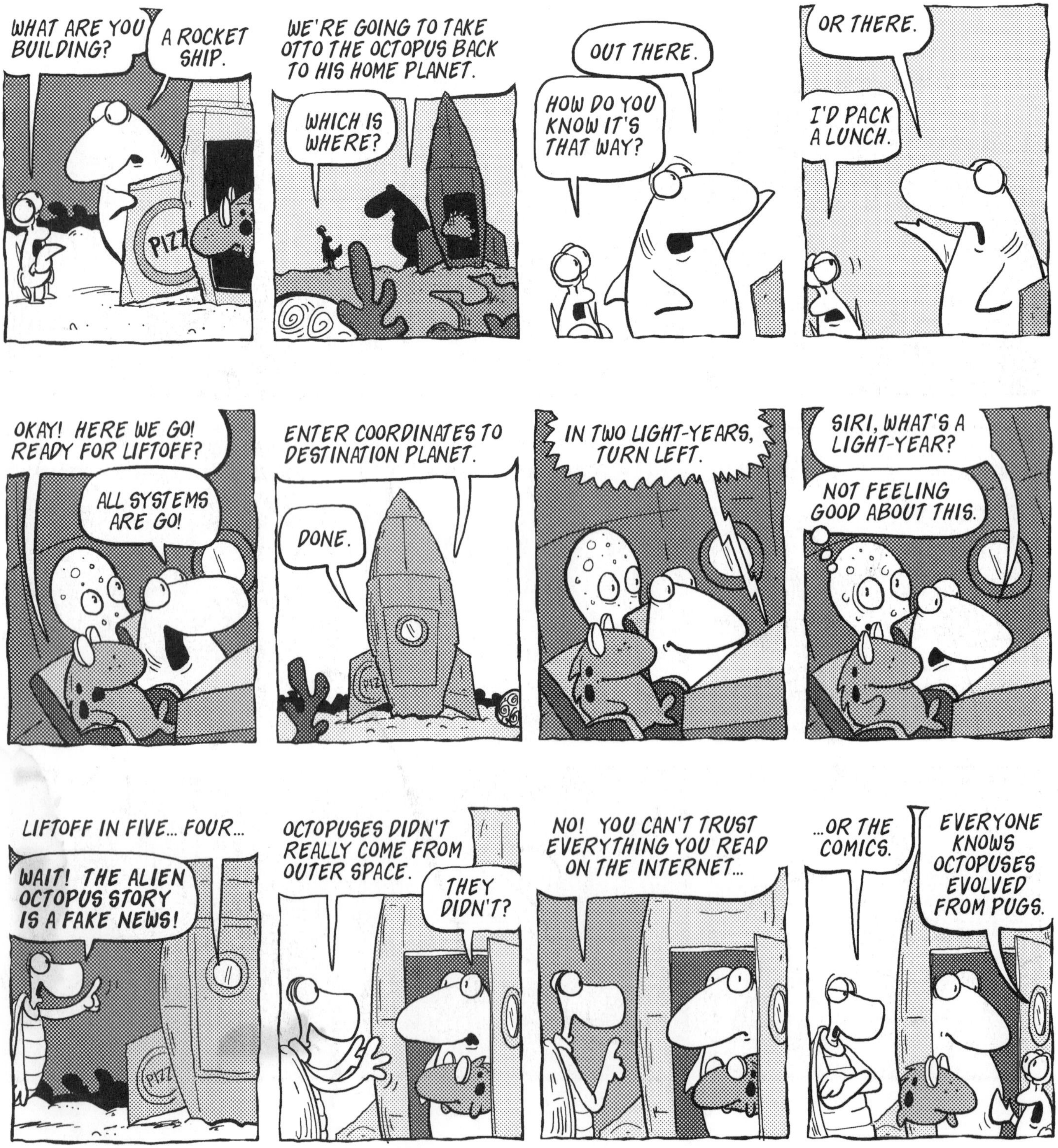
WHAT ARE YOU BUILDING?
A ROCKET SHIP.
WE'RE GOING TO TAKE OTTO THE OCTOPUS BACK TO HIS HOME PLANET.
WHICH IS WHERE?
OUT THERE.
HOW DO YOU KNOW IT'S THAT WAY?
OR THERE.
I'D PACK A LUNCH.
OKAY! HERE WE GO! READY FOR LIFTOFF?
ALL SYSTEMS ARE GO!
ENTER COORDINATES TO DESTINATION PLANET.
DONE.
IN TWO LIGHT-YEARS, TURN LEFT.
SIRI, WHAT'S A LIGHT-YEAR?
NOT FEELING GOOD ABOUT THIS.
LIFTOFF IN FIVE... FOUR...
WAIT! THE ALIEN OCTOPUS STORY IS A FAKE NEWS!
OCTOPUSES DIDN'T REALLY COME FROM OUTER SPACE.
THEY DIDN'T?
NO! YOU CAN'T TRUST EVERYTHING YOU READ ON THE INTERNET...
...OR THE COMICS.
EVERYONE KNOWS OCTOPUSES EVOLVED FROM PUGS.

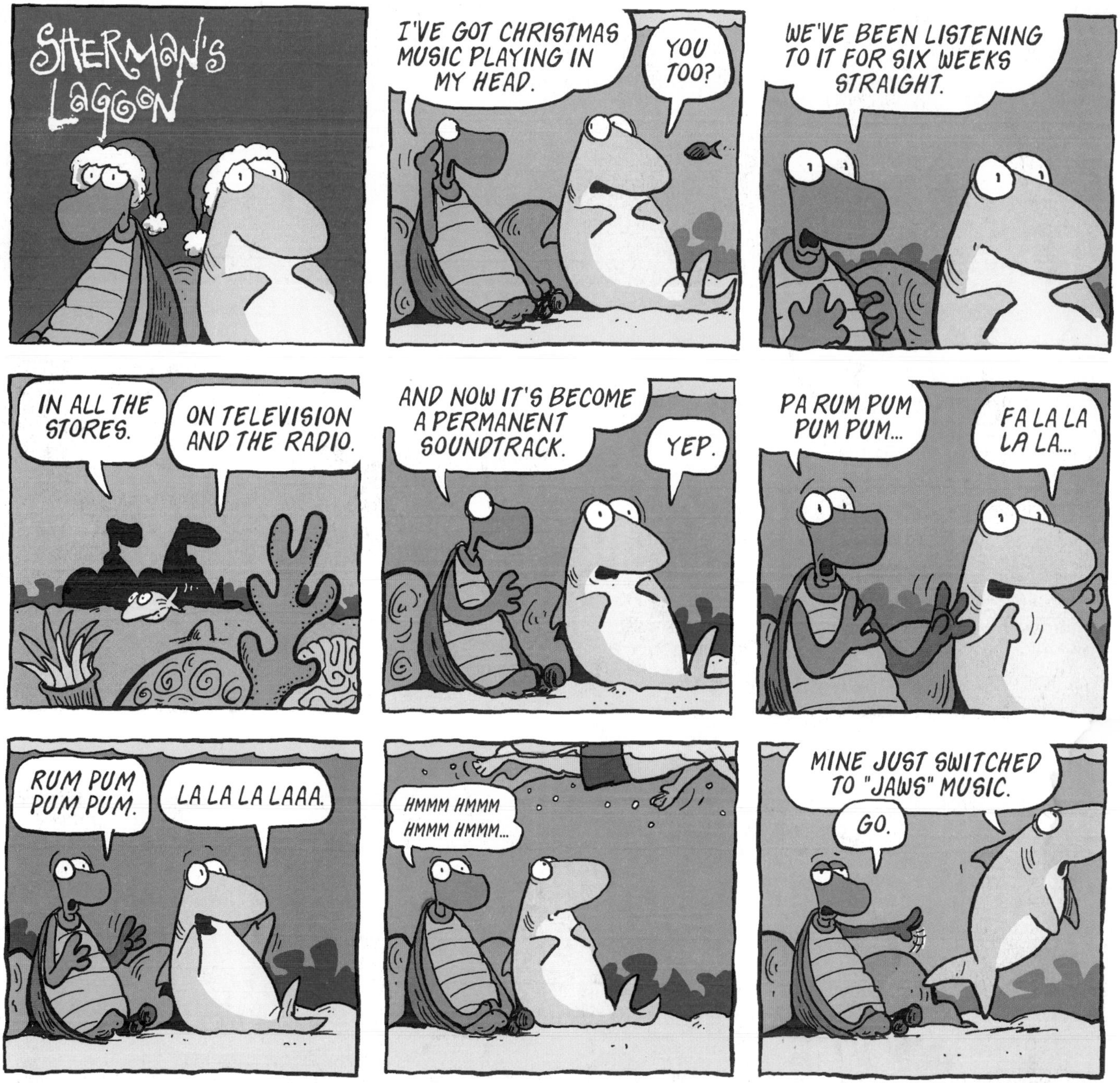
SHERMAN'S LAGOON
I'VE GOT CHRISTMAS MUSIC PLAYING IN MY HEAD.
YOU TOO?
WE'VE BEEN LISTENING TO IT FOR SIX WEEKS STRAIGHT.
IN ALL THE STORES.
ON TELEVISION AND THE RADIO.
AND NOW IT'S BECOME A PERMANENT SOUNDTRACK.
YEP.
PA RUM PUM PUM PUM...
FA LA LA LA LA...
RUM PUM PUM PUM.
LA LA LA LAAA.
HMMM HMMM HMMM HMMM...
MINE JUST SWITCHED TO "JAWS" MUSIC.
GO.

Sherman's Lagoon is syndicated internationally by King Features Syndicate, Inc. For information, write King Features Syndicate, Inc., 300 West Fifty-Seventh Street, New York, NY 10019.

Andrews McMeel Publishing
a division of Andrews McMeel Universal
1130 Walnut Street, Kansas City, Missouri 64106

www.andrewsmcmeel.com

19 20 21 22 23 SDB 10 9 8 7 6 5 4 3 2 1

ISBN: 978-1-5248-5179-8

Library of Congress Control Number: 2019935715

Sherman's Lagoon may be viewed on the Internet at
www.shermanslagoon.com.

─── **ATTENTION: SCHOOLS AND BUSINESSES** ───

Andrews McMeel books are available at quantity discounts with bulk purchase for educational, business, or sales promotional use. For information, please e-mail the Andrews McMeel Publishing Special Sales Department: specialsales@amuniversal.com.

5